UNCERTAIN TRANSITION

D1270686

UNCERTAIN TRANSITION

Ethnographies of Change in the Postsocialist World

edited by
MICHAEL BURAWOY
and
KATHERINE VERDERY

ROWMAN & LITTLEFIELD PUBLISHERS, INC.
Lanham • Boulder • New York • Oxford

ROWMAN & LITTLEFIELD PUBLISHERS, INC.

Published in the United States of America
by Rowman & Littlefield Publishers, Inc.
4720 Boston Way, Lanham, Maryland 20706

12 Hid's Copse Road
Cumnor Hill, Oxford OX2 9JJ, England

British Library Cataloguing in Publication Information Available

Library of Congress Cataloging-in-Publication Data

Uncertain transition : ethnographies of change in the postsocialist
   world / edited by Michael Burawoy and Katherine Verdery.
      p. cm.
     Based on the papers presented at the conference "Ethnographies in
transition" held in March 1996, at the University of California,
Berkeley.
     Includes bibliographical references and index.
     ISBN 0-8476-9042-3 (cloth : alk. paper). — ISBN 0-8476-9043-1
(pbk. : alk. paper)
     1. Europe, Eastern—Social conditions—1989– —Congress.
2. Post-communism—Europe, Eastern—Congresses. 3. Social change—
Europe, Eastern—Congresses. 4. Russia (Federation)—Social
conditions—1991– —Congresses. 5. Post-communism—Russia
(Federation)—Congresses. 6. Social change—Russia (Federation)—
Congresses. I. Burawoy, Michael. II. Verdery, Katherine.
HN380.7.A8U5   1999
306'.0947—dc21   98-28144
                                                    CIP

Printed in the United States of America

♾ ™ The paper used in this publication meets the minimum requirements of
American National Standard for Information Sciences—Permanence of Paper
for Printed Library Materials, ANSI Z39.48-1984.

Contents

Acknowledgments

This volume began with a conference Vicki Bonnell, director of the Center for Slavic and East European Studies, University of California, Berkeley, invited Michael Burawoy to organize. The conference, "Ethnographies of Transition: The Political and Cultural Dimensions of Emergent Market Economies in Russia and Eastern Europe," was held in March 1996. We are grateful to four sources of funding that enabled us to hold the conference and that helped pay for production of the present volume: the Center for Slavic and East European Studies (Director Vicki Bonnell) and the Institute of International Studies (Director Michael Watts), University of California, Berkeley; the Social Science Research Council; the Joint Committee on Eastern Europe of the American Council of Learned Societies and the Social Science Research Council. The staff of the Berkeley Center—particularly Barbara Voytek and Monique Nowicki—were indispensable in making this event successful; our warm thanks to them. We would also like to thank Dean Birkenkamp for his interest in our project and Scott Horst for his editorship.

Also present at the conference were several people who served as discussants or paper givers and much improved our deliberations but who did not contribute chapters to the volume: Vicki Bonnell, Manuel Castells, Simon Clarke, Ellen Comisso, Ken Jowitt, Emma Kiselyova, Gail Kligman, Martha Lampland, Carole Nagengast, Ákos Róna-Tas, David Stark, Andrew Walder, Michael Watts, and Lin Xiu. We thank them for helping to make the event so stimulating.

Introduction

Michael Burawoy and Katherine Verdery

The epochal transformations that have swept through the former Soviet Union and Eastern Europe have prompted stark visions of the future and the past. At one extreme we find the partisans of modernity who claim that the disintegration of communism is the final victory of modernity's great achievements, market economy and liberal democracy. We have arrived at both the end of ideology and the end of history; there will be no more forks in the road. At the other extreme are those who view the end of communism as the twilight of modernity. The collapse of the administered society marks the exhaustion of the enlightenment project to direct and regulate the world we inhabit. Modernity has spiraled out of control into a new, as yet unknown orbit of postmodernity. Between these two grand narratives lie more cautious appraisals that see change in less apocalyptic terms, that see evolution rather than revolution, that see hybrid societies rather than polar extremes.

These cognitive maps of the "Second Great Transformation" focus on macro structures of state and economy. They leave little space for the micro world of day-to-day life, for the cumulative impact of what Akos Róna-Tas (1997) has called "small transformations." In conventional portraits of the "transition" the micro is determined or is an expression of structures, policies, and ideologies of a macro character, with little theorization of the unintended consequences brought about locally by political and cultural contestation intertwined with economic struggles. To explore these unintended consequences is one aim of our collection of ethnographies.

In so doing, we challenge those analyses that account for the confusions and shortcomings of the transition process as "socialist legacies" or "culture." Repeatedly, we find that what may appear as "restorations"

1

of patterns familiar from socialism are something quite different: direct *responses* to the new market initiatives, produced *by* them, rather than remnants of an older mentality. In other words, we find that what looks familiar has causes that are fairly novel. At the same time, however, we acknowledge that people's responses to a situation may often appear as holdovers precisely because they employ a language and symbols adapted from previous orders. This does not mean their vision of the world has been so "corrupted" by the socialist experience as to make them unfit for other ways of life; it means only that action employs symbols and words that are not created de novo but develop using the forms already known, even if with new senses and to new ends.

Our view of the relation between macro structures and everyday practices is that the collapse of party states and administered economies broke down macro structures, thereby creating space for micro worlds to produce autonomous effects that may have unexpected influence over the structures that have been emerging. In the language of Jürgen Habermas (1987), the disintegration of the system world has given freer rein for life-worlds to stamp themselves on the emerging economic and political order. The transformation of party states in the context of changes in the global regime of accumulation has radically shifted the rules of the game, the parameters of action within which actors pursue their daily routines and practices. This presents an opportunity for local improvisations that may press either in novel directions or toward a "return" to socialism, as several of our chapters show. Both innovation and reversion are responses to unstable environments, at least as much as they are evidence of socialism's legacies or its culture. Our insistence on this point distinguishes the present volume from many other writings in "transitology."

It is precisely the sudden importance of the micro processes lodged in moments of transformation that privileges an ethnographic approach. Aggregate statistics and compendia of decrees and laws tell us little without complementary close descriptions of how people—ranging from farmers to factory workers, from traders to bureaucrats, from managers to welfare clients—are responding to the uncertainties they face. From their calculations, improvisations, and decisions will emerge the elements of new structurings. Thus, even an ephemeral moment captured ethnographically will reveal something of the conflicts and alternatives thrown up by the destructuring effects of the end of state socialism. This way of viewing ethnography and the transformation has a corollary related to *time*. Because the postsocialist moment means constant change in the parameters of action, actors tend to strategize within time horizons that are short. New laws keep appearing, taxation policy is continually shifting, inflation makes long-term calculations difficult, and fluctuating interest rates make investment risky. This contraction of time horizons in the aftermath of 1989 gives unaccustomed validity to ethnographic research, whose temporal constitution now more closely approximates that of the actors whose behavior it reports.

In addition to justifying the special insights of ethnography into the rhythm of change in postsocialist society, we might also indicate the social *spaces* on which the ethnographic eye might be most fruitfully trained: distribution and consumption, altered production, ideas about property and technology, the rural economy, and welfare institutions. We will justify each of these briefly now, then explore them at greater length as we summarize the chapters.

(1) Because socialism was a system organized around state-controlled redistribution, dismantling those channels produces a relative vacuum of mechanisms for exchange and distribution; therefore finance, trade, and other forms of exchange move to the fore as sites of innovation (Humphrey [chapter 1], Woodruff [chapter 3]). The same is true with marketing techniques and consumption, neglected under socialism and central to market economies (Dunn [chapter 4]). (2) Industrial production was at the heart of socialist systems and (perhaps in consequence) has proven very difficult to change. An uncertain economic environment precludes the long time horizons necessary for transformative investments in production. Especially here, old patterns seem to reproduce themselves despite the introduction of new practices (Ashwin [chapter 4], Dunn [chapter 8]). (3) Socialist systems operated with characteristic, noncapitalist definitions of property and technology. Significant departures from these definitions, as in computerization (Lass [chapter 9]) and the legal redefinition of property rights (Verdery [chapter 2]), have outpaced the necessary changes in social and cultural relations that would sustain the anticipated economic breakthroughs. (4) Under socialism, rural economies underwent perhaps the most dramatic, repressive, and destructive transformations. Rural responses to the challenge of markets have included both an increase in rural "entrepreneurship" and apparent retrenchment to older forms of production, whether the collective farm (Creed [chapter 7]) or peasant subsistence production (Zbierski [chapter 6]). Here as elsewhere, however, these forms are adaptations to the new environment as much as the persistence of old habits. (5) Socialist states had characteristic welfare organizations, as well as characteristic gender regimes that intersected with these organizations. Under the new liberal dispensation, universalistic welfare provisions are being dismantled in favor of targeted and means-tested benefits (Haney [chapter 5]). Clients respond by defending their inherited rights against the new disciplinary apparatuses (and, in Haney's chapter, within a specific history of gender relations).

From this conceptualization of the times, spaces, structures, and "agencies" of the transition from socialism, our chapters will show the complex relations of socialist and postsocialist life worlds, emphasizing unintended consequences and the way the past enters the present, not as legacy but as novel adaptation. Our approach inclines us to see the antici-pated "transition" as much less certain than some observers might have it—hence our title.

Theories of Transition

When we speak of transition,[1] we think of a *process* connecting the past to the future. What we discover, however, are theories of transition often committed to some pregiven future or rooted in an unyielding past. Thus, on the one side we have economists who debate whether a revolutionary break or a negotiated transition is the most effective way of climbing out of the socialist abyss into the promised world of capitalism. As they debate the character of the change, they generally think of only one future: textbook capitalism. On the other side, historians, political scientists, and sociologists debate the impact of the past. Those who understand communist society as a totalitarian system emphasize discontinuity: once collapsed, communism leaves behind only rubble. Those who saw, beyond and within the party state, an autonomous realm of society regard the latter as laying the foundations for a postcommunist order. They see continuity where totalitarian theory sees rupture. Table I.1 schematizes the contours of conventional transitology.

The simplest model of transition is the one proposed by political scientists and historians of the totalitarian school, from Hannah Arendt (1951) to Martin Malia (1994). In this view the political system completely colonized the life world; there was no realm of autonomy. Communism was based on terror and atomism; its disintegration entailed the extinction of the entire order. Communism was totalitarian and therefore collapsed totally, having lost all resources of regeneration and restoration.

Table I.1   Models of Transition

Path Advocated	Point of Orientation	
	Origin	Destination
Revolution	Totalitarian (extinction)	Neoliberal (genesis)
Evolution	Society (legacy)	Institutional (incubation)

For the defenders of totalitarian theory, communism was such an evil order that anything would be better. They are more interested in celebrating the extinction than in organizing genesis, more interested in salivating over the carcass than in wondering what might be served up next. Here, neoliberal economics comes to the rescue by insisting that markets can spontaneously create a new world if the old can first be destroyed. Shock therapy's package of price liberalization, stabilization, and privatization aims to dissolve the past by the fastest means possible. Not only does the past have no redeeming features, but to slow the reforms would be to court opposition and abort the transition (Lipton and Sachs 1990). It is neoliberalism's pious hope that destruction is the vehicle for genesis.

How, then, do neoliberals comprehend the recession that has afflicted much of Eastern Europe, particularly the former Soviet Union, with unprecedented economic decline? Some, such as Maxim Boycko, Andrei Schleifer, and Robert Vishny (1995), interpret it as a sign of success, since the more quickly the old Soviet economy reaches the bottom of the valley the sooner it will rise up the other side. Others, such as Jeffrey Sachs (1994), who are less sanguine, blame international agencies, especially the International Monetary Fund (IMF), for failing to come to Russia's aid in the early months when reform stood a chance. Yet others, such as Anders Åslund (1995), argue that forces of the past, from Stalinist managers to Soviet culture, obstruct the progress of the market economy. The solution should therefore have been even stronger medicine. At least these theorists recognize that with the collapse of the party state not all is destroyed, even if its legacies go unexamined.

Neoliberal orthodoxy and its neoclassical underpinnings do not go uncontested. Harking back to Schumpeter, institutional economists such as Kazimierz Poznansky (1993) and Marshall Goldman (1994), as well as critics of neoclassical economics from within such as János Kornai (1990, 1994) and Joseph Stiglitz (1994), are aghast at what has been accomplished in the name of the market, at the wreckage shock therapy has left behind. Rather than promoting a mission of destruction, they argue for building the new within the framework of the old. A market economy requires an institutional framework within which to incubate. Such theorists hold up China as an exemplary case of evolutionary transition, a market economy nurtured and protected within the womb of the party state.

Institutional theory diverges from its neoclassical competitor in the way it marks out the distinctiveness of capitalism. Neoclassical theory regards the administered socialist economy as allocationally inefficient. Only market economies, so the argument goes, can match supply and demand. Peter Murrell (1991), one of the leading defenders of evolutionary economics, however, claims there is no evidence that Western capitalist economies are more efficient in distribution. Rather, what distinguishes the market from the administered economy is its dynamic efficiency, its ability to innovate. For this, however, a stable institutional environment is needed that encourages risk taking under competition. If some Eastern European countries have done better than Russia, so the argument goes, it is because they possess a more stable environment, a more consolidated financial infrastructure, lower rates of inflation and interest, more predictable tax collection, more secure property rights, and a more effective rule of law (Murrell 1993). Shock therapy is the wrong medicine not only because of its single-minded concern to destroy but also because it destabilizes the institutional framework of economic decisionmaking. Still, among such evolutionary economists, there is little indication as to how these institutions might take root because there is no study of the micro processes of transition.

As with neoliberal theory, evolutionary economics is oriented to the future and is also prescriptive. It views shock therapy as simply the wrong medicine, undermining the very end it seeks to achieve. Those who pay more attention to the past argue that shock therapy is not only foolhardy but impossible. From Andrew Arato (1981) to Moshe Lewin (1985) and Stephen Cohen (1985), from Iván Szelényi (1988) to Elemér Hankiss (1990), commentators argue that socialist civil society percolated outside (and even within) the formal apparatuses of power, supplying the necessary lubricant for the party state to function even while challenging its monopoly of power. Whether the black market or the second economy, extended kinship ties or private agricultural plots, networks of barter relations or the pushers that promoted them, the collapse of the party state did not eliminate these economic and social forms but caused their greater flowering.

Thus, sociologists have discovered various legacies inherited from the socialist order, legacies variously interpreted as path dependency, cultural persistence, or circulation of elites. More sophisticated theories talk about the reconfiguration of elements from the past, recombinant forms of property (Stark 1996). As things change, so do they remain the same. David Stark and László Bruszt (1998) explore the idea of the reconstitution of inherited networks that take on new institutional forms between state and market. These descriptions come close to the micro foundations of the new economic order, but even they fail to grasp theoretically the specificity of the transition as a process.

A focus on the day-to-day realities of postsocialism reveals a much more ambiguous account of the transformation announced with such fanfare by theories of modernization and of market and democratic transition. Each of these theories has a limited view of the interaction and interpenetration of system and life world, macro and micro, global and local; we need instead to attend much more to how the unfolding uncertainties of macro institutions affect practices within micro worlds and also to how family, work, and community are refashioning themselves—often in opposition to what governments intend. In the ethnographies that follow, we try to show that the conventional metaphors—extinction, genesis, incubation, and legacy—are limited because they give insufficient integrity to the creative and resistive processes of everyday practice. Indeed, we find time and again that every step forward in the direction of the market produces forces opposed. In reaction to the iron law of market expansion, we discover the iron law of market resistance.

Collapse and Recomposition

For totalitarian theory the collapse of the party state entails the breakdown of the entire order, including the institutions of day-to-day life. To be sure, daily life under postsocialism is beset with uncertainty, but it manages to recompose itself even in countries where the political system had permeated it the most deeply and repressively (for example, in the Soviet Union and Romania) and in spaces where the collapse was felt most intensely (for example, in distributive processes and property rights).

Definitive of the administered economy are the central appropriation and redistribution of goods and services. It is this redistributive process that collapses with the Soviet order, the more dramatically the more reliant that order was on the planning mechanism. In its wake, the redistributive apparatus leaves spaces into which multiple forms of exchange and diverse traders expand. Not surprisingly, it is in this sphere of exchange that we find the most innovation and turmoil. Caroline Humphrey describes the proliferation of Russian traders, from the managers of new private conglomerates and their "brokers" to resellers, shuttlers, entrepreneurs, and retailers. This is no return to pre-Soviet trading patterns but an entirely novel configuration of disorder, whose contours form around the disintegration of the vertical pyramid that had attached regions to the center. Regional autonomies are magnified, creating both the reality and the consciousness of uneven development, exacerbated and dramatized by traders who exploit such unevenness.

Long viewed as parasites on the real producers of goods, traders are now held responsible for regional poverty, for the inflow of trash and the outflow of valuables. A visible source of popular anxiety, traders provoke political reactions. Regional governments introduce residence requirements, licensing laws, restrictions on mobility, or what Humphrey calls new citizenship regimes in attempts to restrict and regulate these outsiders in the interests of local inhabitants. This leads to defensive reactions, the formation of exclusive kin networks playing on pan-ethnic or diasporic loyalties to form cross-border patterns of trust and protection.

Just as attenuation of redistributive channels creates spaces for multiple (dis)orders of trade in post-Soviet Russia, so Katherine Verdery shows how the liquidation of collective farms in Transylvania ushers in the recomposition of rural property relations. Romania's Law 18 of 1991 calls for decollectivization and decrees that the land be returned to its previous owners, who must cultivate it or lose it. Nonresidents and those who lack the means of cultivation can loan their land back to the village "association," which will work it on their behalf for a percentage of the crop. The association effectively replaces the collective, often managed by the same staff and drawing on the old members as farm laborers while landowners become shareholders. But from then on, associations face the dilemma of any capitalist firm—how much revenue to reinvest and how much to return as dividends. They have to keep their members from withdrawing their land while continuing to be economically viable. With the level of trust thin, time horizons diminish, and the association finds itself eating away at its future.

New property rights are at work within old relations to produce new social dynamics and a new field of action for villagers. Verdery's description of the struggles over ownership of a granary highlights the new forces that can be mobilized. Ionescu, a recent immigrant to the village, is barred from buying the granary by the district judge (an old-timer), who rules the granary to be a public good unavailable for purchase. The judge appeals to substantive rather than procedural law. The entire village is swept up in the controversy, largely in opposition to Ionescu. The villagers do not want their granary, which they built with their own volunteer labor, to fall into the hands of an outsider who, as a renter capitalist, would charge them for its use. Thus, they find themselves opposing individual private ownership and favoring collective forms, despite Ionescu's argument that his ownership would bring greater benefits to the village than does the elite-dominated association. Clearly, from the point of view of the villagers, markets have their own distinctive irrationality.

In both Buryatia (Russia) and Transylvania, the new order cultivates entrepreneurs and traders who threaten the integrity of local or regional communities, offering old elites the opportunity to mobilize the support of the population. The breakdown of Soviet structures—the redistributive plan or the collective farm—causes old interests to congeal around new hybrid institutions. Disintegration begets innovation, which in turn stimulates reaction.

Market Therapy and Economic Retreat

If totalitarian theory is misguided in predicting total collapse, and if rolling back the party state can stimulate both defensive and innovative moves from local communities, then how should we understand the consequences of shock therapy, whose premise is that civil society is not resilient but weak? Neoliberal theory accounts for the failure of its shock therapy programs by appealing to exogenous factors over which it has no control—foot dragging by international agencies, for instance, or obdurate legacies of the past.

David Woodruff's study of three regional economies in Russia suggests, by contrast, that shock therapy is not obstructed by exogenous factors but creates its own barriers. He shows how the spread of barter relations is not a legacy of the past but follows from the monetization of the economy. Price liberalization and privatization were succeeded in 1993 by the third prong of shock therapy—namely, stabilization—increasing interest rates, reducing cheap loans, and raising taxes. Enterprises now find their bank accounts frozen so that funds flowing into those accounts are immediately and forcibly siphoned off to pay taxation and utility bills. Managers therefore take their enterprises out of the monetary circuit and turn to barter relations. Whereas in the previous system the expansion of barter signified affluence and surplus products, it now signifies bankruptcy. It is a product of shock therapy rather than the legacy of a paternalistic Soviet state.

Even more clearly than Humphrey and Verdery, Woodruff shows that the expansion of barter relations intensifies regional autarky, encouraging local elites to forge a united front against the center. Governments orchestrate relations among enterprises so that regional debt is concentrated in those companies that have the greatest bargaining power with the center. These prove to be the power companies, whose bankruptcy threatens to devastate the local economy. This prospect can be translated into a compelling claim for subsidies, loans, and bailouts.

Shock therapy at first makes great strides toward marketization but then creates its own barriers in the regions, which are strengthened by the demise of the administered economy. By restructuring interests, innovative policies from the center produce their own undoing. The same applies to forces operating within enterprises. Elizabeth Dunn describes how the Western marketing strategies introduced into a Polish fruit-processing plant lead to a backlash among workers and salespeople. The marketers take command of the company, seeking out new consumer niches for their product by appealing to youthful, "with it," antisocialist sentiment. They deploy the same ideology against workers by associating them with socialism and its rigid bureaucracy. Workers, for their part, claim it was their flexibility and ingenuity that had made the company such a socialist success; their resourcefulness could as well be turned to the advantage of capitalist flexibility. Salespeople face different dilemmas. They aspire to Western market principles but find themselves trapped between retailers who demand the same old rewards and marketers who deny them those inducements.

Once more, then, market initiatives are stymied by the real interests they engender. These interests are organized within the firm but are couched in the language of socialism and capitalism, maneuvering between constructions of past and future. Even in postcommunist Poland, site of "successful" shock therapy where the conditions for market growth were often the most propitious in the region, the same is true. Here as elsewhere, although the shocks applied to the "body economic" may have produced positive results at first, they often gave way to deeper pathologies resulting from rational reactions to the treatment itself.

New Institutions and Historical Memory

Evolutionary economists condemn the destructiveness of neoliberal therapy and the expectation that a sufficiently large dose should do the trick. Instead, they argue, markets will produce economic growth only under the protective influence of a broad range of stabilizing institutions. Even when such institutions are introduced, however, they do not always have the intended effects: they, too, court resistance based on meanings and expectations drawn from the past. No less than policies, institutions too are disrupted by a restive and resistive society.

Lynne Haney explores the consequences of attempts to establish a liberal welfare regime in Hungary targeted at the poor and needy, one that aims to discipline its clients for the market. Her study compares welfare regimes in terms of their publicly enunciated policies, the actual practices of their welfare apparatuses (the organization of caseworkers and their work), and the strategies of female clients to advance their interests as mothers, wives, and workers. Based on interviews, archives, and participant observations, Haney discovers three welfare regimes since the inception of socialism: the 1950s established a *familial* regime that relied on existing institutions (family and enterprise) to deal with social security; the 1970s established a *maternalist* regime based on mothers as object and recipient of welfare; the 1990s consolidate a *liberal* regime to dispense welfare on the basis of calculated material needs.

The maternalist regime was a response to demographic and economic problems; it was designed to reduce the costs of Hungary's welfare state and to absorb the social consequences of the late 1960s economic reforms (and feminists might object to its "naturalizing" women's maternal role toward these ends). In part continuous with the goals of the maternalist regime, the liberal regime was the handmaiden of neoliberal economic policies of the late 1980s. Female welfare clients, however, experienced this democratic and market transition as a contraction of the space within which they could pursue their interests. Under the maternalist regime they could negotiate an expanded identity from mother to wife and defend their interests against wayward husbands and fathers, whereas the liberal regime confined them to a bureaucratic accounting of needs. Outraged by this diminution of rights and narrowing of claims, women appealed back to the prior maternalist regime in the name of the identity it had promoted—the identity of mother. This appeal to the past is more than a strategic maneuver to defend interests in the present: the past frames the present, imbuing it with distinctive meaning.

Similarly, Slawomira Zbierski-Salameh shows the way Polish peasants orient themselves to market opportunities based on their experience with the post-Solidarity reforms of the socialist 1980s. She asks why peasants retreat from the market toward "closed-cycle" subsistence production instead of exploring new market possibilities. This is especially puzzling given that the peasantry, especially in the area Zbierski studied, was already endowed with that great asset—private property.

Her answer comes in two parts. First, shock therapy, far from destroying the administered economy, actually strengthened the monopolistic position of the state procurement centers that regulate the peasantry's entry into the market, dictate prices, and control quality. Banks extended credit under terms that made investment impossible. It was not just maladapted institutions, however, but also their meanings that impeded entrepreneurship and risk taking. Under martial law, agrarian reforms had encouraged peasants to expand production into new areas; inputs were subsidized, and consumer markets were accessible. With liberalization, the price of inputs spiraled out of control as consumer prices were held down by cheap imports from Western Europe. Peasants, caught in a price scissors, retreated from the market—just as Woodruff's Russian enterprises turned to barter (chapter 3).

To interpret this unexpected behavior, Zbierski draws on Adam Przeworski's theory of impediments to the transition from capitalism to socialism. Because they were doing relatively well under the protected market of socialism, peasants were less than enthusiastic about tightening their belts in the hope of eventual economic improvement. Feeling trapped rather than empowered by the new market forces, they shortened their time horizons and turned inward toward subsistence production while organizing collective protest against the post-1989 Solidarity government.

Both Zbierski's peasants and Haney's welfare workers find themselves surrounded by new institutions designed to promote a new capitalist economy. Both appeal to the "good old days" to defend themselves against these institutions. Just as neoliberal policies generate retreat away from the market, capitalist institutions provoke their own forms of resistance, recalling the radiant past.

Legacy and Restoration

We turn finally to the argument that the party state's collapse entails strengthening the civil society inherited from the old order. We have already seen that civil society, whether flourishing trade, the return to barter, or protests against welfare and shock therapy, is not some cultural lag—an inherited legacy—but is refashioned out of the old as a response to exigencies of the present. The final three chapters make this especially clear in the way they link economic change to political restoration.

Gerald Creed asks whether rural support for the Bulgarian Socialist Party is a legacy of the past—resistant socialism—or something created under pressures of transition—socialist resistance. Bulgarian villagers, he argues, respond to the transition by trying to preserve institutions that have both symbolic and material importance for them, specifically the cooperative. The anticommunist party (Union of Democratic Forces, or UDF) looked on the cooperative as a quintessential symbol of communism, one that sheltered communist elites who were dragooning villagers into supporting the socialists. The UDF therefore sought to liquidate the cooperatives and return land to the previous owners, thinking this would win the support of the rural population. The exact opposite occurred. As in Verdery's Transylvania, the rural population regrouped around its erstwhile communist elites. Rural people condemned those who laid waste to the countryside and destroyed the buildings they had erected with their own hands; they resisted liquidation of the cooperatives that had given them a new identity as multioccupational villagers rather than simple peasants, seeing themselves now as threatened with repeasantization. Without the cooperative and access to its equipment and materials, they knew their farming would be impoverished. Therefore, they sabotaged government plans by squabbling over the redistribution of land and the reconstitution of cooperatives and by voting socialist.

Whereas Polish villagers embraced the peasant identity nurtured and protected under socialism, even marching on the government in its name, Bulgarian villagers voted socialist for fear of losing their collective farms and having to become mere peasants. In both cases resistance to market transformation occurs, but it takes diametrically opposed forms because of the different institutions in which the rural population had been organized under socialism.

We see the same pattern at work in the Siberian coal mines studied by Sarah Ashwin. In 1989 and again in 1991, these mines were the scene of the most militant opposition to the communist regime, with miners demanding radical democratic reforms. It was on the backs of those miners that Boris Yeltsin first came to power in Russia. The nucleus of such working-class radicalism lay in the work collective, especially in the distinctive forms of solidarity constructed in the immediate work group. With economic reform, however, workers gave up their attachment to the work collective, which was no longer capable of dispensing rewards, and shifted their loyalties to family and family-based survival strategies on the one hand and toward a larger collective on the other. Rather than mobilize their work groups for effective reform, they preferred to change their leadership, supporting authoritarian managers and—beyond these—politicians capable of delivering resources in times of increased scarcity. As in Creed's analysis, so in Ashwin's: a challenge to the locus of group identity is met with an appeal to leaders who have the interest and the resources to defend the collectivity in question. Those leaders are often former communists. Stripped of their ideology, they remain the most powerful and effective rulers, still able to mobilize support from "alienated" collectivities.

Andrew Lass describes similar patterns of "restoration" around the computerization of the Czech and Slovak library systems. Whereas importing a self-contained, standardized business like McDonalds works fairly smoothly, the transfer of an on-line catalog that would make the contents of all major libraries easily accessible comes up against preexisting layers of competitive social relations that resist unification around the new technology and the old library cultures of manuscript preservation. With this argument we come full circle. We began by showing how dismantling the party state led to the reconfiguration of everyday worlds, how market-promoting policies caused a retreat from markets, how building new institutions generated new resistances; finally, we show how the decline of the old order brought pressures to resurrect the very features and personnel that had initially been rejected.

Lass goes further, however, in trying to illuminate just how these seeming continuities arise—and how complex a matter this is. Why is it that CASLIN (Czech and Slovak Library Information Network) does not function more like similar electronic arrangements in, say, the United States? More broadly, wherein lie the resistances to Western blueprints for transformation? Our other authors have answered this broader question (explicitly or implicitly) in terms of new configurations of interest, systemic constraints on action, or attachments to certain identities. Transitologists often answer it by invoking "culture," that amorphous, omnibus concept so readily employed as an explanatory variable when all else fails. Inspired by phenomenology and the sociology of Bourdieu (sources rather different from those of our other authors), Lass explores the question in a very nuanced way. He writes of *habitus*, of structured dispositions and horizons of sense, of patterned feelings and discourses, of webs of connection—what he calls *worlds*. All of these phenomena enter into a micropolitics of daily existence that infuses externally imposed projects with intentions and directionalities divergent from those that were planned. If, as we argued earlier, the transformation of socialism entails the weakening of broader structures and a consequent opportunity for daily practices to influence disproportionately the restructuring that ensues, then Lass has helped us to identify what we should attend to in those daily practices. Hence, once again, ethnography.

Market and Countermarket

In addition to these insights concerning how new life worlds and new structures are constituted from below, what further lessons do the chapters in this volume suggest? We point to four.

The first lesson is that we cannot separate the economic from the political and the cultural. In the imagination of policymakers, the economic is a series of purely economic interventions—privatization, price liberalizations or levers controlling inflation, interest rates, budget deficits, and the like. When these interventions meet everyday life, however, the resistance they encounter is not just economic but cultural and political as well. The economy is always thoroughly embedded in a variety of noneconomic practices. There can be no pure economy, only a political and cultural economy. This lesson is important both for scholars who seek to understand the transformations of postsocialism and also for the policymakers who produce them.

The second lesson is that we cannot conceive of the transition as either rooted in the past or tied to an imagined future. Transition is a process suspended between the two. Policies emanate from the center and encounter resistance, which reverberates back as unintended consequences demanding correction. Policy and reaction enter into a continual interaction that makes up the process of the transition. This process is therefore not a unilinear one of moving from one stage to the next, as projected in neoliberal plans, but a combined and uneven one having multiple trajectories. (It is for this reason that we tend to prefer the term *transforma-*

tion, which has fewer teleological resonances than *transition.*) That is, policies combine with preexisting circumstances in different ways to produce different outcomes and reactions. This combination means the process is also uneven, affecting different regions and, within regions, different sectors at different rates.

The third lesson of these chapters is that we should be wary of reducing the transition to a debate between revolutionary and evolutionary perspectives, both of which presume progressive development. On the contrary, our case studies show that in the present world context the shift to a market economy brings with it "regressive" and "progressive" dynamics simultaneously. We can usefully develop the concept of involution, adopted by Zbierski, to capture the economic changes taking place in postcommunist countries—such as the dominance of exchange over production, with the former expanding at the expense of the latter and forcing populations into primitive *dis*accumulation with a retreat into subsistence. In the extreme case—Russia—the successive stages of shock therapy have pushed the country more and more toward a Third World economy: plundered for its natural resources, opened to cheap foreign commodities, increasingly run by an emergent parasitic financial oligarchy.

The final lesson follows from the third, namely, that we should be explicit about the comparisons we draw between postcommunist and other countries. In comparing the former with ideal-typical conceptions of the West—textbook notions of the free market and liberal democracy—one sees transition societies only in terms of deficits and misses their specificity, their distinctive dynamics. We might better compare those countries with each other than with the Western models they supposedly emulate. Why does the Russian economy continue to decline year in, year out, while the Chinese economy continues to grow? Why has the Polish economy done better in some respects than the much acclaimed Hungarian and Czech models? The answers to these questions will be found not just in how macro policies—privatization, stabilization, liberalization, and so on—are crafted but in the micro responses to them, in the ways people and their communities absorb, manipulate, or reject the new market parameters of action.

Just as Karl Polanyi analyzed communal resistance to the market expansion of the mid-nineteenth century, so at the end of the twentieth century we witness similar communal reactions to the market in postcommunist societies—selective appropriation, evasive improvisation, explicit resistance, and the emergence of new terrains of struggle. In both cases the context is a burgeoning capitalist economy of ever-more-global scope that is drawing countries into vast exchange networks of many forms, from barter to trade to global finance. As Polanyi showed, whereas incorporation into these networks brings affluence for some, for many it brings poverty, marginality, and exclusion from modern means of existence. Our ethnographies illuminate the micro processes through which this second transformation takes place.

Notes

1. Some students of the postsocialist world question the use of this term (for example, Nelson, Tilly, and Walker 1998; Stark and Bruszt 1998). Because the word is so often used in policy circles with the presumption that a kind of ideal-typical free-market capitalism and liberal democracy will result from the collapse of socialism, anyone who entertains some skepticism about the end point might better use another word, such as *transformation*. The skepticism might be over whether the result will be capitalism or over what *form* of capitalism may result. Because our title already indicates this skepticism, we proceed with the word *transition*, suitably humbled.

References

Arato, Andrew. 1981. Civil Society vs. the State. *Telos* 47: 23–47.

Arendt, Hannah. 1951. *The Origins of Totalitarianism*. New York: Harcourt, Brace, and Jovanovich.

Åslund, Anders. 1995. *How Russia Became a Market Economy*. Washington, D.C.: Brookings Institution.

Boycko, Maxim, Andrei Schleifer, and Robert Vishny. 1995. *Privatizing Russia*. Cambridge: MIT Press.

Cohen, Stephen F. 1985. *Rethinking the Soviet Experience*. New York: Oxford University Press.

Goldman, Marshall I. 1994. *Lost Opportunity*. New York: Norton.

Habermas, Jürgen. 1987. *The Theory of Communicative Action. Volume Two: Lifeworld and System: A Critique of Functionalist Reason*. Boston: Beacon Press.

Hankiss, Elemér. 1990. *Eastern European Alternatives*. Oxford: Clarendon Press.

Kornai, János. 1990. *The Road to a Free Economy*. New York: Norton.

———. 1994. Transformational Recession: The Main Causes. *Journal of Comparative Economics* 19: 39–63.

Lewin, Moshe. 1985. *The Making of the Soviet System*. New York: Pantheon Books.

Lipton, David, and Jeffrey Sachs. 1990. Creating a Market Economy in Eastern Europe—The Case of Poland. *Brookings Papers on Economic Activity* 1: 75–147.

Malia, Martin. 1994. *The Soviet Tragedy*. New York: Free Press.

Murrell, Peter. 1991. Can Neoclassical Economics Underpin the Reform of Centrally Planned Economics? *Journal of Economic Perspectives* 5(4): 59–78.

————. 1993. What Is Shock Therapy? What Did It Do in Poland and Russia? *Post-Soviet Affairs* 9(2): 111–140.

Nelson, Joan M., Charles Tilly, and Lee Walker, eds. 1998. *Transforming Post-Communist Political Economies*. Washington, D.C.: National Academy Press.

Poznanski, Kazimierz Z. 1993. Restructuring Property Rights in Poland: A Study in Evolutionary Politics. *East European Politics and Societies* 7(3): 395–421.

Róna-Tas Ákos. 1997. *The Great Surprise of the Small Transformation: The Demise of Communism and the Rise of the Private Sector in Hungary*. Ann Arbor: University of Michigan Press.

Sachs, Jeffrey. 1994. Toward Glasnost in the IMF. *Challenge* 47(3): 4–11.

Stark, David. 1996. Recombinant Property in Eastern European Capitalism. *American Journal of Sociology* 101: 993–1027.

Stark, David, and László Bruszt. 1998. *Postsocialist Pathways: Transforming Politics and Property in East Central Europe*. Cambridge: Cambridge University Press.

Stiglitz, Joseph. 1994. *Whither Socialism?* Cambridge: MIT Press.

Szelényi, Iván. 1988. *Socialist Entrepreneurs*. Madison: University of Wisconsin Press.

1

Traders, "Disorder," and Citizenship Regimes in Provincial Russia

Caroline Humphrey

After more than sixty years as an instrument of the state plan, trade in Russia has erupted as one of the most volatile elements in the present economy and society. This chapter describes the new forms of trading and investigates what can be learned from them about the current social transformations in provincial Russia.

Burawoy and Krotov (1993) have suggested that the post-Soviet Russian economy is dominated by "merchant capital," meaning that enterprises seek profit from commerce rather than through the transformation of production. In the sphere of production, much of the old Soviet structure remains. Furthermore, merchant capital, Burawoy and Krotov argue, does not spontaneously evolve into modern capitalism; rather, like the past alliance between merchant capital and feudal dominant classes, the present clientelistic links between Russian managers and organs of political power prevent the growth of an autonomous bourgeoisie (1993: 65): I argue here that Burawoy and Krotov are correct about the persistence of the earlier organization of production and are right to query the assumption that when liberalized, trade inevitably takes a Western capitalist form. But events since the early 1990s have overtaken their diagnosis: new players on the scene are unaccounted for by Burawoy and Krotov's scenario. In any case, we need to think in different theoretical terms.

The last few years in provincial Russia have seen an enormous burgeoning of petty trade, unforeseen in the merchant capitalism scenario. Significantly, a large proportion of petty trade is international and consists of "shuttlers" traveling abroad to bring in manufactures for sale. Directly related to the explosion of small trade are the breakup and subdivision of former state enterprises, which have shed much of their labor. The dynamics of petty trading are highly volatile: successful individuals move into small wholesaling and then into large wholesaling, but many small traders fail. Despite this, there is an endless sporadic flow of people into trade, prompted as much by absolute necessity as by the desire to make a profit. Although some wealthy private firms have emerged in the economic interstices where money can be made, in the provinces their number is small.

These days the idea of merchant capitalism applies perhaps least of all to the former state and collective enterprises. Even relatively successful enterprises of this type have strong incentives, for reasons explained later, not to show a profit. The majority totter on the edge of ruin or are bankrupt. They experience a great shortage of money, and many operate almost entirely by barter (see chapter 3, this volume). In summer 1996, industrial workers went for months without being paid, but agricultural workers had not received money wages for years. Since the early 1990s the subsistence sphere has greatly expanded. Ordinary people—whether in industry or agriculture, whether urban or rural—rely on their own vegetable plots, exchanges with relatives, and forest gathering to provide basic food. By contrast, petty trade and the wealthy private firms, the sources of clothing, domestic utensils, cigarettes, alcohol, etc. on the one hand, and oil products, cars, and luxury goods on the other, operate entirely by money. This need for cash in a barter-and-subsistence economy is one of the main sources of "traders," people who need money to purchase things they cannot produce themselves.

Many provinces of Russia cannot balance their budgets. They rely on financial subsidies from Moscow. This means that, very generally, money circulates through regional governmental budgets only to certain parts of the population: key industries (power, transport), state employees (administrators, doctors, teachers), and state dependents (pensioners, invalids, war veterans). Successful traders reap this cash, giving rise to a number of support industries for the rich New Russians, as they are called, such as car-repair firms, security teams, and builders of their new houses. These money flows do not penetrate far, however, and great numbers of people have irregular access to money and, in the countryside, virtually no access.

The intellectual problem in analyzing this situation lies in trying to comprehend an unprecedented and fluid set of circumstances. Unlike China, where a centuries-old pattern of petty capitalism quickly reestablished itself after the reforms in the early 1980s (Gates 1996), Russia does not appear to be reverting to its prerevolutionary combination of family merchant houses and great periodic fairs. In fact, Russians seem surprised by what is happening with their trade. In comparison with China, Russian trade is atraditional, in the sense that it is inventing its own new culture as it goes. It is doing this, however, not in a blank field but in an economic terrain inhabited by the disintegrating and unwieldy former state enterprises, as well as by local governments desperate to keep at least part of those enterprises alive.

The vocabulary of holistic schemes seems inadequate to explain what is happening. If a term like *the transition* is debatable because it is often taken to imply that postsocialist economies are coming to resemble Western capitalist economies (but which one?), how much more questionable is a term like *merchant capitalism?* Not only is an analogy between Russia in the late twentieth century and the distant past of Europe debatable, but the theoretical concept of a stage or an epoch characterized by an interrelated structure may limit our understanding of the current circumstances of widespread and erratic change. Woodruff's seminal article, "Barter of the Bankrupt" (see chapter 3) points rightly to the need to understand local politics and its fitful relationship—even its frequent contradiction—to Moscow's attempt to regulate the flow of money.

Above all, applying the idiom of Marxist historical schemata to contemporary experience almost inevitably denies the ethnography of representations. The notion of a class-based, stable ideology cannot deal with those features to which anthropologists have access and that are peculiarly important in the unstable conditions of Russia today—namely, the nontheorized and most various frameworks and values through which people understand the world. It is essential, in my view, for an ethnography to include these representations, since they both inform economic action and create reactions to that action. I argue that the forms taken by the surge of mass trade are greatly influenced by these views.

The reactions to the facts of trade emerge from the underswell of the habitus of people's life, which was formed in Soviet times but is now undirected and contradictory. The great difficulty in describing this phenomenon lies in its inarticulacy and emotion-driven character. It may seem surprising to use such terms in relation to trade, but it should be remembered that present trading activities developed from an illegal pursuit, without a vocabulary of its own legitimacy, and that Russian precedents for "normal" trade lie in generations that precede the longest memories. This means the stereotypes characterizing trade from the inside are more powerful than the emerging idioms to conceptualize it from inside. Contrast, for example, the modest domestic expression traders use for their profit, *navarka*, the grease that emerges on the top of soup, with the passionate, generalized denunciation of an elderly man (one of many who made similar statements): "What is the source of Russia's misfortunes? Traders. They should be put away. They just make money for themselves, not for society." Since the early 1990s government responses have again repeatedly controlled, liberated, and abruptly regulated traders in various ways. These public reactions have various immediate purposes, but I shall argue that their ultimate sources lie in evolving ideas of order, in concepts of identity and territoriality, and in different political cultures. An ethnographically adequate account of trade in present Russia therefore has to describe not only the various trading activities but representations of those activities and, most difficult of all, the sources of such representations, and it should be phrased in a way that incorporates the reactive and dynamic nature of the phenomena.

To get at the contradictory dynamics affecting trade it is necessary to uncover the emotion-charged, unrationalized values that are derived from people's ambivalence to the realization of the Soviet state structure. The state's organization penetrated the consciousness of all people, but here it underwent a culturally varied transformation (sometimes oppositional in character, especially among non-Russians [Humphrey 1989]). I shall argue that the historically formed sense of "us" against the state—that is, an identity defined by the state but required to act in relation to it—has given rise to a plethora of localisms. These localisms exist at district, county, and province levels and have deepened and become mutually competitive in recent years with the weakening legitimacy of all-Russian structures. Soviet organization of production and distribution gave each the ideal character of a self-reproducing social whole, a tendency emphasized by the local "self-government" rhetoric of Yeltsin's program.

This chapter shows how uncontrolled movement violates the sense of order pertaining to bounded wholes. The defensive territoriality now exists in incoherent confrontation with the simultaneous realization of globalized desires and demands. Trade brings in desirable goods, but it also carries out valuables, and it inevitably breaches the frontiers of jealously guarded domains. International trade, including that with the states of the former Soviet Union, arouses both the most desire and the most anxiety. Markets and border crossings are places where "disorder" (*bezproyadok*) is feared. I will argue that the acute confrontation of trade with localism is an active component in the emergence of new citizenship regimes in Russia. In addition, I will try to explain why Russians stereotype traders together with smugglers, profiteers, speculators, racketeers, and 'criminal-genic elements' and how the vast accumulation of legislation regulating trade is actively affecting what it means to be a citizen in Russia.

Expansion of Cross-Border Trade

In the historical long duration, Russian state policy toward trade has been characterized by autocratic centralized control with a few temporary windows of quasi-free trade. Even if short-lived relaxations were sometimes more or less forced on it, the Tsarist government succeeded in retaining a remarkably constipated trade policy. At the tiny number of international border trade posts, the fiscal demands of the state always tended to outweigh the need to keep prices down and goods flowing.[1] However, after the Soviet era in which trade was under state control *tout simple,* the liberalization of international trade and visa regulations in the perestroika years led to a probably irreversible change. Beginning in April 1991, all Soviet citizens were allowed to take part in international trade (Butler 1991: xxiii).

There was an immediate rush of small traders to bring back foreign goods for sale. Six years later, large numbers of people still engage in this trade. It was estimated, for example, that in 1992 about half of the population of Irkutsk took part,[2] and in 1996, according to information from the Business Round-Table of Russia, around 30 million people (41 percent of Russia's working population) were engaged in the international petty commodities shuttle trade and services tied to that trade (Nikitina 1996).

On the whole, the export of Russian goods is not carried out by the independent shuttlers. Rather, the collapse of many industries and the hazy, complex process of privatization has provided an unprecedented opportunity for unscrupulous officials and managers. This process involved the extraordinarily widespread selling off and removal of former state property, seen by many as a gigantic rip-off in which not only the goods themselves but many of the profits have been transferred outside Russian frontiers—that is, to hard-currency accounts.[3] It has been estimated that values equivalent to the total state reserves of dollars and gold are removed from Russia each year, often by illegal means.[4] The breakup of the USSR also encouraged the illicit removal of goods internally among republics because they did not take action against crimes committed on one another's territory (Handelman 1994: 19). Recently, an ever-increasing number of goods has been designated as having strategic value and not to be exported.[5] But previously, entire regional governments (e.g., Kalmykia in 1992) were involved in the turning of state (i.e., "no one's") property into marketable commodities, and violations of export regulations continue to be widely reported. At present, much energy at federal and province[5] levels is expended to control the outflow of goods.

The mass character of trade gives the subject its importance in post-Soviet society. In the context of post-Soviet values, the voluntaristic, profiteering, and boundary-crossing character of trade still makes it seem nonroutine, almost transgressive, and for that reason trade is coming to be the site of citizens' conflicts. Only as of 1995 or so did a few organizations emerge that dared to mention traders' rights. These groups are often in conflict with provincial governments. Two such groups in the city of Ulan-Ude in Buryatia are *Grazhdanskoye Yedinstvo* (Civil Unity) and the Association for the Support of Small and Middle Entrepreneurship of Buryatia. In 1996 these groups were struggling against a recent Buryat government resolution that replaced the existing system of licensing alcohol sales with a "humiliating" auction of licenses and other restrictions. Significantly, and presumably because traders include such a large part of the population, Civil Unity argued that the resolution is contrary to federal law and contravenes the civil rights guaranteed in the constitution. The group proposed to organize a mass referendum of the population, the only way to force the provincial government to reconsider the issue.[7]

This chapter focuses on the individuals and firms I call "traders," defined as those who aim to profit from middlemen activities involving goods and services. This category is heterogeneous, with a number of rapidly changing forms, but it has the advantage of coinciding with the indigenous concept of *torgovtsy* as people not involved in productive labor. In terms of functions, it might be feasible to make the familiar distinctions among wholesalers, retailers, brokers, financiers, and so forth, but in Russia today individuals and firms may take on one, some, or all of these functions. From an anthropological point of view, it is more useful to try to discover the evolving types of traders defined by indigenous categories, as this can tell us about how traders are beginning to fit into and generate an emergent citizenship regime. Later I outline the dynamics of six such types: *biznesmen* (businesspeople), *brokery* (brokers), *predprinimateli* (entrepreneurs), *chelnoki* (shuttlers), *kommersanty* (trader-retailers), and *perekupshchiki* (resellers) as a first step in this rather uncharted domain. A further highly important indigenous category is that politely known as *torgovyye menshinstva* (trading minorities).

Some Terms for a Contextualization of Trade in Russia

The economic environment in which traders operate is dominated by productive enterprises such as the extractive and processing plants, collective farms, and factories that were state managed under the Soviet regime. I refer to them as corporations in that since the reforms they have charters (*ustav*) legitimizing them as separate legal entities with rights distinct from those of their members.[8] Such production units now engage in buying and selling, bartering, and so forth. I will argue later along the lines of Clarke (1992), however, that in the post-Soviet economic collapse these enterprises are not dominated primarily by the profit motive but rather are concerned with survival and the social protection of their members. There is a spectrum here. Perhaps the majority of corporations

in rural areas could be called "neosocialist corporations" because socialism (as indigenously defined) is not dead in Russia. Other enterprises,
which enter the current fray with a mixture of communitarian, strategic,
and commercial motives, might be termed "postsocialist corporations."
A third, small category of corporations consists of firms created by independent entrepreneurs that are frankly commercial in outlook. The aim
of these distinctions is not to make an absolute differentiation between
institutions on the ground, which would be difficult, but to problematize
the different ways in which Russian citizens are constructing new economic institutions.

Along with production corporations, the other major actors are the
state organizations—including government and municipal bureaucracies—and educational, cultural, and health institutions. It is a peculiarity
of Russian life that many of these organizations also act like economic
corporations. For example, a rural middle school often has its own housing, agricultural land, tractors, and livestock; supplies its own food and
heating; and engages in trade within the district. The trend toward institutional self-sufficiency has increased recently with ministerial budget
cuts and late payment of running costs and wages. Nevertheless, state
employees (the *byudzhetniki* as they are known) are much envied since,
along with pensioners, they are essentially the only people in rural areas
with access to money wages.

Trade is giving rise to new social categories. It is in this context that I
employ the idea of the *citizenship regime.*⁹ The term refers to the political
categorization of citizens by government agencies, even if such a classification is not set out in any document. The term thus refers to a practice
rather than a charter. At present, a post-Soviet citizenship regime is being
formed. A flood of new laws constantly appears; these laws are of several
types and originate from various levels of government, thus affecting the
legal capacities of people of various statuses. For example, in Moscow in
one week in November 1995, the following were issued: one codex (*ko-
deks*), five decrees (*ukaz*), fifteen resolutions (*postanovleniye*), one in-
struction (*ukazakniye*), one law (*zakon*), and thirteen orders (*rasporyaz-
heniye*); and these applied variously to citizens of the Russian Federation,
citizens of Moscow, Russian citizens living permanently abroad, pensioners of Moscow, citizens of Kalinin Oblast, and so forth.¹⁰ With the declaration of sovereignty by various constituent parts of the Russian Federation, local regulations now elaborate—and sometimes conflict
with—those from Moscow. Many laws are ignored or not known about,
but a basic bureaucratic portfolio is still part of post-Soviet life, notably
papers proving one's place of birth, official ethnicity, and membership in
a corporation; passports for internal and foreign use and for registration

of domicile; work record; housing entitlement; and professional qualifications.

To engage in trade, one must acquire the status of either a "physical person" (*fizicheskoye litso,* the right to trade as an individual) or a "juridical person" (*yuridicheskoye litso,* the right to trade as a company). In Russian parlance one "buys" these rights; that is, one purchases a license for a given period.[11] Even someone who sells pine nuts on a street corner must have a license and must keep a book showing the source and cost of acquisitions, the price of each sale, and the profit on each transaction. Taxes are charged on all profits.[12] Physical persons are limited to a small turnover. Juridical persons are subject to dramatically increased taxes on profits, reaching 90 percent in larger firms, and must also keep a professional accountant and a further set of licenses, such as licenses for import, export, storage, and sale premises of various kinds; employment of laborers; compliance with sanitary regulations; and so forth. The amount of regulation is difficult to comprehend and impossible to describe fully here, but one example is that a truck must have a license not only to be on the road but also to travel to given regions. A trader I know was greatly hampered by the fact that her truck was not licensed to go into the neighboring province in Russia.

Such regulations are widely flouted, thus putting traders in an uncertain relationship with the law and placing them in the hands of alternative networks. A further concept to introduce at this point involves social relations of trust. In trade, these relations tend overwhelmingly to be personal relations and are different from the structure of state posts, even for people who are trading on behalf of state or former state institutions.

After a brief window of liberalization in the period 1991–1993, in which it was hoped that free trade would encourage Russian manufacturing, state policy concerning the role of trade has wavered. Indeed, the official import-export trade, from which the state derives considerable income, is generally estimated to be far outweighed by the illegal flood of goods in and out.[13] Now, the Russian government sees nonpayment of taxes and customs duties as one of its major problems. Traders are viewed as uncontrolled elements to be pounced on for fiscal purposes. An example is seen in the resolution of the Russian Federation, brought into force on 1 August 1996, limiting the untaxed import of international goods by physical persons (i.e., shuttle traders) to a value of U.S.\$1,000 and 50 kg. The Government Customs Committee hopes this law will bring increased customs duties of 2 trillion rubles (\$400 million) per month into the state treasury. Russians laugh at this. They predict the new law will only put weak traders out of business, whereas the others will redouble their bribes to the customs people, and prices on the street will go up (Nikitina 1996). The almost universal attitude is that trade is not only largely unprotected by the state but is carried on more in the face than under the aegis of state laws and policies.

In any event, traders have long since elaborated their own means of establishing trust in the context of their particular activities. At the very least, you can trust yourself. The phenomenon of the shuttler, someone who personally travels to Turkey, China, and other countries to buy and bring back goods, is one result. Shuttlers often use close kin to sell for them while they go on their next journey, but for the wider links required to obtain start-up capital, establish reliable sources of goods, obtain licenses, find "friendly" customs and railway officials, and so forth, a range of new ties is emerging that differs in various communities, as is described more fully later. Among Russians, family feeling (*semeinost'*) is often no longer strong enough to support these functions, and the ritualized trade friendships that had flourished between Buryats and Russians, Russians and Chinese in prerevolutionary times no longer exist. Bruno (1996) has made the interesting point that women often attribute their success as entrepreneurs to their ability to deal with people and their reputation for greater trustworthiness than men. Banks are still widely avoided—it is feared they may crash or arbitrarily freeze personal accounts. As a result, even in fairly large transactions payments are commonly made in person and in cash.[14] Anyone with a departure ticket at an airport can expect someone in his or her network of contacts to materialize at their elbow, such as that old school chum with a mysterious wad of cash in a plastic bag to be delivered to the "red-haired woman with a McDonalds T-shirt" at the other end.

Both barter deals and the pursuit of cash make peculiar demands on personal trust. Barter requires security for future and repeat transactions and engenders local dependencies (Humphrey 1991; Woodruff, chapter 3 [this volume]), but it is worth mentioning here that money, which is so scarce in present Russian circumstances, also becomes a barterable commodity. To obtain it, personal networks must be scoured. I was present when my Buryat host, the long-standing director of a government horticultural research station, needed money to pay the electric bill. Last quarter she had paid the electric company with several thousand fruit tree saplings, but this time the company insisted on money. Indeed, it had cut off the electricity for a weekend, to my host's indignation. After several telephone calls to the director of the electric company, an old friend/enemy, to no avail, my host said, "Well, I'll try Lydia Ivanovna for the money, though she's a devil, because she owes me for those black currants last year." The call went: "Lydiushka, my dear, how is your health? And your wonderful daughter Tanya, how did her exams go? . . . The thing is, I need money, just a few million, by next Tuesday. What, you haven't got any? Now I'm sure those workers of yours would appreciate some raspberries; they are really exceptional this year." Appealing to every known tie and blandishment is one technique (with strategic use made of the formal/informal word for "you"), but equally possible, according to the relationship being played out, are threats and shouting, groveling, haughtiness, or exercising naked power. Such personalization of transactions is common virtually throughout the economic field, which is one reason it makes no sense to divide the Russian economy into informal and formal sectors.

The pervasive atmosphere is one of fear of infringement, theft, and violent robbery; and, indeed, these are common. This fear is seen in countless incidents, from seemingly trivial threats, like the roadside trader who scratches a skull and crossbones on his temporarily vacated space, to confrontations over disputed use of former state property ("Do you want to kill me with that bulldozer of yours?" as one factory manager screamed dramatically, hoping to deter some "wretched Armenians" from digging up pipes on "his" territory). No one seems to consider calling the police; most common is the appeal to higher power—in other words, to protection. Here it is interesting that Russians refer to both patrons in the legitimate power structure and racketeers by the same term, *krysha,* meaning roof. A small enterprise manager needs a "roof" up in the ministry or among the circle of the province bosses. For street traders the "roof" is much lower and of more dubious help. Without exception, traders pay both legitimate site fees to the town council ("for clearing rubbish and keeping order") and bungs to racketeers who divide up the streets ("to keep others off your patch").

The term *mafiya* is also widely bandied about, perhaps because although criminal organizations clearly exist with histories that go back to Soviet times, today the shadowy tentacles of armed protection are evident in the most respectable areas of public life—and the two are not easily distinguishable.[15] All banks have their own, normally immaculate armed security guards,[16] as do hotels for foreigners and shops with expensive imported goods. But the protection racketeers also cultivate an aura of reliability and popularity (in Ulan-Ude they are "former sportsmen," the Boxers, Wrestlers, and others who have divided up the town). Cossacks and quasi-military squads also stalk the markets "to keep order." Although Russians do distinguish legitimate protection from illegitimate protection at the ends of this spectrum, it makes more sense to recognize that a widespread need for security exists and that provisions for protection can arise from within ordinary social groups, as well as being provided by outside agencies (Varese 1994).[17]

Some traders are indeed linked with criminal activities, notably making fake vodka, counterfeiting money,[18] and selling drugs.[19] Furthermore, the boundary that had separated protection from trade, tenaciously upheld in most criminal circles during the Soviet period, has been greatly eroded, which means racket organizations themselves sometimes engage in trade (see discussion of "thieves in law" and "authorities" in the underworld in Handelman 1994: 3–32). But the almost hysterical fear of criminal deception among ordinary people—the feverish inspection of dollar bills, the countless ingenious tests for "real" vodka—seems disproportionate and has deeper cultural sources, as Lemon (1996) argues. Petty traders are vulnerable in their interstitial position. The more they employ protection, the more society in general tends to mistrust them.

Disintegrating Corporations

This section attempts to describe how the breakdown of enterprises as social groups is generating a peculiarly post-Soviet form of anxiety and how the combined effects of the economic crisis and local government control prevent corporations from taking effective action.

In southeast Siberia, despite the reforms, not all enterprises have changed their status to privatized types.[20] Especially in agriculture, many Soviet enterprises simply remain in place, and even those with the new status of joint-stock company or farmers' association are still referred to colloquially as *kolkhoz*. In industry, many of the huge monolithic organizations of Soviet times have been broken up into their constituent parts. The former Trans-Baikal Timber Corporation, Zabaikalles, for example, has become a series of separate production and processing units located all over the republic (Kurochkin 1995). In either case, my material shows that such a provincial enterprise still sees itself as a productive unit concerned with reproducing itself as a *kollektiv*.[21] In other words, there seems to be a significant lag between popular values and juridical changes, which affects how people act. What the corporations are reproducing is not a monetary fund or an economic capacity to supply a product but a social community that is specific in its localization at a certain place and in its occupational characteristics. Clarke (1992: 7) aptly refers to this community as "the primary unit of soviet society" and argues for the continued vitality of this "state within the state" in the postsocialist period (1992: 27).

One reform that is changing the social nature of the corporation is the relinquishing in 1993–1994 of a range of social functions to the local administration, the lowest branch of the state.[22] Pensions, insurance, education, and medicine have gradually been handed over. This removal of social responsibilities has been the first step in the disintegration of the enterprise-based *kollektiv*. The dire economic situation of virtually all agricultural corporations has forced them to make bitter decisions, and in this situation the crumbling of the boundaries of the community creates anger and anxiety.[23] The cumulative destabilizing effects of the economic crisis and the shedding of social responsibilities can be seen clearly in the following example.

The Onokhoi Wood-Products Company, formerly a branch of the giant state Zabaikalles, has a population of 5,000 people, and its situation is desperate. When it decided to privatize as an open joint-stock company, 51 percent of the shares were taken over by the *kollektiv,* 20 percent were retained by the state, and 29 percent were sold on the open market. "All would have been well," people now say, if the open shares had not been bought up by outsiders, the "Tyumen representatives," who also succeeded in having their leader chosen to be the director. As things began to go wrong and salaries were not paid, some members of the *kollektiv* began to sell their shares, which were also quickly bought up by the Tyumen people.

The battle for control between insiders and outside shareholders is a common occurrence in Russia (Clarke 1992: 13–14), and one reason for such tension is the feeling that only insiders will care for the corporation as a whole. In fact, the explanation for the failure of Onokhoi lies less in callous decisions made by the outsiders from Tyumen, as local people feared, than in the disappearance of purchasers in Kazakhstan, the Urals, and other regions with the breakup of the USSR. This situation was compounded by rising interest rates on loans, the high cost of electricity, increased customs charges, and higher federal and local taxes. By late 1994, a product sellable for a ruble cost 1 ruble 35 kopeks to produce. Still, it was decided "at any price to strive to preserve the *kollektiv* and survive until better days." As there was no money, wages were paid in furniture. "Take it, sell it, and survive!" workers were told. Meanwhile, management also tried to supply the members with food, obtained by barter for Onokhoi wood products.

The Onokhoi workers went on strike in August 1994, demanding work and wages, and the Tyumen director was replaced by a local man. But try as they might, management and the trade union were unable to preserve the *kollektiv* as a source of work. Half of the 2,150 jobs were annulled, and many of those with jobs were put on short time or given obligatory holidays. The director expressed the hope that those out of work could manage on the private plots provided by the firm and on the "gifts of the taiga forest." His next words are telling with regard to attitudes toward enterprise-based trade:

> "In the recent past the company processed 250,000 cubic metres of timber in six months, but in 1994 this was reduced to 17,500 cubic metres. And although our main suppliers remain the same, the Kurbinsk and Khandaga-

tai forestry companies, no one is going to give raw materials for free. So to give work at least to our sawing workshops we were forced (true, in only small amounts) to obtain unconditioned wood from Irkutsk Oblast and even from commercial traders from the Amur. And it was just the same with selling. We have no way out but to sell to private traders, or to barter our goods for food." "The Onokhoitsy are flapping like fish on ice," observed the journalist sadly. (Nikolayev 1994)

Some significant points emerge from this example with regard to the conditions for trade. Even though the firm has undergone a major change in status, having been freed from state control,[24] (1) the aim of both buying and selling is not to establish a slimmed-down, efficient firm but to provide work, food, and other sustenance for an existing community; (2) nevertheless, forced by the economic crisis, the firm sheds jobs and puts people on short time; (3) there is a reluctance to trade with unaccustomed partners, particularly private traders; and (4) large numbers of people, still in some sense in Onokhoi, now have to fend for themselves.

Trade by such firms is enmeshed in government regulations that make it disadvantageous to show a profit. Visible profit of juridical persons, as mentioned, is very heavily taxed, and a profitable enterprise might be refused government commodity credit (*tovarnyy kredit*). This is the system, especially elaborated in agriculture, whereby the government secures a supply of future products in return for loans in the form of gas, spare parts, and other commodities. Enterprises are forced to participate because they cannot find alternative buyers willing to gamble on future production. One of the aims of the commodity credit system, as a government official told me, is to keep enterprises going while not making money available to them, because in their theoretically independent status they are not trusted to use it "in the right ways." All of this reduces former state enterprises' capacity to trade. But many people justify the system ideologically. For the old guard there is simply a stark opposition: there are "two ways of living one's life," one based on honest production inside the corporation and the other on nonproductive, selfish business that provides no work for anyone else (Shelkunova 1995).

Many people are forced into petty trade. They belong to a corporation, live there, and yet have no employment there. Others work but receive no pay. "How do you manage when the wages are not paid?" I asked one librarian. "What can I do?" she replied. "First I borrow. Then I stand on the street corner and sell things."

Sense of Place, Frontiers, and the "Great Trash Road"

The Soviet regime introduced a powerful administrative hierarchy of functional departmentalization combined with territorialization. A citizen's status came to be defined most notably by attachment to a work collective, a unit located in an administrative subsection of the state (republic, autonomous republic, oblast, raion, and so forth). At each level, from republics downward through the administrative hierarchy to enterprises, units were recipients in the redistributive economy of scarcity (see Verdery 1991). At the same time, units were territorially defined. Although there were important social exceptions to the principle of territoriality, such as ethnicity, professional qualifications, or membership in the Communist Party, an entire range of control policies in the late Soviet period had the effect of deepening that principle (policies involving registration of domicile, access to work, wage differentials, and housing).

I suggest that after the collapse of the USSR, disintegration of the Communist Party and many all-union departmental structures left regionality to flourish in new ways. Not only has the old *propiska* residence permit been replaced by an even more stringent registration system, but an emotional identification with place has emerged with articulate force and has become an active generator of the emerging citizenship regimes. The raising of the status of certain provinces, local elections, the unilateral declaration of free trade zones, the publicity given to provincial budgets, wide differences between regions in the buying power of the ruble, and so forth have contributed to this emergence. A symptom is the recent formation of numerous *zemlyachestva* (societies of people from the same district). These groups exist at different levels in Russia as a whole but also within provinces. In Buryatia, for example, there are societies for people from Barguzin district, Ol'hon district, and so forth. Whereas their overt aims are usually cultural, the *zemlyachestva* also seem to act as lobbies and networks.[25]

Yet, the specter of further splitting apart has made frontiers the focus of tension. The "sacred frontier" of Soviet times has not disappeared, although it has been displaced from the USSR to the Russian border, and it is credited with a long pre-Soviet history. For example, in an article entitled "Ashamed on Behalf of State Power . . ." (*Za derzhavy obidno . . .*), Gomelev (1995) describes how the proud customs service battles at its frontier posts to maintain the Russian Customs Charter of 1633—a charter more legendary than practical, one imagines—against the disorderly flows of goods. At the same time, seamlessly attached to the official ideology but different from it is the people's attachment to their places. Place, people, and local enterprises, all tied together (as workmates, schoolmates, *zemlyaki*—district coresidents—and so forth), are the social sites for these "natural" attachments, and they can also emerge at different levels, from the brigade seen as a *kollektiv* to the enterprise, the district, the republic, and to Russia itself. A Buryat colleague told me he was traveling in Chita Oblast with a young nephew. When they were returning home the boy looked eagerly at the map to search for the boundary with Buryatia, and as they passed through an undifferentiated steppe he saw a signpost and announced happily, "At last we have entered our homeland (*rodnaya zemlya*)."[26] The existence of traders, I argue, cuts right across the loyalties sharpened in the new battle for existence. Not only do traders not "earn their rights" by productive labor in one or another corporation, but they cross institutional/territorial boundaries and make money from the very discontinuities other people feel obliged to observe. They jar against people's sense of identity. They are thought to *take out* the property felt to belong legitimately to honored collectivities that are above mere law. By contrast, as will be shown later, what they *bring in* is disvalued.

A 1996 Russian presidential decree illustrates the crystallization of the concern with communities, borders, and illicit trade. According to this decree, 1,500 km of unprotected state frontier in Transbaikalia is to be guarded against incoming "contraband, narcotics, weapons, and illegal immigrants" by a new frontier guard consisting of local volunteers, first Cossacks but also hunters, shepherds, and others. These people will be given various concessions, but, more important, they will have the right to verify documents, stop transport, and "control the border regime." The local community will be "full owners" (*polnymi khozyayevami*) of the border zone.[27]

Border anxiety translates from the international frontier to certain territories and sites inside the country. The frontier of Russia with China and Mongolia physically consists of a high fence and a ploughed-up strip of land on much of the Russian side, with watchposts and lights near crossings. Foreigners are not allowed near border zones. The border is also furnished in places with infrared, radiowave, electronic surveillance equipment and "automated control of the activity of security personnel" (Fedin 1995). These same techniques are being borrowed to provide security perimeters for large installations and enterprises inside Russia where theft has become endemic, ranging from petrol stores to gas suppliers to nuclear power stations (Fedin 1995: 1). No technical measures, however, can counteract the disloyal trade that operates from inside an enterprise or administrative unit. Compounding this sense of uncontrollable flux is the fact that not only people but also goods are changing status: products that were formerly "ours" are now foreign (e.g., Armenian brandy).

A symptom of the contradictory obsession with territoriality is the continued existence of GAI, the state transport inspection. GAI posts still exist on every main road out of all cities, ostensibly to check vehicles for roadworthiness and similar factors. In fact, the GAI regularly stops trade vehicles and extracts "tribute" (*dan'*, as people say) simply for passage.

Larger sums are taken for the slightest infringement of traffic regulations or the appearance of carrying smuggled goods, provoking the cynical view that the more restrictions exist, the more can be milked from them by the very people who are supposed to uphold them. This is a vicious circle. Provinces create their own economic conditions, differences between these conditions give rise to trade and smuggling, regulations to counteract smuggling give rise to bribery and tribute taking, and the effect is sharpened differences between the units since prices are hiked up in the places for which goods are destined. So it is no surprise that at a higher level of operation republics, too, act as arbitrary requisitioners (e.g., the Ukraine takes 10 percent of the electricity Russia sends to Chechnya [Polukeyev 1995]).

If there is one prevailing fear that valuable goods are flowing out, there is another that "rubbish" is coming in, brought by human caravans.[28] This explains the expression "the Great Trash Road"[29] (alluding to the Great Silk Road) that brings a current of flimsy clothes and trinkets into Russia from "Asia"—a vague concept here including China, Turkey, and the Near Abroad (the successor states of Central Asia and Trans-Caucasus). One senses several multilayered evaluations of this situation. On the one hand it is perhaps seen as a fatal weakness for Russians to desire such things, as suggested by the derogatory words used for the goods. But at the same time consumption of these items of international currency gives Russian citizens the feeling that they are at last participating in the global arena of fashion and technology. Perhaps most prominent is a third sense of being cheated, since most people are well aware that the flaunted labels of Adidas, Coty, and Levi-Strauss are counterfeited in the shadowy sweatshops of "Asia." As a result, the impulse is to reject the "trash" and search farther afield to South Korea, Malaysia, Japan, and Western Europe for genuine goods of high quality.

Six Types of Traders and Their Dynamics

To obtain some heuristic purchase on the confusion of current economic life, I divide traders into six categories, but this is not meant to imply that they are altogether separate from one another on the ground or that the types are fixed and permanent. The first two categories are "businesspeople," the managers who run new private conglomerates, and "brokers," those who trade on behalf of state and former state enterprises.

The Siberian provinces are unlike the metropolitan and industrial regions because of the relative absence of private business conglomerates. I know of only two in Ulan-Ude: Arig Us, which developed from the former state trading organ into a construction firm that also sells gasoline and other commodities, and Motom, which began as a Lada concession and expanded into car repairs, furniture making, banking, and retailing. Both are at least temporarily highly profitable, have wide national and international trade links, and are multifaceted operations. But even at the cutting edge of provincial capitalism, these firms have close relations with the Buryat government.[30] Arig Us, no doubt benefiting from government concessions, joined with the government to set up Prodsoyuz, an organization to help the faltering stalwarts of state industry (engineering, sugar, wool processing, and so on). Prodsoyuz has a special relationship with a clearing bank (the Oktyabr' Bank, no less) to reschedule outstanding debts between the various participating companies and allows them to borrow from the clearing bank at low rates of interest. Local people suspect the association of "monopolizing credit," to the disadvantage of small competitors. In other words, the new capitalists are tied into local political-economic structures, and their financial clout allows them some leeway in manipulating their immediate trading context.

Operating at the level of the single enterprise, brokers typically take charge of marketing part of the main product or subsidiary products in return for difficult-to-find inputs. They travel around, search out buyers, and let people know of goods available in their own enterprise. For example, in 1993 a broker from a collective farm in Chita Oblast arranged to sell milk from his company to a dairy in China for the next three years in return for supplies of flour, rice, and sugar. The brokers involved in such deals are almost always close associates, relatives, or friends of the managers or local government officials. Their origins can often be traced back to the crafty "suppliers" (*snabzhentsi*) of Soviet days. Taking a wage and modest personal profit from these operations, the "broker" strives to set up regular agreements, although this is often impossible. Many brokers take pride in supplying their community with much-needed goods ("I feed the whole *kollektiv*"). Brokers, however, have also been agents in illegal strategies to move local goods across the frontier to the golden land of China.[31]

With regard to citizenship regimes, both businesspeople and brokers are understood to be representatives (*predstaviteli*) of corporations, and they are well supplied with the legitimating documents of core citizenship. Their being known is the guarantee of their trustworthiness inside the corporation, and its weight is behind them in dealings with the outside. Some significant factors, however, differentiate the two groups. The businesspeople tend to be young and well educated, sometimes with training in the United States or other capitalist countries. They often have an unorthodox entrepreneurial spark. For example, Motom started when two young Buryats were sent to buy sheep but used the money instead to buy tires and eventually set up their own company dealing in secondhand cars. Motom's present retail business, two sleek supermarkets, monopolizes the small niche for expensive foreign goods that are otherwise locally unavailable. Furthermore, the personnel of government and big business are interchangeable: the career of a likely young operator moves easily among posts in the postelection administration, major firms in the locality, and government agencies acting in a commercial capacity.

The reverse is true of brokers whose future seems less secure. Breakdown of trust ("We found he was trading on his own behalf") has led many state and former state enterprises to get rid of their brokers. The functions of trade often devolve onto the directors, who are normally trained in manufacturing and unused to trade. Many complained to me that they are unable to attend to production, as they spend most of their time traveling around searching for buyers or negotiating for credits. Barter deals can include the very fabric of the enterprise. "I have a lot of buildings," said one director. "People often ask me to pay in buildings, but I don't agree—or at least I haven't agreed yet." Finally, the rapacious environment of the present virtually compels successful businesspeople to employ their own security. The faltering enterprises, however, cannot afford that luxury. They are regularly subject to theft, often by their own employees. The director-broker thus has to negotiate both internally and externally to keep the workers on his or her side. "One of my biggest headaches is to find flowers for Women's Day," the same director told me. "Where the heck can I get them when I only have flour to pay with?"

Turning now to discuss traders outside the corporations, it is necessary to give a brief résumé of post-Soviet mass trade. The era began with the relaxation of border restrictions around 1988–1989.[32] By train, plane, and coach, tourist groups would set off for Mongolia; in fact, they were trading caravans, often sent by farms, factories, or institutes.[33] Curiously, they returned stuffed to the roof with Soviet-produced but unobtainable (*defisitniye*) goods. The reason for this is that Mongolia had been sent large quantities of such high-quality products by the USSR for the privileged specialists and army officers based there, but these people were now leaving the country. The Soviet goods soon ran out, and the buses carried back Mongolian leather jackets, hats, and winter coats. Before long every family in Transbaikalia was replete with Mongolian goods. By 1991 the shelves in Transbaikalia were empty of goods to sell in Mongolia, and a coupon system was introduced. Local residents were limited, for example, to buying one school exercise book, and even for such a trivial purchase one had to stand in line and show a passport and residence permit.[34] Subsequently, the policy was reversed, and prices rose.

In 1991 the China trade opened up, although China never became a mass destination because of language problems and the unfamiliar culture. The trade with China suddenly expanded enormously, but it was carried out by increasingly professional operators. At this point we see the crystallization of the more or less distinct categories of independent traders whom I call resellers, shuttlers, entrepreneurs, and trader-retailers.

I begin with shuttlers, whose activities are a direct outcome of the history just outlined. Shuttlers (*chelnoki*) are so called because they personally travel with the goods they buy and sell. Their Mongolian equivalents are called *gahaichin*, which means "pig keeper" (a pejorative term for the manly pastoralists of the steppes), but the pigs in question are huge bales of goods, barely carryable by two people. In China the Russian shuttlers are called "hoovers" from their habit of buying everything on sight. They take back mostly clothes, trainers, and cheap brand-name products to sell. Shuttlers travel in groups for reasons of security, and as regulations on the border are tightened they have to make illicit arrangements with customs officials and train guards to accommodate their goods. What is in demand in China is not Russian consumer goods but Western money, and that is what shuttlers export. In Russia they sell Chinese goods at kiosks or at the market for rubles, change the money into dollars, fly to China with the dollars, buy a new bundle of goods, and head back to Russia or Mongolia by train.

It is more difficult for the Mongolian *gahaichin*. In the period 1990–1992 there were trading rows of Mongols in the Ulan-Ude market. But they were forced to pay extra-high protection money to Buryat gangs and were shortly forced out by local shuttlers, so they spread their activities deep into Russia along the railway lines and up to Moscow. Their numbers were later curtailed by laws reimposing visa restrictions for Mongolian citizens in Russia. Completely unprotected, they are often attacked and robbed. When addressed they say they are Buryats, as Russian citizens are subject to fewer fines and less violence from foreigners.

Meanwhile, local shuttlers have flourished, but there is high turnover in this category. The shuttlers are restricted by the personal nature of their business: an eager crowd of relatives and friends awaits each transport in the expectation they will be given a share. At the petty sales end, marketplaces tend to be glutted, and shuttlers are unable to spread out into the countryside to make sales; at the upper end wholesalers (*optoviki*) are increasingly taking over trade routes. The poor quality of most Chinese goods has caused a fall in demand. As a result, shuttlers are flying to South Korea, Singapore, Turkey, and even Japan. To break into wholesale trade requires storage space, licenses, vehicles, and so forth—in other words official contacts, which shuttlers, archetypal marginals who sail close to the wind, rarely have.

The contacts essential for shuttlers are resellers and trader-retailers. Resellers (*perckupshchiki*) are mostly people who can no longer depend on corporations. They include pensioners or children with highly limited

routes (buying in one part of the city and reselling at a higher price some-
where else), people who sell domestic products such as honey or knitted
shawls on behalf of relatives, and people who trade vodka on credit to
circles of neighbors. Most resellers act as individuals or tiny close-knit
groups and often have no license, but they are not totally estranged from
the society of trade. They have clientlike relationships with their suppliers.

Trader-retailers (*kommersanty*) have the capital to purchase a kiosk in
town or a vehicle to travel to the villages, buying local products such as
meat, as well as selling vodka and other goods. The future once seemed
bright for them, but that is no longer the case. The days of the sell-off of
collective farm livestock have ended,[35] and people now never sell their
own meat through a trader if they can sell it themselves. Furthermore, the
lack of money in villages means buying consumer goods there has virtually ceased. A typical village has one or two bright little private shops belonging to trader-retailers that are barely trading or are even boarded up,
together with a store belonging to that old Soviet stalwart, the Consumer
Cooperative.[36] Both types probably make most of their money from
vodka; but villagers say they prefer the Co-op, although it has higher
prices, because it retains the old "reliable, honest" bureaucracy and sells
unprofitable useful things like matches, unlike the shady *kommersanty*.[37]

The most dynamic actors are those freelance traders I call entrepreneurs (*predprinimateli*). Some are rich and powerful; others lead a pre-
carious existence. In general, they operate on a larger and more irregular
scale than the shuttlers, which allows them to make windfall profits from
international import-export.[38] Many entrepreneurial firms are joint ventures with roving Korean, Vietnamese, or other foreign businesspeople
who supply the initial capital and international links. When demand
plays on globalized desires and fashions, the entrepreneur needs access to
fast travel and communications. Adept manipulation of the legal system,
an aptitude for risk, and a thirst for the freedom money offers are characteristic of entrepreneurs. It is my impression that opportunities for risky
major deals are becoming scarcer; there is too little money in the provinces. Entrepreneurs fall back on safer options, wholesaling if they are
successful or purchasing a kiosk or a concession[39] if less so.

It is also significant that many people are latent traders—that is, they
have purchased licenses to trade as physical persons without actually
doing so. This seems to indicate a change in attitudes toward trading.
Not only does trade, unusually, now appear as a safety net, but the idea
that having a license provides possibilities for economic good fortune is
highly important for many people. It goes along, in my view, with striving
for the sense of freedom gained from having money. As Simmel wrote
(1978: 306–312), having money is different from having specific objects

in that whereas the latter constrain the owner, the abstract nature of money allows maximal enjoyment of almost any object and the pleasure of further use and fructifying of money itself. Woodruff points out (in this volume) that this implies the presence of a fully monetized economy. In the context of Russia, which is very unevenly monetized, the dollar is much more "moneylike" than the ruble; it gives a greater sense of mastery—the ability to be an actor in the world market. This explains to some extent the eagerness of entrepreneurs to set up foreign-dollar bank accounts and their reluctance to trap good money in productive investments at home. Yet as Lemon (1996: 60) demonstrates, the dollar also has a powerful antivalue. "Trade for dollars," she writes, "drains the nation of its characteristic treasures. . . . For Russians, it is the self as a 'national being' that is alienated or thought endangered by wrong exchanges and foreign currency." The Russian government is currently developing laws to block currency transfers abroad, and it is widely believed that these laws will harm small traders.[40]

Trading Minorities

The ambivalence aroused by trade in general is crystallized into antagonism in the case of diaspora traders, who are accused more than any others of creating "disorder." Localism reinforces itself with racist stereotypes. In southeast Siberia, the two main diaspora groups are the "Kavkaztsy"[41] and the Chinese. Each has an established economic niche, which differentiates them from the wide-ranging ad hoc operations of the entrepreneurs. Socially, the two diasporas are very different from each other. The Kavkaztsy established a market role in Soviet times as purveyors of fruit, vegetables, and flowers, and they expanded through the now half-forgotten perestroika cooperatives to dominate marketplaces in a series of towns. The Kavkaztsy of Irkutsk fought off an attempt at penetration by Central Asians in the early 1990s (Dyatlov 1995: 5–6). When military events erupted in the Caucasus, supply lines were cut, leading the Kavkaztsy to operate as middlemen buying supplies from Central Asian wholesalers at low prices. But they managed to send money back to their republics. They have begun to divide functionally and to fight among themselves: the Azerbaijanis control the marketplaces and keep the Chechens out, whereas from 1992 onward the Chechens have taken over finance (including forging promissory notes and counterfeiting currency). In spring 1993 police discovered 500 million rubles in the possession of a Chechen group in Irkutsk, along with twenty-five false promissory notes worth 6.5 milliard rubles (Dyatlov 1995: 9–10). Russians feed on such news, which adds to their stereotypes of the Kavkaztsy as flamboyant, sexually disgraceful, and violent. Around this time, the mayor of the city said, "A Chechen mafia controls the whole of Irkutsk."

It is far from clear, however, whether this is really the case. As Dyatlov establishes (1995: 6–10), the vast majority both of criminal groups in the city[42] and of crimes are attributable to indigenous inhabitants. Nevertheless, the general assumption is that the Kavkaztsy "generate crime."[43] As a result, the Kavkaztsy have had to find Russians as fronts under which to register their companies and to hire indigenous people to run their kiosks. "They are there, although you can't see them," is still the assumption. In this connection, special measures were enacted by the Irkutsk city Soviet in 1993 to control and establish residence quotas for citizens from the Near Abroad and the Caucasus. Thus by 1994, when fears of Chechen terrorism had been added to the mix, the MVD (Ministry of Internal Affairs) was able to state that all 250 Chechens in the city were known and controlled, and all had residence permits and established businesses; therefore, they would be unlikely to engage in terrorist acts (Dyatlov 1995: 10).

By 1996 it was no longer the Chechens but a Georgian gang that was the focus of fear. In June seven members of the gang were shot in a cafe by Russians. A police report makes it clear, however, that the issue was one of territorial dispute rather than ethnic conflict. Both groups are multiethnic; the "Georgian" group in Irkutsk includes Russians, Buryats, and Jews as well as Georgians. Interestingly, the war is largely ideological, concerned with the old criminal traditions that separate theft and anti-state crime on the one hand from business-related crime on the other. The Russian gang is headed by a "thief in law" nicknamed Tyurik, who owns shares in the Bratsk aluminum factory and now lives in Spain. The Georgians, by contrast, advocate the older, "pure" criminal tradition that eschews contacts with business.[44] Despite such newspaper reports, people in general do not understand the distinctions among gangs and firmly link trade, crime, and disorder with "blacks" in a mutually self-reinforcing circle.

The Chinese traders create no such fears of violence, but they have also evoked the erection of severe new barriers in the citizenship regime. The fear here is akin to the yellow peril myth, that Chinese economic penetration will be followed by a political expansion with millions of immigrants swamping Siberia. Chinese are said to be already present in great numbers as market sellers, guest workers, entrepreneurs, retailers, cleaners, and students.[45] Many are hidden from officialdom, as they live on expired visas and pay no taxes. As with the Kavkaztsy, it is rumored that, as they are not apparent in cities, a large number of Chinese live in outlying towns and villages. Chinese traders are said to have moved from shuttling to create a solid infrastructure of their own markets, joint ventures, hotels, restaurants, shops, dormitories, and undercover financial institutions in most Siberian cities, and anxiety is expressed that they are widely buying immovable property behind Russian names.

In fact, it seems that Chinese contract workers and students, both invited by Siberian institutions during the early 1990s, greatly outnumber traders. In those years Chinese traders bought timber semimanufactures, gasoline, and technical components and sold the usual clothes, shoes, and consumer goods. More recently, they ceased buying Russian goods and exported the money from retail sales back to China, a procedure said to involve an underground banking system (Dyatlov 1995: 16–24).[46] Since early 1994, Chinese economic activity in Siberia has been cut drastically by local authorities eager to "protect national interests." Contract workers have been sent back to China, Chinese business investment has virtually ceased, and Russian sales in China have been correspondingly cut— all of which has created an economic disaster for the region (Minakir 1996). A policy of harassment (*bytovaya nepriyazn*) was instituted throughout the Far East toward those who had obtained legal residence status (Minakir 1996: 22). Petty traders have been reduced to a trickle. In Ulan-Ude I estimate that only thirty to forty Chinese traders and one large Chinese shop remain.

Unlike the Kavkaztsy, the Chinese traders in Siberia do not have their own mafialike protection gangs, perhaps because of a different solution to problems involving trust. With their family ties and internal discipline (perhaps related to the still fearsome political regime in China), the Chinese are mutually collaborative. The Kavkaztsy, on the other hand, belong to antagonistic ethnic groups and to different clans with traditions of armed revenge. With mistrust pervasive among their traders, the Kavkaztsy have tended to secure their transactions through more violent means.

The Chinese are not accorded the frightened respect given the Kavkaztsy. Rather, despised for their strange mildness, they are often attacked by local nationalists. In Irkutsk the annual holidays of the Special Air Forces, the army, and the Cossacks are occasions for regular attacks on Chinese markets (Dyatlov 1995: 24–25). During 1993 some patriotic organizations associated with the nationalist Vladimir Zhirinovsky's party were set up to "strengthen Russians" and to combat the presence of foreigners, "who have many rights and no responsibilities." A militarized terrorist group, calling itself Partner Ltd., founded a special Freedom Movement sector to "liberate" the region from foreign mafias. More broadly, continual complaints were made to the authorities about speculation, nonpayment of taxes, fictive marriages to obtain residence permits, and so forth on the part of the Chinese traders. In December 1994 the Irkutsk administration reacted with yet another crackdown, despite the fact that new regulations had been put in force in 1993. State security organized two massive operations, named *Foreigner* and *Signal,* that checked all firms, markets, and dormitories. The relatively small results, only 302 Chinese deported and 1,380 arrested, were said to reflect the cunning of the incomers and the corruption of local officials in hiding presumed illegalities.

This is not an isolated instance. In Ulan-Ude in summer 1995 there was also a crackdown on all foreign retailers of consumer goods in the central market; all were deprived of their licenses. This action aroused some protest and engendered a call for setting up a new committee to protect the rights of entrepreneurs against administrative organs.[47] By summer 1996 Kavkaz retailers were rarely seen in the city, and Chinese traders had been confined to a market in the Elevator District of the city, where they were sequestered humiliatingly in their own compound behind a wire fence. This was far the busiest part of the market.

The Aesthetics of "Disorder"

The familiar Soviet landscape of the city, replicated in town after town, seems to arouse an unexpected protectiveness. The city should develop and reproduce itself as an expression of the people's progress, it is felt. Thus, neither unfinished municipal buildings, with heaps of bricks and tangled, unused pipes, nor the disintegrating fragments of the past are regarded as constituting "disorder." Old boards of honor with half of the letters gone, rotted plaques of Lenin, and the broken swings and playthings of a closed kindergarten are left just as they were, and people pass them without comment.

But the physical evidence of new individual activities is not seen as the people's doing. Trading is kept away spatially from government buildings and otherwise seems "disorderly" wherever it happens. Pavement sellers by a shop door "get in the way"; when confined in a market, they "create dirt." A foreign or colorful appearance is noted immediately, registered, and resented. In Ulan-Ude the result has been that original-looking trading stalls have virtually disappeared. Kiosks and stalls, by local regulation, must be of a given size (recently increased, to the traders' irritation). Many places have lines of identical stalls, nameless, and all painted the same color. Seeing this, people say with satisfaction, "At last there is some order in our markets."

I am much taken with Lemon's (1996: 45) interpretation of the post-Soviet market as a quasi-theatrical stage on which roles are played. This description seems to be borne out by the numerous street traders who are beginners; unlike the blasé professionals, they often look apologetic, uncomfortable at being there at all.

In general, in Russia laws and bureaucracy are popularly seen as the outcome of the desire for order. People are willing to tolerate what might seem to be excessive proliferations of rules because those rules represent civilization, which tames the seething, disorderly nature of the Russian people. This disorganized passionate nature is something people are also secretly proud of. But in the cultural structure of self-analysis, there are always scapegoats for the negative aspect of disorder. For many people, even those engaged in it, trade plays this role.

Conclusion

Trade in Russia has burgeoned in a particular direction. The functions of state-planned internal exchange have not been efficiently replaced by trade but limp along in a crippled version of the Soviet system. Meanwhile, mass trade—with its search for any kind of profit—has been produced, but is also limited, by the drastic reduction of incomes. What success has occurred in trade is closely connected to consumers' expanded horizons to embrace the entire world. As a result, although a few large firms linked to government have been able to dominate profitable aspects of home production (oil products, cars, and similar products), the activity of small traders is overwhelmingly concerned with selling imports and images of foreign glamour. Since the early 1990s demand and desire have moved to sources further and further outward. One after another, the earlier suppliers failed to satisfy—Central Asian underground workshops, Eastern Europe, Mongolia, and China, in turn, came to glut the markets and be pushed aside. The expansion of the network of suppliers to distant and expensive places will probably result in a gradual professionalization of the import trade and the relegation of the new traders-in-desperation to the lowliest reselling roles.

Yet, simultaneous with this process is another, conceptual one that is also progressive. In this view it is native Russian products that are valued—almost supervalued, as though nothing the rest of the world can produce can compensate for their loss (Humphrey 1995). As the products of native labor, these goods have an almost noneconomic value. It is acceptable for other people to want these excellent products, but it somehow seems immoral when they are traded away. Simultaneously, incoming goods are devalued. Is this what years of learning the labor theory of value have come to? In fact, such an inchoate sense of value parallels the real selling off of (mostly state) property hastily and disadvantageously. Indignation at this process taps the contradictory facts that, on the one hand, Russians do cherish concepts of production collectives to which they are attached, and they feel loss if the *kollektiv* disintegrates, but on the other hand, it is they themselves who stand at the warehouse doors ready to make a deal. When identifiable "traders"—people defined as not engaged in production—are perceived as the perpetrators, however, the sense arises that now there are "outsiders" on the raid. Thus, added to the thicket of legislation by which the nested sovereign units of the country seek to define themselves is growing regulation concerned specifically with defense against the types of trade that have become so prominent in Russia. Taken together, this legislation is producing new citizenship regimes. These serve not only to exclude trading diasporas but also to limit the activities of home-based traders.

I have argued that this process marks a fundamental shift in the way society is perceived to be organized. If the perception of tsarist times was of a vertical hierarchy, which was replaced by the Soviet pyramidal territorial structure, the recent shift is to a more horizontal, relatively egalitarian territoriality.[48] The jostling for equal status relates to obtaining subsidies from Moscow, as well as to regional freedom of action, but the upper linkages with the center have become shifting and uncertain. The collectivities invoked in contemporary loyalties and exclusions are essentially those created by the Soviet administrative structure. It is significant that with all of the historical revelations of the arbitrariness of these created administrative units and the alterations and amalgamations the Soviets themselves introduced, few boundaries have been changed in the slightest since the collapse of the USSR. What did collapse in the early 1990s was the former solid pyramid as defining the relation between units. Revealed now by the retraction of Soviet homogenizing governmentality is the variety of idiosyncratic resources (ethnicity, culture, environment, religion, and the like) that can be used in defining regional identity.

Trade in general operates by making a profit from the difference between the state of affairs in one place and that in another, and this means that traders, almost by definition, will infringe the boundaries between regionally defined units. The peculiar position this situation creates for traders in Russia defines their essentially post-Soviet character. I have tried to show in this chapter how, from the smallest units such as the Onokhoi Wood-Products Company to a large city like Irkutsk, trade is generating anxieties of several kinds. The resulting citizenship regime first creates privileges and subsidies for core members (these have varied during the period under study but include distribution of goods, allocation of vegetable plots, entitlement to coupons, differential wage structures, and access to government loans) and, second, discriminates against various categories of outsiders (for example, through quotas on residence, refusals of licenses and charters, strategic tariffs on imports, and arbitrary removal of trading rights). The legal citizenship regime is nevertheless benign compared with the torrent of aggression traders suffer in everyday life.

Regionalization is further promoted by the mass exodus of industry and agriculture from the price mechanism and the substitution of barter for money transactions (see Woodruff, chapter 3, this volume). The information required (who wants 20,000 saplings or 50 easy chairs?) and the trust networks necessary for ongoing barter tend to be local. Furthermore, barter, although a type of trade, undercuts the existence of traders; it always seems cheaper in the short run to exchange goods than to pay for traders' profits. Yet, in the Russian provincial economy today, apart from state agencies only private traders have money. Provincial governments have seized what they see as a double opportunity: if electoral popularity is enhanced by accommodating local sentiments regarding "order," the fiscal coffers can be filled by hitting traders hard. As a result, small traders are hedged around by taxes and restrictions on every side, and the few profitable firms are supported in quasi-monopolistic positions. Perhaps the fact that they have money—money that can be spent in China or Turkey, money that can be "used voluntaristically"—is what makes traders seem so enviably dangerous. They are a challenge to governments that seek to maintain power by controlling the distribution of money. But, paradoxically, if trade were to be freed up and supported by positive public images, the separatisms that are a much more real danger for Russia today would have less foundation in economic practice.

Notes

Acknowledgments: I am grateful to the History and Economics Centre, King's College, Cambridge, for financial support while I was doing research for this chapter. Many thanks to Victoria Bonnell, Roberts Kilis, David Sneath, and the participants in the Ethnographies of Transition conference who read earlier drafts and made valuable comments.

1. During the nineteenth and early twentieth centuries only two or three trade posts were found along the entire border with China and Mongolia (Khokhlov 1987: 67).

2. Dyatlov (1995) writes, for example, that in 1992, 49 percent of the citizens of Irkutsk were personally involved in trading. That figure had declined to 21 percent by late 1994.

3. "The characteristic of Russian business is that it produces almost nothing," writes Gomelev (1995: 2). "The 'New Russians' take legendary profits by re-selling what we succeeded in creating during the years of Soviet power, and their highest goal is selling across the frontier."

4. Each year $10–$12 billion escapes from Russia, a total of around $45 billion during the period 1991–1995; state reserves amounted to $12 billion (*Moskovskii Komsomolets,* 28 Nov. 1995: 1).

5. The restrictions on export of strategic goods began in 1993 (Handelman 1994: 114). In eastern Siberia such goods include rails and engineering parts, deer organs, food, KamAZ trucks, glass, antiquities and art objects, medicines, precious metals, and weapons (Gomelev 1995). Several of these items are still exported by local governments with agreement from Moscow.

6. I use the term *province* here for both oblasts and republics within the Russian Federation.

7. *Pravda Buryatii* [Ulan-Ude], 3 August 1996: 1.

8. In the Soviet period state enterprises did not have charters because they were regarded as branches of the state. Collective farms had charters, but they were identical to one another and were not effective as a basis for independent economic activity. The terminology for current charters, such as the *aktsionernoye obshchesvo*, the *tovarishestvo s ogranichestvennoi otvetstvennostyu*, and others, is largely the same as that used in tsarist times; see Owen (1991).

9. I acknowledge the work of David Anderson (1995), who introduced this term in his Ph.D. thesis on Evenki reindeer herding in north Siberia. The term is intended to be historically neutral, but I acknowledge that it is not indigenous.

10. *Kommersant* [Moscow], 28 Nov. 1995: 8.

11. The cost of a license to trade as a physical person was 400,000 rubles a year in 1996 in Ulan-Ude, about one month's worker's wages.

12. Physical persons were liable for taxes of 12 percent of profits in Ulan-Ude in 1996.

13. Some estimates are given in Handelman (1994) and Gomelev (1995). In 1994, before the Russian currency was made convertible, a single customs' haul at the Ulan-Ude airport uncovered an attempt to export illegally U.S.$18.6 Million (Gomelev 1995).

14. Personal checks are virtually unheard of in the provinces, mainly because people do not trust that they will be honored. Bank transfers have recently become more common in transactions between firms.

15. Security staff are often recruited from former KGB, police, and military personnel.

16. Usually a band of handpicked friends of the director of the bank. They are employed to watch the employees of the bank as much as to protect top managers (Tanya Zhimbieva, personal communication).

17. Hiring security guards may be more than a matter of protection. The anthropologist, David Sneath, suggested to me that the Soviet era generated a model of inclusive institutionism that reproduced in miniature many of the functions of the state and that modern corporations may reproduce that model.

18. Dollars are the most valued, and also the most suspect, form of money (Lemon 1996). In eastern Siberia counterfeit dollars are rumored to come from China. Most currency exchanges have special machines to detect counterfeit notes.

19. The cannabis trade is active in south Siberia, but it seems a relatively makeshift affair. In summer naked men run through fields where wild hemp is growing, accumulating the pollen on their bodies. The pollen is scraped off with a knife, rolled into a ball, and sold. Local people know this activity goes on but do not interfere because of threats from drug-running gangs.

20. In February 1994, the latest date for which exact figures are available, of the 206 collective and state farms in Buryatia about 53 percent (60 collective and 49 state farms) had made no change to their status; 6 state farms had become collective farms; of the 97 farms that "privatized," 60 became associations, 20 became limited companies, 4 became agricultural cooperatives, 5 became joint-stock companies, and 8 became subsidiaries of other enterprises (*Buryatia* [Ulan-Ude], 17 Feb. 1994: 3). As the tempo of privatization has slowed since 1994 and several farms have reversed privatization, it can be estimated that even nominal privatization in agriculture is still little over 50 percent.

21. An example from agriculture is the Buryat Unegetei specialized vegetable farm, which has remained a state farm (*sovkhoz*) on the old Soviet model. In hard times in 1995, it was helped by an entrepreneurial support scheme of the Buryat government, which bought Dutch seed potatoes and offered them to the state farm for a return of 15 percent of the profits. The government got its return, but when asked if the farm made a profit the director replied:

"No. We remained a state farm, i.e., government property. We thought of becoming a joint-stock company, but we decided not to because of our difficult financial position. Last year vegetables gave us 800 million rubles income, but our 900 cows gave us 460 million of losses. If I submitted (*podchinil'sya*) to logical reasoning and economic calculation I would get rid of the cows. But that would mean getting rid of work for our people. I repeat, the vegetables saved us. After all, they cannot import fresh vegetables from the west. But our difficulty is that even here we did not sell our product but made a 'gift' of it. To this day we have not been paid for it. On paper the farm looks good, but in real life—terrible." (Shelkunova 1995: 2).

Note how the director associates economic dependency with a state farm type of enterprise and clearly does not take seriously the idea of giving up the cows and firing part of the workforce.

22. The 1992 presidential edict to this effect was only gradually implemented. The socialist enterprise had controlled the land in both public and private use, as well as the housing stock, central heating, lighting and roads, medical facilities, transport, clubs, kindergartens, and sporting facilities; in the agricultural sector it provided firewood, fodder, fertilizer, young livestock, seed, and use of machinery to its members for their private plots. Some enterprises also constructed their own medical centers, paid teachers, built schools, and provided school buses for their members. By 1996 enterprises varied in the extent to which they had relinquished these responsibilities.

23. As the director of a Buryat collective farm explained:

"In deciding economic matters in the conditions of the wild, and to us very unfamiliar, market, we do everything not to leave people without work, because the principle of collectivism is highest of all for us. So we decided to go in for production which does not cost much but needs a lot of labour. Namely, herding horses and increasing our stock of Kazakh white-head cattle for meat. We have given up mechanised cleaning-out, watering, heated fodders and even electrical lighting, and we have gone back to horse carts for transport. In a word, we have turned backwards, to the distant past. And for our own internal use we have decided to keep some sheep, pigs, and foxes for fur. . . . A problem which much concerns us [is] that 10 hectares of our best fields were never given back to us by Kyren. And by the petrol pump at the edge of our land our fields are being trampled by their cattle. The Kyren village administration does not lift a finger to help fence off our fields, and all this is made worse by a 24-hour commercial shop they have set up—night and day their drunken louts attack and steal from our people. When will the district administration take a decision to get rid of that spreader of moral decay?" (Uskeyev 1994: 2)

24. Nevertheless, there was some indignation within the firm because the state had not used its 20 percent shareholding rights to intervene and had not agreed to liquidate the firm's debts (Nikolayev 1994).

25. People active in setting up a *zemlyachestvo* told me they had experienced initial hostility from the provincial government because the group might provide "parallel power." To gain control of the localism movement, the Buryat government set up its own local cultural organizations in each district.

26. Attachment to place emerges in local religious cults in Buryatia at sites often placed at the entrances and exits of communities based on enterprises and of rural districts.

27. *Argumenty I Fakty* [Moscow] no. 32, 1996: 14.

28. Gomelev (1995) describes the "shameful" nature of the inward trade goods registered by Irkutsk customs in 1994: 255 tons of food (which should have been produced internally, he implies), 3 tons of calculating and computer equipment, and 2,096 tons of alcohol.

29. In Russian, the *Velikii Shmotkovyi Put'*.

30. Government credits are important here, but there are also more symbolic ties. For example, the two firms have offices in government-owned property in the center of town, and Arig Us has a plane named *Buryatia*, often used by government officials, with the firm's logo painted on it.

31. For example, valuable copper is sold to an agent who acknowledges receipt of "metallic waste" and resells it to the firm (for which service the agent receives a fee). Now officially consisting of metallic waste, the consignment is sold abroad, and customs agents are bribed to look the other way or it is simply hoped that no inspection will take place.

32. In Soviet times, visas had been needed to travel to Mongolia and China, and even people with relatives abroad were restricted to one visit per year, whereas most people were unable to travel at all. Everyone knew, however, that these visits to relatives were used to obtain valuable goods for resale.

33. An unprecedented rise in agreements to "cooperate" between Russian and Mongolian collective and state farms, factories, and similar organizations covered the emergence of mass trade. For Russians in Transbaikaliya, Buryat friends were suddenly in great demand to act as interpreters in Mongolia.

34. Balzhan Zhimbiev, personal communication, referring to Ulan-Ude in 1992.

35. When the collective farms came to terms with the unprofitability of live-

stock and were also instructed to privatize (around 1992–1994), great numbers of animals were sold.

36. Set up in the 1920s, Consumer Cooperatives originally operated shops locally on the basis of members' fees. Later, the organization became a huge state-supported operation that conducted international trade, operated its own bakeries, and had a monopoly retail position in rural areas.

37. This prejudice among local people is not well-founded; the co-ops I visited did not necessarily sell useful items. Items on sale at a private village shop included three rolls of toilet paper, two German deodorant sprays, one bottle of shampoo, bandages, a few bars of three types of soap, toothpaste, one pair of jeans, a few pairs of children's shoes and socks, a tablecloth, one pair of women's evening shoes, two tins of liver paste, and a few packets of biscuits, tea, soda, and salt. Vodka was also sold but was kept under the counter. This shop was operating at a loss, according to the owner.

38. An example is a Buryat entrepreneur who had a contact in distant Rostov-on-Don, arranged to sell fruit conserves from Rostov in Mongolia, and, after several visits to Ulaanbaatar, obtained a consignment of Chinese oranges and mandarins in Mongolia just in time to ship them to sell in Buryatia for the new year. The entire operation was conducted through barter. A less successful example is the Mongolian entrepreneur who set up a factory sewing leather coats in Ulaanbaatar. He and his family lived in Russia and stayed in Irkutsk, Bratsk, Angarsk, and Ulan-Ude in search of partners. His best hope was an Angarsk oil company, which he hoped would buy his coats for its workers and would also accept a consignment for resale by its commercial department. In return, he aimed to obtain several cisterns of gasoline to sell in China, which would enable him to bring back a huge consignment of goods to sell in Russia. Nothing came of the plan.

39. A new type of trader is the "dealer" (*diler*), who obtains a concession to sell an international product, such as the magazine *Marie-Claire,* in a local market.

40. A presidential edict of 1 January 1996 gives the state the right to confiscate from a Russian firm the full value of imported goods if the goods do not arrive in Russia within 160 days of the order. The reason for this edict is that Russian firms were fraudulently "ordering" goods abroad, sending payment immediately, and arranging for the payment to be put in a foreign bank account as the goods "failed to turn up." The law states that if the importer does not have the money, the firm's bank will be charged. The edict will hit small firms, since banks will not risk lending them money for foreign orders unless the firms can show at least twice the value of the order on their account books (*Moskovskii Komsomolets* [Moscow], 28 Nov. 1995: 2).

41. *Kavkaztsy* is the politest term by which these people are known locally (*chernozhopyye,* black-assed, is another). I put inverted quotation marks around "Kavkaztsy" to show that this is a general appellation by Siberians, who often neither know nor care about the traders' ethnic identity.

42. In 1993, there were apparently 455 criminal groups known to the police in Irkutsk Oblast, of which 30 were "ethnic"; of the 369 groups known in 1994, only 9 were ethnic (Dyatlov, Demid, and Palyutina 1995: 8).

43. An interesting article by Dyatlov and colleagues (1995) discusses local reactions to the trial of an Azerbaijani vegetable trader accused of raping a local Russian girl. The girl's mother, hearing he was to be allowed out on bail, shot and killed the accused as he emerged from jail. The city of Irkutsk was in an uproar over these events, and hundreds of letters were written to the local papers. The great majority of residents defended the mother. What is significant is that relatively few of those assailing the accused attacked him for his specific ethnicity (Azerbaijani). Rather, they railed at him for being an outsider (*chuzhak*) and a trader: "We are in our own home; why should we be afraid of foreigners in our own country? They all trade; not one of them works."

44. *Informpolis* [Irkutsk], no. 30 (174), 25 June 1996: 3.

45. Dyatlov (1995) estimates that 2.5 million Chinese were living in Russia in 1993, of which 1 million were long-term residents. In Irkutsk, according to official figures, there were 40,000 arrivals during 1994; according to nonofficial estimates there were 72,000 to 110,000 arrivals. These figures seem greatly exaggerated. According to Minakir (1996) there were no more than 50,000 to 80,000 Chinese immigrants in the entire Far Eastern territory of Russia.

46. The mechanism is for the trader to bring in goods, sell them to a Russian contact, and put the money in an underground Chinese bank, receiving a note whereby the sum can be recovered in China in yuan for the next trade trip. The Chinese bank can use the rubles received to purchase real estate or set up a joint venture, but most of the rubles are converted to dollars for illegal export back to China. It is said that 10 to 15 Chinese a day are arrested at the Irkutsk airport as money couriers (Dyatlov 1995: 16).

47. *Pravda Buryatii* [Ulan-Ude], 9 Aug. 1995: 2.

48. In the face of demands for sovereignty and ethnic unification, a presidential decree in the early 1990s made certain "lower" autonomous okrugs equal in status to republics and oblasts inside the federation, thus giving them equal representation in Moscow and the opportunity to obtain direct credits from the center. This policy effectively disarmed the rhetoric of ethnic unification, since the okrugs could now operate with the center directly and gained no advantage from joining up with ethnic brethren.

References

Anderson, David. 1995. *National Identity and Belonging in Arctic Siberia: An Ethnography of Evenkis and Dolgans ar Khantaiskoye Ozero in the Taimyr Autonomous District*. Ph.D. Dissertation, University of Cambridge.

Bruno, Marta. 1996. Women and the Culture of Entrepreneurship. In *Post-Soviet Women: From the Baltic to Central Asia*, ed. M. Buckley. Cambridge: Cambridge University Press.

Burawoy, Michael, and Pavel Krotov. 1993. "The Economic Basis of Russia's Political Crisis. *New Left Review* 198: 49–70.

Butler, W. E. 1991. *The Customs Code of the USSR and the Law on the Customs Tariff of the USSR*, intro. and tr. W. E. Butler. London and Moscow: Interlist.

Clarke, Simon. 1992. Privatization and the Development of Capitalism in Russia. *New Left Review* 196: 3–27.

Dyatlov, V. 1995. "Torgovyye men'shinstva" sovremennogo Irkutska: problema stabil'nosti i konflikta v rossiiskoi provinstii. Ms.

Dyatlov, V., D. Demid, and E. Palyutina. 1995. "Kavkaztsy" v rossiiskoi provintsii: kriminal'nyi episod kak indikator urovnya mezhetnicheskoi naprazhennosti. *Acta Eurasica* [Moscow], 1 (1): 46–63.

Fedin, E. 1995. Chto godit'sya po granitse podoidet i TEKu. *Business Moskovskiye Novosti,* 20 September 1995: 1.

Gates, Hill. 1996. *China's Motor: A Thousand Years of Petty Capitalism.* Ithaca, N.Y.: Cornell University Press.

Gomelev, L. 1995. "Za derzhavy obidno . . ." *Pravda Buryatii* [Ulan-Ude], 17 March 1995: 2.

Handelman, Stephen. 1994. *Comrade Criminal: The Theft of the Second Russian Revolution.* London: Michael Joseph.

Humphrey, Caroline. 1989. Janus-Faced Signs: The Language of Politics of an Ethnic Minority in the Soviet Union. In *Social Anthropology and the Politics of Language,* ed. R. Grillo. Sociological Review Monograph 36. London: Routledge.

———. 1991. "Icebergs," Barter and the Mafia in Provincial Russia. *Anthropology Today* 7(2): 8–13.

———. 1995. Creating a Culture of Disillusionment: Consumption in Moscow in 1993, a Chronicle of Changing Times. In *Worlds Apart,* ed. D. Miller. London: Routledge.

Khokhlov, A. N. 1987. The Kyakhta Trade and Its Effect on Russian and Chinese Policy in the 18th and 19th Centuries. In *Chapters from the History of Russo-Chinese Relations: 17th–19th Centuries,* ed. S. L. Tikhvinsky. Moscow: Progress.

Kurochkin, V. 1995. Nesbyvshiyesya nadezhdy. *Pravda Buryatii* [Ulan-Ude], 17 March 1995: 2.

Lemon, Alaina. 1996. *Indic Diaspora, Soviet History, Russian Home: Political Performances and Sincere Ironies in Romani Cultures.* Ph.D. Dissertation, University of Chicago.

Minakir, P. A. 1996. Kitaiskaya immigratsiya na rossiiskom dal'nem vostoke: regional'nyye, natsional'nyye and mezhdunarodnyye aspekty problemy. Unpublished paper given at the international conference, Migration in Post-Soviet Space, Minsk.

Nikitina, E. 1996. "Chelnoki" tonut v more poshlin. *Argumenty i Fakty* [Moscow] 32: 7.

Nikolayev, V. 1994. Onokhoiskii peredel 1. Kombinat zakryt. Vsekh ushli . . . po yagodu, 2. Mama, mama, chto my budem delat' . . . *Pravda Buryatii* [Ulan-Ude], 8 Sept. 1994: 2, and 9 Sept. 1994: 2.

Owen, Thomas C. 1981. *Capitalism and Politics in Russia: A Social History of the Moscow Merchants, 1855–1905.* Cambridge: Cambridge University Press.

———. 1991. *The Corporation Under Russian Law, 1800–1917: A Study in Tsarist Economic Policy.* Cambridge: Cambridge University Press.

Polukeyev, O. 1995. Bandity ubivayut, GAIshniki obirayut. *Business Moskov-skiye Novosti,* 20 Sept. 1995: 4.

Shelkunova, Olga. 1995. Shturman v stikhii rynka. *Pravda Buryatii* [Ulan-Ude], 31 May 1995: 2.

Simmel, Georg. 1978. *The Philosophy of Money,* tr. Tom Bottomore and David Frisby. London: Routledge and Kegan Paul.

Uskeyev, B. Ne do zhiru, no . . . zhivem. *Pravda Buryatii* [Ulan-Ude], 22 July 1994: 2.

Varese, Frederico. 1994. Is Sicily the Future of Russia? Private Protection and the Rise of the Russian Mafia. *European Journal of Sociology* 35: 224–258.

Verdery, Katherine. 1991. Theorizing Socialism: A Prologue to the "Transition." *American Anthropologist* 18: 419–439.

2

Fuzzy Property: Rights, Power, and Identity in Transylvania's Decollectivization

Katherine Verdery

An especially challenging area of transformation in the former socialist world—challenging for both social policy and social theory—concerns the (re)creation of private property rights from the collective property of socialism. Property rights are changing in more than postsocialist contexts, but those contexts differ profoundly from others. In no Western country undergoing the privatization of socialized assets has social production existed on anything like the scale of that in the former socialist bloc. Moreover, in the latter instances public enterprise operated in political, economic, and jural systems governed by totally different rules from those of liberal capitalism, making the creation of postsocialist private property rights an entirely different proposition from the divestitures of public property in countries like Britain, France, or the United States.

For these reasons, the process amply deserves the fast-growing corpus of literature devoted to it. This literature treats such issues as the theoretical relationship among private property, markets, and democratic politics (e.g., Comisso 1991; Riker and Weimer 1993); the process of transforming public property into private and the consequences of this transformation for economic development and state power (e.g., Frydman and Rapaczynski 1994; Frydman, Rapaczynski, and Earle 1993; Kiss 1994; Staniszkis 1991; Stark 1992; Voszka 1991); the justifying ideologies of transformed property rights and their social effects (e.g., Appel 1995; Maurel 1994a, 1994b; Verdery 1994); and the nature of the new rights being exercised (e.g., Comisso 1991; Cornea 1993; Hann 1993a, 1993b; Stark 1996). Reports to date on emerging property forms speak not of a wholesale shift from public to private ownership but rather of mixes of

53

the two: different social actors hold different bundles of rights, and the definitions of the status of property are blurred and ambiguous.[1]

Among the tasks these investigations facilitate is a deeper inquiry into the very concept of property itself—what it means, and how property regimes are socially produced. Such an inquiry should also explore the ideological aspect of privatization as a centerpiece of the transition, for the neoliberal project of transforming public into private property has more than just a practical aim (ostensibly easing the creation of markets, not to mention the interface with global capital); it has great ideological significance as well. This significance goes beyond the mere fact of constantly pressing for *private* property. If we see the transition as a project of cultural engineering in which fundamental social ideas are resignified—including not only "markets," "democracy," and "private property" but also ideas about entitlement, accountability, and responsibility—then the (re)creation of private property is evidently a critical locus for this cultural project. The reason is that neoliberal property notions so often emphasize *rights* (entitlement) and *obligations* (accountability), whose subjects are normatively *individuals* (physical or jural) exercising *exclusive* rights. From this vantage point, all other arrangements look fuzzy.

My purposes in this chapter are twofold. First, I suggest that to understand "property" in postsocialist contexts, one must go beyond defining it in terms of rights and obligations that assume individualized property subjects. I prefer instead a property analysis that invokes the total system of social, cultural, and political relations and inquires into, rather than assumes, the nature of property conceptions (cf. Hann 1993, 1993b; Ghani 1996). That is, I seek to broaden the way we study the "property" aspect of postsocialism. Second, I chronicle a specific moment in which a specific set of property conceptions was taking shape that favored not individual but collective property rights based in collective labor. By investigating this moment, I hope to show the social processes through which a new property regime is being produced, one that seems to incorporate older ideas from socialism. My data come from Aurel Vlaicu, a Transylvanian village undergoing decollectivization. The breakup of its collective farm has resulted in a complex array of property forms and claims, antithetical to what I believe the neoliberal architects of privatization had in mind—hence I label the outcome "fuzzy property."

I begin by describing some of the overlapping rights and claims to land that prevailed in this community as of 1996, and I argue that these rights and claims have meaning only in a larger enabling context. I then present an episode in which collective property forms with overlapping rights were strengthened at the expense of exclusive individual ownership. Using ethnographic methods, I seek to document transitional dynamics that might otherwise remain invisible—although not in their long-term effects. In this episode we see the intersection of interests and dispositions that served to maintain complex (fuzzy) property rights at a moment when they might have been altered. We see as well how these rights are bound up with power relations, with social identities and notions of self, and with embeddedness in social networks. Both parts of my discussion explore different reasons why emerging property forms seem fuzzy from the vantage point of an idealized image of exclusive private property; both parts seek to show the processes and calculations generating this fuzziness.

I speak of "fuzzy property" in part to ironize simplistic notions of private ownership, and I leave the notion somewhat vague since property rights can appear indistinct for a variety of reasons. Different people may contest ownership of a single object, complicating the assessment of use rights, obligations, and claims to revenue. If property is a relationship between persons with respect to things, then conflicting definitions of that relationship give the things in question ambiguous status. Property rights may also appear ambiguous because several different social actors enjoy overlapping claims to something; for example, the sovereign may have the right to allocate and recover use rights to certain lands as well as have a claim on their fruits, whereas households actually exercise these use rights and perform all of the labor, yet lineage heads claim managerial rights and a share of the harvest. In such cases, the hierarchy of rights and obligations may in fact be very *un*ambiguous, but from the point of view of privatization programs such as those being implemented in the former socialist bloc the rights appear fuzzy because of their complex interrelations and the multiplicity of actors holding them. Yet other reasons for fuzziness appear if we define property (following Ghani 1996) as a bundle of powers crystallized into practices of exclusion and inclusion within routinized rules.[2] Fuzziness, then, will lie precisely in the *lack* of routinized rules and crystallized practices around private property in the context of postsocialism, as well as in the constraints on exercising bundles of powers. My term *fuzzy property* covers all of these forms of indistinct, ambiguous, and partial property rights.

The chief social actors in the scenarios to follow are residents of the village of Aurel Vlaicu (county Hunedoara, Romania), where I conducted research during 1993–1994 and 1996;[3] the mayor and other officials of the commune in which Vlaicu is located; and a new organizational form, the Aurel Vlaicu Agricultural Association. This last requires explanation. Throughout Romania (and some other countries of the region as well), the return of land to its former owners entailed the liquidation of collective farms (in Romanian, *cooperative agricole de producţie,* or CAPs), sometimes accompanied by the creation of new entities, associations (*asociații*).[4] The association is a kind of producers' cooperative whose raison d'être is that few of the new proprietors own the equipment necessary for cultivating their newly returned land, and many are too old to carry out the work of farming it. Moreover, in the Romanian case, many new landowners do not even live in villages, for the restitution process permitted *all* heirs of former owners, even those living in distant cities, to claim family land. To ensure that newly private land would not go uncultivated, thus requiring massive food imports, the government encouraged people to form associations.

Legally, an association takes a form that is neither a limited liability nor a joint-stock company but is called a "commercial society"; it has a different tax regime from that of those other, more explicitly profit-oriented forms.[5] In the Aurel Vlaicu association, members joined with some form of social capital and are free to leave at any time.[6] All of its members contributed their social capital in the form of land, which had been returned to their families by Romania's law on property restitution, known as the Law on Agricultural Land Resources, or Law 18/1991. It was understood that the owners held and would retain ownership rights to the land placed in the association; they transferred managerial rights over cultivation in exchange for a payment from the harvest.[7]

My discussion is restricted to the Aurel Vlaicu association, successor to the village's collective farm (CAP), and it excludes the complex and overlapping rights, obligations, and claims to the land in the *state* farms (IASs).[8] Because Law 18 left IASs intact as state property, with component landowners reduced to shareholders having no rights of use or alienation, IASs retained a more complex mix of public and private than associations; their directors could manipulate that distinction creatively, producing what Stark (1996) calls "recombinant property." I focus here, however, on complex property rights at their fuzziest: those lying at the interface of collective and individual, with minimal state mediation. In the next section I offer a general description of the formal system of property rights involving the Vlaicu association to show the complexity of those rights and their implications in both local and wider organizations of power.

Complexly Overlapping Rights

As of 1996, there were numerous sources of ambiguity in property rights in the Transylvanian countryside.[9] Among the most important was the slow process through which owners acquired title to their land. Although Law 18 was passed in February 1991, three years later under a quarter of Romania's entitled households had received their property deed (*titlu de proprietate*), a figure that had increased to 63 percent by mid-1996.[10] Only in autumn 1995 did anyone in Vlaicu acquire one. In 1991 all claimants received a temporary property affidavit (*adeverință*), but that did not endow them with full proprietary rights, which were to follow only with subsequent registration and titling. Bearers of an affidavit held only rights to use the land and take its fruits; they could not sell it or use it as collateral on a loan (although the affidavit did obligate them to pay taxes on it). Strictly speaking, then, until villagers obtained title in 1995, those who placed their land with the association did so as not-yet-owners allocating rights of control they technically did not have full capacity to cede.[11]

Law 18 established a number of fairly stringent constraints on an individual's private property rights—that is, it set up a hierarchy of prior rights and claims. For instance, it constrained the land's use: owners of agricultural land do not have the right to leave it uncultivated, on penalty of a fine; those holding use rights and not cultivating the land lose those rights after two years (Law 18/1991, articles 53–55). Nor have they the right to change the category of its use—say, from vineyard to pasture or arable to house plot—except under certain conditions and only by permission of the Ministry of Agriculture (art. 56, 57, and 69). There are constraints on acquisition as well. Persons who in 1991 failed to register their claim to land within a specific time (initially thirty days, extended to forty-five) lost their right to claim ownership altogether; the property right reverted to the state. No one was permitted to claim the return of more than ten hectares (ha.) per family (art. 8 and 9) or to acquire thereafter more than 100 ha. total (art. 46). Persons having land not in the collectives but in state farms received no ownership or use rights to that land, only a claim to a share of the state farm's revenues (art. 34).[12] Finally, although the wording of the law is not entirely clear on this point, it appears to make all sales of agricultural land contingent on the prior exercise of rights of preemption by an organization called the Agency for Rural Development and Planning (art. 48)—which, as of mid-1998, did not yet exist. Owners were thus unable to dispose of their land as they pleased within a legal framework.[13]

Such provisions, together with the fact that anyone wishing to regain property title to earlier-owned lands had to file a request (*cerere*) to that effect, suggest that "the state" holds the most inclusive prior rights over disposal and use. Law 18 therefore (re)constitutes a paternalist state as the ultimate landlord, one empowered to disaggregate property rights and allocate them selectively downward to other actors through the process of "reconstituting or constituting the right of property" Law 18 was designed to inaugurate. This set of state powers is not unique to postsocialism; every major legal system empowers the state to limit property rights (although the content of those limitations varies).[14] Further, in practice these state powers are not absolute. Law 18 specifically allocates to "common law," for instance, the division of a holding among its rightful heirs (art. 12). Moreover, because nearly all of the constraints on land use and sale listed earlier have been violated (in the case I know best, and presumably throughout Romania as well), we see that although the state may occupy the first rung in a "hierarchy of estates" of administration over land (cf. Gluckman 1943), it lacks adequate sanctioning power to enforce its priority.

Although these provisions may seem unambiguous enough, they are complicated by a significant historical fact: because of the way collective farms were formed—by the "voluntary" donation of land rather than by a law expropriating it—de jure the land in a collective farm always remained the social property not of the state as a whole but of that specific collective. The same is true of the other objects of property rights held by CAPs, such as the fixed capital (e.g., barns and other outbuildings) produced through members' collective labor or paid for by the goods sold from that labor (cf. Maurel 1994b: 11–12). Without first nationalizing the land of collective farms, the state had no way of acquiring the prior rights noted earlier, but Law 18 did not nationalize that land. The land therefore cannot, technically speaking, be restored to its prior owners by an act of state (Law 18) but only by action of the collective farm body dissolving itself. Absent such action,[15] according to a notary with whom I discussed this matter, Law 18 effectively disbands the collectives by the same means used to constitute them in the first place—state violence—as if to acknowledge that because the "consent" used in collectivizing was a fiction, there is no reason to secure owners' consent now to reverse that process. It is clear, then, that from a legalistic point of view, there is much ambiguity in the source and allocation of rights to the property of CAPs. We are probably better served to speak of property as a bundle not of rights (which may be moot) but rather of *powers*.

While usurping the rights of individuals and local collectivities to decide their collective's fate by formal consent, Law 18 further biased the constitution of subsequent property rights in a collective rather than an individual direction: it gave associations as jural entities the edge in acquiring property of moribund CAPs. A crucial clause reads as follows:

Zootechnic constructions, workshops for small manufactures, machinery, equipment, and other such fixed means belonging to the disbanded CAP, as well as the land underneath these and the land necessary to using them, and also vineyards and orchards and animals all become the property of the members of associations of a private nature (*asociaţii de tip privat*) having the status of jural persons, if these are established. The rights of former CAP members to the above-mentioned goods will be set as a value proportional to the land area the CAP received from them and the volume of work they gave the CAP. (art. 28)

In a word, CAPs would "morph" into associations, the social capital of which was assigned to the members as shares by an algorithm linking one's total land and labor contributions to the CAP.[16] The algorithm gave individualized contour to a collective entity without actually carving out an individual's share. Only those villagers who chose not to belong to the association were to be separated out fully from the collective and paid in money or kind for their share of the fixed capital. Thus conceived, the law presented the transformation of CAPs into associations as the "default option"; their disaggregation into fully individual proprietorships required extra work. We see clearly in this situation a systemic bias toward quasi-collective property arrangements.

In some Romanian settlements, villagers chose to transform the CAP directly into one or more associations without first dividing the land among former owners. In Vlaicu, however, before an association could organize, a few people occupied land—mostly the land they had once owned—and began to work it. This set off a chain reaction that ended in reassigning private property rights to all former owners in the location of their old plots; something similar happened in many other villages. The process of reimpropriation proved extremely complex and resulted in considerable ambiguity in the ownership status of land (see Verdery 1994 for a detailed description of these problems). In consequence, for many villagers in Vlaicu and elsewhere, in 1998 it was still not clear exactly who "owned" what parcel. Differences of opinion and overt conflicts persisted; legal challenges continue to hold up the process of clarification, for one can go to court only when one has a deed, but it is precisely over who should have the deed that many parties want to litigate. As villagers fight over these issues, local officials often usurp the contending owners' usufruct rights, cultivating the land and disposing of the product themselves.[17]

The individual who has managed to obtain undisputed title to a specific surface area of former CAP land theoretically holds all of the rights of use, enjoyment, and disposal not reserved for the state. Serious contextual constraints exist, however, on the exercise of these rights. One concerns the possibilities for disposing of one's products, because of inadequate channels for distribution. A household of two or three people will use about 600 kg of wheat a year for its own needs (average yields for this region are around 3,000 kg per hectare [kg/ha.]). Anything over that amount will be useful mainly if it is sold, and the cash from sale will be necessary to pay for next year's plowing and harvesting. But without an auto or a cart to drive to market and the time to remain there to sell, one may have difficulty exchanging the product for cash. An alternative has been to contract part of the product to a state monopoly organization called Romcereal, but this means accepting the state price for grain—generally lower than the market price.[18] A second alternative is to give one's land to other, landless villagers in sharecropping arrangements for half of the harvest, which economizes the cash needed for production and easily disposes of half of the product. That alternative is limited, however, by landless villagers' lack of implements, farm equipment, and cash and by their loss of interest once they secure land of their own. A third alternative—feeding excess grain to animals, which are simpler to market than grain—is available only to households with adequate labor to tend them. Thus, a rudimentary distribution infrastructure limits the possibilities for disposing of the fruits of one's possessions—and this is true not just for individual owner/farmers but for the association and its members as well.

An even more important constraint on exercising ownership rights concerns production, for few people who received their land owned the implements necessary for cultivating it. The instruments they had donated to the collective in the 1950s had long since rusted away, and no substitutes were provided. People who had given cattle to the CAP received an equivalent number in 1991, which they might use as draft animals; but to profit from their animals they would have to acquire plows, harrows, seeders, threshers, fertilizer, and all of the other means involved in a cycle of agricultural production. Ideally, they might buy tractors and combines as well. In the early 1990s, however, the price of agricultural implements kept going up disproportionately to the price of agricultural produce, and loans were hard to obtain.[19] Without cold cash it was hard to acquire implements or have one's land worked, and without these it was hard to acquire cold cash. This simple conundrum caused many to decide to place some or all of their land with the association rather than attempt to work it themselves as exclusive private owners. Given the lack of implements, the association was the only possibility standing between ownership and the forfeiture of one's rights from noncultivation.

Having joined the association, one entered a realm of intricately overlapping rights, obligations, and claims. Let us take as an example a widow who is too old to manage the work on her newly acquired three hectares. If she turns them over to the association, she loses the right to farm her land on her own or to allocate its use to a third party, and she alienates most (but not all) of the rights to its day-to-day management; still, she can tell the agronomist what crops she wants as payment and in what proportions. She can specify, for example, that she wants some sugar beets, potatoes, corn, and wheat in specific proportions and cash instead of barley. That is, she has the right to influence the use of her land even if she is not farming it directly. Her choices obligate her to pay certain amounts of money (according to the areas being sown with particular crops) for the cost of plowing and to provide the necessary labor for labor-intensive tasks, such as hoeing and weeding corn, since the association has no independent labor force for such work.

Although our widow can specify the *proportions* of various products and cash she will receive as revenue from her land, she has lost virtually all control over the *amounts* (except for the rows of corn she hoes, where her effort and timing do affect the outcome). These amounts enter into a complex politics within the association leadership. One agronomist of the Vlaicu association, for instance, wanted to be popular with the villagers and to prove that he was as good as the previous fellow, even at the expense of the association's long-term prospects. After the harvest, he paid for the inputs and salaries and then divided the entire remainder among members (each received about 1,000 kg/ha. given to the association), reserving nothing to renew production the following year—by which time he had left the village. Two and three years later, members received only 400 and 550 kg/ha., respectively, for the new agronomist had persuaded the council to buy two tractors and related equipment with the association's income, docking members' pay for the cost and interest on the loan. If our widow had experienced extensive cash needs during those years, she would have been in trouble.[20] If she were clairvoyant, she might have taken her land out of the association to avoid having to contribute to the future purchase of tractors; otherwise, she has lost income and automatically become part owner of the tractors, since she helped to buy them.[21] On the other hand, should she decide—as many Vlaicenii do—to keep, say, a hectare of her land out of the association and work it herself, she might (if her timing and connections are right) use an association tractor to plow that hectare.[22]

The association to which the widow gives her land acquires the rights to manage and use it and to take its fruits, some of which must be redistributed to her. That is, by taking land the association incurs obligations to cultivate it and to generate revenue for redistribution. In summer 1994, the Vlaicu association ran out of money to pay for the plowing, sowing, and harvesting of about 25 ha., for which it was nonetheless obligated to deliver a product. The agronomist cast about for someone else who would do the work and pay the owners in a sort of subcontracting arrangement. Because everyone giving land has a claim on revenues, *every* member of the association would have received less had the 25 ha. gone uncultivated. That is, the rights of each member limit the rights of others to the product from their land, or, to put it differently, people have overlapping rights to the revenues, which they are obligated to share with other members.

In the following year (1995), a similar subcontracting arrangement resolved the problem that for rotational purposes the association needed to plant more corn than members were prepared to work; a third party contracted to plant the difference. This and the previous example show overlapping rights and obligations with respect to both revenues and use: the association has the right to allocate the use rights that have been allocated to it so as to fulfill its obligations to the claims of the owners. The subcontracting arrangements produced a third tier in the hierarchy of use rights, a third claimant to the surface area; "owners" had allocated these rights to the association, which allocated them to a third party. Each tier of claimants expected revenues from that surface, and in 1995 the top two tiers also exercised certain rights to the product that constrained managerial decisions at the tiers below. The allocation of rights to land, although complex, is not chaotic; from the viewpoint of a Western ideology of exclusive individual ownership, however, these overlapping rights ambiguate the land's property status.

People's rights do not only overlap, they also conflict. In 1996, when hail and floods affected certain fields in Vlaicu but not others, owners in the unaffected areas began to urge individuated revenues. Instead of using a production average for the whole farm in determining members' payment, they said, the association should use the precise yields of each owner's actual parcels. That is, individual rights to revenue should supersede the collective claims on which the association bases its risk-sharing and paperwork-reducing strategies. The agronomist rejected this proposal, but it underscores the complex calculation of individual and collective property claims.

Although technically the association acquires managerial and use rights when owners give it land, its leaders' managerial rights and control over the product are further circumscribed by the property structure it inherited and by its relations with both members and the state. Leaders are obliged to create revenue for members under conditions that are far from optimal. To begin with, the structure of the fields they have received to work is highly unsuited to sensible cultivation. The land commission that restored land to its owners failed to consolidate fields;[23] worse yet, the restitution of people's original plots meant breaking the association's holdings into myriad small parcels scattered among the fields of nonmembers. Because the association finds it technically impossible to work very tiny parcels, it cannot accept every piece of land people want to give it, and this reduces the scale of its operations.[24]

Constraints inherent in the association's relationship with its members come from such factors as the members' right to withdraw their land at will and problems with labor. As owners, members have the right to withdraw their land. Indeed, at first some Vlaicenii would wait until the association plowed their land and then withdraw it, leaving the association to pay for the plowing.[25] Others withdrew land once their pay dropped following the purchase of the tractors. To form a rational cultivation plan, in 1995 and 1996 the leaders suggested three-year contracts. Because the contracts would restrict owners' rights to withdraw, members—fearing further erosion of their receipts—resisted.

Members' rights of withdrawal are in turn limited, however, by whether there are other ways to have their land cultivated. In villages where (unlike Vlaicu) very few people have tractors with which to plow for others, members may in effect be powerless to withdraw their land; associations can control them by threatening expulsion, which might mean being unable to have one's land worked at all. Where associations have less power over members' withdrawing their land (as in Vlaicu), the leaders were at least initially inclined to maximize pay to members at the expense of rational long-term planning. Rather than withhold payment to buy needed equipment or supplies, they sought to pay members more in an attempt to keep them. Part of the reason is the association's history as a morph of the CAP: village "individualists," fomenting an anticollectivist climate, would gloat over members if the association's pay was low and would say "See? The association is ripping you off just like the CAP!" The Vlaicu association's statute reserves 20 percent of earnings for costs and reinvestment, but according to the president, in 1994 it was withholding only 10 percent for salaries and expenses; if it withheld more, it feared, nonmembers would provoke departures by painting the association as "just like the old CAP." From these examples we see that who has use rights to allocate and under what conditions is a complex function of local wealth, the effects of prior management decisions, and the varied local histories of collectivization.

Further checks on the association's exercise of its managerial capacities come from problems with the labor supply, coupled with members' right to determine their crop profile and form of payment. The generally low technical and financial endowment of agriculture means that, like CAPs before them, associations must rely on the manual labor of their members to carry out labor-intensive tasks such as hoeing and weeding. Many members are not physically capable of, or not locally resident for, this purpose; they tend not to ask for payment in crops whose hoeing and harvesting requirements they cannot meet—especially root crops and corn. This is particularly true of members residing in cities, who hold three-fourths of the Vlaicu association's land and, according to the agronomist, generally want payment only in wheat and cash. Although no farm can plant wheat year after year on the bulk of its surface area without crop rotation, nonetheless, the Vlaicu association has been forced to err in that direction. In summer 1996, desperate for soil replenishment, the agronomist planted much more corn than local members could hoe and harvest. She thus risked large expenditures for day labor (but only after exploring local garrisoned soldiers and convicts—staples of the old CAP—as possible sources of labor). Therefore, members' capacity to work, their right to determine their revenue, and their right to dispose of their land compromise leaders' optimal management and risk taking.

So, too, does the association's dependency on the state for mechanized inputs, credits, and prices—a dependency the agronomist believes is much greater now than it was for the CAPs. Associations' right to inherit the fixed capital of the CAPs did little to endow them with tractors and combines, for CAPs in Romania, unlike other socialist countries, generally did not have this equipment; it was provided by machinery stations (SMAs) on the Soviet model. After 1989 the SMAs changed their names to Agromecs but remained state institutions, slated for eventual privatization. Associations lacking equipment were compelled to use their services; the fees, however, were exorbitant, set to support the antiquated machinery and the leftover bureaucracy of paper pushers. In Vlaicu, the high cost of hiring this equipment was what led the association to buy tractors and auxiliary implements. Reducing that source of dependency on the state, however, exposed it to another: the vagaries of government policies relating to credits and interest rates. Organizations like this one are supposed to have privileged access to agricultural credits at 15 percent interest. But these credits turn out to be available only to certain special friends of local banks, with all others borrowing at rates as high as 100 percent that vary at the whim (or so it seems) of the government-controlled central bank. Further worsening one's exposure to such insecure rates are the state-set prices to which associations—given inadequate distribution channels—are virtually tied. Problems with obtaining cheap credits are probably the most important constraint on what associations can do with the use rights they enjoy.

Having begun this section by emphasizing the rights and obligations that supposedly accrue to owners and managers, I have found it increasingly necessary to qualify those rights by noting the systemic constraints on people's exercise of them. In so doing, I support Hann's observation that to consider property only as a matter of rights and obligations is inadequate: "There are many persons and families in Hungary today for whom the current rhetoric about widening choice and extending property rights must seem a sick joke: . . . they cannot become entrepreneurial farmers because they lack the basic capital resources, and their social rights are being whittled away all the time" (Hann 1993a: 313). Exclusive individual ownership rights to land, which many in both Eastern Europe and the West see as the goal of decollectivization, are effectively constituted only within a total field of relations among institutions, policies, and social actors. These relations shape what actors are able to do with property, modifying the "rights" to which they may be entitled and the "obligations" to which they can be held.

Fuzzy property, in the examples given here, consists of complexly overlapping use and revenue rights lodged in external conditions that give the holders of those rights incomplete powers for exercising them. The external conditions include such "legacies of socialism" as a systemic bias against individual ownership and in favor of state or quasi-collective forms. For something more closely approaching exclusive individual proprietorship to emerge would require not so much clearer legal specification of who has what rights—these rights are fairly clear—but modifications in the surrounding economy that would permit individuals to acquire the means of cultivation affordably and to dispose of their product profitably while outcompeting quasi-collective associational forms. That, in turn, depends on various parties' electoral fortunes, intergovernmental relations, decisions by international lending agencies, and other factors not usually included in discussions of property.

If property is more than just rights and obligations, as I have been suggesting, it is also more than just the surrounding political economy; it entails complex meanings, often revolving around ideas about labor, persons, community, and kinship. These meanings are not necessarily those of Western privatization programs. Postsocialist property regimes will gradually develop from repeated interactions between macrosystemic fields of force and the meanings, behaviors, and values of the people caught up in them. In the next section, I explore the dynamics of transition in Romania's property regime by examining a specific event that helps to reveal more fully the meanings of property. In this event, individual ownership rights were asserted and rejected in favor of persisting fuzzy property and collective rights. Behind this outcome lay not only a certain set of power relations but also convictions about social justice and self-actualization. I offer considerable detail on this case to provide evidence of a sort rare in literature on postsocialism: the ethnography of cultural reproduction.

The Trial: Individual Versus Collective Claims

Sitting in the office of the Vlaicu association one day in November 1993, I learned that its agronomist and accountant had wasted their morning in court. They told a complicated story about the liquidation of the collective farm, an irregular auction of a granary, a resulting lawsuit decided against the plaintiff—a villager I'll call Ionescu—and an appeal aimed at annulling the auction. A few weeks later I ran into Ionescu on the street. He greeted me with enthusiasm and invited me to hear his side of the story, encouraging me as well to ask certain other people for their opinions. Among those he mentioned was Iosif, a good friend of mine who has distinguished himself since 1989 with entrepreneurial activities. "Iosif and I are trying to do something good here," said Ionescu, "create a *real* association, with a granary, a bakery . . . not a *socialist* association [i.e., like the existing one] but one on an American model."[26]

My curiosity piqued, I asked both Iosif and his mother, Ana, about Ionescu's case.[27] Ana replied with feeling that the granary should belong to everyone, not just to Ionescu, adding, "He's boasted all over the village that he'll get the granary and will never have to work again, just live off renting it out. Shouldn't it belong to the village rather than to just one person? The whole village built it, after all." Iosif disagreed, saying that Ionescu had been the victim of a breach of the law. Law 18 had special procedures for auctioning off the goods of collective farms, he said, procedures that had been closely followed until suddenly the officers of the prospective association had realized they would need a granary; at that point they had interfered with the auction unlawfully, and Ionescu was right to sue them. Agreeing with his mother that it would of course be better to have the granary used by one hundred people than by one, Iosif nonetheless felt larger principles were at stake here: do we or don't we respect the law, and do we or don't we give property to individuals who will take good care of it (as the association, he feels, does not)?

These four brief conversations—with the two association officers, with Ionescu, with my friend Iosif, and with Ana—set the coordinates of what proved to be a villagewide controversy over privatization. Virtually all of the significant issues appeared in these commentaries. I spent the next several months filling them out by attending the sessions of the court case, discussing it with the plaintiff and defendants as well as with the presiding judge, and asking many other villagers for their opinions. Because I was not present for the critical auction, I cannot say what happened there, but I am fairly confident of what was at issue in the case: a clash between procedural issues on the one hand and the "public good" on the other and between the conditions promoting individual entrepreneurship as against certain values of community. These conflicts lie at the heart of privatization all over Eastern Europe; they are also central to producing a new property regime with specific conceptions of "property," as well as specific conditions that either favor or impede autonomous individual action and ownership relations.

I should emphasize a salient feature of this case: it is about the privatization of a good that, unlike land, had not been privately owned before. It thus resembles privatization of the industries built up during the socialist period that are visibly the product of people's labor in that time when collective labor produced collective products having no "owners." Land, by contrast, has prior owners; its privatization creates conflicts between those owners and others who feel entitled to a share by their work in the collective (see Verdery 1994: 1105–6). With the Vlaicu granary that sort of conflict was not present, and this brought the question of public good more cleanly into view.

As best I can determine, the events leading to the dispute went something like this. Law 18/1991, providing for the liquidation of collective farms and the return of their land and animals to the former owners, unleashed chaotic activity, for the terms within which everything was to be resolved were fairly short and no one really knew how to do what they were supposed to be doing.[28] The law gave each CAP fifteen days to constitute a so-called liquidation commission, and each commission had nine months to dissolve the CAP (art. 26). As I have noted, the law foresaw the possibility of setting up associations, privileged recipients of the fixed capital of the old CAPs, which would otherwise be sold at auction and the proceeds distributed to members according to the algorithm noted earlier.

In Vlaicu—and presumably not there alone—it took some time to form an association. A few villagers began occupying their land and evidently intended to work it not in association but by themselves; others were still too dazed at the prospect of regaining their land to think clearly about its disposition. Some of the personnel of the old CAP wanted to form an association but were having trouble figuring out how to do so. On 5 July 1991, when the association was still just an idea and not yet a jural entity, the village liquidation commission put in the newspaper the notice required by law, stating that every Thursday from 10:00 to 2:00 "until the patrimony [of the CAP] is liquidated," public auctions would be held for the sale or rental of buildings and the sale of equipment and other objects.[29] One aim was to obtain enough money finally to launch the association. Its first official meeting had already taken place (in March 1992), but its legal incorporation would occur five months later, in August, after several items had already been put up for auction—including three of the five cattle barns, some equipment, and the only available tractor.

By his own report, Ionescu showed up on Thursday, 30 July 1992, in hopes of buying not the granary but a smaller building, the so-called annex.[30] He said he planned to use it as a workshop and shelter for his tractor and tools, with an eye toward eventually forming some kind of agricultural association. Also present at the auction were several people representing the embryonic leadership council of the embryonic Vlaicu association—I'll call them the quasi council. When this group outbid him for the annex, Ionescu asked what other buildings were to be sold; among them was the granary. He asked to make a bid, the quasi council countered, and Ionescu raised the offer. At this point one of the quasi councilors asked that the bidding be stopped so the quasi council could consult with association members on how high they were willing to go. The president of the liquidation commission then suspended the bidding.

These events took place amid considerable confusion. As one of those running the meeting explained to me, "We had no idea how to do an auction, how to proceed with liquidating the CAP; my image of an auction was from American TV movies—standing in front of people and calling out numbers—but that's not how it was happening." Although the liquidation commission had requested a legal aide from the county capital, none turned up. No one knew whether it was acceptable to suspend the bidding, but under the circumstances—in which people representing an embryonic association suddenly realized it could not function without a granary it did not yet have the resources to buy—that seemed the thing to do. The decision was not only logical but also possible because most of the people on the liquidation commission were also on the quasi council of the prospective association.

Deeply upset by what had happened, Ionescu complained to the mayor, who reopened the bidding on Saturday, 1 August 1992. Ionescu refused to bid, saying he had won the real auction held two days earlier and Saturday was not a day listed for auctions. Overriding his objections, the association raised his earlier bid by a small margin and was awarded the granary. Ionescu retained a lawyer, sued the liquidation commission, and lost. He filed an appeal to have the auction annulled for breaching the published terms that auctions were held on Thursdays only. By the time his appeal began (20 January 1994), one-and-a-half years had passed since the auction, and the association was a well-established—indeed, an essential—player in village life.

The appeal took place in two court sessions, which I attended. The judge's questioning sought to establish the precise course of events and pursued several additional points. These points included the size of the association (over 100 member families), its aim (grain cultivation), who built the granary (villagers collectively, through "voluntary" labor in the 1960s), whether it was necessary to the association (*very* necessary, said several witnesses for the defense), why Ionescu came on Saturday and brought others with him if he refused to bid (disputed), whether other large items had been sold on Saturdays despite the terms of the published announcement (they had), the reactions of villagers to Ionescu's bid on the granary (panic and disapproval, said defense witnesses), and why the commission made no public announcement of the auctions that were taking place on days other than Thursday ("an oversight," said the commission's president). The mayor was repeatedly summoned as a witness and failed to appear, submitting instead a written statement—not taken under oath—that the Thursday auction was held only for the annex, that Saturday was assigned for auctioning the granary, and that the granary was essential to the association's success.

At the end of the second session, the lawyers for the two sides summed up their arguments as follows. The plaintiff's lawyer argued to annul the auction for procedural irregularity: (1) two persons who had bid on the granary for the association were also members of the liquidation commission; (2) the law requires publicity since sales are not for a limited number of people but for *any* potential buyer, and because the publicity had mentioned only Thursdays, the Saturday auction excluded buyers who might have wanted to come; and (3) it was impossible for the association as such to bid on the granary in July, for it acquired legal status only in August. Thus, the quasi council could bid only as private individuals, which would mean they had no grounds for suspending the auction to consult with anyone else. The lawyer emphasized that the manner of the auction contravened the interests of the public and of former CAP members since the lack of publicity kept potentially higher-bidding participants from attending, which reduced the proceeds from sales that could be distributed to villagers.

The defense lawyer rejected the suit, saying (1) the plaintiff could have bid on Saturday (he had done so for earlier purchases) but did not; (2) he had insisted on exceeding the mandate of the Thursday auction, which, as shown in the mayor's deposition, was only for the annex and not the granary; (3) as someone pursuing a private outcome, he was not legally qualified to sue in the *public* interest; and (4) because article 28 of Law 18 specifies that the fixed assets of CAPs automatically become the property of associations, the granary never had to be put up for auction. The lawyer called into question the very notion of "public good" used by the prosecution, asking whose interests were to be protected by wide publicity—those of people in cities and towns far from the place where items are being sold, who would have little reason to want a granary in a small village and might do antisocial things with it?

The summaries made it clear that completely different principles were at war. One was that because article 28 of Law 18 privileged new collective farms, the auction need never have occurred, in which case all other arguments were moot. Upholding the law in the broadest sense was thus compatible with ruling against the plaintiff. Alternatively, because Law 18 gave precise instructions about the conduct of auctions (which in my view had clearly been breached), one could argue to uphold the law by ruling in the plaintiff's favor. There was also the matter of the association's legal status at the time of the auction, which might or might not be seen as adequate to qualify it for inclusion under article 28 of Law 18.

Then there were questions about just what it means to defend the "public good": how should one construe the "interested public" for purposes of selling off collective property, how wide should that public be, and who is qualified to defend its interest?

The question of the public good turned out to be decisive, as I learned from conversations with the presiding judge after the trial was over. The judge is a very unusual person, a true product of the socialist era who, supplementing her "healthy" social origin with intelligence, discipline, and night school courses, worked her way up from cleaning lady to president of the district court. Having resigned her post after the revolution she was soon called back to help handle the avalanche of cases, being one of the few members of the county judiciary's "old guard" whom many younger judges respected. In my frequent contacts with her during my research in 1993–1994,[31] I became persuaded of the genuineness of her convictions and of her dedication to certain values, particularly those promoting social equity; in this, she resembles many of the East German judges portrayed in Markovits's *Imperfect Justice* (1995). I was thus not surprised when she found against the plaintiff and dismissed the case. Her reasons, as she explained them to me, were as follows.

First, given the provisions of Law 18, article 28, the entire auction was unnecessary. Although acknowledging that she could have ruled strictly against the association since it had no jural status at the time of the auction, she preferred to see the evidence that it was forming as sufficient grounds for applying article 28 and awarding it the CAP's fixed property. Behind this preference stood, second, her belief that the law should protect the interest of the greater number—the members of the association rather than a single individual. In this case the plaintiff could not claim to be defending the social interest himself, for a larger social interest was represented by the defendants, and he could not sue for protection of his personal interest since he had forfeited that interest by not bidding on Saturday when he had the chance. The judge described her overall philosophy of judicial decisions: that because any decision has social consequences, her job is to determine them and judge according to the greater public good. At this moment in Romania's history, she said, it was more important than ever to render decisions according to the morality of a case, as long as the outcomes are consistent with legal norms. Given that there is right on both sides in many of the cases related to Law 18, the best principle is to make a decision that serves the greater need or, alternatively, does the lesser injury. To my suggestion that in a transforming Romania the public good might also be served by promoting private ownership that would contribute to solving Romania's economic crisis, she agreed in principle, but Ionescu was not, she thought, the kind of person who would act in that way.

Whatever the reasons for the judge's decision,[32] the effect of her decision was to deny legal sanction to those who would move an object from an ambiguous status, subject to overlapping claims and rights on the part of individual owners and collectivity, into Ionescu's clearly defined, exclusive private ownership. By her sentence the granary remained the property of the association, "belonging" to all and managed by their representatives. The sentence thus augments the larger patrimony of collective or unindividualized property in Romania that includes associations, state farms, and other state-owned enterprises.[33] Each member has a claim on the granary—in fact, multiple claims similar to those described previously—motivated not only by his or her present share in the revenues that might help to maintain it but by conceptions about the role of labor in property owning. Here the projects of the judge, local authorities, and association leaders that intersected in ruling the granary a collective good come together with conceptions and values held by many villagers.

As I went on my rounds during those weeks, the trial was a prime topic of conversation, and the overwhelming opinion was that the association should win. Included in the file for the case was a full list of association members, over seventy of whom (65 percent) had signed a statement expressing the widespread view that the granary had been built with their labor and they in no way agreed that it should become Ionescu's property. After the verdict I heard repeatedly one or more elements of the following "collective" opinion: "It's very good that he lost the trial. He never worked in the CAP a day in his life. We all built that granary; it was hard work, and he didn't do any of it. There are many of us; we aren't a single person trying to become rich overnight! He's the kind of person who never really liked to work, was always looking for a way to get by easy—he even boasted he'd get this granary and never have to work again, just live off the interest! He's not even from here. Why should it go to a single individual when it's the work of all of us and we need it? You can't give the wealth of everyone to a single person!"[34] Only four people (of the over thirty families from whom I noted an opinion) dissented from such views, and each had good reason. About half of the villagers who expressed an opinion against Ionescu were members of the association; most of the others had received some land and were farming it themselves. A small number were "inmigrants" (like Ionescu) who had received no land, had little possibility of benefiting from the granary, and thus might have sided with him; but even many of those people saw the granary as a public good, usable (for a fee) not just by the association and its members but by everyone.

The widespread opposition to Ionescu's suit, then, did not rest chiefly on the prospect of benefiting from the granary if he lost, even though the structure's utility was clearly significant. Further, it was not a simple question of "locals" against "inmigrants," although that division did play a role. Rather, I believe it was a reaction against certain aspects of the construction of capitalist individualism that, unfortunately, Ionescu represents, as well as against the notion of private property associated with it. Implicated in both are deeply held values concerning community and the definition of self in relation to work. To explain this and to show why Ionescu's suit catalyzed so vigorous a reaction among his fellow villagers, I should say a further word about his personal characteristics.

Ionescu is not a native-born Vlaicean; he comes from a neighboring village and married into Vlaicu in the 1960s. His in-laws, likewise, were not native to Vlaicu but had moved there from a hill village; by local status conceptions they are "strangers" (*străini*), "inmovers" (*veniți* or *venituri*) of relatively poor hillbilly origin, held in some contempt by locals. Having no land, the family gave nothing to the collective farm at its formation and were not regular members. Ionescu had served as the village bus driver during the 1970s and had gained a certain sympathy; this was easily reversed, however, following his 1980 visit to a brother in the United States, from which he returned full of "American" ideas about how to get rich without working hard.[35] From then on he conformed to the stereotype of capitalist enrichment that was central to Communist Party propaganda. For years Vlaicenii had been laughing behind his back at his plans for one or another venture in which other people would put in the effort and he would "contribute the brains" and reap the profits.

Why are these details significant? Because they limn the system of self-conceptions and social boundaries within which Vlaicenii constructed the public good and the public property that would serve it. The core of village reaction to Ionescu's case (echoing language used by the judge in her conversations with me) was that the granary is a public good and should not be monopolized by a single person. It is a public good not because it was part of the collective farm but because it contains the labor of all those who lived in the village when the collective was formed in 1959. Villagers had built the buildings of the CAP in their "free" time through "voluntary" labor, with coercive work norms to urge their voluntarism along. In a certain sense these buildings embody the common suffering of all those who lost land to the collective; the structures are everyone's congealed labor, but alongside their sweat are blood and tears (cf. Creed 1998: 239). Anyone (such as Ionescu) who did not participate in that experience but wants to appropriate its result finds himself facing the community from the outside.

This notion that the structures of the CAP in some sense represent villagers' personal substance appeared in the comment of a local functionary who observed, concerning the looting of the CAP buildings in many settlements throughout Romania, "The buildings of the CAP weren't *communist,* they were *people's work.*" The same notion appears even more starkly in the procedure by which villagers in Noul Român (in southern Romania) decided to dismantle their CAP buildings. They marked off with a tape measure separate sections for each family, the area corresponding precisely to the amount of work each family had given to the collective; each family then took the building materials from its section.[36] In Ionescu's trial, the public good had a comparable connection with labor through ideas about creation and destruction. Association members and others were worried that because there would be no public constraints on what Ionescu might do with his property, he might repeat what he had done with a small CAP structure he had brought earlier: destroy it to use the building material for other purposes. With this, a part of the community's very "self" would vanish, leaving no residue among its members. (Ionescu, by contrast, saw the destructive potential not in himself but in the way the granary and other CAP buildings were being treated by the association. He complained that the association stored corrosive substances that ruined the buildings, whereas he would repair and improve them in the interests of the entire village. When I told Ionescu that the judge believed her decision defended the public good, he challenged that notion: "If she wants to defend the public good, she should have come here and taken a look at the deteriorating barns and garage.")

The same connection between owning and working appears in villagers' opposition to Ionescu as "lazy," as "not liking to work." People drew a contrast between we who work and he who is lazy. More to the point, he wants to be lazy *at our expense.* Vlaicenii could become positively apoplectic at the rumor that Ionescu would buy the granary and then *rent it back* to people to store their grain; thus, they would sweat in the fields and he would sit with his feet up, profiting from their efforts in the present as well as in the past. Community property would thus be used to exploit community members. One woman put the problem thus: "The whole village is saying 'Why should he get the results of our work?'" In short, private appropriation from the fruits of collective labor is wrong.[37] The rumor about Ionescu's intentions fueled his difficulties, then, because villagers so strongly associate possession with work.[38] From among numerous comments supportive of this point, I cite one woman's succinct summary in telling me why a certain piece of land should belong to her: "It's mine because I worked it" (*e al meu că eu l-am slujit*). We can only conclude that John Locke is alive and well in Transylvania.

Public reaction against Ionescu, therefore, rested on property conceptions involving what "community" and "person" consist of and how self is formed in relation to them. Central to both were notions concerning kinship and labor. Ionescu was placed outside the boundaries of community because he acted (or was suspected of acting) individualistically, like someone with no kin, and because he was seen as not valuing labor and the things built up from it; further, his labor was not congealed in the public goods he wished to appropriate. Also at issue, I believe, was the larger—and very painful—process of seeking meaning for ruined lives. All villagers, especially the elderly who lived through the devastating experience of collectivization that many felt as intensely as a live amputation, are struggling to recast and revalorize the past forty years. For these purposes, ideas about work, possession, social embeddedness, and community are vital.

After the judge's decision, feelings subsided except among Ionescu and his few allies, who protested that the judge was a "communist" and the legal process in Romania a farce. One of them complained that the so-called collective interest should not overwhelm respect for correct procedure. Others summed up the collective-versus-individual issue by observing that Ionescu had erred in thinking he could take on the whole village. More unnerving was the word that spread from those opposed to Ionescu's plans. Several villagers had sworn, it was said, that had he won the trial they would have burned down the granary rather than have it become his. From this we see clearly the depth of the passions the case aroused over matters of owning, public versus private, destruction, and appropriated work.

As for the granary qua public property, three years after the trial things stood as follows. The harvest of all land worked by the association automatically goes into the granary; according to the leaders, however, no villager, whether an association member or not, will be allowed to deposit grain harvested from nonassociation land.[39] Not all villagers appear to realize this, insisting to my hypothetical question that of course they could use it if they paid a fee "because it's ours." Some maintenance work has been done on the granary, but the leaders admitted it was difficult to get the members to approve necessary expenditures for maintenance if those expenditures would diminish their revenue, already eroded from buying the two tractors. The overlapping rights and responsibilities concerning this public good thus remain somewhat uncertain.

My discussion has shown that many in the village preferred to maintain a situation of ambiguous and overlapping property rights rather than promote their disaggregation; instead of entering the exclusive private ownership of any one person, the granary remained "ours," with pieces of our work embedded in it. The reasons for this preference, I have argued, have in part to do with the benefits villagers saw in having a collectively owned structure they could use in the absence of proper storage facilities of their own—that is, the lack of a storage and distribution infrastructure directly affected their interest in the building. At least as important, however, were people's sentiments about work, self, and the acceptable appropriation of the fruits of their labor, sentiments marshaled in revalorizing fractured lives and recreating meaning. It was not villagers' preferences and strivings, of course, but those of the judge that determined the trial's outcome. And although her reasons emphasized defense of the public good—which she did not see as resting in individual private property relations—more than ideas about self and work, "property" for both her and the villagers emerges with a distinctively collective coloring.

Because judge's and villagers' preferences intersected in the judge's decisions, most villagers had the sense that justice was done. For them, the trial built credibility for the legal system and the larger political order standing behind it, legitimating certain communal values over those of exclusive individual ownership and gain. These values were reinforced not because of a corrupt, captive, or Stalinist judiciary but rather because the trial mobilized deeply held senses of self and valued notions about community.

Conclusion

What does the material presented in this chapter suggest about ownership, about the relations we think of as property, and about the postsocialist transformation? First it underscores the truth, easily forgotten, that "property" is about social relations, relations among persons rather than between persons and things. It shows that one cannot set *things* off as wholly separate from the persons who exercise property rights, for property is also about self and definitions of selfhood; it is about relative investments of activity and of self in things and about the sense of worth entailed in those investments. Property is therefore about the boundaries between self and nonself—and as this material shows, such "self" is not necessarily individual but can also be collective. Property understood collectively lacks the clear edges of an ideologized notion of exclusive private owning; it is, in this sense, fuzzy.

Second, my material suggests that postsocialist ownership patterns generate these kinds of fuzziness because of the complexly overlapping rights, obligations, and claims that emerge from socialist property relations. These rights and claims have just begun to crystallize into routines and practices, and what should be bundles of powers are still far from empowering. In part, property remains fuzzy because in conditions of general economic uncertainty people prefer arrangements that obscure individual liability and separate obligations from assets (cf. Stark 1996: 1019–21). We might express the point in a metaphor: just as the crystallization of a snowflake depends on the ambient temperature, the crystallization of exclusive private ownership depends on the ambient conditions and the relations among actors in an overall field of power. Thus, to see the snowflake itself as representing "property" is inapt (we might say it is just the tip of the iceberg). This point and the preceding one together suggest that to understand postsocialist property we must look beyond both *things* and the *rights* claimed to them, focusing instead on meanings, relations, and powers.

Finally, this material shows the transition as a process in which new constellations of possibility and constraint work on notions of value, both inherited and emergent, to produce postsocialist property regimes only messily related to their Western blueprint. The changes inaugurated in 1989 created new fields of action in which socialism's "legacies"—such as forms of collectivism—are not simply reproduced but are revalorized within the struggles that mobilize them. Before Ionescu's trial, if a different kind of person with a different project had bid on the Vlaicu granary, it is possible that villagers would not have defended collective rights with such vigor; after the trial, however, I believe that definition of rights is more robust. Here is where ethnography—ethnography not just *of* but *in* the transition—is unparalleled as a path into histories of the future.

Notes

Acknowledgments: I owe special thanks to the following people for valuable comment on this chapter: Michael Burawoy, Elizabeth Dunn, Gail Kligman, Mary Poovey, and Kim Scheppele. Discussants at the conference, particularly Ken Jowitt, also did much to improve it. The research reported here was supported by field grants from the International Research and Exchanges Board (IREX) and the National Science Foundation.

1. As to whether these mixed ambiguous forms are good or bad, opinions vary. For Staniszkis (1991), they are the route to Polish capitalism; for Cornea (1993), they are a ticket to economic stagnation and communist restoration; and for Stark (1996), they are flexible forms that are likely to prove adaptive in the shift to market economies.

2. Ghani's full definition is considerably longer: "Among stratified communities, property in land can be defined as a: (1) bundle of powers (2) crystallized into marked forms of practice (3) having routinized rules of the game (4) regulating domains of rights of inclusion and exclusion (5) in cultural traditions where persons, objects, rights and obligations are defined (6) thereby setting forth fields of maneuver over control and access to land (7) leading either to certain forms being sanctioned through power (8) or to the reconstitution of the bundle of powers in new forms" (Ghani 1996: 3).

3. The 1993–1994 research was supported by IREX; research in summer 1996 was funded by the National Science Foundation.

4. For a description of liquidating collective farms, see Verdery 1994.

5. Associations are not governed by Law 31, concerning the privatization of state property, but by Law 36, concerning the use of property given in usufruct.

6. At exit they may take all of their social capital provided they leave behind a minimum value of 10,000 lei. When the association's statute was written in August 1992, members' minimum required contribution was set at 10,000 lei, "taken as the value of one hectare of land." By summer 1996, however, a hectare of land was valued at around 3 to 3.5 million lei.

7. This payment was in part negotiated between the association and each member and in part fixed by the association independently as a function of its financial needs and the decisions of its leadership council. These decisions varied widely from one village to the next. For example, whereas the Vlaicu association's first agronomist preferred to ensure members' satisfaction at the expense of acquiring machinery that would have greatly improved the performance of the association, agronomists in other villages decided differently. Vlaicu association members received about 1,000 kg of wheat for each hectare they had placed in the association that year, compared with 350 kg per hectare in the neighboring association in Romos, whose agronomist underpaid members for the first two years and bought tractors, seeders, spreaders, and other agricultural implements.

8. State farms were run as state enterprises with salaried labor and an appointed director. Much—but by no means all—state farm land came from expropriating large landowners, political prisoners or "war criminals." Collective farms, by contrast, were formed from "voluntary" donations of land by villagers who thereby became CAPs' members and labor force. Members were not paid a fixed salary but received various forms of remuneration in cash and kind. The two kinds of farm had different jural statuses. Before 1989, about 60 percent of Romania's agricultural land was in collective farms and 30 percent in state institutions, with the remainder in individual private farms.

9. I specify "Transylvania" because the property regime differed in Romania's other regions in ways that make some of what I learned in my Transylvanian research not completely applicable elsewhere in that country. See Verdery 1994: 1077–78 for an explanation.

10. These figures are courtesy of the Romanian Ministry of Agriculture.

11. Some villagers understood this technicality when pressed about it, but many did not. One man asserted that from the moment he planted his land it was "his" whether he had a piece of paper or not, and thus he can do whatever he wants with it, including place it with the association. In his view, property rights do not require ratification by any subordinate authority but only (in Lockean fashion) the mixing of one's labor with an object.

12. A law passed in 1994 allows for the eventual disaggregation of state farms and the return of at least some of their lands to the original owners after the year 2000.

13. As of my research in summer 1996, many persons who had bought or sold land and informed me they had not done so with all of the formalities— registration in the new cadaster—because "it's not possible" (*nu se poate*), but they were unable to explain why that was so. Notaries with whom I discussed the problem claimed no official transfer could be recorded in the absence of an

Agency for Rural Development and Planning; the wording of Law 18, however, states that circulation of land is free with certain exceptions, noting only that land "may" be sold through the exercise of rights of preemption accomplished by the state through that agency, giving first refusal to relatives and neighbors (art. 48).

14. Thanks to Kim Scheppele for this point.

15. I received contradictory replies to my question as to whether Vlaicu's collective farm members had formally voted for its dissolution. The interim mayor who had run the 1990 meeting at which Vlaicenii had divided up the farm's dairy cattle by lot felt their doing so constituted a vote to dissolve, but he did not recall having actually put the question to a vote (indeed, he seemed disconcerted when I raised the point).

16. Law 18 does not specify how these two quantities are to be linked. The Vlaicu CAP liquidation commission, following instructions from the county capital, weighed people's donated land as worth 40 percent and their labor in the CAP as 60 percent of their claim on the goods of the old CAP.

17. For details, see Verdery 1994.

18. This possibility is available only for wheat. The relative prices of state and open market for wheat in 1995 were (respectively) 250 lei/kg and around 300 lei/kg; in early 1996 the state raised its price to 350 lei/kg against a projected 500 lei/kg on the open market. In response to natural calamities that threatened to reduce yields to half their 1995 levels, in June 1996 the state price was raised to 450 lei/kg.

19. In June 1996, the agronomist of Vlaicu's association told me she would need the wheat harvest of 100 ha. to buy a tractor she could have bought two years earlier with the harvest of 50 ha.

20. During this period a methane gas line was being laid in the village at considerable cost to residents, making them more vulnerable to even small fluctuations in their income from the association.

21. To my knowledge, the Vlaicu association has no provision for returning to members their share of these fixed means if they decide to withdraw their land; it simply restores to them the land's use.

22. In conversation with the association's agronomist and chief accountant, I learned that they view the new implements as belonging to the members and will rent them out at low cost once work on the association's fields is completed. So far, those who have benefited the most from this possibility have tended to be members of the association's council, but other members also reported having plowed with an association tractor.

23. The reasons given for this failure included the refusal of many owners to accept land on any other place but the spot where they had had it before, even if that meant repossessing a 2 ha. farm in ten tiny parcels.

24. Some associations did consolidate fields, whereas in others those who wanted to farm independently were given parcels other than the ones their families had owned before.

25. The leaders put a stop to this practice by requiring payment for plowing in advance.

26. One should not make too much of this; Ionescu was, after all, appealing to *me*.

27. The two people in question were about seventy and forty-five years of age at the time; Ionescu was about fifty-five.

28. People had thirty days from when the law went into effect to make their claims on the basis of several possible kinds of evidence, which might, in fact, conflict and to which many villagers lacked ready access. Urbanites wanting to claim village lands had even more difficulty doing so if they lived any distance from their natal villages. The entire process of restoring ownership rights was to be completed within ninety days of the law's promulgation (art. 10 par. 5).

29. *Cuvîntul liber* (Deva), 5 July 1991. The term *patrimony* is widely used in Romania to indicate collective property. I do not have space here to explore this fascinating concept.

30. This auction is thus taking place well after the nine-month cutoff point at which all CAPs were to have been liquidated.

31. By arrangement with the vice president of the county court, I sat in this judge's courtroom three or four times a month and listened to cases, specifically attending to those about land. By the time the lawsuit against the association came up, I knew the judge reasonably well and had engaged in a number of discussions with her. I was sent to this particular judge because many of the other judges had much less experience and therefore were less often assigned difficult cases pertaining to Law 18.

Readers might wonder at the effect of my presence on the judge's decision. In my conversations with her outside the courtroom prior to the sentence, I had made it clear that I did not know enough about the law to have a position on the case; when she asked me to clarify something for her, however, I answered in a way she might have interpreted as defending the plaintiff. Since it was clear from our other dealings that she took my opinions seriously, her deciding against the plaintiff indicates that she was not influenced by what she might have thought was my view. Both parties to the case believed, however, that she was probably more scrupulous in defending her judgment knowing she would have to discuss it with me at the end.

32. Candidates include genuine conviction, a bribe from the defendants, orders from county authorities, and so on.

33. To preserve the association's ambiguous status not only enables a potentially larger pooled income for the members (they need not pay to rent storage space); it also shores up the position of those networks among the rural elite, including the association's own leadership council, for which the persistence of collective property—which the council defends as in the collective weal—brings possibilities for personal gain through various forms of political capitalism (see Verdery 1994; Stark 1996). The judge's ruling thus promotes this elite *as a collectivity* by preserving parts of its collective resource base rather than by individualizing ownership resources.

34. Kim Scheppele (personal communication) has found similar popular sentiments in petitions from villagers to the constitutional court in Hungary.

35. This opinion was circulating well before the end of party rule. I had met Ionescu during my first trip to Vlaicu in 1973–1974 when he was fairly well regarded (for an inmigrant), but during my visits in the 1980s I found opinions of

him had somewhat soured because of his behavior since his return from the United States.

36. I have this report from Prof. Aurel Răduțiu of Cluj.

37. By comparison, none of the three villagers who bought CAP cattle barns at auction is in Ionescu's position because all have used the structures they bought to start their own firms (a dairy farm, a pig farm, and a store); they are not living as rentiers but are working.

38. For further detail on this point, see Verdery 1994: 1105–6; Lampland 1995: 100–103.

39. This policy had been put to the test the previous year, I was told, when a record harvest left some members with so much grain from the fields they were working on their own that they asked the association for storage space and were denied it. The reason given was that Vlaicenii working on their own often do not use treated seed, pesticides, or herbicides and therefore can corrupt the harvested crop by mixing their own harvest with it in storage.

References

Appel, Hilary. 1995. Justice and the Reformulation of Property Rights in the Czech Republic. *East European Politics and Societies* 9 (1): 22–40.

Comisso, Ellen. 1991. Property Rights, Liberalism, and the Transition from "Actually Existing" Socialism. *East European Politics and Societies* 5 (1): 162–188.

Cornea, Andrei. 1993. Directocrația remaniază guvernul. *22* (5, 16–22 March): 7–8.

Creed, Gerald. 1998. *Domesticating Revolution: From Socialist Reform to Ambivalent Transition in a Bulgarian Village.* University Park, Pa.: Pennsylvania State University Press.

Frydman, Roman, and Andrzej Rapaczynski. 1994. *Privatization in Eastern Europe: Is the State Withering Away?* Budapest: Central European University Press.

Frydman, Roman, Andrzej Rapaczynski, John S. Earle et al. 1993. *The Privatization Process in Central Europe.* Budapest: Central European University Press.

Ghani, Ashraf. 1996. Production and Reproduction of Property as a Bundle of Powers: Afghanistan 1774–1901. Paper presented at the Agrarian Studies Program, Yale University.

Gluckman, Max. 1943. Essays on Lozi Land and Royal Property. Rhodes-Livingston papers, no. 10.

Hann, C. M. 1993a. From Production to Property: Decollectivization and the Family-Land Relationship in Contemporary Hungary. *Man* 28: 299–320.

———. 1993b. Property Relations in the New Eastern Europe: The Case of Specialist Cooperatives in Hungary. In *The Curtain Rises: Rethinking Culture, Ideology, and the State in Eastern Europe,* ed. Hermine G. DeSoto and David G. Anderson. Atlantic Highlands N.J.: Humanities, 99–121.

Kiss, Yudit. 1994. Privatization Paradoxes in East Central Europe. *East European Politics and Societies* 8: 122–152.

Lampland, Martha. 1995. *The Object of Labor: Commodification in Socialist Hungary.* Chicago: University of Chicago Press.

Markovits, Inga. 1995. *Imperfect Justice: An East-West German Diary.* Oxford: Clarendon Press.

Maurel, Marie-Claude. 1994a. *La transition post-collectiviste: mutations agraires en Europe centrale.* Paris: Editions L'Harmattan.

———. 1994b. Terre, capital, travail: vers de nouveau rapports sociaux en Europe centrale. *Cahiers Internationaux de Sociologie* 96: 7–32.

Riker, William H., and David L. Weimer. 1993. The Economic and Political Liberalization of Socialism: The Fundamental Problems of Property Rights. *Social Philosophy and Policy* 10 (2): 79–102.

Staniszkis, Jadwiga. 1991. "Political Capitalism" in Poland. *East European Politics and Societies* 5 (1): 127–141.

Stark, David. 1992. Path Dependence and Privatization Strategies in East Central Europe. *East European Politics and Societies* 6 (1): 17–54.

———. 1996. Recombinant Property in East European Capitalism. *American Journal of Sociology* 101 (4): 993–1027.

Verdery, Katherine. 1994. The Elasticity of Land: Problems of Property Restitution in Transylvania. *Slavic Review* 53 (4): 1071–1109.

Voszka, Eva. 1991. From Twilight to Twilight: Transformation of the Ownership Structure in the Big Industries. *Acta Oeconomica* 43 (3–4): 281–296.

3

Barter of the Bankrupt: The Politics of Demonetization in Russia's Federal State

David Woodruff

From the Politics of Monetary Policy to the Politics of Monetization

Desperation is the mother of invention. In 1994, as post-Soviet Russia entered its third year with a fall in production unprecedented in its short and depressing economic history, the country's impoverished industrial enterprises turned increasingly to barter. The spread of barter occurred despite falling inflation rates and in no way constituted a hyperinflationary "flight from money."[1]

This process of demonetization bears directly on the central issues of contemporary Russian politics: state power and national integration. As some classic analyses have demonstrated, the arrival of the money economy must be examined in tandem with the growth of state power.[2] Although money exchange appears to be more convenient than barter because it obviates the "double coincidence of wants," standardized and repeated patterns of barter transactions do not suffer from this difficulty and are capable of sustaining relatively complex economies (Humphrey 1985: 56–57). Thoroughgoing monetization of economic activity issues only from the aggressive insistence of the fiscal organs of the state (Schumpeter 1991: 108). The state's aggressiveness in this regard is usually held to stem from the complementarity between state building and monetization of the economy. Money exchange facilitates taxation and national integration; state standardization of money and taxation in money promote its use. As an aspect of state building, the process of monetization cannot be free of political conflict. Control over a unified currency and monetary policy is a powerful instrument in the hands of national authorities and thus inevitably becomes entwined in struggles over the degree of national economic and political integration. The concentration of power at a national level, embodied in the dominion of central authorities over the monetary and financial order, can only be the result of the sort of organized coercion and political negotiation that gave rise to the other powers of the national state.[3]

To draw analogies between Russia's present state-building project and earlier models may appear anachronistic. After all, Russia embarked on its market reforms with both a national currency and the institutions of money taxation in place, however imperfectly the latter were adapted to new circumstances. But although Moscow's possession of these attributes of a capitalist nation-state certainly represented an accommodation (albeit one-sided) between central and local authorities, this accommodation was reached under the circumstances of a planned economy. Price liberalization in January 1992, which entirely transformed the nature of money, made this accommodation instantly obsolete.

The profound and ongoing renegotiation of the relations between center and regions in Russia has important methodological consequences for studying the politics of economic reform.[4] Literature that concentrates on the *politics of monetary policy* in post-Soviet Russia necessarily focuses on decisions made in Moscow to print more or less money (e.g., Lipton and Sachs 1992; Åslund 1995). It therefore regards as resolved the very issues raised most sharply by the simultaneous end of the Soviet Union and the command economy: the terms of Russia's national economic and political integration and the capacity of its state to maintain and promote that integration. Furthermore, the unjustified assumption that the major influence on practices of exchange is the ability of central authorities to broadcast and implement their commitment to hard money systematically obscures the state-building dilemmas facing Russian federal and local officials. These dilemmas can be adequately grasped only through careful attention to the conflict-ridden political and institutional contexts in which exchange takes place and to the efforts of local and central authorities to affect those contexts. In short, Russia's situation demands a focus not on the politics of monetary policy but on the *politics of monetization:* the clash of political and administrative interests affected by the prevalence of monetary or nonmonetary exchange.

This chapter argues that the partial but very substantial demonetization of the Russian economy in 1993 and 1994 must be traced to fundamental institutional and political asymmetries between central and local authorities. Officials on the two levels of Russia's government have very different attitudes toward the project of achieving monetized exchange and implementing the attendant principles of consumer sovereignty, hard budget constraints, and the price mechanism. While monetization and fiscal imperatives go hand in hand for Russian central authorities, local authorities find themselves in a far more ambiguous situation for two reasons. First, to a large extent a presumed ability to tax *particular* economic actors in kind is hardwired into the social infrastructure of Russia. For example, power and heating stations are often located on the territory of industrial plants even when they service residential consumers as well. Second, although local authorities also find it more convenient to tax in money, when circumstances require it they are far better situated to organize new forms of taxation in kind than are central authorities.

Monetization affects local and central authorities differently with regard not only to their fiscal situation but also to their political imperatives. As the literature on the "politics of stabilization" emphasizes, the burdens of market-oriented policies are more politically transparent than the benefits. Governments agreeing to the liquidation of a factory that has run out of money must be able to allow themselves the luxury of abstraction, since the pain of the policy is felt by a concrete and compact group whereas most of the benefits, should they eventually appear, will accrue to scattered individuals who are unlikely even to recognize their shared interests, much less act on those interests politically (Nelson 1993). This dilemma affects both local and central authorities in Russia, but their thresholds of political tolerance are very different and have displayed a tendency to diverge over time. For a local government, the failure of a single factory employing several thousand people may seem an unacceptable disaster, whereas Moscow has grudgingly come to see it as acceptable. The failure of a power system that provides heat to millions of people in a Siberian winter, however, is a disaster unacceptable to Moscow as well.[5]

Although to some extent such judgments of acceptability can be made in anticipation of political pressure, there are also threshold effects built into Russia's administrative structure, which serves as something like a corporatist system of representation for Russia's industries. Under central planning, industry was grouped into sectors under the direction of particular ministries. Because of the importance of lobbying for scarce resources, the role of the ministries was as much representational as managerial. Reforms under Mikhail Gorbachev and Boris Yeltsin have eliminated many ministries (although some managed a tenuous resurrection as a loose quasi-private enterprise grouping or "concern"), consolidated others, and reduced still others to "committees" of nebulous authority and mandate. Nevertheless, sectors of industry retain representation in the Council of Ministers, whose power to make most critical decisions on economic policy has rendered both parliaments virtual sideshows. Problems that can be presented as those of sectors are heard at the top. Prob-

lems of the individual enterprise can increasingly find a hearing only on
the local level, whether through formal consultative institutions (such as
the energy commissions that set local electric power rates), through meetings of local authorities with industrialists' organizations of varying degrees of coherency, or simply through direct informal contacts between
enterprise directors and local officials. Thus, the structure of industry's
political representation tends to make central authorities more responsive to those issues that affect enterprises qua sectors as opposed to those
affecting enterprises sharing other possible characteristics such as regional location or competitive position. For a province, by contrast, the
voice of the individual enterprise is institutionally much louder.

Focusing on the electric power and heat sector, this chapter investigates the way these institutional and political differences in the situation
of local and national authorities affect Russia's effort to move to a
money-driven economy.[6] Because virtually all actors in the economy have
dealings with this sector, it proves a particularly useful place from which
to observe shifts in exchange practices in the broader economy. These
practices have seen dramatic shifts over time. In fall 1993, electric power
companies throughout Russia began to discover that fewer and fewer of
their customers were paying their bills. And increasingly, those customers
that did pay offered not money but unsold goods of their own production. Over the next year, overdue debt to electrical power companies
swelled from about 5 percent to about 17 percent of all debt overdue to
Russian industry (*Segodnia* [Moscow], 9/1/94). Meanwhile, by February
1994 around half of all payments to electric power companies were made
in kind, and barter seems to have continued to rise from that point; in at
least some regions barter accounted for over 75 percent of payments by
summer of that year (see Tables 3.1 and 3.2). To reiterate, the barter
boom occurred on the background of falling inflation rates.

To understand how the different institutional and political concomi-
tants of monetization for central and local authorities issued in nonpayments and payments in kind for electric power, one must start from two
straightforward questions. First, what made Russia's enterprises stop
paying their power bills? The short answer is that by late summer 1993
many had run out of money, and in a context in which price liberalization
had encouraged economic actors to count their money better, it had become much harder to find loans for all but the most certain ventures. The
second question is, why did electric power companies refrain from cutting power to those who failed to pay? There are two reasons. One is that
this extremely serious sanction may destroy the enterprise in question
without returning the debt, since Russia lacks effective bankruptcy mechanisms that could compensate creditors after a company shuts down. A
second common reason power companies fail to disconnect chronic debt-

Table 3.1   Payments in Kind to Two Regional Power Systems

Dal'energo (Maritime Province)		Krasnoyarskenergo (Krasnoyarsk Province)	
Date	% of Payments in Kind	Date	% of Payments in Kind
All of 1993	25	All of 1992 (est.)	5
January 1994	64	First quarter 1993	32
February 1994	60	First semester 1993	30
March 1994	62	First nine months 1993	37
April 1994	75	All of 1993	45
May 1994	83	First quarter 1994	77
June 1994	93	Second quarter 1994 (est.)	80
July 1994	100		

Sources: Data from Dal'energo and Krasnoyarskenergo. Krasnoyarsk estimates were made by the commercial director, who supplied other numbers on the basis of accounting documents. Although no claim of representativeness can be made for these data, Krasnoyarsk tends to have some of the cheapest electricity in the country, whereas the Maritime Province at least until 1994 had among the most expensive electric rates. This suggests that a desire to avoid paying especially high prices cannot be a major cause of barter.

ors is that local authorities will not let them, both because for them shutting down an enterprise in this way is an unacceptable disaster and because they see electrical energy as a relatively resilient sector.[7] This resilience stems from several sources, among them two purely political ones: first, that local authorities count on Moscow's unwillingness to allow a particular power system to shut down and, second, that electrical energy *as a sector* has strong representation in Moscow.

But the resilience of the electric power company is not the only precondition of local governments' pursuit of these policies. They must also be willing to tolerate economic activity by enterprises that can be taxed only in kind, for the institutional mechanism by which electric power companies collect their bills—direct withdrawal from bank accounts with no requirement of owner approval—is the same one used by the tax authorities. Nonpayments and barter payments to electric power companies can come only from those firms that have no officially visible money. Although the budget gets its share first, on the whole a firm paying its power bill in kind pays its taxes either in kind or not at all. And, indeed, as in-kind payments for electricity were rising, local governments increasingly began to accept taxes in the products of their local enterprises. The spread of such "barter of the bankrupt" sowed chaos in the price mechanism and placed huge strains on interregional exchange.

In short, capacity for in-kind taxation, however imperfect, allows local authorities to ease the situation of local enterprises by staying the hand of local power companies whose aggressive moves to collect their debts might force industry to remain in the visible money economy. Such actions work to transfer the difficulties of local industry onto the sectors whose lobbying on the national level provides the toughest test of Moscow's commitment to hard budget constraints.[8] As an upshot of this bilevel politics, barter and nonpayments spread, the bases of market calculation crumble, and the central government's fiscal and political capacities to pursue monetary stabilization weaken. At the same time, the government's decaying capacity to spend money where it wants leaves it increasingly unable to cope with the challenges to national integration these processes present.

The balance of the chapter is divided into five sections. The first criticizes views of the nonpayments crisis based on arguments about reform "credibility." It argues that a breakdown of old mechanisms of the soft budget constraint *preceded* the major growth of nonpayments starting in late summer 1993. The second question presents data on the growth of barter from that same period. Focusing on the strategic interaction of electric power companies and their debtors in the context of local politics, it offers an explanation of how nonpayments and barter can result from this interaction. The section also examines some of the mechanisms that make this barter trade at least marginally feasible economically for the power companies and presents arguments as to why this barter exchange can in no way be viewed as a market phenomenon. The third section compares local and federal fiscal reactions to demonetization, arguing that central authorities lacked the capacity to insist effectively on monetization. Local authorities, by contrast, had both reasons and capacities to use taxation in kind to adapt to the spread of barter. The fourth section discusses how problems raised for the electric sector by nonpayments and barter became issues on the national stage and posed fundamental challenges to national integration.

The concluding section reinterprets the politics of nonpayments and barter in electrical energy in terms of Karl Polanyi's theory of the "double movement," the struggle between the principles of market liberalism and social protection. Adapting Polanyi's argument about the overwhelming political power of human communal morality to an image of a more institutionalized and less functional political process, the conclusion shows how Russia's federal structure imparted a character to its double movement that threatened to blow Russian society apart rather than bring it together.

Transformation of the Nonpayments Crisis and the Hardening of Budget Constraints

The growth of nonpayment for electrical energy from fall 1993 was the latest incarnation of an issue that had dominated discussions of economic policy in Russia ever since price liberalization in January 1992: the "non-payments crisis."[9] Simply put, many Russian enterprises find their customers are not paying their bills on time or at all. In turn, they face their own suppliers with empty hands: since we're not getting paid, how can we pay you? These suppliers then offer the same justification to their suppliers, who have suppliers of their own, and so on. With the ramification and interweaving of such chains of debt, nonpayments at times have reached extraordinary proportions. One economist has estimated that in the first six months of 1992 half of all bills for transactions between firms were not paid (Rostowski 1993: 131). Even though nonpayments shrank in real terms through much of 1993, outstanding overdue bills as of January 1, 1994, were still equal to over 11 percent of total 1993 production (*Finansy*, no. 3, 1994: 73).

The rapidly expanding literature on the nonpayments crisis has focused largely on the motivations of the individual enterprise in deciding to ship goods without payment. The individual enterprise is seen as an autonomous agent making a decision it must believe to be in its interest, so those enterprises not demanding payment in advance must believe the state will intervene to make the debts good later. The persistence of this old psychology of the "soft budget constraint" demonstrates that lack of reform credibility explains nonpayments (Odling-Smee and Lorie 1993; Bigman and Leite 1993; Ickes and Ryterman 1992).

In this section I will raise three objections to credibility approaches to the explanation of nonpayments, two relatively briefly and a third at length. First, the fundamental premise that Russian enterprises are autonomous actors making independent decisions about whether to deliver their products to nonpaying customers is inaccurate. As the next section will discuss in more detail, continually since price liberalization, especially in the sectors of fuel and electrical energy, local (and occasionally national) officials have directed enterprises to provide goods before payment is received and have hindered energetic efforts at debt collection.[10] Enterprises that believed their debtors would be rescued would obviously not need to be strong-armed in this fashion.

A second failing of credibility arguments is their lack of attention to the concrete institutional structures within which different sectors of Russian industry operate. In fact, credibility arguments cannot explain the sectoral structure of the nonpayments crisis. Purely economic accounts tend to divide industry into three sectors: upstream, midstream, and downstream (Rostowski 1993: 136–137; Ickes and Ryterman 1992: 354). On this view, downstream industries, closest to final customers, who must pay cash, are the least likely to become large creditors; since they are forced to regard apparent falloffs in demand as permanent, for them the credibility of reforms is in essence automatic. Upstream and intermediate industries, by contrast, should have both large payables and large receivables, as they finance production through not paying for supplies and continue to ship goods to customers they believe will soon come into the money needed to pay.

Figures 3.1 and 3.2 graph a measure of how many overdue payables and receivables different sectors were generating per ruble of production at various dates in 1993.[11] The mean rate of arrears generation was set equal to zero, so sectors displayed above the axis were generating more nonpayments per unit of production than the average and those below less. The pattern is very stable over the first eight months of 1993 and to some extent shows results similar to what would be expected from applying the upstream-intermediate-downstream classification. The food and light industry sectors, which sell largely to final consumers, accumulate both categories of arrears rather slowly in relative terms. As expected, ferrous metallurgy, a largely intermediate sector, has large quantities of overdue payables and receivables. Chemical and petrochemical products probably also fall largely in the intermediate realm and have a high nonpayments rate, as do the intermediate goods producers in the construction materials sector. The low rate of arrears generation in the nonferrous metallurgy sector probably represents its focus on export opportunities—in essence, nonferrous metallurgy has become a final-demand sector. Machine building and metal working, which among other things includes passenger cars, represents a mix of intermediate and final producers, as does the wood sector.

Figure 3.1   Late Receivables by Sector, 1993

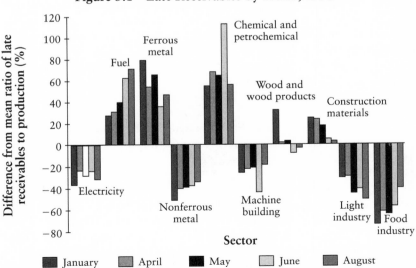

Figure 3.2   Late Payables by Sector, 1993

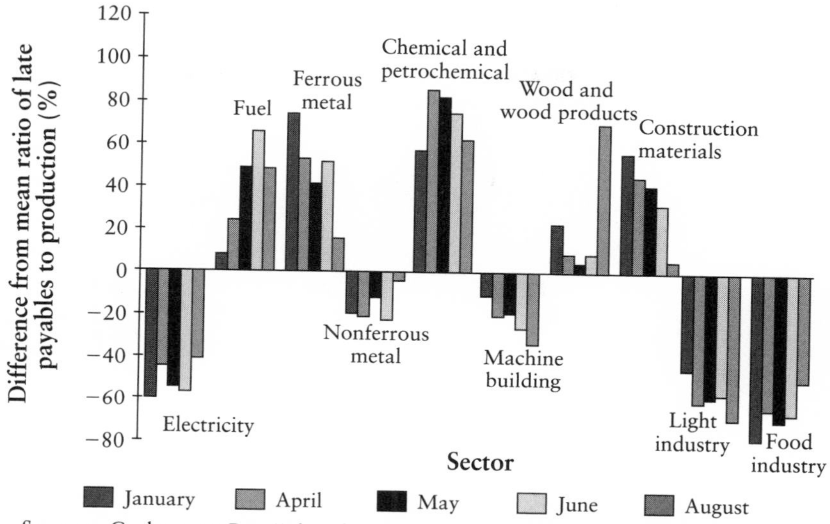

Sources: Goskomstat Rossii data from *Sotsial'no-ekonomicheskoe polozhenie Rossii-skoi Federatsii 1993 goda*, no. 2 (1993); *Sotsial'no-ekonomicheskoe polozhenie Rossiiskoi Federatsii 1993 goda*, nos. 6–7 (1993); *O razvitii ekonomicheskikh reform v Rossiiskoi Federatsii (dopolnitel'nye dannye za ianvar' avgust-1993 goda)*.

It is difficult, however, to explain in these terms the striking difference between the position of electric power and that of the fuel complex. Why is it that as of mid-1993 electricity was generating arrears at so much lower a rate, despite the fact that both sectors were far from final demand? Here a crucial institutional factor must be introduced. As noted earlier, power companies have the right to deduct their bills directly from their customers' bank accounts.[12] If customers have money they are holding legally, power companies can take it. Whereas crude oil and natural gas suppliers also have the right to use direct deduction, downstream refiners and distributors do not; neither do coal producers. As a result, it is much harder for the fuel industry to collect its bills.[13] Thus, the explanation for the sectoral structure of the nonpayments crisis through mid-1993 lies as much with institutional structures in the payments system as it does with the tendency of various sectors to give more or less credit to Moscow's commitment to ending subsidies and bailouts.

A final objection to credibility approaches to nonpayments will be argued at greater length. Starting in October 1993, real (constant-ruble) levels of nonpayments began to grow (see Figure 3.3).[14] Yet, were credibility accounts correct, one would not expect a jump in nonpayments from this date. First, the violent dispersal of parliament in early October

Figure 3.3   Real Overdue Receivables as Percentage of Their January 1, 1993, Level

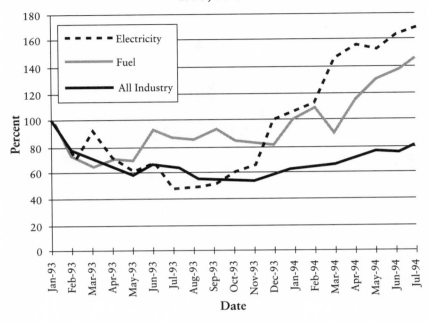

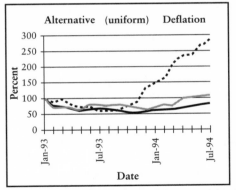

Sources: Nonpayments series and partial sectoral composition from the Economic Trends Center, Government of Russia, in *Segodnia* (Moscow) 9/1/94, 11. Figures for the first of the month. Deflation of "All Industry" figures is by the industry price index (IPI) from *Russian Economic Trends: Monthly Update*, 10/17/94, although the weighting of this index is not likely to be entirely appropriate (I thank Gregory Grossman for pointing this out to me). Electricity and fuel figures deflated by the incomplete series of sectoral price figures from *Russian Economic Trends* 3, no. 2: 37; missing price data were interpolated on the assumption of a constant month-on-month growth rate (except for the final month's figure, which was extrapolated). Deflation of all three series by the IPI, for which there is a complete series, produces an even more dramatic apparent relative growth for electricity, as shown in the lower diagram.

seemed to portend increased government ability to implement its commitment to monetary restriction and the elimination of cheap credits. The spirit of the moment was captured in the declaration of the minister of finance that "we have crushed the rebellion, [and] we will crush the inflation" (quoted in Sapir 1994: 164; cf. *Delovoi Mir* [Moscow], 10/13/93).[15]

Second, even before such pronouncements, the soft budget constraints invoked by the credibility school had been dramatically undermined for reasons that had as much to do with the institutional frailties of the Russian state as with a commitment to monetary tightening. The credibility theorists seem to presume that a belief about the state's eventual willingness to subsidize is sufficient to provoke profligate behavior by enterprises. Yet, judgments about whether the state is *able* to subsidize are equally important. Moreover, the soft budget constraint mechanism depends crucially on actors analytically and empirically distinct from the subsidizing authority. Without their cooperation it cannot operate.

In short, a credible commitment to subsidize that would inspire enterprise profligacy involves a complex institutional structure, the presence of which cannot simply be assumed. A close examination of Janos Kornai's theory of the soft budget constraint proves the point. Kornai offers a theory of the causes of the widespread willingness of socialist firms to run themselves into debt their sales will not allow them to repay (Kornai 1986). Three actors are involved: the softly constrained firm itself, its creditors, and the "paternalistic" state. The state steps in to rescue the firm after it has made the unsustainable expenditures, which were financed by the creditors (who may themselves have been parts of the state). Without this two-phase structure (first the loan-financed spending, then the bailout), the notion of the soft budget constraint is incoherent.[16] Only the expectation of future political successes in extracting subsidy can shape economic behavior, since a firm would have to regard any past subsidies unlikely to be repeated as an exhaustible resource.

The impact of the soft budget constraint—that is, of enterprises' willingness to run into unsustainable debt—can therefore be undermined from one of two directions. Budget constraints can be tightened *laterally* simply by creditors' reluctance to extend the credit needed to run up debts. Or they can be tightened *vertically* by a state that refuses to provide financial help to ailing enterprises or that finds itself incapable of making the required expenditures. By mid-1993 Russian enterprises found budget constraints dramatically hardening both laterally and vertically. After July 1, 1992, payment regimes for almost all interenterprise trade were determined exclusively by the enterprises, and most enterprises sought to switch to payment in advance. In part, the shift to prepayment reflected the well-known difficulties recovering damages through the state arbitration system; earlier, banks would at least send payments for bills in the order received if and when money arrived in the debtor's bank account. With the end of automatic bank bill collection, the general willingness of enterprises to extend credit to their customers shrank. As Figure 3.3 reveals, nonpayments declined in real terms in all but one of the months from January 1993 to October 1993.

Reduced interenterprise loans were not the only component of the lateral hardening of the budget constraint. After bank reforms in 1988, many enterprises had been able to create "pocket" banks that would extend loans on easy terms. As the situation unfolded, however, these banks began to demand increasing independence to channel credit to profitable uses as they experienced heavy pressure from the Central Bank to keep their cash flow positive.[17] Inflation helped to provide a means to realize this increased demand for independence. Because banks were forbidden to exceed fixed ratios between capital and assets (loans), inflation meant they constantly had to issue new stock. Since this process occurred in the context of shrinking enterprise financial power, it gave bank management expanded influence, as enterprise shares in the capital stock shrank and stock became divided among larger numbers of smaller investors or fell into the hands of management itself.[18] Finally, as interest rates became significantly higher than inflation in 1994, banks began to display increased apprehension over whether loan applicants would be able to repay their debts.

The tendency for lateral sources of credit to dry up was matched by a vertical hardening of budget constraints that stemmed as much from the Russian state's institutional weakness as from increased monetarist resolve. The government relies on commercial banks as the distribution mechanism for virtually all of the large volumes of earmarked credits given out by the Central Bank and the Ministry of Finance. But officials' ability to monitor the use of these loans is very weak, and many recipients appear to prefer to resell them at a higher interest rate than direct them to the production-supporting uses for which they were intended.[19] In June 1993, probably in response to this difficulty, the Central Bank implemented a policy of pegging its interest rates to near-market levels (*Voprosy Ekonomiki*, no. 6, 1993: 4–6). Distributing commercial banks began to be vested with increased financial responsibility for loaned funds, which made banks unwilling even to pass on funds designated for enterprises unlikely to pay them back.[20]

By spring 1994, refusal by commercial banks to distribute centralized credits seems to have reached epidemic proportions.[21] The scope of this phenomenon can be gathered from the fact that although the Central Bank authorized 1.3 trillion rubles in credits for the electric power industry in the first nine months of 1994, only 503 billion rubles in loans were actually made. Commercial banks, worried that their clients would default on the loans and leave the bankers with the liability for repayment, had refused to distribute 60 percent of the authorized loans (*Finansovye Izvestiia* [Moscow], 12/27/94).

A second set of institutional incapacities that contributed to the vertical hardening of budget constraints involved federal government problems with delivering promised subsidies to their intended recipients before their value had been eroded by inflation. Federal budget expenditures are made through an awkward system that passes expenditures through many agencies on the way to their intended recipient. Aside from the unintentional bureaucratic tangles the system creates, inflationary conditions give each link in this chain incentives to capture "float" on the money by delaying payment.[22] As a result, subsidies can be largely worthless by the time they arrive at their intended destination.

The effects of this inadvertent lowering of subsidies were reinforced by the deliberate policy of the Ministry of Finance, run throughout 1993 by committed monetarist Boris Fedorov, who sequestered many promised expenditures because of shortfalls in budget income (*Segodnia* [Moscow], 12/8/93, 9). In combination with the institutional weaknesses of the federal spending apparatus, by the end of 1993 this policy essentially left Moscow unable to make a credible commitment to subsidize.[23] Many promised subsidies simply never arrived. Although their intended recipients could not tell whether such failures were caused by a breakdown in disbursement institutions or by limitations imposed by revenue shortfalls, it mattered little from the vantage point of the weight of the government's word.

In short, from summer 1992 onward, budget constraints on Russian firms grew even harder. Creditors were increasingly less willing to loan money to enterprises in anticipation of an eventual government bailout. Banks grew more and more independent and jealous of their bottom line and began to refuse to bear responsibility for the return of even government loans intended to help their customers. And the government itself, as much through institutional incapacity as political commitment, rescued failing firms less and less frequently. By late 1993, enterprises maintaining a belief in the softness of their budget constraints would have appeared to be engaged in little more than wishful thinking.

Yet, as mentioned earlier, it was at precisely that moment that nonpayments began to rise in real terms after a long decline. Especially sharp rises occurred in nonpayments for electric power, which accounted for an ever-larger share of new nonpayments (see Figures 3.3 and 3.4). Although the electric power sector made up only around 7 percent of the ruble value of industrial production in early 1993, it accounted for over 38 percent of the real growth in nonpayments from October 1993 to July

**Figure 3.4   Electricity Nonpayments as a Percentage of Total
Nonpayments, November 1992–July 1994**

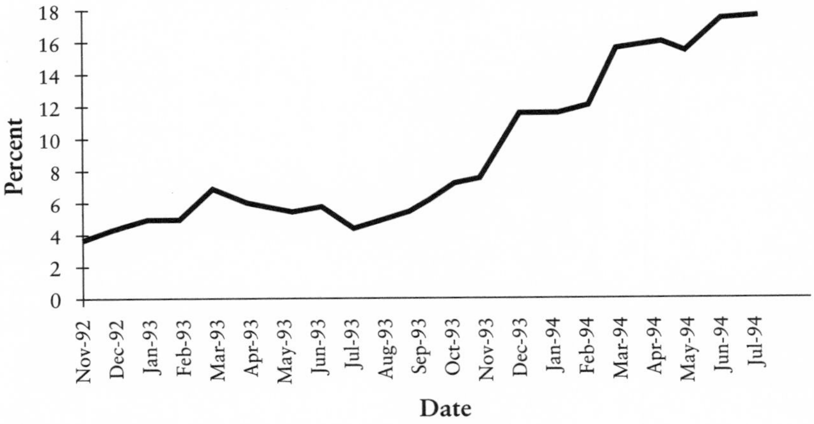

Source: Segodnia (Moscow), 9/1/94, 11.

1994.[24] By the end of May 1994, the relative success of power companies
in extracting payment from their customers was already a thing of the
past; now only fuel producers had more nonpayments from their customers relative to output (*Russian Economic Trends* 3, no. 2, 1994: 33).

In this section I leveled two empirical criticisms against credibility explanations of nonpayments: that they incorrectly predict the sectoral
structure of nonpayments and that nonpayments increased from late
1993 in circumstances in which there was every reason to believe the
credibility of hard budget constraints was fairly high. I also advanced one
methodological criticism, arguing that deductive accounts based on an
image of enterprises making autonomous decisions about whether to ship
goods without payment will be wrong because that image is fundamentally inaccurate. In the next section I build on this methodological point
to develop a model of the interaction between electric power companies
and their debtors in the context of local politics, in an effort to explain
the explosion in electric power nonpayments from fall 1993.

The Barter of the Bankrupt: No Money and No Markets

Given electric power companies' direct deduction rights, the boom in
nonpayments to this sector reflected the fact that enormous numbers of
enterprises simply had no money in their official bank accounts by late
1993. Yet, nonpayments figures alone understate the scope of this phe-

nomenon. Although full data are not available, it appears that through-out Russia even those enterprises that did pay their power bills increas-ingly did so in kind. A Russian business weekly claimed that by February 1994 half of all payments for electricity in the country were in kind (*Kommersant*, 2/15/94, 31). Trends in all three of the very different Rus-sian provinces visited for this study reflected these national develop-ments.[25] Two regional power companies furnished data reflecting a dra-matic increase in payments in kind that moved in parallel with the general trend for growing nonpayments described earlier (see Tables 3.1 and 3.2). In both regions, by summer 1994 over 75 percent of electric power payments made were done in kind.[26] Like nonpayment, in-kind payment could occur only with a complete absence of funds in enterprise bank accounts.

The growth of payments in kind and nonpayments to electric power companies poses two sets of questions. First, why did the process of hard-ening lateral budget constraints fail to extend to this sector? What made power companies less able to mount the vigorous defense of their finan-cial position that had increasingly become the norm in Russian economic life? Second, why did firms offer payment in kind rather than in money? What was the origin of the goods, and what made it feasible for the power company to accept them?

Among suppliers to industrial enterprises, electrical power companies are in a unique position. Industry's absolute dependence on electrical power means its disconnection destroys industry's capacity to make money. In some cases—especially in the chemical and metallurgical in-dustries—disconnection may also destroy delicate continuous-process equipment.[27] As a result of their possession of only a single and very de-structive sanction, when enterprise bank accounts began to empty conta-giously in the second half of 1993 and the direct deduction rights that had held nonpayments for electricity to a minimum stopped working, electric power companies suddenly found themselves in a weak strategic position vis-à-vis their debtors.[28]

Power companies' most obvious coercive mechanism, disconnection, is not a very credible threat for reasons both political and economic. Cut-ting off the power in retaliation for nonpayments is difficult politically because regulations adopted in 1992 mandate that local authorities must give approval before any shutdown is carried out.[29] Although such ap-proval is not impossible to win, it is given rarely and, at best, grudg-ingly.[30] Local authorities usually force the power company to refrain from cutoffs while promising some subsidies—and possibly invoking the essentially inoperative bankruptcy mechanism against those enterprises chronically failing to pay their bills.[31]

Even if approval can be won for a cutoff of electrical power, an enterprise that is shut down will be unable to earn money to pay back its debts, so the benefits may be minimal. As officials in two different regions put it, to shut off enterprises with any prospects whatsoever would be "to cut off the branch we are sitting on."[32] Given that Russia's bankruptcy provisions are weak and virtually untested, power companies' chances of recovering their debts from shuttered enterprises' assets are all but nil. Therefore, power companies are likely to attempt to disconnect the power of only those enterprises they view as likely to yield nothing but an endless stream of nonpayments.[33] Payment in kind, although, as explained later, less attractive than payment in money, is usually much preferred to no payment at all.

Given that the power company's single sanction is too destructive and politically difficult to be very credible, it is unsurprising that many enterprises arrange to ignore their electric bills. But what explains the fact that some bills are paid, at least in kind? First, as noted in the preceding section, enterprises that keep money in their official bank accounts will have to pay for electricity, so to avoid paying for electricity is also to leave the officially visible money economy, which involves certain costs.[34] (Sometimes, however, it is possible to combine the benefits of an official bank account with successful evasion of the power company's bill collectors. One common scheme cited by power company officials involves the transformation of subdivisions into legally independent firms with their own bank accounts but no institutional relationship with the electric power company. Electricity debts stemming from the operations of the subdivisions accumulate in the bank account of the parent enterprise, which is kept empty.[35]) A second reason an enterprise may pay its electric bill is that without an absolute belief in its political immunity, it has reason to offer at least some payment to the power company to keep it from starting to engineer a shutdown.

These are reasons bills were paid at all. But why were some bills paid in kind? In-kind payment may have been the only choice for enterprises worried about the threat of disconnection but that had already chosen to leave the officially visible money economy as a way of avoiding payment of taxes and debts. One should not conclude, however, that all enterprises with empty bank accounts were, in fact, doing a flourishing business in the clandestine economy. The renewed growth in nonpayments from fall 1993 was accompanied by an ever-more prominent phenomenon known as the *krizis sbyta,* or sales crisis. A study that examined tax documents for five enterprises in each of Russia's regions found that approximately a quarter of 1992 production went unsold, as did 14.5 percent of production in the first half of 1993 (*Segodnia* [Moscow], 6/11/93, 12).

The accumulation of such inventories is somewhat puzzling, since although constantly shrinking demand can explain the lack of sales at original prices, it cannot explain why prices on such goods were not cut. The answer must be sought in the concrete institutional structures of economic calculation in Russia today. Substantial evidence shows that accounting rules imposed by the tax system are a major cause of the stickiness of prices. Until August 1994, tax regulations designed to avoid the underdeclaring of revenues forbade enterprises to sell anything they produced for less than the cost of production (*sebestoimost'*) plus at least some profit.[36] The definition of production costs is hardly self-evident.[37] Regulations can force the inclusion of overhead and depreciation costs on equipment that is not being used, for instance.[38] Faced with lack of demand at the price their accounting departments determined in line with tax law requirements, enterprises were forced to let goods accumulate in warehouses in hopes that inflation would eventually lower the real price sufficiently to allow buyers to be found.[39] Or they had to find a way of showing paper receipts satisfactory to the tax organs.

Barter provided one answer to this problem, allowing some sales to take place that could not have happened in the official money economy. Faced with the choice of receiving no payment at all, power companies were willing to accept payment in kind at the "price" determined by the fixed profitability markup over the cost of production.[40]

Of course, the power company must then sell the goods taken in payment at a profitability markup over *that* price or the tax authorities will raise serious objections.[41] Sometimes a power company, through its own commercial organization, is able to make a money sale its customer was not. Such goods have in essence been transferred to a marketing agent who can realize economies of scope in selling goods from a wide variety of producers unable to sell them themselves. As the head of the company in Krasnoyarsk put it, "The quality of these products was perfectly good, and there was no reason we couldn't sell them. But selling them took time and commercial expertise that the factories couldn't command." Krasnoyarskenergo thus organized a commercial network through a subsidiary bank to deal with sales.[42]

If the good cannot be sold at its official accounting-determined money price, then the price may somehow be "lowered."[43] This lowering cannot show up in the accounting. One method—difficult because of the lack of contract enforcement mechanisms—is to sell the goods on credit at terms that inadequately reflect inflation. A second is to pass the goods on further through what one can call "price ratification" barter—that is, essentially to follow the strategy of the enterprise that made the in-kind payment in the first place. Many potential traders are also stuck with goods they cannot sell for money at the accounting price. When barter is carried out at the ratios between cost-plus-markup prices, which often seems to be the case,[44] on paper both sides show that they took in the necessary amount. (In one such deal in Krasnoyarsk, for instance, the power company accepted railroad ties in payment for electricity from a local sawmill and was later able to trade them for pipes it needed from a factory in the western part of Russia.) Although such mechanisms may allow markets creakily and partially to clear, they do not generate prices that are in any way useful in the planning of production.

To summarize the arguments of this section: when nonpayments to electric power companies began to increase in fall 1993, power companies were usually unable to insist on payment because they were in a weak strategic situation.[45] The only threat they had available, to disconnect nonpaying customers, was likely to be blocked by local authorities and in any event was too damaging to be credible in most cases (especially without effective bankruptcy procedures that would allow debts to be taken from the assets of an enterprise that had failed). Payment was made in money by firms that had decided that the benefits of retaining an official bank account outweighed the cost of paying electric bills (and taxes) in full and on time. Firms with empty bank accounts, whether these stemmed from deliberately hiding income or simply from the inability to make any sales at the prices mandated by the tax system, could sometimes be coerced into making payment for electricity in kind. The "prices" for such goods in terms of the electricity debt they canceled tended to be unrealistically high compared with what the goods would have brought if sold on the open market, although power companies had some ability to sell for money even goods their customers had been unable to sell. When money sales were impossible, however, in-kind payment for electricity bred more barter by power companies themselves.

The mode of exchange spreading through these complicated processes can be described as the barter of the bankrupt, in-kind exchange carried on by firms whose official (and often unofficial) monetary position consists of nothing but debts. For enterprises in this situation, any money receipts transferred to the bank instantly disappear to pay for back taxes and the other categories of automatically deducted payments. Barter allows such firms to continue with some production and sales, although usually at a much-reduced level (cf. Burawoy 1996). Perhaps because of Adam Smith's famous invocation of the human propensity to "truck and barter," post-Soviet barter is sometimes seen as a sign of the spread of market calculation. Yet, if one accepts as definitive of the market the principles of consumer sovereignty, the price mechanism, and hard budget constraints, then the barter of the bankrupt flourishing in Russia's regions in 1994 was clearly of a nonmarket character. In the barter of the bankrupt production is sovereign, not consumers: creditors are forced into purchase of a good they would not otherwise have acquired. The price mechanism does not operate. Prices are set subsequent to production according to the enterprise's conception of its costs; they are not prior prices driving production through the urge for money profit. And as power companies are forced to extend credit to their customers and eventually to cancel it by accepting goods at markup prices, they enact the two-phase scenario of the soft budget constraint described earlier.

Local and Federal Fiscal Responses to the Barter of the Bankrupt

> In the conditions of the crisis of payments, barter exchange operations between enterprises are constantly growing, and likewise the practice of making payments to local budgets with [enterprises'] production. In such barter transactions money funds are naturally not transferred to the enterprises' bank accounts, and therefore there are no tax receipts for the budget system.
>
> —Vladimir Gusev, director of the Russian Federation
> State Tax Service, *Finansy,* no. 11, 1994: 5

Power companies trying to force delinquent customers to pay their bills in money should have had an ally in the state. The empty bank accounts of enterprises operating outside the visible money economy frustrate not only electricity suppliers but also the agents of the fisc. As states drive to expand their tax capacity, they tend to embrace the slogan "pay in money or pay the consequences." As Joseph Schumpeter put in a classic essay, "Tax bill in hand, the state penetrated the private economies and won increasing dominion over them. The tax [state] brings money and calculating spirit into corners in which they do not dwell as yet, and thus becomes a formative factor in the very organism which has developed it" (Schumpeter 1991: 108). A full explanation of the spread of barter must include not only reason parties to exchange choose this form of it but also an account of why the state does not eliminate barter.

I can begin this account by considering the situation of local authorities when faced with the decision of whether to authorize the shutdown of an enterprise not paying its electric bills. They confront a choice between eliminating an enterprise in serious trouble and forcing the power company to bear some costs. Authorities see the latter choice as feasible largely because they perceive electricity producers as relatively resilient in the face of nonpayments and barter. Some of the reasons for this resilience are the political factors analyzed more closely in the next section: the electric power sector has relatively strong political influence in Moscow, and in crisis situations central authorities are usually willing to supply emergency funds.

But there are other reasons power companies are relatively resilient.

First, the very low ratio of variable to fixed costs in the operation of power plants makes the short-term opportunity costs of supplying electricity for free rather low, although in the long term this practice amounts to a drawing down of the fixed investments in the plants. Second, in the immediate post–price liberalization period electric companies accumulated significant financial power. Indeed, local authorities and many employees of other industries often believe power companies benefited disproportionately in early stages of reform when price rises, although regulated, nevertheless allowed power companies to pay very high wages. Thus, when power companies also began to face harder times with nonpayments, some sentiment held that earlier gains compensated for present difficulties.[46] In at least a temporary and practical fashion there was some truth to this idea. Power companies had used their financial strength to build up their shares in the capital stock of local banks, which in some cases enables the extraction of loans even from bankers who are uncertain of the prospects for repayment.[47] (As already noted, by 1994 bankers were becoming increasingly resistant to such pressure.)

The relative financial resilience of electricity producers may explain why forcing them to bear the costs of nonpayments and barter is feasible, but it does not compel such a choice. The roots of local leaders' great hesitation to agree to shut down a nonpaying enterprise lie in weighty political and practical considerations. In the pattern familiar from the long stream of literature inspired by Mancur Olson's *Logic of Collective Action* (Olson 1965), an aggressive policy in support of electricity producers has many enemies with a minimum of collective action problems and few organized supporters. Although the coherence and power of Russia's "directors' corps" have often been drastically overstated, the shared opposition among leaders of large industrial enterprises to high electricity prices and vigorous bill collection can rapidly give rise to at least a tactical alliance when required.[48] In Primorskii province, which inherited a weak and expensive power system from the Soviet period, opposition to a local administration that had strongly backed the electric power company helped to produce an exceptionally coherent alliance of industrialists that managed to remove the province's governor in spring 1993.[49]

No industrialist bloc of comparable strength emerged in the other provinces studied, however, and the importance of local political pressure in blocking aggressive electricity bill collection should not be overestimated. Russia's provincial governors are still largely appointed rather than elected. They can plausibly make the case for their own irreplaceability by arguing that central aid for their province depends on the goodwill of the president and that the president is more likely to show such goodwill toward his or her own appointees. The fact that virtually every provincial governor was elected to the Federation Council in late 1993 suggests the governors' structural strength on the local political scene. It therefore seems plausible that provincial governors might see it as politically feasible to adopt a somewhat stricter attitude toward electricity debtors.

It is difficult to see, however, what reasoning would push them to adopt such an attitude. The argument at the core of the literature on the politics of stabilization is that politicians must endure the suffering of the organizationally and politically visible victims of reform in the interests of the organizationally and politically invisible beneficiaries. Such an argument can appeal only to leaders who can conceive of themselves as representing the entire community to which the postulated eventual benefits of market reform would accrue. For leaders of subnational jurisdictions it is likely to be less than compelling.

This is especially true to the extent that local leaders are likely to be rather bereft of alternatives to the social and infrastructural services provided by enterprises that would be shut down (cf. Wallich 1994: 81). Russia's extraordinary housing shortage minimizes opportunities for labor mobility, and the empty coffers of local budgets are unable to cope with present tasks, let alone unemployment compensation (Wallich 1994: 77). Tolerating enterprise tax and bill evasion allows enterprises to pay their workers at least some salaries.[50] Moreover, the Soviet state had no reason to distinguish between public and private infrastructure; thus, the sewage or heating in sections of major cities or in entire smaller ones may be technologically inseparable from that of the industrial enterprises around which they were built. As a result, shutdown would mean massive and expensive problems for which there are no funds.

All of this makes local governments willing to ignore or even to facilitate firms' exit from the officially visible money economy and gives them strong reason to hope that current levels of final demand are artificially low and will increase at some point. (If credibility arguments have some impact, the appropriate locus is thus the local government more than the enterprise.) In one of the provinces visited for this study, Samara, which has a highly militarized industrial economy, the administration official who would have to agree to shutdowns believed nonpayments were caused by the government's failure to pay for the defense industry production it ordered in 1993. Shutdowns would thus attack the symptom rather than the cause of nonpayments and were "not a solution to the problem."[51] Key officials in a Siberian province investigated, Krasnoyarsk, were explicitly antimonetarist, believing money should be printed as necessary to service the current level of nominal transactions in the economy. In the meantime, as a deputy governor put it, "until the central government has corrected its line . . . it is necessary maximally to retreat from monetary circulation on the territory of the province, that is, to strengthen the mutual ties of enterprises, and try to carry out payments in kind [*tovayrne vzaimoraschety.*"[52] To the extent that barter on such motivations allows production and sale of goods to continue, the view that final monetary demand is artificially limited becomes something of a self-fulfilling prophecy.

Relative power company resilience, fears of political opposition, unwillingness to suffer the burdens of a harsh policy when the benefits might accrue elsewhere, an absence of alternatives to the social and infrastructural services vested with enterprises under state socialism, and hopes that the economic depression will eventually pass, then, all contributed to local authorities' reluctance to allow the electricity cutoffs that would drive firms into the visible money economy or out of business.

Whatever the motives, the policy of tolerating the barter of the bankrupt had important fiscal consequences. As the epigraph for this section indicates, tax officials are painfully aware that enterprises' in-kind receipts cannot easily be taxed, even if officially recorded. The huge growth in so-called tax undercollections (*nedoimki*) starting in fall 1993 gives some idea of the magnitude of the problem. By "undercollections" Russian authorities mean taxes officially assessed on the basis of a firm's records but that the firm has no money to pay. Both barter (when declared) and nonpayments produce undercollections.[53] At the end of the first half of 1994, undercollections to the federal budget had reached 7.5 trillion rubles, an amount equal to a quarter of the tax revenues actually collected (see Figure 3.5).[54] Because the tax authorities, like electric power companies, had the right to deduct payments automatically from bank accounts, the growth of undercollections also indicated a widespread exit from the visible money economy.

Unsurprisingly, Russia's national authorities reacted to this situation with measures designed to improve tax collection. Most of these measures, many of which were spelled out in President Yeltsin's May 1994 orders on the economy, concentrated on making it more difficult for enterprises to conceal money held in banks (*Rossiiskaia Gazeta* [Moscow], 5/25/94). A tax regulation in June, however, gave fiscal authorities new powers to confiscate and sell property and production from delinquent enterprises. Although one newspaper described the order as "a return to federal taxes collected both in money and in kind," in fact the intent was to convert any confiscated goods into money. In practice, this meant the state would attempt to sell for money any goods its producers had been unable to sell. Although little evidence is available on the implementation of this measure, the administrative difficulties involved are manifest. The volume of undercollections to all levels of the budget system as of September 1, 1994, represented well over $39,000 per employee of the State

Figure 3.5   Undercollections (federal budget), January 1993–July 1994

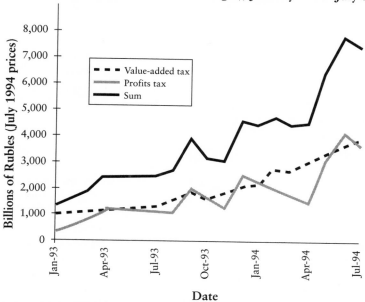

Date

Source: Segodnia (Moscow) 9/1/94, 11. Deflation by Consumer Price Index. For the first half of 1993, only quarterly data are available; missing figures have been interpolated on the assumption of a constant month-on-month growth rate.

Tax Service and the State Tax Police.[55] The conditions under which such a large volume of sales was to be made were not propitious. The measure called for tax authorities to attempt to sell production at the enterprises' cost-markup price, with permission to reduce the price after two months if no sales had been made. If warehouse space was unavailable, confiscated goods were to be stored on the premises of the tax-delinquent enterprise until they could be sold (*Kommersant-Daily* [Moscow], 6/30/94, 2).

Whatever the actual administrative outcome, the federal attempt to generate money income forcibly from tax delinquents operating outside the money economy follows the typical pattern of state-driven monetization. The response of local authorities was different in essence. For the reasons already indicated, local governments in the regions visited for this study (and, all evidence indicates, elsewhere in Russia) did not launch efforts to bring enterprises into the visible money economy for tax purposes; instead, they moved to accept goods from those enterprises that could not pay their taxes in money. For local governments, such collection of taxes *in natura* was not a way station preceding a subsequent money sale of those goods. Rather, local authorities' efforts focused on finding ways to make direct use of these goods or to barter them for other goods needed locally.

Taxation in kind was organized largely by clearing operations (*zachety*) in which accumulated local tax debts were canceled in return for the production of debtor enterprises. When possible, authorities made direct use of those goods. The Krasnoyarsk administration, for example, used building materials accepted as taxes from local firms for construction projects financed by the budget.[56] Authorities also made a largely unsuccessful effort to convince schoolteachers to accept their salaries in sausages and other food goods paid as taxes by local producers (*Krasnoiarskii Komsomolets* [Krasnoyarsk], 6/4/94). When goods available as in-kind tax payments cannot be put to direct use, some way of exchanging them must be found; here the clearing operations become more complicated. Often, tax arrears from the local power company are canceled in return for production from one of the power company's debtors for which the power company has no use. One province administration that had been unable to pay for medicine for a local hospital intended to solve the problem by retiring tax arrears it was owed by the local power company, which in return would supply medicine it, in turn, had accepted as payment from one of its debtors (*Finansy*, no. 10, 1994: 28). I encountered similar arrangements in two of the provinces visited for this study.[57]

These anecdotes illustrate how local administrations, unable to insist on monetization, were able to create some capacity to tax in kind and to use this capacity to maintain critical local services. In so doing, they were drawn into arranging multilateral barter deals that made operation in the barter economy more practicable for local firms (by overcoming the problem of the "double coincidence of wants" required for a barter transaction). Local governments' ability to tolerate the operation of firms outside the visible money economy because of in-kind taxation capabilities thus provides a crucial facilitating circumstance for the increase of barter.

It is difficult to gauge the scale of local in-kind taxation.[58] One indicator that its scale had become fairly significant by late 1994 comes from the reaction of federal tax authorities. Most taxes in Russia are divided between local and federal budgets according to percentages that vary by the tax. In-kind taxes accepted by local governments count against only the local portions of taxes, however, and thus are not shared with the federal budget.[59] By late fall 1994, the head of the State Tax Service was beginning to express concerns about this practice (as seen in the quotation that opens this section), and in December new regulations were promulgated to give federal authorities better information on the scale of taxation in kind.[60]

The concern of federal tax officials over local in-kind taxation underscores the distinct situations in which central and local authorities find themselves with respect to the imperatives of monetization. In his *Philosophy of Money*, Georg Simmel suggests that the term *independence*, in contrast to autarkic nondependence, should be used to refer not to a lack of dependence on others in general but to an absence of *concrete* dependencies on *particular* ways of providing for given needs (Simmel 1990: 300–301). Independence in Simmel's sense is a precondition for a single-minded pursuit of money income. The fiscal organs of an ideal-typical "independent" state are indifferent to the substance of the economic activity carried on by tax-paying organizations and individuals and are concerned only that such activity yield taxable money revenues. Organizationally, the collection and spending of tax revenue can be entirely isolated. What this implies is, as Max Weber noted, a "fully developed money economy" (Weber 1978: 199) on which everything necessary to the state's functioning can be purchased.

Russia's local authorities find themselves in a situation far from this ideal type of Simmelian independence; indeed, they find themselves enmeshed in a thicket of concrete dependencies. The clearest example is that of power companies, also in tax arrears as a result of nonpayments by their customers. No local government could take the attitude that it would simply dismantle and sell furnaces and power lines in response to an inability to pay taxes in money. Power companies are a far end of what is clearly a spectrum of indispensability. Yet, the leaders of Russia's provinces have inherited an economy built on the premise that no enterprise would ever cease production. As a result, large enterprises tend to cluster very close to this extreme of indispensability. Weber argued that "a political body based purely on deliveries in kind does not promote the development of capitalism. On the contrary, it hinders it to the extent to which it involves rigid binding of the structure of production in a form which, from a point of view of profit making enterprise, is irrational" (Weber 1978: 199). The in-kind taxation of local government does not bind local enterprise to unprofitable activities. Rather, it represents the rigid binding of local government itself to the foundations of the local natural economy—and local government's consequent inability to become the agent of capitalism monetization.

Moving Moscow: Regional and Sectoral Lobbying

The government can fire all the provincial governors, but no fuel oil will appear as a result. The risk of freezing the towns and villages will remain, however. And if this happens, the money will be found, and the fuel oil will be shipped. Why let things go all the way to a crisis?

—A provincial governor to a deputy premier[61]

Any government, even if it is monetarist three times over, will have to give money under the threat that there will be no light and no heat in Moscow.

—Sergei Glazev[62]

The facility of power companies and local governments in adapting to the barter of the bankrupt should not mask the huge problems it presents to them. Despite the best efforts of those forced to organize barter trade, what Russians increasingly term "live" money (to distinguish it from in-kind income whether in the form of goods or the so-called promissory notes that are usually mere facilitators of multilateral barter exchange) is still indispensable to make many purchases and, above all, to pay salaries.[63] This situation forces appeals to Moscow. There are two channels whereby the problems created by the concentration of nonpayments in the fuel and energy complex reach Moscow as demands for subsidy: through the lobbying of regional leaders and that of sectoral ones.

The pattern of regional lobbying is determined by the structure of the electrical power system each province inherited from the Soviet era, which sets up political tasks that must be fulfilled if electric power is to be used as a source of subsidy. The nature of these tasks can be seen through a comparison of the three regions visited for this study: Samara province in European Russia, Krasnoyarsk Territory in central Siberia, and the Maritime Territory (Primorskii *krai*) in the Far East on the Korean and Chinese borders. In Samara and Krasnoyarsk, which are home to hydropower plants, enormous investments in the energy sector were made in the Soviet era. Here the issue is one of ownership. The fate of these power stations as the national system was partially privatized in 1993 became the object of major center-region controversy. The privatization scheme mandated that all power stations above a particular size should remain the property of the federal system, whereas smaller and more out-of-date stations were to become local property (*Kommersant-Daily* 1/15/93). Because the intent of the national power company was to set prices that would reflect investment levels sufficient to reproduce systemwide capacity,[64] under this plan regions home to large hydropower plants would not capture particular price benefits from those plants. Local ownership of power plants also provides at least some additional control over their behavior, which may help in efforts to block aggressive debt collecting.

As a result, local leaders in Samara and Krasnoyarsk fought to retain control over their hydropower plants. In Samara, although executive authorities discussed the need to acquire ownership of the local plant, they never seriously opened the battle for it. Instead, a strategy of projecting to Moscow an image of a loyal and proreform region paid off in a series of special orders from Yeltsin and the Council of Ministers that, among other things, mandated special low prices for Samara consumers on the output of the hydropower plant.[65] Krasnoyarsk adopted a more aggressive approach of challenging the constitutionality of the privatization order that was to strip it of ownership of its much larger hydropower systems. After winning its case before the Constitutional Court, the province was able to work out a deal for shared ownership that retained substantial local control in price policy.[66]

Other regions with less fortunate inheritances from the Soviet period have found that in the context of hardening lateral budget constraints, nonpayments to electrical power companies quickly raise bedrock problems with keeping the furnaces running. Regions dependent on fuel shipments from outside their borders are in an especially difficult position, as out-region coal mines and oil refineries are little interested in barter and are increasingly unwilling to ship without payment in advance.[67]

Such regions, of which the Maritime province is one, thoroughly depend on central subsidies. In late 1993 the leadership of this province sought to combine a policy of defending debtor enterprises from power company cutoff efforts while extracting money from Moscow on the basis of critically low levels of coal supplies (*Vladivostok*, 11/19/93; *Novosti* [Vladivostok], 10/12/93). Although Moscow regularly promised money to purchase coal, it appears to have delivered inconsistently at best, and suppliers stopped shipment in the face of nonpayments (*Zolotoi Rog*, 1/11/94). Moscow's orders to out-region suppliers to deliver coal without prepayment also appear to have been ignored. As a result, the province struggled through a winter of brownouts and no hot water. All of this led to a desperate local political struggle over whether to pursue more vigorous electrical power debt collection to yield "live money" for out-region supplies (*Krasnoe Znamia* [Vladivostok], 2/19/94). In June 1994 the local governor—who, as noted earlier, had come to power a year earlier at the head of a movement of industrialists united above all by anger at the high prices and aggressive debt collection of the power company—ordered the cutoff of any enterprises more than a month overdue in payments (*Krasnoe Znamia* [Vladivostok], 6/20/94). Still, for the first eight months of 1994, the Maritime province's Dal'energo power company was paid for only about 64 percent of the electricity it supplied, and that payment was largely in kind.[68]

The logic of the Maritime province's strategy was that expressed in the quotes at the outset of this section: the threat of letting power systems fail seems so serious as to be incredible. But the upshot was merely to demonstrate how limited Moscow's capacity is to deliver money reliably where it has promised. As already described, the practical problem facing the Russian state no longer consists of making a credible commitment to monetary restraint but of making a credible commitment to subsidize. Nevertheless, many regions find few alternatives to asking for such subsidies.

The problems raised by nonpayments and payment in kind for electricity become converted to demands for subsidy through a second channel: direct lobbying by the branch ministry for fuel and energy (Mintopenergo). At a meeting in June 1994 on preparations for the coming winter, for example, Mintopenergo officials argued that because of nonpayments they would need central support to ensure having enough money to pay for winter stockpiles (*Rossiiskaia Gazeta* [Moscow], 6/25/94). Under the leadership of Iurii Shafranik, former governor of the oil-rich Tiumen' province who took over the post in January 1993, the ministry mounted continual press campaigns to draw attention to the nonpayments problem (which, as noted previously, began seriously to affect the fuel sector earlier than the electrical power sector). The major causes of nonpayments for fuel appear to have been the absence of direct deduction rights and the great technical difficulties in cutting off customers (especially for drilling operations), reinforced by the anticutoff lobbying of local authorities. As electricity nonpayments expanded, the ministry broadened its lobbying to address that issue as well.

In general, the fuel and electricity sector has been successful at lobbying for credits for itself, but that leaves fuel and energy producers paying interest on loans made to cover customer nonpayments. As one oil industry executive put it, "They've made us into a source of indirect subsidies for the entire economy, and then they suggest that we take out a loan to improve our situation" (*Kommersant-Daily* [Moscow], 1/12/93). Increasingly, Shafranik's lobbying has focused on convincing central authorities to hand out loans to nonpaying customers, which the customers will use to pay off their debts to the energy sector (e.g., Shafranik, Kozyrev, and Samsuev 1994). The idea languished for over a year, but a special government commission on nonpayments established in summer 1994 appears to have approved at least a limited version. (Commercial banks, as argued earlier, are unlikely to want to serve as intermediaries for these loans.)

The commission, in spite of its ritual invocation of the experience of various regions in dealing with nonpayments, seems to have included no representatives of the regions while giving heavy weight to sectoral concerns (*Rossiiskie Vesti* [Moscow], 8/13/94, 1). Yet, the energy sector's efforts to procure low-interest loans for its customers demonstrate that the sector has become, in effect, a lobbyist for the regional leaders whose actions helped to generate the nonpayments problem in the first place.

Conclusion: The Triple Movement

Starting with summer 1993, more and more of Russia's state-owned or newly private enterprises dropped out of the officially visible money economy as their bank accounts emptied, inventories of unsold goods gathered dust, potential creditors followed the newly audible counsel of their pocketbooks and refused to finance money-losing ventures, and the central government's ability to choose the recipients of its largesse continued to decline. As a result, power company access to enterprise bank accounts was no longer an effective bill collection mechanism, and nonpayments to electric companies began to rise. Threats to disconnect nonpayers proved largely hollow because of the devastating nature of the sanction and the interference of local authorities. At best, the threat of disconnection could extract barter payment at effectively a much lower price.

Local authorities' willingness to permit costs to be pushed onto the electric power sector stemmed on the one hand from their belief in the resilience of that sector and on the other hand from their ability to organize in-kind taxation of electricity customers whose empty bank accounts signified their exit from the visible money economy. This belief was in part a result of political factors: the strength of corporate organizations representing the fuel and energy complex and the perception of Moscow's unwillingness to permit a wintertime collapse of systems that ensured the population's heat.

In the remainder of this chapter I propose to reanalyze the story just recounted in terms of Polanyi's theory of the "double movement." By this term Polanyi meant the struggle "between two organizing principles in society . . . the principle of economic liberalism . . . [and] the principle of social protection aiming at the conservation of man and nature as well as productive organization" (Polanyi 1965: 132). Although Polanyi suggests that each principle is associated with "definite social forces," he insists that the clashes and alliances provoked by the monetary interests of these social forces are insufficient to explain the rise of protection. Indeed, arguments focusing on interest-driven class actions "all but completely obstructed an over-all view of market society, and of the function of protectionism [broadly understood] in such a society. . . . Ultimately, what made things happen were the interests of society as a whole, though their defense fell primarily to one section of the population in preference to another" (Polanyi 1965: 152, 161–62).

This structural-functionalist image of an amoeba society continually generating and retracting interest group pseudopodia as necessary to defend its survival may seem outlandish in the context of contemporary political economy. Surely one cannot ascribe all deviations from the most consistent market liberalisms to a universal urge for the "self-protection of society"; if this were adequate, the entire thriving school of comparative politics that focuses on the shaping of a variety of market economies under the impact of political struggles would be irrelevant. Indeed, even the movements for trade protection and against the deflationary strictures of the gold standard, which Polanyi cites as examples of the defense of societywide interests, have since been less mystically and rather convincingly analyzed in terms of social forces by Peter Gourevitch (Gourevitch 1986); Gregory Luebbert compellingly reconceived the same political struggles as a reaction to the emergence of labor as a political force (Luebbert 1991). Therefore, can any explanatory leverage be salvaged from Polanyi's emphasis on an innate tendency to defend "the human and natural components of the social fabric" (Polanyi 1965: 120)?

What Polanyi offers is the insight that there is a social sine qua non, that whatever the specifics of politics, the prospect of hideous social cataclysms will force a policy reaction out of all but the rarest and most virulent regimes. Although one can debate whether the demise of, say, Junker agriculture should qualify for characterization in Polanyi's apocalyptic terms, it is possible to move his approach beyond an ethereal functionalism when the social fabric is *concretely institutionalized,* when bedrock tasks of social reproduction are the direct responsibility of identifiable organizations.

For Russian local administrations, the social fabric and the economic fabric are one. The absence of possibilities for labor mobility, the prevalence of one-factory towns, and the intertwining of "public" and "private" physical infrastructures make virtually imperative "the defense of productive organization" emphasized by Polanyi as one aspect of the double movement (cf. Wallich 1994: 81). Local enterprise efforts at survival are coextensive with survival of critical sections of the local community. For local politics, then, ethereal functionalism, although a huge oversimplification, is nonetheless a forgivable one. In only one of the three cases studied here did local authorities attempt to allow the hardening of budget constraints against local productive organization, and this plan ended with the political coalescence of industrialists and a change of the local regime.[69] In the other two cases, local authorities maintained soft budget constraints as long as resources allowed.

For Polanyi, the society whose impulse for self-protection drove the double movement was territorially coextensive with the national state. The glue of this society was most of all the national currency, which fused individuals into a nation, into a "social unit" vested with a shared instinct for protection against the destructive effects of self-regulating markets (Polanyi 1965: 201–205, 214–215; Glasman 1994: 61–62). For contemporary Russia, with its two levels of government, this straightforward identity of society and state through the nexus of the monetary system cannot be assumed. As a result, Russia's "double movement" has three phases rather than two and displays the potential to destroy rather than promote national integration. The spread of the market principle through society—seen in the lateral hardening of budget constraints analyzed in the section on the transformation of the nonpayments crisis—ran into roadblocks first on the local level and then on the national level. As local administrations scrambled with ever-decreasing effectiveness to defend local industry from destruction, they found themselves condoning or even promoting the demolition of the price mechanism and a massive exit of industry from the money economy. This exit threatened the integration of the broader Russian economic and social space, and it left regions with vital dependencies on other parts of the country facing disaster as barter proved to have largely local purchasing power.

With the prospect of this disaster begins the final phase of Russia's "triple movement." Even Moscow encounters the social fabric in concrete, institutional form when the fate of entire regional power systems is at stake. The ability to distribute money with real cross-regional purchasing power is both the emblem and the key institution of the Russian national integration that alone can avert such disasters. Given the crumbling of state structures and the fiscal difficulties posed by the widespread shift to barter, the issue becomes how long Moscow will be able to play this role.

Notes

Acknowledgments: Many thanks to Neil Fligstein, Gregory Grossman, Ken Jowitt, Barbara Lehmbruch, Robert Powell, and audiences at Berkeley and MIT to whom I presented earlier versions of this chapter. Particular thanks to Michael Burawoy for his valuable comments on this article and for sharing his work with me. I am especially grateful to Kiren Chaudhry for suggestions and conversation; my intellectual debt to her goes far beyond what the academic conventions of citation can capture. Remaining factual errors and analytical failures are my responsibility alone. Research for this chapter was facilitated by a Social Science Research Council fellowship I held in 1992–1994.

1. One should discount entirely the recent claim that "regardless of earlier Russian inclinations to barter, the economy has become thoroughly monetized" (Åslund 1995: 5). This claim is apparently meant to relate to the period during which his book was being written (March–August 1994 [Åslund 1995: xi]). For the skeptical, in the first seven months of 1994, less than half of the payments made to the Russian rail system were in money (*Kommersant* [Moscow], no. 31,

8/23/94, 23). Like the electric power sector studied in this chapter, the railway system has dealings with an enormous number of economic actors and can be taken as giving at least some indication of exchange practices in the broader economy. Inflation (Consumer Price Index) fell from 20 percent per month in October 1993 to 6 percent in July 1994. *Russian Economic Trends* 3, no. 2 (1994): 123–124.

2. See Weber 1978: 196–197, 963–964; Simmel 1990: 185–187, 395–397; Schumpeter 1991: 108; Polanyi 1965: 201–205, 214–215.

3. For some relevant case histories of the process of consolidating a national monetary order, see Holtfrerich 1989: 216–240; Hammond 1957; and especially Chaudhry 1997, chapter 2, where this process is situated in the broader context of the twin tasks of state building and market building.

4. As Gavin Helf (1994: 10) argues, "The struggle to reintegrate [the] fragmented polity is the field on which economic, political, social and even constitutional reforms are played out, and defines the parameters of debate and limits to these other 'transitions.' "

5. The point that central and local authorities are at loggerheads because the former are trying to promote economic reform whereas the latter must deal with the social consequences of reform was made to me very forcefully by Iurii Moskvich, presidential representative for Krasnoyarsk *krai*. Compare Philip Hanson (1994: 23–28) and the discussion of "how oblast coping mechanisms may undermine stabilization" (Wallich 1994: 80–81).

6. Electric power and heating (almost always provided through large stations serving entire neighborhoods rather than by furnaces in individual buildings) are institutionally united in Russia; co-generation (use of the heating network of water heated for steam to turn electricity-generating turbines) often makes the unification physical as well.

7. This argument comes in part from the Russian business weekly *Kommersant* [Moscow], 2/15/94, 31: "By agreement with the local administration power supply enterprises can pull the plug on chronic nonpayers. But this still [is] only a threat, with a very limited sphere of action. Local administrations give such permission very rarely, and the main thing is that all the same one won't get the debt back this way. It is true that for liquidating the debt one can take production of the debtor. . . . And at present up to half of all payments are made with such barter."

8. The earliest mention I have seen of a special place for the fuel and energy complex (or TEK by its Russian initials) in the nonpayments crisis is in Zhuravlev (1992: 4). "Consumers of fuel and energy resources, and this is in essence the entire national economy, are forced to cover their lack of liquidity by delaying payments to the TEK, to which the Central Bank lacks the 'moral' right to refuse loans."

9. A terminological note: I have chosen to use the term *nonpayments crisis* (*krizis neplatezhei*) because this is how the issue is discussed in Russia. There is a certain amount of linguistic flux over what counts as nonpayments, whether to look from the side of receivables (*debitorskaia zadolzhennost'*) or the side of payables (*kreditorskaia zadolzhennost'*) and whether to include in the category only

overdue receivables (payables) or all of them. One should be wary, therefore, of sentences such as "*obshchii ob"em neplatezhei ravniaetsia . . .*" (the general volume of nonpayments is equal to . . .) since the choice among the four possible referents of *neplatezhi* will be driven to some extent by political considerations. *Neplatezhi* are coming to be most often defined, however, as overdue receivables. I will use "nonpayments" in this sense unless the context indicates otherwise.

10. For an example of federal authorities ordering shipment of fuels without prepayment, see "O neotlozhnykh merakh po obespecheniiu nefteproduktami pervoocherednykh gosudarstvennykh nuzhd" [On urgent measures for supply of oil products for immediate state needs], Presidential order no. 413-rp, in *Sobranie Aktov Prezidenta i Pravitel'stva Rossiiskoi Federatsii*, no. 5 (3 August 1992): 292–293. See also *Delo* [Samara], 4/23/93.

11. The measure was constructed by dividing total outstanding payables and receivables in arrears as of these dates by the ruble value of production from January to May 1993 (this denominator was chosen only because of data availability; naturally, it would be better to use monthly production data). For each sector, this score was divided by the average score for all sectors listed here (weighted according to the volume of production), and then one was subtracted so a final result of zero would represent the average rate of generation of payables or receivables.

12. For electrical power, the railroads, and crude oil and natural gas suppliers, the old payment order system was retained. Under that system the supplier notifies the payer's bank that a payment is due, and the payment is automatically sent (this is known as *bezaktseptnoe sniatie*) (de Boissieu, Cohen, and de Pontbriand 1993: 111; *Segodnia* [Moscow], 2/22/94). Electrical energy producers' rights in this regard were confirmed in interviews with officials at power systems in Samara, Krasnoyarsk, and Vladivostok in 1994. Until May 1994, arrears for electrical energy were assessed very high fines of 2 percent a day; after that they were dropped to 0.5 percent a day. Interview with the chief engineer at Energonadzor (Samaraenergo), May 1994.

13. The problems are especially great in the oil sector, where drillers, refiners, and sellers are in different organizations at best very weakly coordinated by the new oil "concerns" intended to unite the industry "from the well to the gas pump." Drillers find it very difficult to reduce production in the face of nonpayments since once a well is taken off-line, bringing it back on is both difficult and expensive (interview with the chief economist for *Kuibyshevneft'*, Samara, April 1994). And without their own storage facilities, drillers are forced to ship their products regardless of whether payment is likely to be forthcoming. Refiners, who do not have direct deduction rights, are now trying to sell their production to commercial structures, which are able to pay in advance. This allows them to avoid the official oil distribution system (the *nefteprodukty*), the branches of which do not pay in advance and are more subject to local administration political pressure (*Delo* [Samara], 10/8/93, 7; *Kommersant-Daily* [Moscow], 2/19/94, 6). Samara province's largest refinery has taken over all sales functions from the *nefteprodukty* and has tried to switch to 100 percent payment in advance, although as demand continued to fall into 1994 it was forced to ship to its whole-

salers on credit (*Za peredovuiu tekhniku* [Novokuibyshevsk] [newsletter of the Novokuibyshevskii Refinery], 12/17/93; *ABV: Ezhenedel'naia Regional'naia Delovaia Gazeta* [Samara], 2/16–23/94, 2).

14. The importance of October is shown by the fact that nonpayments (overdue receivables) jumped to 72 percent of the month's production from 54 percent the previous month (*Kommersant* [Moscow], 2/1/94, 4–5), although some of that increase may have been the result of a one-time adjustment in the method of calculating these nonpayments (*Voprosy Ekonomiki*, no. 1 [1994]: 53).

15. In fact, monthly wholesale inflation fell from 19 percent in October 1993 to only 6 percent by August 1994 at the same time as nonpayments increased (*Russian Economic Trends* 4, no. 2 (1994): 149). This fact is particularly uncomfortable for those inclined to find the roots of both nonpayments and high inflation in the lack of reform "credibility."

16. As János Kornai puts it (1986: 4) with regard to the classical budget constraint, "The budget constraint is a constraint on ex ante variables . . . based on expectations concerning . . . *future* financial situation" (emphasis added).

17. On the "pocket banks" see Hellman (1993), which predicts their increasing efforts to achieve autonomy. Such efforts are described by Burawoy (1994), who demonstrates that in early 1993 their impact was muted by a pattern of local government influence over local Central Bank branch operation. The cases I studied did not display this pattern.

18. This mechanism was described to me by the director of a Vladivostok commercial bank (interview, October 1993), the executive director of a holding company uniting many former state-owned factories (interview, November 1993), and the head of the Central Bank office for Krasnoyarsk territory (interview, June 1994). For statistics reflecting banks' bumping up against asset limits defined by their capital stock, see *Finansovye Izvestiia* [Moscow], 5/15–21/93, 3. The history of the Samara province's largest bank, which originally drew capital from large state enterprises, provides a good example of this trend. The bank's fifth issuance of stock in late 1993 saw the share of stock held by the four largest stockholders shrink from 47.6 percent to 32.8 percent, with only one stockholder owning as much as 10 percent. This decline was followed by a recapitalization of profit designed to increase the shares held by original bank founders, but by spring 1994 the bank's leadership was still able to announce that a much tighter approach to crediting bank founders would be followed. Interview with the bank's vice president, 29 April 1994; interview with the chief economist for a founding enterprise, 29 April 1994; see also *Delo* [Samara], 12/3/93, 4, and 3/4–18/94, 4; *Samarskie Izvestiia,* [Samara], 3/16/94, 1.

19. In interviews, a number of bankers involved in distributing centralized loans cited their sense that Central Bank control over their use was minimal, although Central Bank officials tended to assert the opposite. For a discussion of the diverting of earmarked credits and a claim of extremely weak state control in this area by the country's then chief prosecutor, a political opponent of the government, see *Trud* [Moscow], 8/4/93, 2.

20. Burawoy 1994: 591. Representative is a May 1993 government resolution that vested responsibility for return of new government investment loans in a

commercial bank that was supposed to distribute them (*Rossiiskie Vesti,* [Moscow], 5/25/93, 4). Such responsibility is obviously very real. In spring 1994 one Samara bank took out full-page ads in all of the local newspapers to ask to be spared from distributing centralized credits to farmers because of its fear that the credits would not be repaid; for example, *Samaraskie Izvestiia* [Samara], 4/7/94, 7. Bankers also assert that once taxes are taken into account, even central credits clients repay are a money-losing proposition (banks are allowed to charge only 3 percent more per annum on these loans than the rate at which they received the money from the Central Bank.) *Samaraskie Izvestiia* [Samara], 4/7/94, 7; interview with a Samara comercial bank vice president, 29 April 1994.

21. Interview with the chiefs of the Central Bank head office for Samara province (25 April 1994) and Krasnoyarsk territory (June 1994). Also *Business-MN,* no. 18 (11 May 1994): 1; *Delo* [Samara], 3/18/94, 8.

22. At least that is the picture drawn by officials of the new *kaznacheistvo,* or treasury office, still being set up in 1994, which was supposed to improve the federal government's capacity to manage payments. Interviews in Vladivostok, Samara, Krasnoyarsk.

23. One common form of subsidy is low-interest loans distributed through commercial banks the budget is supposed to compensate for the difference between the low interest rate and the one at which they purchase loaned money from the Central Bank. For instance, such a system was supposed to be used for loans to assure seasonal shipments to isolated far northern regions (*Kommersant* [Moscow], no. 28 [1993]: 27). According to the head of the Central Bank office for Krasnoyarsk territory, there were great difficulties getting such compensation monies out of the federal government despite the fact that they had been officially promised (interview, June 1994). For an early example of banks' refusal to distribute low-interest loans because federal budget compensation was not paid on time, see the discussion from a provincial legislature reported in *Materialy dvenadtsatoi sessii Nizhegorodskogo oblastnogo Soveta narodnykh deputatov dvadtsat' pervogo sozyva, 22–23 sentiabria 1992* (Nizhnii Novorod, 1992), 69–71.

24. Calculated from data sources cited for Figure 3.3. Production figures for the first five months of 1993 are from Goskomstat Rossii, *Sotsial'no-ekonomicheskoe polozhenie Rossiiskoi Federatsii v 1993 goda,* no. 6 (1993): 81.

25. The provinces were Samara *oblast'* in European Russia, Krasnoyarsk *krai* in Siberia, and Primorskii *krai* in the Far East. Data from these cases are used in this section and the next to substantiate an argument about processes that are national in scope; some systematic comparisons are made below.

26. The deputy governor of Krasnoyarsk *krai,* who headed the territory's energy committee, disputed the accuracy of these figures, arguing that the power company would not be able to function in such a case; she conceded that occasionally the barter percentage had reached as high as 50 percent (interview, July 1994).

27. With regard to the chemical industry, this factor was cited by a local power company in *Delo* [Samara], 11/12/93.

28. The argument offered here parallels one proposed earlier in Sapir (1993: 42). Sapir drew on Schelling (1960) to explain with coercive deficiency and deter-

rence games what he saw as the prevalence of price restraint in Russian interenterprise relations in circumstances of mutual supplies of weakly substitutable goods.

29. Interview with Samaraenergo officials, April 1994.

30. *Kommersant* [Moscow], no. 5, 2/15/94, 31; interview with deputy governor for the energy and transport sectors, Samara province, April 1994.

31. Interview with official at Samaraenergo, April 1994. Compare *Volzhskaia Kommuna*, (Samara) 2/8/94, 1. For a parallel story from Vladivostok, see *Novosti* [Vladivostok], 10/12/93, 2. Other utilities suppliers find themselves in a similar situation with respect to local authorities; it was reported in 1995, for instance, that some local administrations had used special police units to prevent the natural gas monopoly *Gazprom* from disconnecting its nonpaying customers. *Monitor* (electronic newsletter of the James Foundation) 1, no. 31 (13 June 1995).

32. Interviews at Samaraenergo (April 1994) and Krasnoyarskenergo (July 1994). On the other hand, both power companies had made efforts—in Samara's case, even successful ones—to invoke cutoffs. (Evidence of attempts to invoke cutoffs in Krasnoyarsk comes from a July 1994 interview with the head of the energy commission for Krasnoyarsk *krai*.)

33. Samara power company officials, for instance, were gathering data on world prices for goods made by their major debtors in an effort to convince local authorities of the futility of keeping these plants afloat.

34. If enterprises had not valued their official bank accounts, electricity payments would have evaporated long before they did. Without an official bank account, it is impossible to get a legal loan, and even subsidized loans that arrive on an "arrested" account are transferred immediately to creditors with direct deduction rights. Sachs (1994: 59–60) argues that in deciding whether to go "underground," enterprises must weigh the loss of "some public goods being provided by the government," such as contract enforcement, against the benefits of avoiding taxes. Although Sachs is surely right to argue that the state's inability to provide public goods promotes an exit from the visible money economy, the income elasticity of demand for these public goods may be just as important: some enterprises leave the officially visible money economy because they cannot afford to stay in it. Another potential motive: in informal conversation it is often reported that various rackets now have excellent access to bank account data, which is a good reason to keep one's bank account empty.

35. Interviews at Samaraenergo (April 1994) and Dal'energo (August 1994). For a published example, see *Moskovskie Novosti*, 5/8–15/94, 8.

36. The regulation stems from revisions to the tax code passed by the Supreme Soviet in late 1992 and was confirmed in correspondence from central to local tax authorities; for the law, see *Normativnye akty po finansam, nalogam, strakhovaniiu i bukhgalterskomu uchetu*, no. 2 (1993): 35–36; for confirmations, the same publication, no. 11 (1993): 54; no. 12 (1993): 25. Implementation of this regulation was discussed in an interview (July 1994) with officials of the tax inspectorate, Krasnoyarsk *krai*. They noted that originally this regulation was supposed to have forbidden enterprises to sell below "market" prices; the point was

to avoid the widespread practice of declaring a lower price in tax documents than in actuality. With market prices for many goods unavailable, however, the officials applied a rule of costs plus a fixed profit markup. Extensive evidence reveals the impact of this regulation on enterprise pricing behavior. It was cited in a number of widely separated interviews I conducted, especially by energy system officials unable to cut prices on goods they had received in barter. Former economics minister Andrei Nechaev cited this regulation as a major economic problem in *Moscow News*, 9/2–8/94, 9. Accounting rules increasing amortization leading to increased on-paper production costs drew protests for forcing unsustainable price rises; see *Volzhskaia Kommuna* [Samara], 2/12/94, 1. Finally, the seriousness of the problem was underscored by the issuance of a Presidential Order, published in *Kommersant* [Moscow], no. 31, 8/23/94, 60, which very slightly softens pricing rules. The order allows sale for money below production costs with special prior permission of the tax authorities once there are demonstrable failures at selling the product at the markup price. Barter transactions must take place at the same price as recent money sales or, if there are none, at least at production costs.

37. This should not be surprising since "the seemingly objective facts of contemporary life are themselves shaped by accounting conventions" (Block 1990: 32).

38. Interviews in the industry department for Samara province (May 1994).

39. Interview with city government economic officials in Lesozavodsk, Maritime province (August 1994).

40. The "price" of these goods is actually the amount of ruble-denominated electricity debt that will be canceled. This pricing practice was described by officials at all three power systems studied. Costs plus markup represent a lower boundary set by the fact that these transactions must be official (and therefore must follow the tax rules on pricing discussed earlier) if they are to do the paying enterprises any good in terms of clearing debts on their bank accounts or avoiding fines. Power company officials, however, find it very hard to monitor or affect the prices at which they are transferred goods under barter payments. Krasnoyarskenergo officials reported that they had discovered that many enterprises had multiple prices for their goods, with a special, higher one reserved for the power company. (A sawmill executive in Krasnoyarsk *krai* confirmed this practice.) At Dal'energo no monitoring capacity existed, although plans were in the works to create a new service to deal with this issue. Samaraenergo officials were under the impression that they took in goods at the same prices other customers paid for them.

41. Interviews at Samaraenergo (April 1994) and Krasnoyarskenergo (July 1994).

42. Story and quote from Rosenbaum (1995: 147–151). The goods referred to in the quote remained after the power company had tried to minimize the amount of in-kind debt payment it would have to accept by organizing (under the name of *wechsels*, or promissory notes) what were in essence multilateral barter exchanges between itself and its suppliers. A similar although less organized system was already functioning during my visit in June 1994. Samaraenergo also had a

special commercial section to sell goods received in barter, whereas at Dal'energo this function was handled by the supply division (where "commercial" skills tended to concentrate under the shortage economy). For plans to introduce a similar system for the entire power network, see *Finansovye Izvestiia* [Moscow], 2/17–23/4, 2.

43. These strategies are drawn from interviews with officials at Krasnoyarskenergo (July 1994). I should stress that they themselves did not think of barter as a way of lowering the price of the good; rather, they simply bartered what they were unable to sell for money. Lowering the money price was not an option.

44. Interviews at Samaraenergo (April 1994) and Krasnoyarskenergo (June 1994); interview with livestock feed factory director in Primorskii *krai* (August 1994); interview with Krasnoyarsk deputy governor for economic policy (June 1994); interview with Samara deputy governor for economic policy (May 1994) (in the last two cases the discussion concerned pricing for barter taxes). Since barter that took place at other ratios would in some cases be a tax violation, those I interviewed would have been unlikely to mention it.

45. Åslund (1995: 211) suggests that "the energy enterprises, especially Gazprom, were the last to cut deliveries if they were not paid, because they counted on Chernomyrdin's help." Although, as noted in the section "Moving Moscow: Regional and Sectional Lobbying," the fuel and energy sector was relatively successful in lobbying for central assistance, it is a mistake to suggest that as a result that sector was unconcerned about extracting payment. Immediate payment from a customer is *very* much preferred to the at best eventual and at any rate unreliable compensation from the state described in the preceding section.

46. For representative sentiments along these lines, see *Samarskie Izvestiia* [Samara], 3/12/94, 1; *Delovaia Sibir'* [Novosibirsk], 6/4–10/93, 5; this theme was also constantly raised in my interviews in Vladivostok in fall 1993.

47. See the figures on Dal'energo loans in *Krasnoe Znamia* [Vladovostok], 9/28/93, 1.

48. For an example in Samara province, see *Volzhskaia Kommuna* [Samara], 2/8/94, 1, and *Delo* [Samara], 2/11/94, 1.

49. The directors' discontent focused largely around prices rather than collection of bills; the fact that the anti–power company bias of the new local regime also involved blocking shutdowns when the problem of nonpayments became more acute subsequently became fairly clear (interviews in Vladivostok, October and November 1993, June 1994).

50. The mayor of a small Siberian town made this point rather explicitly in a July 1994 interview; concern for the fate of employees was also cited by the assistant governor for energy and transport, Samara province (May 1994), as a reason not to disconnect the power of those behind in their electricity debts.

51. Interview with the assistant governor for energy and transport, Samara province (May 1994). They have occasionally allowed shutdowns, as in *Delo* [Samara], 8/20/93, 1; here, local enterprises were trying to get the government involved.

52. Deputy Governor V. D. Kuz'min, paraphrased in *Krasnoiarskii Rabochii* [Krasnoyarsk], 5/6/94, 1. Kuz'min confirmed the accuracy of this quote and expanded on his monetary policy views in an interview (June 1994).

53. These are not the only causes, however. According to the head of the State Tax Service, a substantial portion of undercollections by the federal budget in 1994 stemmed from a decision to grant delays in making tax payments to defense enterprises that had not been paid for output produced in response to over-optimistic defense procurement purchasing orders. See *Finansy*, no. 11 (1994): 5. On problems with financing and organizing defense procurement, see *Finansy*, no. 2 (1995): 3–7.

54. This figure somewhat understates undercollections since it refers only to the two most important taxes, the profits tax and the value-added tax. Tax receipts for the federal budget from *Finansy*, no. 9 (1994): 61. The scale of under-collections can also be gauged by the fact that the minister of finance estimates the federal budget losses from direct tax evasion to be much smaller than the losses from undercollections; *Finansy*, no. 12 (1994): 4. For a clear explanation of undercollections see *Segodnia* [Moscow], 7/5/94, 12.

55. Calculated from *Finansy*, no. 11 (1994): 6. For employment figures of these agencies as of 1 January 1994, see *Voprosy Ekonomiki*, no. 1 (1994): 81.

56. Interview with the deputy governor for economic policy, July 1994. For instances of local tax remissions in return for social services supplied by enterprises, see Wallich (1994: 81).

57. This system was the most strongly developed in Samara (interview at Samaraenergo, April 1994), interview with the deputy governor for economic policy, May 1994; and plans were in the works in Krasnoyarsk (interview at Krasnoyarskenergo, July 1994; interview with deputy governor for the wood industry, June 1994). Primorskii province had also accepted taxes in kind (interview with tax inspectorate official, August 1994), but it proved impossible to ascertain the further fate of the goods accepted in this way.

58. The only official interviewed in any of the three provinces who would guess at a figure was the deputy governor for economic policy in Krasnoyarsk, who estimated that 15 to 20 percent of Krasnoyarsk's budget income in the first quarter of 1994 was in kind (interview, July 1994).

59. Tax inspectorate officials in Krasnoyarsk (July 1994) and Vladivostok (August 1994) reported that goods had been accepted only in payment of local portions of taxes.

60. See *Normativnye akty po finansam, nalogam, strakhovaniiu i bukhgalterskomu uchetu (prilozhenie k zhurnalu "Finansy")*, no. 2 (1995): 30–33.

61. Remark made at a government conference call on winter problems, reported in *Segodnia*, 11/25/93, 2.

62. *Segodnia* [Moscow], 12/11/93, 10.

63. In 1994 it became fairly common for salaries to be paid in kind, with workers forced to consume or sell production no one had bought for money.

64. Interview with the deputy governor in charge of energy policy, Krasnoyarsk, July 1994. On the price policy implications of hydroplant privatization, see *Izvestiia* [Moscow], 9/22/93, 4.

65. On privatization of the hydropower plant, see *Delo* [Samara], 5/7/93, 1; 11/10/93, 13. On local leadership's lobbying and the eventual decision to reduce hydroplant power rates for local consumers see *Delo* [Samara], 3/19/93, 1; 12/

31/93, 9; *Volzhskaia Kommuna* [Samara], 3/22/94, 1. For evidence of the Samara leadership's consistent proreform and progovernment image, see *ABV: Ezhene-del'naia Regional'naia Delovaia Gazeta* [Samara], 2/9–15/94, 1; as an example, the governor seriously toned down the angry demands of local industrialists before agreeing to sign an appeal they had drafted to the government; *Volzhskaia Kommuna* [Samara], 2/8/94, 1; *Delo* [Samara], 2/11/94, 1.

66. See *Delovaia Sibir'* [Novosibirsk], 4/9–15/93, 3; *Krasnoiarskii Rabochii* [Krasnoyarsk], 6/10/93, 1; *Izvestiia* [Moscow], 9/22/93, 4; interview with the head of the state property committee for Krasnoyarsk territory, June 1994.

67. On barter, interview at Dal'energo (August 1994); Primor'e had previously been able to barter fish for out-region fuel. On demands for money payment by out-region suppliers, see *Krasnoe Znamia* [Vladivostok], 6/20/94, 1; 2/19/94, 3. By contrast, Krasnoyarsk was able to fuel its coal-fired plants with local coal by organizing barter; interview with the assistant governor for economic policy, June 1994; Samara purchased natural gas for its furnaces by bartering cars from the giant VAZ plant (interview with assistant governor for energy policy, May 1994); by early 194 VAZ's cars were increasingly hard to sell, and the plan seemed likely to come under strain.

68. Calculated from information provided by Dal'energo.

69. In the Maritime province. For a similar functionalist account on the level of the country as a whole, see Murrell (1993: 111–140), where the social organicism is drawn from Hayek. But here the oversimplification is no longer excusable, as the victory of the forces of loose money proved highly transitory.

References

Åslund, Anders. 1995. *How Russia Became a Market Economy*. Washington, D.C.: Brookings Institution.

Bigman, David, and Sergio Pereira Leite. 1993. Enterprise Arrears in Russia: Causes and Policy Options. International Monetary Fund Working Paper. WP/93/61.

Block, Fred. 1990. *Post-Industrial Possibilities: A Critique of Economic Discourse*. Berkeley: University of California Press.

de Boissieu, Christian, Daniel Cohen, and Gaël de Pontbriand. 1993. Gérer la dette interentreprises. *Économie Internationale* 54 (second trimester): 105–120.

Burawoy, Michael. 1994. Why Coupon Socialism Never Stood a Chance in Russia: The Political Conditions of Economic Transition. *Politics and Society* 22 (4): 585–594.

Burawoy, Michael. 1996. The State and Economic Involution—Russia Through a China Lens. *World Development* 24 (6): 1105–1117.

Chaudhry, Kiren Aziz. 1997. *The Price of Wealth: International Capital Flows and the Political Economy of Late Development*. Ithaca, N.Y.: Cornell University Press.

Glasman, Maurice. 1994. The Great Deformation: Polanyi, Poland and the Terrors of Planned Spontaneity. In *The New Great Transformation? Change and*

Continuity in East-Central Europe, edited by C. G. A. Bryant and E. Mokrzycki. London: Routledge.

Gourevitch, Peter. 1986. *Politics in Hard Times.* Ithaca, N.Y.: Cornell University Press.

Hammond, Bray. 1957. *Banks and Politics in America from the Revolution to the Civil War.* Princeton: Princeton University Press.

Hanson, Philip. 1994. The Center Versus the Periphery in Russian Economic Policy. *RFE-RL Research Report* 3 (17): 23–28.

Helf, Gavin. 1994. *All the Russians: Center, Core and Periphery in Soviet and Post-Soviet Russia.* Unpublished dissertation: University of California at Berkeley.

Hellman, Joel. 1993. *Breaking the Bank: Bureaucrats and the Creation of Markets in a Transitional Economy.* Unpublished dissertation: Columbia University.

Holtfrerich, Carl-Ludwig. 1989. *The Monetary Unification Process in Nineteenth-Century Germany: Relevance and Lessons for Europe Today. In A European Central Bank? Perspectives on Monetary Unification after Ten Years of the EMS,* ed. M. D. Cecco and A. Giovanni. Cambridge: Cambridge University Press.

Humphrey, Caroline. 1985. Barter and Economic Disintegration. *Man (n.s.)* 21 (4): 48–72.

Ickes, Barry W., and Randi Ryterman. 1992. The Interenterprise Arrears Crisis in Russia. *Post-Soviet Affairs* 8 (4): 331–361.

Kornai, János. 1986. The Soft Budget Constraint. *Kyklos* 39 (1): 3–30.

Lipton, David, and Jeffrey Sachs. 1992. Prospects for Russia's Economic Reforms. In *Brookings Papers on Economic Activity* (2): 213–283.

Luebbert, Gregory M. 1991. *Liberalism, Fascism, or Social Democracy.* London: Oxford University Press.

Murrell, Peter. 1993. What is Shock Therapy? What Did It Do in Poland and Russia? *Post-Soviet Affairs* 9 (2): 111–140.

Nelson, Joan. 1993. The Politics of Economic Transformation: Is Third World Experience Relevant in Eastern Europe? *World Politics* 45 (3): 441–460.

Odling-Smee, John, and Henri Lorie. 1993. The Economic Reform Process in Russia. International Monetary Fund Working Paper. WP/93/55.

Olson, Mancur, Jr. 1965. *The Logic of Collective Action: Public Goods and the Theory of Groups.* New York: Schocken.

Polanyi, Karl. 1965. *The Great Transformation: The Political and Economic Origins of Our Time.* Boston: Beacon.

Rosenbaum, Andrew. 1995. A Land of Buried Treasure. *Euromoney* (April): 147–151.

Rostowski, Jacek. 1993. The Inter-enterprise Debt Explosion in the Former Soviet Union: Causes, Consequences, Cures. *Communist Economies and Economic Transformation* 5 (2): 131–159.

Sachs, Jeffrey. 1994. Russia's Struggle with Stabilization: Conceptual Issues and Evidence. *World Bank Research Observer,* Annual Conference Supplement: 57–80.

Sapir, Jacques. 1993. "Inflation, stabilisation et dynamiques régionales en Russie: Analyse des trajectoires macroéconomiques et de leurs fondements micro et mésoéconomiques." Paris: Centre d'Études des Modes d'Industrialisation.

―――. 1994. Conversion of Russian Defense Industries: A Macroeconomic and Regional Perspective. In *Privatization, Conversion, and Enterprise Reform in Russia*, ed. M. McFaul and T. Perlmutter. Boulder: Westview.

Schelling, Thomas. 1960. *The Strategy of Conflict*. Cambridge: Harvard University Press.

Schumpeter, Joseph. 1991. The Crisis of the Tax State. In *The Economics and Sociology of Capitalism*, ed. R. Swedberg. Princeton: Princeton University Press.

Shafranik, Iu. K., A. G. Kozyrev, and A. L. Samusev. 1994. TEK v usloviiakh krizisa [The fuel and energy complex in crisis conditions]. *Eko: Ekonomika i organizatsiia promyshlennogo proizvodstva* 1: 63–74.

Simmel, Georg. 1990. *The Philosophy of Money*. Tr. Tom Bottomore and David Frisby from a first draft by Kaethe Mengelberg. Second enlarged ed. London: Routledge.

Wallich, Christine. 1994. Intergovernmental Finances: Stabilization, Privatization, and Growth. In *Russia and the Challenge of Fiscal Federalism*, ed. C. Wallich. Washington, D.C.: World Bank.

Weber, Max. 1978. *Economy and Society: An Outline of Interpretive Sociology*, ed. G. Roth and C. Wittich. Berkeley: University of California Press.

Zhuravlev, Sergei. 1992. Ideal'naia institutsional'no-psikhologicheskaia sreda dlia 'plohkhogo' nachala reform v Rossii [The ideal institutional-psychological environment for a 'bad' start to reform in Russia]. *Informatsionnyi Biulleten' Rabochego Tsentra Ekonomicheskikh Reform* [Moscow] (3): 2–10.

4

Slick Salesmen and Simple People: Negotiated Capitalism in a Privatized Polish Firm

Elizabeth Dunn

When privatization plans based on neoliberal economic theory were introduced into Eastern Europe, they were supposed to catalyze a chain reaction that would transform both the economy and society. Privatization was supposed, above all, to create owners with *interests*—a personal stake in the success or failure of the enterprise (Staniszkis 1992). Because these owners would have personal interests, they would be forced to adopt modern, efficient business practices or face going out of business. According to the logic of the neoliberals, this plan would remedy socialism's inefficiencies in both production and distribution and would create enterprises that would be competitive on the global market. One of the most significant means developed for promoting this adoption of "modern" business practices was capital privatization, the sale of a state-owned enterprise to a transnational corporation based in the West. Transnational firms were supposed to transfer both financial capital and know-how to state-owned enterprises (Kozminski 1993: 35). A neoliberal take on privatization might also assume that once these practices were brought to Eastern Europe they would quickly become hegemonic because of the combination of market pressures and their obviously superior efficiency.

In this chapter I look at a firm that, at first glance, could be a poster child for neoliberal privatization programs. Alima-Gerber (AG), a formerly state-owned fruit and vegetable processor purchased by Gerber Baby Foods in 1992, has instituted a wide variety of practices taken straight from U.S. management such as quality assurance, flexible labor practices (including contract labor and outsourcing), marketing and sales techniques, and employee training. Yet, on closer inspection, these techniques are less powerful than they might appear. Despite the intentions of those who institute the techniques, their effects are often blunted, transmuted, or compromised. The case of AG shows that neither private ownership nor the introduction of U.S. business practices, with associated ideologies of persons and their relationships, necessarily means transferring whole and intact a certain form of organization from the West. Rather, these practices and ideologies are filtered through local cultural formations and historical experiences. They can then be constantly negotiated in those terms. In a manner similar to the way decollectivized agricultural land becomes "fuzzy property" in Romania (Verdery, chapter 2, this volume), privatized firms and their management practices in Poland become "fuzzy" arenas for dispute and interpretation rather than imposed structures identical to those found in the West.

The Transformation of Alima

The transformation of Alima is a result of privatization, the sale to Gerber, and Gerber's attempt to introduce its own management techniques in Poland. Four of the most significant practices Gerber brought to Alima are quality control, marketing and sales techniques, a plan for restructuring the labor force, and a sales technique called "image marketing." All of these practices have arisen from Gerber's strategic vision for the firm.

Alima is a small fruit and vegetable processing plant in Rzeszów in southeastern Poland. It was one of the first firms sold by the Ministry of Privatization under right-wing Minister Janusz Lewandowski in early 1992. Although multiple firms bid on Alima, Lewandowski and his aides chose Gerber to take over Alima particularly because of Gerber's knowledge of sales and marketing issues such as niche marketing and brand management.[1]

After Gerber acquired Alima, it began making extensive changes. The firm sent a management team from Fremont, Michigan, to restructure the plant and to institute new procedures. Alima-Gerber's new strategy was to increase consumption of its products by making high-quality goods aimed at niche markets. Improving quality meant, first, renovating the physical plant and adding both a new baby food line and quality control laboratories. It also meant introducing stringent quality control protocols that involved numerous tests—each specified in excruciating detail—on every batch of product. The data from each test are entered onto a report form, which is then sent to the quality control labs. A full set of test results for one batch of product often exceeds eighty pages.

Reshaping Alima also meant making significant changes in the number and composition of the labor force. Although Alima's management had already substantially reduced the labor force while preparing for privatization,[2] the new management of Alima-Gerber sought even further reductions. Under a system of voluntary and compensated layoffs, 474 employees left the firm—about one-third of the total (Klimczak 1994). At the same time, AG also decided to outsource many of its services. Laundry, cafeteria, cleaning, and security personnel were given the choice of accepting the layoff or moving to the shop floor, and their service jobs were given to employees of independent contractors. Since the number of shop-floor workers accepting the layoff exceeded management's expectations, it also hired contract labor for the shop floor.[3] Outsourcing and contract labor gave the firm the ability to adapt the size of the labor force to changes in production that resulted either from the agricultural season or changes in the product line (producing pineapple juice, for example, takes fewer laborers than apple juice, which is made from apples rather than from imported concentrate). At the same time the layoffs were being planned, the firm hired a significant number of new, full-time employees. These new employees were sales representatives in cities all over Poland or marketing department employees in both Rzeszów and Warsaw. No employees from production were moved into these jobs, and only a few employees from other divisions were moved to either sales or marketing.

Finally, Gerber brought the idea of niche or image marketing to Alima. When Gerber first took over Alima, the company recognized that the domestic market would buy too little of the existing baby food or children's juice lines to make the enterprise profitable. The first answer to that problem was to try exporting to foreign markets: products for Russia and the Czech Republic, a line of puddings for the French market, and foods approved by religious authorities for Israel and the Middle East. Export was never a successful strategy; however, Gerber discontinued all export to Western Europe from Poland, and export to other regions did not make up the shortfall. Meanwhile, the expensive machinery and laboratory equipment were not being amortized. The high-tech production facility in division 4, for example, sat idle roughly 50 percent of the time (excluding nights and weekends).[4]

In response to this dilemma, AG devised another strategy. Whereas growth in the baby food market was slow, growth in the beverage market was skyrocketing. Poles consumed 197 percent more juice in 1995 than they had in 1992. Although 1995 per capital consumption had reached 7.9 liters, AG officials believed that as Poles obtained more disposable income their consumption could reach average Western European levels (15 liters per capita per year) or even German levels (38 liters per capita).[5] Alima had a long history of experience making juices for children. The company's Bobo Frut brand juices for infants had been produced since the 1960s and were widely acknowledged to be a superior product, even under socialism. The Junior Frut juices for toddlers and older children, introduced in the early 1990s, were not an overwhelming financial success but were also known as a good product. The juice market for small children, however, had lower growth potential: AG already controlled about 80 percent of the market. Instead, AG decided to attempt to resegment the domestic market to sell a new product. Frugo, a new juice drink, was aimed at thirteen- to eighteen-year-olds, the age group with the lowest per capital consumption of juices. To sell this product more effectively to teens, marketers attempted to create a new social identity that (the ads implied) could be purchased along with the product. The image was one of a dynamic, mobile, fashionable young person. As an employee from the marketing division explained, "A product for everybody is a product for nobody. Nobody identifies with it. That's why Frugo is aimed especially at youth. Frugo will be a part of the young world like no other brand. It will be a fragment of their culture."

The management practices brought in by Gerber were lauded in the press and displayed as a mark of the firm's successful transformation. Yet, the process was not so simple. As I discovered, Gerber's management practices were substantially changed as they were moved to Alima.

Capitalism in the Vernacular

Despite Gerber's attempts to transfer its management techniques to Alima intact, they continue to be articulated through local cultural beliefs and historical experiences. This situation results in part from a shift in management: the U.S. managers have been phased out and replaced with Poles, most of whom have extensive experience in the United States or with U.S. firms (Barlik 1996). By the time I arrived at Alima in 1995 to do field research, I was the only American working in the firm full-time.

Although many local cultural schemata are used to translate U.S. management practices, the most significant is a dichotomy between socialism and capitalism. Many related terms are grouped under these headings in a manner similar to the dichotomy Ladislav Holy (1992) found in Czechoslovakia. There, the planned economy is associated with stagnation, irrationality, and ideological constructions subject to politics, whereas the market economy is associated with civilization, modernity, development, rationality, and pragmatism. Similarly, a number of related terms are grouped together at Alima.

Socialism	*Capitalism*
Backwardness	Modernity, civilization
Stasis	Dynamism, movement
Inadaptability	Flexibility
Age	Youth

Drabness	Colorfulness
Deprivation	Satisfaction of wants
Obedience	Critical self-reflection
Collectivism	Individualism
Gifts	Sales
Personalized relationships based on "connections"	Impersonal relations based on rational calculation

These dichotomies are reiterated through many management practices and are mapped onto persons to create differences among them (Martin 1992). Whereas some kinds of people are constructed as young, modern, and dynamic, others are made out to be old, passive, and incapable of changing to meet new circumstances.

One iteration of this phenomenon was seen in the advertising campaigns for Frugo, a new drink for teenagers. Describing the genesis of the marketing strategy at the Frugo launch party, the advertisers and marketers depicted the situation as if there were a well-defined group with an unfulfilled need. From the advertisements, however, it was not clear that this group or its need existed prior to the product. To sell the product, then, the advertisements had to define the target group—teens—as a distinct social entity (see also Mintz 1982: 158). Distinguishing teens from babies and toddlers was easy: AG removed all traces of the Gerber name from the product, except for a small company name and address on the back of the label, and ensured that when the product was put in stores it was placed on shelves next to soft drinks and juices for adults rather than on the Gerber racks. Distinguishing teens from adults was a knottier problem. The Frugo advertisements showed a youngster dressed in fashionably baggy clothes, spray-painting graffiti, set against a dynamic background of color and noise. In contrast, the advertisements also showed images of static, drab, fat adults. These images of adults were essentially caricatures of the socialist life world; in one commercial, for example, the adult is a fat woman in black clothes and a beret, sitting against a red background. She says aggressively, "Fruit? They want fruit? When I was young, we often lacked *beets!* And they're asking for fruit!" Such images indexed and mocked the ideas of noble suffering and sacrifices for a radiant future contained in socialist ideology and propaganda.[6] They also indexed qualities such as drabness, passivity, immobility, and unresponsiveness to needs and desires, all of which are imputed to the socialist system.

Critical to this strategy was the creation of difference: if both the product and the targeted consumer were not somehow "different" from others, this specialized product would not be needed. As anthropologist Sidney Mintz writes (1982: 158), "Making the product 'right' for the consumer requires continuous redefinition and division of the groups in which he, as an individual consumer, defines himself. The deliberate postulation of new groups . . . helps to impart reality to what are supposedly new needs."

In hiring and training sales representatives at AG, a similar image marketing strategy of redefinition and division of groups occurs: in which one group of employees is assigned the qualities of capitalism, whereas others are deemed products of socialism. Sales representatives are hired to fill vacancies in a department that has existed only since 1993. They are believed to have special qualities that make them different from other employees and similar to the product they sell; they are supposedly dynamic, agile, and assertive, which also makes them fit for a new department and a new kind of firm. I saw how this "sales representative" identity was created when I sat in on a day of job interviews for a vacancy in Lublin. All of the nine candidates for the position were men and, with one exception, were under age thirty.[7] The interviewing team, which included the district manager and the director of sales, was led by Irena, a psychologist and the firm's recruitment specialist.

Irena began by asking the candidates what they were looking for in a job and how they envisioned a day's work. Without exception, all nine candidates responded that they wanted to be sales representatives because they liked *ruch,* movement or circulation, and abhorred the idea of sitting behind a desk. Then Irena asked them about their job experience. Most had already been in four or five jobs despite the fact that they had graduated from university only four or five years ago. Short job tenure did not bother Irena. She told me later that not only is it typical for people to have worked six months here and five months there but that she never expects sales representatives to stay for long; keeping the 100 sales rep jobs filled is a full-time job for her.

After the last candidate left, the four of us discussed, analyzed, and compared the job seekers. Irena was partial to a man she called "the rugby player." In her opinion, his athleticism made him a desirable candidate since he would have the strength, aggression, and dynamism needed in a sales representative. Irena dismissed another candidate as too quiet and still; she said she felt he was "hiding something." The interview process is designed to allow Irena to make such judgments about the personality and predisposition of the candidates. According to her, experience in this type of work is less important than predisposition. You can train someone to sell, she said, but you cannot train them to have more energy, to move faster, or to be extroverted.

The idea of internal dispositions as a critical element of sales representatives is reinforced in the training they receive. Each new hire is shown a video about how to be a sales representative. The video focuses on self-presentation: how to make internal dispositions such as vitality, friendliness, and self-confidence manifest through dress, speech, and body language. The aim is to convert these internal qualities into physical activity that will elicit another form of activity—purchase—from wholesalers and grocery store managers.

Later, all of the sales reps are invited to an annual two-day sales training seminar at which topics such as negotiation skills, creative thinking, and business ethics are taught. The point of the training is not, however, to transfer a certain body of facts. Instead, through a set of simulations, games, exercises, and explanations of human psychology, sales representatives are asked to examine their "mentalities," to search within their character and transform their thinking. In this way, they supposedly become more intensely energetic, mobile, and outgoing and more effectively externalize these qualities so as to display them to potential customers.

The sales reps and the company together engage in a form of image or niche marketing parallel to that used in the Frugo advertising. First, in the hiring process the sales reps sell themselves; like the product, which is supposed to transfer its qualities to the consumer, the sales reps bill themselves as employees who will transfer their qualities to both firm and product. The firm uses them to construct a mimetic relationship among firm, product, employee, and consumer. As the assistant director of sales told a group of new sales reps, "Trust in, and the opinion of, our products are [conveyed] through your persons" (*Ufność i opinia naszych productów są przez wasze osoby*). Another sales manager told his reps, "A sales representative is a calling card from our firm." Jarek and Mietek, two sales representatives from Warsaw, emphasized to me that they are truly the company's representatives and that their appearance, demeanor, and actions create images of the company and its products in the minds of the clients. The formal job description says that sales reps' duties include "developing and maintaining the trust and faith of clients through pleasant and friendly relations and an elegant look." The goal of all this is to create another sort of identity between the sales representatives and the product: if the sales reps move quickly, circulate among clients, and elicit trust and goodwill from them, the product will also circulate quickly through the store. The product will come in from the firm, pass through the store, and go out the door in customers' bags, whereas money will trace the path in reverse, thus hastening the circulation of capital.

As in the Frugo commercials, the niche as sales reps for these dynamic people is created in opposition to an image of other people as static and uncomprehending. In this case, the foil is the shop-floor worker, who is seen as the antithesis of the sales representative. In one of the job interviews the candidate mentioned that in another firm he had worked for,

production workers were given the option of interviewing for sales representative jobs. AG's director of sales and the Lublin area manager were
clearly horrified by this idea, saying that the characters of the two jobs
are far too different for people to move between them. The director commented that because the two jobs are so different in character, the people
in the positions must also have different characters; hence, switching between the two jobs is impossible.[8]

When I asked Alima employees in other departments such as sales,
marketing, and operations why shop-floor workers could not be moved
to other jobs within the corporation or could not be organized in such a
way that they took greater responsibility for production, the response
was inevitably "they are simple people" *(One są proste ludzi). Proste* carries a variety of meanings: although it literally means "uncomplicated"
or "straightforward," it is often a euphemism for "unintelligent." This
view of the workers as unthinking—or incapable of thought—permeates
the production process, particularly in the quality assurance protocols.
Shop-floor workers do conduct some of the tests on products at various
stages of the production process. Strict written protocols exist for how
these tests should be conducted since, as a quality control manager told
sales representatives, "people can forget how to do the tests, or they can
forget to do them. They might feel bad or have a quarrel or something
and forget the tests or do them wrong. That's why we have directions on
the report pages and why there are directions in the binders at each station." (No similar directions are written out for sales reps or for the president of the company, although presumably they might also have bad days
or quarrels.) Moreover, even the shop-floor workers who do the tests are
not permitted or required to analyze the data received or to make changes
in the production process. In general, any decisions about the quality of
the product or the production process must be made after samples have
been sent to the quality control laboratories for testing and a manager
has made a decision about adjustments to the production process, which
can take days.

A view of workers as merely physical labor, not thinking beings, also
shows up in the training procedures for shop-floor workers. Rather than
being trained in "thinking skills" or interpersonal relations, shop-floor
workers in general attend only two types of training: an occupational
health and safety class mandated by the Polish government and classes
for training and certification on the operation of different kinds of machinery. The courses are cursory and aim at delivering a specific body of
minute and detailed facts. For example, whereas the in-class exercises for
sales representatives ask them to rate their "reactions to conflict and dis-
agreement," the examination for the occupational health and safety
course asks, "After working four hours, how many minutes is a break?"

and provides multiple-choice answers. Workers who take the course and who must pass the examination to keep their jobs are allowed to cheat. When I took the exam, the members of my brigade circulated a list of the question numbers and the letters of the correct answers during the test. The health and safety inspector saw what was happening and even encouraged it—if one of us lost track of the number-letter correspondences and marked down the wrong answer, he corrected it before the paper was handed in. In this way, workers are deemed incapable not only of critical thinking, self-reflection, and making decisions but also of understanding even simple concepts and memorizing facts.

The lack of self-reflection and thought employees outside the shop floor attribute to shop-floor workers also leads them to categorize production workers as unable to understand changes in the economy and therefore in business practice, which, in turn, makes them unfit for other jobs in the company. Shop-floor workers are not just subsumed under a Fordist separation of mental and manual laborers (Braverman 1974)—which would be strange enough in a factory that professes to carry out flexible production. They are constructed as products of the socialist system who are unable to adapt to changing economic conditions precisely *because* they lack the ability to think. For example, a member of the marketing department said, "These old people who worked here before, they don't understand the need for marketing. Marketing only started in 1993, and it was never in Poland before then. These people on production used to only have to produce as much as they could; they never had to worry about selling it. They didn't understand then why marketing was needed, and they don't understand now." Here, the marketer equated work experience, location within the domain of production rather than distribution, lack of understanding, and the socialist system.

Although no one actually calls the shop-floor workers "socialist" in the sense of members of a political party (especially since many were affiliated with Solidarity), they are clearly associated with "the way things were before" and the inefficiencies of the socialist system. One such affiliation was seen in the general belief that shop-floor workers are older than other employees, even though a survey I conducted showed that the average worker on the line was only about thirty-three—just slightly older than the cutoff age for newly hired sales representatives, which is thirty. As one former manager told me, shop-floor workers are capable only of taking orders because "the U.S. touchy-feely 'I'm not your boss, I'm your coach, we're a team' thing doesn't work with people who are used to being order receivers. As long as a vertical hierarchy is kept in place, it works okay. But modern management doesn't work with these older people. They grew up in a different system. You can't reconvert forty or fifty years of a person's life." The image of shop-floor workers as "older" reflects not their chronological ages but the fact that they began to work at a younger age rather than continuing in the educational system, so even thirty-five-year-olds had fifteen years of experience working under the socialist system. Thus, calling them "older" is a way of tying them to the socialist era.

Another way of constituting the workers as "persons of socialism," if not socialists, is to talk about their unwillingness to excel or take risks. The personnel manager, for example, told me that it is extremely difficult to get shop-floor workers to accept the idea of bonuses or salary differentials based on merit because they are used to collectivism. "Do you love individualism as an American?" he asked me. "The people here [on production] don't. They fear it, fear being alone. For them, being part of the mass is strength." This association with masses and collectives indexes the politics of the socialist era. One of the failings of socialism, the manager believes, was that it did not recognize individual talents or initiative. In a study he conducted, the personnel manager found that 60 percent of Alima workers did not work independently. He said this meant there was no way to reward or encourage those people who did excellent work—so no one did any.

The qualities (and lack thereof) assigned to persons by management ideology reflect the dichotomy between socialism and capitalism. The Frugo advertisements contrasted images of immobile, backward, old socialist persons with a young, dynamic, mobile one. Descriptions of shop-floor workers and sales representatives also contrast socialism and capitalism: on the one hand there are people associated with production, backwardness, a lack of critical or analytic thought, collective consciousness, and an inability to innovate; on the other hand there are highly mobile, active, modern individualists associated with sales who continually learn because of their self-awareness. The set of ideas associated with forty years of socialism is mapped onto persons so they become embodiments of "the way things used to be." Just as advocates of a market economy believed socialism was unreformable, shop-floor workers are seen as untrainable and unchangeable (Kornai 1992: xxv; cf. Martin 1992). In management ideologies, shop floor workers' only flexibility lies in their aggregate number within the firm: they can be hired or fired to change the size of the labor force.[9]

A view of shop-floor workers that sees them as untrainable, whether because of disposition or lack of native intelligence, is an integral part of flexible production in multinational firms. As Melissa Wright (1996, chapter 3) points out in her study of the Mexican maquiladoras owned by U.S. firms, for some workers to be constituted as "trainable" others must be made "untrainable." In the post-Fordist organization of production within multinational corporations, "unskilled" workers are "the uniform constant for reading everyone else as comparatively more skilled and legitimately more powerful" (Wright 1996: 200). In a similar manner, for some employees to have "dispositions" that make them more amenable to sales, some other group of workers has to be classified as lacking those traits. This phenomenon shows up clearly in the new job evaluation system designed during my time at AG, which was directly related to issues of salary. Under this system each job is evaluated against criteria such as the education, creativity, responsibility, teamwork, decisionmaking requirements, physical strength, difficulty of work conditions, and dexterity required to do the job. Points are assigned to each category. According to the director of personnel, this is an *objective* means of determining the concrete value of each job to the firm, in contrast to the *political* criteria used under the socialist system (see also Kopertynska 1995; Oleksyn 1995; and Gick, Tarczynska, and Bernat 1995). Not surprisingly, the post of "production worker" receives the fewest points. Except for difficulty of work conditions, physical strength necessary, and monotony, "production worker" is the baseline against which all other categories are measured.

These ideological constructs might be dismissed as irrelevant if the material stakes involved were not so high. As AG's personnel manager observed, the point of these systems is to legitimate differences in pay in an "objective" manner and to avoid controversy (see also Oleksyn 1995: 20). He added, "People have to understand the disproportions in pay now. Salary has to be an individual secret, but I can't be ashamed of earning more than another person if I'm good. People have to understand, simply, why some people earn more than others. They have to understand that others get more because they have more education, experience, and merit." Merit, of course, is defined in ways that disadvantage shopfloor workers.

These workers do not simply accept such differences, however, or leave them undisputed. Using their own concepts of the experience of socialism, they challenge the definitions of themselves as *proste* and inflexible and seek other bases on which to determine the allocation of resources within the firm. They reinterpret socialism in an attempt to break up the associations that put them at a disadvantage in the present while appropriating parts of the powerful new ideology of Western business.

Alternate Interpretations of Socialism

Because the new management techniques being instantiated at AG are filtered through the culturally constructed dichotomy between socialism and capitalism, arguments against them can be made by discussing the meaning and interpretation of the terms the dichotomy encompasses. That is, the dichotomy does not go unchallenged; the terms within it are often recategorized and used to dispute management practices. This challenge is intentional on the part of shop-floor workers, who argue that their experience under socialism makes them *better* workers for a capitalist firm than those with no socialist history because they can more quickly adjust to batch production and create higher-quality products. In this way, they reinterpret "socialism" as a symbol and recontextualize it so that arguments about the character of socialist production become disputes about the organization of capitalist production. Such reconfigurations and negotiations go on constantly, and they disrupt the company's attempts to institute U.S. management techniques.

During my first few days at AG I asked Ula, one of the union representative, if she believed what I had heard in Warsaw, that workers who worked under socialism cannot change and cannot adapt to the new requirements of capitalist enterprises. She responded, "What do they think we did all these years? We built this firm, we built this Poland under socialism! What was there before here, after the war—nothing. The lumpenproletariat, who didn't work, weren't many. We all worked hard to build this factory, to build Poland. So they can't tell us we don't know what we are doing, that we have nothing to contribute. You can't say that all was bad under socialism. What was bad under socialism will be bad under capitalism, and it has to go. What was good under socialism will be good now, and it has to stay." I asked what was good and what had to stay. She replied, "Well, everything. This was a really good firm. It's not like there wasn't an economy under socialism. We made profits, and that has to stay. There don't have to be many changes here, because this was the best firm in Poland." Ula's lecture significantly complicates the idea that what was socialist was inefficient and bad and what is capitalist is necessarily better. She, like many other workers, believes parts of the way work was organized under socialism are, in fact, suitable for use under the new constraints of the capitalist enterprise. Workers with long experience, she asserts, are not merely repositories of "bad habits" but have expertise that can make the firm successful as a capitalist enterprise.

I saw this expertise during my stint in AG's division 4, which produces either baby foods or Frugo. Baby foods for Russia, Saudi Arabia, Israel, and Kuwait, as well as Poland, came off the line on the days we made baby food. During one shift we often made four or five different kinds of baby food, each destined for a different market. Even if we made only carrot-beef baby food all day, the recipe and the packaging had to be changed between batches since, as everyone assured me, each nationality has "different tastes," and Polish babies will not eat food made for American babies.[10] Often, however, we had to do more than change recipes;

we had to shut down the line after a small batch of forty or fifty thousand jars, wash everything, reset all of the machinery, and begin production of a completely new product. Depending on the degree of change (meats to fruits takes longer to switch since new machines must be brought on-line, and changing bottle sizes entails having mechanics move parts on all of the machinery), we could have the line down and back up again in under thirty minutes. In all, the division 4 brigades could produce forty-one different kinds of baby food and four kinds of Frugo, not including different recipes for the same product.

This kind of small batch production with extremely quick changeover times is a hallmark of flexible specialization in production (Piore and Sabel 1984). I marveled at how, as the last bottle of a batch passed each station, the workers in my brigade could quickly clean their machines, reset them, and move to whatever stations the next batch called for without being directed by supervisors. Workers moved quickly from sterilizer to pasteurizer, for example, when we switched from meats to fruit. Workers who were no longer needed at their stations were quickly dispatched to the vegetable-processing area to peel carrots or potatoes or to another division to begin fermentation testing on finished juice products. When I commented to Jolanta, my brigade supervisor, on how smoothly the changeovers went, she replied, "Oh yes! These are universal people—our brigade workers can do any job in this factory." This "universalism" is a means for production workers to defend their jobs against both lay-offs and being replaced at prestigious stations by lower-paid temporary workers. They constantly assert that although unskilled laborers might be able to replace workers with years of experience at certain tasks, there is no way unskilled labor could ever replace them at the full range of the various tasks they are called on to perform. In making this kind of assertion the core workers adopt much of the language of flexibility and mobility management and the sales reps call on as their own ideological justification: the ability to move quickly between tasks and to adapt to changing conditions without wasting time.

The production workers do not ground their assertions of flexibility in their individual characters, however, or in terms of Western management jargon, as do the sales representatives. Instead, they call on their histories as production workers under socialism. Jolanta, a supervisor, explained that before Gerber bought Alima, Alima made literally hundreds of different products, not only juices for babies but also ketchups, jams, canned dinners, frozen vegetables, and fruit-based liqueurs. The constant shifts in production had little to do with consumer demand but instead were driven by the kind of produce being delivered to Alima by local farmers. Since Alima was bound to accept all of the produce grown by contracting farmers, no matter what its quality, products were constantly being developed to take advantage of the available produce. (Liqueur, for example, was a way to use fruit that had been delivered rotten and that was therefore no longer suitable for consumption by children.) Jolanta asserted that the constant shifts in the production array made workers highly flexible; since they had to switch jobs all the time, they learned a wide variety of skills and could move quickly between tasks.

Here, then, is a set of traits presented in the language of "flexibility," an ideology with great power in the firm. Yet, it is a different kind of flexibility from that of the sales representatives. The sales reps base their assertions of flexibility on their *specialization,* especially on the specialization of their characters and personalities. The production workers, on the other hand, use historical experience to assert that their *generalism* makes them flexible. The sales reps, whose claims to special efficacy are based on personality characteristics, also base their claims on their *individuality*—their uniqueness, competitiveness, and ability (or need) to work alone. This contrasts starkly with the shop-floor workers' claims to flexibility based on the *interchangeability* of experienced workers within and among the brigades.

Shop-floor workers base their claims to flexibility and interchangeability on the continuity of their work community. Core workers argue that since they have worked together for so many years, they are uniquely suited to smooth over the difficulties and irregularities of production by coordinating their labor among themselves. This ideology often sets them in conflict with the firm's managers, almost all of whom came to AG after privatization and who lack experience in the community. These managers try to increase workers' productivity and flexibility by setting up competition between individuals, whether through merit bonuses for good evaluations or by individual quotas on tasks such as fermentation testing. Permanent full-time shop-floor workers see this policy as divisive and counterproductive since it will make it impossible or impractical for them to help one another, thereby breaking apart the community, limiting interchangeability, and impeding the smooth flow of work. Danka, a worker with fifteen years' experience, told me that once individual merit bonuses were put into effect, mutual aid among workers would end. "Then nothing will get done around here," she snorted (cf. Humphrey and Ashwin, chapters 1 and 8, this volume).

It is debatable whether the historical experience of socialism makes workers somehow more flexible. Certainly, the kind of flexibility required by socialism was different from that required by capitalist production since socialist production required adaptation to uneven quality and supply of inputs rather than to consumer demand.[11] What is significant here, however, is that shop-floor workers reconstitute socialism (as both a social and an economic system) as a symbol in the present. They refit specific aspects of state socialism and historical experience into a new context that disrupts the dichotomy proposed by management. Production workers do so to challenge the system that devalues them and their labor and to renegotiate the terms under which they are evaluated. Workers do not argue that socialism or the socialist organization of production was wonderful; rather, they argue that the experience of socialism's constraints makes them better workers for a capitalist enterprise. Rather than accept a division of mental and manual labor that constitutes them as inflexible, they assert that their experiences and their responses to constraints constituted a flexible response to an inflexible situation (cf. Burawoy and Lukács 1992).

In doing so, workers represent a form of expertise that allows them to regain at least some modicum of control over their labor, their bodies, and their work lives. For example, both Wright (1996) and Aihwa Ong (1987) report that in subsidiaries of multinational firms in Mexico and Malaysia such heavy pressure exists to extract labor value from every minute that workers are not allowed to go on bathroom breaks without permission. Their work is stringently supervised, and even detailed hand movements are specified and monitored. Such tactics have been attempted at AG, including a "bathroom registration" book to determine if certain employees are taking too many breaks. But workers and their immediate supervisors (most of whom are former colleagues with many years of experience in the firm) often subvert these restrictions. For example, when a juice bottler named Malgosia was pregnant, the shift supervisor allowed her to move to a station at which she inspected bottles passing down the line and helped to pull a bottle a minute off for statistical sampling. This job had two main advantages: it was the closest to the restroom, and since three women worked at this station, someone could cover for her if she needed to leave her station briefly. Such a situation is possible only when shop-floor workers are seen as having control over their own bodies, as flexible enough to move from station to station, and as able to coordinate the demands of the task among themselves. Malgosia did not register her absences in the "break book."

Workers throughout the plant often arrange to cover for one another while they smoke a cigarette, have a drink, or attend to personal needs. Shift supervisors and shop forepersons, who have the most years of experience, know that their subordinates understand the production process and can coordinate the work themselves, so they turn a blind eye.[12] After several weeks in which they are ignored by workers and only half-heartedly enforced by shift supervisors, disciplinary technologies such as the break book vanish—until the next time they are reincarnated by managers higher up. During six months in division 1, I never witnessed a new disciplinary policy that was consistently enforced, although several were introduced. This is a strong contrast to what many authors describe in the maquiladoras and Asian assembly plants.[13] I never saw at AG the kind of bodily control seen there—including not only elaborate rules about where people can be on the shop floor but also managers physically readjusting workers' bodies.

Similarly, workers often construct a kind of expertise that allows them to take control of the production process to some degree rather than ceding it entirely to the quality control process. In division 1, which has a juice bottling line, workers rely on their sense of experience and community to control the line speed. As in most production lines, not all of the machines produce at the same rate. The capper can cap more bottles per hour than the packer can pack, for example. This unevenness is a serious problem on the juice line because if a machine at the end of the line slows down and backs the line up to the pasteurizer, hundreds of bottles that are filled but not pasteurized can sit too long in the machine or sit on the line waiting to be pasteurized. Those bottles become contaminated microbiologically and must be thrown away. Hence, the workers running the packer, labeler, pasteurizer, capper, and filler must all be attentive to the speed at which the others are producing, watching for production problems and adjusting the speed at which their machines are running. This situation is complicated by the fact that not all workers at these stations can see one another. To solve this problem, the workers at these key stations have devised a system to signal one another. If the packer is backing up, for example, the lead worker at the packer "hoots" over the deafening din to notify the pasteurizer operator, who signals the person running the capper to slow down.

Likewise, although technically they are supposed to wait for reports from the laboratories, workers often notify one another about defects in the product and work out their own solutions. When the capper was making microscopic cracks in the glass bottles one day, the pasteurizer operator, who detected the flaws when the bottles filled with water, informed the capper operator, who adjusted her machine to screw the caps on more loosely. Such coordination and adjustment, workers told me, result directly from the experience of socialism; workers learned to coordinate among themselves to compensate for defects in raw materials and machinery (see also Burawoy and Lukács 1992). In effect, this situation gives workers power to resist their own deskilling: as long as the line speed is variant and production problems occur that can be fixed immediately, the workers cannot be managed entirely through written protocols or by the "experts" in the laboratories.

Production workers use their reinterpretations of the socialist experience in other significant ways as well. They bring them into play as they attempt to acquire a bigger portion of the firm's resources. This strategy came up in complex ways during battles over sales and marketing budgets.

"People Look on You Differently when You Give Them Presents": Fuzzy Dichotomies

Whereas shop-floor workers often intentionally disrupt management's dichotomy between socialism and capitalism, others have such disruptions forced on them. Sales representatives, for example, have every reason to accept the dichotomy. Yet, because they have clients who expect them to recreate socialism's gift economy, they have to muddy the waters to get the resources they need to meet their clients' demands. They must somehow deal with the discrepancy between a construction that makes them out to be the representatives of capitalism and the "socialist" practices they must use to get sales. In doing so, they enter into a domain in which one of the most important practices mandated by Gerber—the creation of a separate budget line for sales and marketing—goes up for negotiation. Such negotiations are complex. Since the marketing budget battles are about the transformation of socialist reciprocity, they form a spectrum of values and interpretations that leads to conflict. The lines of conflict are not always clear since people in different positions within the firm must contend with the structures and values of the socialist system and with the imperatives of a profit-making business and the rhetoric of Western management. It is not an easy case of "socialist" shop-floor workers versus "capitalist" sales representatives but rather an intricate set of negotiations about the construction of relationships among the firm, its employees, and its customers.

The marketing department has a fixed sum of money that must cover advertising, promotions, and "freebie" giveaway items such as T-shirts and pens with the company's logo. Marketing has decided to focus on television advertising, with a secondary focus on print advertising. Marketers see ads as the most effective form of promotion since they reach a broad spectrum of the population and ensure that dispersed members of a targeted niche market are reached.

The sales representatives disagree strongly with this use of advertising funds; they bemoan the fact that they no longer have pens and T-shirts and plastic bags to give out to their clients, the grocery store managers. The sales reps are caught in a problematic situation: whereas AG marketers and many clients (mostly owners and managers of large private stores) want to create relationships based on mutual profit, impersonal relations between businesses, and a constellation of business practices they label as professionalism, other store managers run formerly state-owned shops as if they were still state owned. Selling to these managers entails using the repertoire of practices developed under state socialism, including building personal relationships through gift giving. Resorting to these tactics, and to the different systems of relationships and value they implied, is often difficult for sales representatives to negotiate.

A salesman named Jarek showed the contradictions in his approach to gift giving in a shop in Lublin. The store manager refused to buy any more creamed turkey (a best-seller) until she had sold the jars of lamb she still had. Jarek, fuming, tried to explain patiently that if people wanted turkey they were not going to buy lamb any more than they would buy apricots. They would simply go to another store and get turkey. She held firm. Outside the shop, Jarek exploded: "If people want coffee, they won't buy tea! They'll go to another shop. Doesn't she know there are other shops around the corner? Stupid Communist, that's what she is!" He continued, telling me that what I was seeing in Poland was actually stranger than what other anthropologists were seeing in, say, Mozambique: "You might expect Mozambique to be weird; it's still a little savage there. But here you have intelligent, civilized people who think like this. This is supposed to be a civilized country. But there are still people who don't understand that people won't buy what they don't want!" Then, more quietly, he muttered, "I bet she would have ordered that turkey if I had given her a present. She bought a lot of stuff when I gave her some pens." "Why don't you give her a present?" I asked. "Because I don't have any, that's why!" he crowed. He seemed happy that he could refuse to use the old system of creating personalized business relationships through gift giving. Yet, when he had gifts with the AG logo, he did give them away in exchange for purchases or concessions from shop owners. "After all," he reflected, "people look on you differently when you have given them a present, don't they?" Other sales reps said they cannot get permission to hold promotions, place their products on advantageous shelf space, or write orders without these promotional items if the store manager had experience under socialism.

Sales reps, then, are in an ambiguous position: they must rely on different strategies depending on the relationship they feel the client wants, either old-style "arranging" with managers of formerly state-owned shops or an emphasis on quality, customer service, and other tenets of nouveau management theory when dealing with managers of new, privately owned, or foreign-owned grocery stores. Caught in the middle of shifting forms of economic relations, they need the tools to deal with different groups of customers who hold very different beliefs about how business is done.

The marketing department constantly battles with the sales representatives over providing promotional items. One marketer screamed in frustration when I brought the issue up in an interview: "Look, we do prepare all this material for *them*! But they don't use their heads about this promotional material. They use it like water, giving it out to everyone. If there is a problem, they just throw ballpoint pens at it. They have to learn to use their heads about it so it's used well. After all, we have no guarantees that this stuff has any effect, and it's very expensive. They have to learn to solve problems other ways!" Another marketer, joining the fray, added, "After all, ballpoint pens do not sell the product. The sales reps' attitude is that the manager of the store has to buy it. That's fine, that's their job. But our attitude is that *mothers* have to buy it. The merchandise has to leave the store, not just go into it. We have a totally different perspective on the market." The marketers, isolated from the demands of socialist reciprocity by their focus on (and distance from) end consumers, see little value in creating personalized relationships and want to push the sales reps toward creating impersonal, "professional" relationships with clients.

The shop-floor workers have a totally different perspective on the marketing budget. Whereas both sales representatives and marketers see the marketing budget as a discrete budget line—that is, money earmarked for some kind of advertising—production workers tend to see the marketing budget as merely a part of the firm's overall budget. Shop-floor workers and union representatives argue that money spent on ballpoint pens and sales reps' cars is money that is not spent on wages. Moreover, shop-floor workers see these items not as tools sales reps use to build relationships with clients to sell more product but as gifts for the sales reps' personal use aimed at building a relationship between the sales reps and the firm. The issue is tendentious and bursts out at odd times; when I was given a small pocket calendar with the firm's logo on it, a shop-floor worker commented sourly, "They have those for everyone but us. But of course, we're not people, we're just Negroes *(murzyny)*." Her interpretation was that the gifts were intended to express a kind of human relationship between the firm and its employees and clients from which production workers, considered machines or slaves, were excluded.

The issue of the cars (which bear the firm's logo and also come out of the sales and marketing budget) was even more tendentious. During contract negotiations between the unions and AG, the sales reps (who are nonunionized) had to send in their car registrations to prove the firm still owned the automobiles and had not given them to the sales reps as gifts. Sales and marketing, in the view of most production workers, divert company funds to nonproductive and unnecessary activities or directly into sales reps' pockets, thereby depriving production workers both of the money and of the relationship they should enjoy with the firm.

The same marketer who dismissed shop-floor workers as "those old people" and insinuated that they were relics of socialism told me workers "don't understand why all this money should be spent on marketing or why sales reps should get cars and good salaries. They look at the money we spend and see it as money that could be given to them. They work hard, they think, and they don't understand why they don't get that money. They see it as coming out of their pockets." What the marketer fails to appreciate is the similarity production workers see between the firm and a family: the resources of one member are the resources of all and should be equally shared. Moreover, most production workers continue to believe the firm has a quasi-parental role toward its employees and should be "caring" for them, both materially and symbolically, in exchange for their labor. In the employee gazette, for example, one union representative wrote about the ongoing need for the firm to provide extra money for the employee social fund, which was one of the most significant ways the firm "cares" for employees and which was teetering on the brink of insolvency. She wrote, "It is hard for me to agree with the thesis that in capitalism everyone must look out for himself. We live together, we work together, and we must help one another. Sometimes people who earn a lot must sacrifice and give a morsel of cake to those who find themselves in difficult circumstances." The same kind of argument was mobilized during contract negotiations when the unionized shop-floor workers demanded a larger share of what they saw as common wealth.

The complexities of arguments about the marketing budget reveal that what is happening at Alima is more than the simple divide between workers who are products of socialism and sales representatives who embody capitalism, or the divide between backward stasis and dynamic modernity as the Frugo commercials imply. The shop-floor workers do use images and practices derived from socialism, but they recontextualize them. If the workers reinterpret the socialist era as a system whose defects made them adaptable, they do so to prove that these same qualities and patterns of work organization make them good employees of a capitalist enterprise. If they argue that they have the expertise necessary to keep production moving smoothly, they do so to show they can create quality products suitable for sale in the market. If they argue that the firm has the responsibilities of the "parent state" (Verdery 1994), they do it to get what they see as their rightful share of the firm's profits.

Similarly, the sales representatives also have complex relations to socialism, both as a symbol and as a set of social practices and habits. Although they often condemn socialism, talk about how awful things were when there was nothing on the shelves, and praise themselves as the representatives of a capitalism that makes goods available, they must also struggle to obtain from the firm the material resources that allow them to reproduce one of the practices they condemn, *so that* they can meet the imperatives of a capitalist enterprise.

These ambiguities and complexities place very real constraints on the firm's strategy and resources. If the firm must increase wages and social benefits and provide gifts for employees, there is less money for ballpoint pens to give to store managers; if it decides on expensive advertising campaigns, there is less money for the social fund; if it prioritizes freebies for customers, there will be fewer złoty for full-page ads in national magazines. Rather than eradicate "socialism" in its entirety and insert a whole new system into the company, Alima-Gerber is in the difficult position of having to negotiate with the historical experience of socialism (as both symbol and recontextualized practices) while operating under the hard budget constraints of a capitalist firm.

Conclusion: Ambiguous Legacies and Fuzzy Management

Clearly, the methods prescribed by Gerber are not universally accepted or implemented. U.S. management practices are filtered through local symbols and historical experiences and are then contested through the new terms to which they have been attached. Workers and sales representatives alike use elements of both capitalist and socialist practice to carry out their jobs; they use parts of Western management theories and talk of socialism (both real and ideal) to legitimate what they do and to make claims on the firm's resources. The ambiguity of both the sales reps' and shop-floor workers' arguments shows that what is happening at AG is a process of negotiation and transformation. Rather than some sort of uniform adaptation of "best" practices, as neoliberal theory might predict, what we see is a variety of ideologies and practices derived from various systems and historical experiences—all being used in contests over how the firm will be reconfigured.

Although the transition is often viewed as something unique in history, the situation is not exactly new. It is similar to what Sara Berry (1993) describes for Africa. She argues that neither colonial governments nor international development agencies have been able to impose new forms of production or social organization hegemonically in their attempts to change agricultural practice, although they have not merely foundered on the shoals of intransigent "native tradition." Instead, Berry argues, attempts to rule Africa through "native custom" opened the door for the continual reinvention of tradition. Fragments of "custom" were brought up and reinterpreted in new contexts (i.e., colonial courts) to bolster claims on land and labor. Often, the "customs" cited by each party were contradictory or were interpreted differently by parties to the dispute. As

Berry points out, the meaning of *custom* was continually changing and was used both with and against European legal and ideological frameworks. Central to this process was the continual redefinition of social identities since claims on resources were contingent on the claimants' position in the traditional social structure. These, too, were up for negotiation. In short, Berry argues that instead of unilaterally changing patterns of production or access to resources, colonial governments and donor agencies have tended to create new social spaces in which social practice, tradition, and identity can be debated. The outcomes of economic restructuring programs hang on the results of these negotiations.

A similar set of points might be made for Eastern Europe. The neoclassical argument hinges on the state lifting barriers to individual initiative through programs such as the privatization of state-owned enterprises, which is supposed to open the door either for the spontaneous generation of a market economy if it is rooted in universal human nature (Holy 1992: 234–237) or for foreign businesspeople to fill the void and create a market economy with their physical and intellectual capital (Sachs 1993; Kozminski 1993). The case of Alima-Gerber, however, challenges the idea that privatization, either alone or in concert with the introduction of Western business practices, is enough to determine what goes on in the firm. The structural constraints of capitalism are insufficient to dictate particular forms of social organization within the firm. Instead, new social spaces, such as sales and marketing departments, and new practices, such as marketing budgets and quality control, create arenas in which people negotiate social identity and organization.

Socialism is brought into this context in a manner analogous to custom in Africa (cf. Creed, chapter 7, this volume), although perhaps often in a devalorizing as well as a legitimating sense. Socialism is not a complete and self-contained system active in the present, just as native custom did not provide a cohesive and unambiguous set of rules. Rather, fragments of the socialist experience are brought forward and inserted into a new context. The past and the present are in the present, but the past is so significantly changed by its location in the present that it becomes an integral part of it. This struggle is not between a new form of capitalist discipline and the legacies of socialism in which those legacies exist merely as anachronisms or stumbling blocks to be overcome.

Negotiations are carried on by people with varying material and historical and cultural resources who have multiple forms of ideology and practice on which to draw. Varying experiences not only of socialism and socialist practice but also of historical traditions, religions, and ideologies of democracy and market economy are all available. This situation increases the potential for varying outcomes and perhaps accounts for startling divergences among countries in the region, as well as for the fact that tsarist-inspired traders (Humphrey, chapter 1, this volume), entre-pratchik bureaucrats-turned-businessmen, and Western MBAs all exist simultaneously. To understand the complexity of the transition depends less on applying macrotheoretical models than on understanding ethnographically how these diverse people negotiate and reshape the structures within which they live.

The outcomes of these small, daily negotiations have real significance for the way economies and societies of Eastern Europe will be configured (cf. Piore and Sabel 1984).[14] The transition, then, is less a movement from one preordained state to another than a period of intensified struggle over resources (Berry 1993: 8; Stark 1991: 19). Thus, we might echo what Berry says about Africa: "Negotiability is not just an inconvenience for foreign investors but a pervasive feature of social and economic life that calls for reconceptualization" (Berry 1993: 13). Negotiability certainly calls for a reconceptualization of the transition in Eastern Europe, a period in which the outcomes of negotiation are more significant than ever before.

Notes

Acknowledgments: Thanks to Katherine Verdery not only for her help in wading through ethnographic details for this chapter but for her support during the fieldwork. Many thanks also to David Karjanen, Lanfranco Blanchetti, Sidney Mintz, Elizabeth Ferry, and Michael Burawoy for their helpful comments on earlier versions. Field research for this project was funded by a grant from the International Research and Exchange Board (IREX), with funds provided by the National Endowment for the Humanities and the U.S. Department of State, which administers the Title VIII Program. The research was also supported by the National Science Foundation and the Society for Human Resource Management Foundation. None of these organizations is responsible for the views expressed.

1. This information was provided by two employees of the Ministry of Privatization who worked on the Alima-Gerber deal.

2. This reduction was accomplished by placing a breathalyzer outside the employee exit after each shift. Employees who had a high blood alcohol content at the end of the shift could be fired for drunkenness, which allowed the firm to dodge the complicated rules for conducting layoffs on any other basis. This policy affected men significantly more than it did women.

3. The 1996 Polish Labor Code attempts to forbid extended use of contract labor by mandating that the third consecutive contract signed by an employee is permanent. This does not mean the temporary agency cannot rotate workers among firms or simply fire employees after two contract periods and hire new workers.

4. This figure was given by the director of operations during a speech to the workers in division 4.

5. These figures were provided by AG marketers during the launch of a new product.

6. This interpretation was provided by two separate AG employees in response to my complaints that I did not understand why everyone else who viewed the ads laughed uproariously.

7. AG has a very strict age limit for newly hired sales reps; they must be under thirty. Irena, the recruitment specialist, says older people just "don't have the strength" to do the job.

8. A pragmatic issue is also at work here for both production workers and sales representatives. Because of the overall shortage of housing in Poland and the great expense of renting or buying a new apartment, it is extremely difficult for employees to relocate in search of better job opportunities.

9. Even such flexibility has associations with capitalism and socialism. Restrictions on firings and layoffs are seen as legacies of the socialist era. New restrictions were included in the 1996 Labor Code, which was written while the postcommunist left-wing party was in power.

10. One day my job was to hack fifty-kilo blocks of frozen butter into little chunks, which were added along with salt to a vat of baby food. When I asked the head of product development why we were adding so much fat and salt, she said Polish babies, like other Poles, had a taste for it and would not eat the low-fat salt-free recipes devised by Gerber.

11. Thanks to Michael Burawoy for reminding me of this point.

12. Discipline for contract workers is significantly more stringent than that for long-term core workers, as is surveillance. For example, during several shifts, my brigade was knocking on bottles with rubber tubes to test for fermentation. A perfectly sealed bottle makes a different sound from one containing highly fermented juice, and discerning between the two sounds is not always easy. Our brigade leader almost never checked the work of experienced workers but often retested all or most of the bottles temporary workers had judged to be defective.

13. Melissa Wright (personal communication) suggests that one of the reasons the workers she observed were so much more stringently controlled was because of the *kind* of work they were doing, which was electronics assembly. The delicate and exacting nature of that work may make minute control over bodily movements more significant than it is in baby food production. This does not explain, however, why there is a much greater emphasis on controlling absences from the line in Wright's cases or why similar strategies of body control are used in other Mexican assembly plants, such as textile manufacture, that are not doing such detailed work (see Fernandez-Kelly 1983).

14. Alima workers have already had a direct effect on privatization. During the privatization process, the Ministry of Privatization decided it was the "owner" of Alima for all intents and purposes and did not involve the workforce in the choice of Gerber or inform workers of events during the negotiation process. When Gerber was announced as the successful bidder, the price of Alima—including investment commitments, contracts with farmers, and guarantees not to lay off workers for a specified period of time—was presented as a fait accompli. The workforce and farmers were furious, and their complaints reached na-

tional newspapers. Lewandowski was later forced to apologize to Alima employees. The Alima case was brought up the first time Lewandowski was brought before a Sejm tribunal to face charges of betraying the national interest, and the Ministry of Privatization subsequently became much less interested in trade sales. The case was also used by the political left as ammunition during the 1993 campaign that brought it to power in the Sejm.

References

Barlik, Ewa. 1996. Polska Kadra, Amerykanska Strategia (Polish Management, American Strategy). *Rzeszpospolita* 16 (4270), January 19.

Berry, Sabra. 1993. *No Condition Is Permanent: The Social Dynamics of Agrarian Change in Sub-Saharan Africa.* Madison: University of Wisconsin Press.

Braverman, Harry. 1974. *Labor and Monopoly Capital.* New York: Monthly Review Press.

Burawoy, Michael, and János Lukács. 1992. *The Radiant Past: Ideology and Reality in Hungary's Road to Capitalism.* Chicago: University of Chicago Press.

Fernandez-Kelly, M. Patricia. 1983. *For We Are Sold, I and My People: Women and Industry in Mexico's Frontier.* Albany: State University of New York Press.

Gick, Alan, Małgorzata Tarczynska, and Małgorzata Bernat. N. D. Metoda Firmy Mercer: Analiyczno-punktowa ocena pracy (The Mercer Method: An Analytical Point-Based Valuation of Work). *Personel*: 30–34.

Holy, Ladislav. 1992. Culture, Market Ideology and Economic Reform in Czechoslovakia. In *Contesting Markets: Analyses of Ideology, Discourse and Practice*, ed. Ray Dilley. Edinburgh: Edinburgh University Press.

Klimczak, Joanna. 1994. W Alimie-Gerber, Dobrowolne Zwolnienia (At Alima-Gerber, Voluntary Layoffs). *Gazeta Wyborcza* 196 (578), August 24.

Kopertynska, Wanda. 1995(?). Wartosciowane Pracy (The Value of Work). *Personel* (date unknown): 43–46.

Kornai, János. 1992. *The Socialist System: The Political Economy of Communism.* Princeton: Princeton University Press.

Kozminski, Andrzej K. 1993. *Catching Up? Organizational and Management Change in the Ex-Socialist Bloc.* Albany: State University of New York Press.

Martin, Emily. 1992. The End of the Body? *American Ethnologist* 19 (1): 121–140.

Mintz, Sidney W. 1982. Choice and Occasion: Sweet Moments. In *The Psychobiology of Human Food Selection,* ed. Lewis M. Barker. Westport, Conn.: Avi.

Oleksyn, Tadeusz. 1995(?). Wartosciowanie Pracy (The Value of Work). *Personel* (date unknown): 20–21.

Ong, Aihwa. 1987. *Spirits of Resistance and Capitalist Discipline: Factory Women in Malaysia.* Albany: State University of New York Press.

Piore, Michael J., and Charles Sabel. 1984. *The Second Industrial Divide: Possibilities for Prosperity.* New York: Basic Books.

Sachs, Jeffrey. 1993. *Poland's Jump to the Market Economy.* Cambridge, Mass.: MIT Press.

Staniszkis, Jadwiga. 1992. *The Ontology of Socialism.* Oxford: Clarendon Press.

Stark, David. 1991. Path Dependence and Privatization Strategies in East Central Europe. *East European Politics and Societies* 6 (1): 17–54.

Verdery, Katherine. 1994. From Parent-State to Family Patriarchs: Gender and Nation in Contemporary Eastern Europe. *East European Politics and Societies* 8 (2): 225–255.

Wright, Melissa. 1996. Third World Women and the Geography of Skill. Ph.D. thesis, Department of Geography and Environmental Engineering, Johns Hopkins University.

5

"But We Are Still Mothers": Gender, the State, and the Construction of Need in Postsocialist Hungary

Lynne Haney

Caseworkers employed in Budapest's Xth district welfare office will remember 13 March 1995 for some time. On that day, female clients converged on their office en masse to protest the *Bokros csomag,* a government proposal to restructure the Hungarian welfare system. Lines of women formed outside the building long before the agency's official office hours. When the doors opened, a stampede of women rushed into the office. Their emotions ran high, fluctuating between anger and fear. "I cried when I heard the news last night," one female client remarked. "I kept my daughter from school to come here and complain." To calm a group of clients gathered around her desk, one caseworker assured them that the reforms would not adversely affect them. "It will be like the aid you already receive," she explained. "Those with low incomes will continue to get support." Unconvinced, a female client retorted, "So just like that aid, nothing will be left in a few months." The others grumbled in agreement. Another woman staged a sit-in at a caseworker's desk, demanding that she ask Prime Minister Gyula Horn to revoke the proposal. As a male security guard escorted the woman out of the office, she quietly repeated, "No one cares any more, but we are still mothers. We are still mothers."

With her comment, this client advanced a profound argument about the nature of the welfare changes under way in Hungary. Hers was a comparative analysis based on what she and her fellow clients had learned from years of experience in the system. For most of their lives, these women had been constituted as mothers within the Hungarian welfare apparatus. Since the late 1960s, they had been enmeshed in a subsystem of welfare that accorded them special privileges. They were entitled to three years of maternity leave, family allowances, sick leave benefits, and child-rearing assistance. Eligibility for these programs was based on motherhood. In postsocialist Hungary, this subsystem of welfare crumbled around these women. In the mid-1980s, maternity leave payments were income based, and child-rearing assistance was means-tested. In the mid-1990s, all other social policies met a similar fate—the entire system of maternity leave grants and family allowances was subjected to income tests and thus was provided only to specific classes of mothers. So although these women were "still mothers," the welfare apparatus no longer accorded them special privileges based on that identity.

Whereas these Hungarian women experienced the current welfare restructuring in comparative and historical terms, the scholarly literature on the welfare states of Eastern Europe has not been systematically comparative or historical. Only since the mid-1990s has the welfare state come into theoretical focus for scholars of Eastern Europe. As with theories of transition more generally, this scholarship tends to be fairly prescriptive in nature. Basing their analyses on idealized notions of the Western welfare state and models of how welfare states "should" operate, these scholars have focused on how to bring Eastern Europe into line with dominant modes of welfare capitalism (Kornai 1993, 1994; Szelényi and Ladányi 1996). In Hungary, many social scientists link their prescriptive arguments to larger claims about the imperatives of the transition to a market economy and how that transition requires scaling back welfare programs (Timar 1991; Kornai 1994; Szalai 1994). Because these analyses take the West as their point of comparison, they fail to explore the dynamics of welfare state development within Hungary; they leave untheorized the historical reconfigurations and reconceptualizations of Hungarian welfare itself. The few analysts who eschew a prescriptive approach and take a historical perspective on Hungarian welfare do so in quantitative terms—focusing on shifts in the cope of social benefits (Ferge 1991; Deacon 1992a), patterns of (re)distribution (Ferge 1992b; Andorka 1996), or the overall amount of welfare transfers (Tóth 1994; Andorka and Tóth 1995). Hence, the existing literature on Hungarian welfare is bifurcated between prescriptive models that compare Western mythology to the Hungarian reality and quantitative models that chart historical alterations in the overall size of the Hungarian social policy apparatus.

The conceptual framework advanced in this chapter will be of a different sort. Rather than take an ideologized image of the Western welfare state as my comparative base, I will examine the dynamics of welfare state transformation within Hungary over time. Instead of conceptualizing this transition in terms of the quantitative categories of size, scope, or amount, I will analyze it for the social conceptions of need it encodes. Drawing on recent feminist welfare state theory and historiography, my analysis will be guided by the notion that all welfare states embody distinct architectures of need—understandings of who is in need and of how their needs should be met (Fraser 1989; Fraser and Gordon 1994). Welfare states not only engage in the (re)distribution of benefits, they also articulate historically specific interpretations of need. These architectures of need are etched out on multiple terrains within welfare states. First, they are articulated through regime policies—inherent in social provisions, public proclamations, and discursive constructions. Second, they are constituted through the practices of actual welfare institutions—embedded in the organization of casework and the professional models ascribed to by state actors. Because welfare policies and practices define social conceptions of need, they draw upon and shape women's identities in complex ways. Hence, welfare regimes must also be examined for the space they accord women to advance their own interests and to maneuver in their everyday lives. Thus, my analysis of Hungarian welfare will operate on three levels, tracing changes in regime policies, practices, and client strategies.

With this conceptual framework, I identify three Hungarian welfare regimes from the inception of state socialism: the welfare society of the period 1948–1968, in which women's needs were familialized through state policies and practices organized around the household and the enterprise; the maternalist welfare state of the period 1968–1985, in which women's needs were maternalized through social provisions and institutions designed to regulate the quality and quantity control of motherhood; and the liberal welfare state of the period 1985–1996, in which women's needs were materialized through means-tested programs and poor-relief agencies aimed at the bureaucratic regulation of material problems. In short, Hungarian welfare has shifted from the familialization to the maternalization to the materialization of women's needs. The origins of these regimes were social, economic, and professional in nature. That is, the regimes arose out of historically specific responses to industrialization, economic reform, demographic shifts, and professionalization. Thus, the key architects of need have also varied in Hungary. Whereas party officials and unions were critical in the creation of the first regime, demographers, economic reformers, and psychologists were central to the formation of the second regime. In contemporary Hungary, sociologists and neoliberal economists are playing the critical roles in the construction of women's needs.

Although the history of Hungarian welfare can be periodized according to these three regimes, this chapter will focus on the contours of and transition between the second and third regimes. It will trace the shift from the maternalization to the materialization of need in Hungary and the ways in which this shift led to the replacement of an old set of maternal identities with a new set of class identities. It will also explore how, along this transition, the space available for women to maneuver and secure their own interests contracted and narrowed.

More specifically, my discussion will begin with an analysis of the welfare apparatus of the final two decades of state socialism. In this section, I unearth the ways motherhood was built into the social policies of the period and how notions of a "good mother" shaped welfare work. I also illuminate how this social conception of need enabled female clients to expand their identities as mothers to protect themselves as wives and women. This discussion is followed by an analysis of the postsocialist welfare regime. Here, I reveal how social class replaced motherhood as the central principle guiding welfare policy and practice. I then show how this focus on material need led to the stigmatization of the "welfare client" and how women resist this stigmatization by reasserting identities inherited from the state socialist period—a sense of entitlement based on motherhood.[1]

The Maternalist Welfare State: Quantity and Quality Control of Motherhood

The roots of the Hungarian welfare state can be traced to the mid-1960s. Before this period, Hungary was structured much like a welfare society in which the well-being of the population was to be secured through existing social institutions (Gal 1969; Ferge 1979). In such an order, the targeted social policies associated with a welfare state were deemed unnecessary—economic planning and work-based provisions were to meet the population's material needs, whereas the family was to fulfill the caring welfare functions.[2] Yet in the mid-1960s this welfare organization changed as the needs of specific social groups rather than social institutions were emphasized. A subsystem of welfare arose to link eligibility to social characteristics other than labor force participation.[3] Motherhood was one such identity. In this period a set of welfare policies and institutions emerged to address the "special" needs of Hungarian mothers. As a result, Hungarian women were placed under the purview of a maternalist welfare apparatus that constituted them as child rearers and fostered a sense of entitlement based on motherhood.

The impetus behind the rise of this maternalist welfare apparatus came from multiple sources. First, it came from demographers concerned with the quantity control of motherhood. After the relegalization of abortion in 1956, the Hungarian birthrate plummeted to record lows. From 1954 to 1962, the birthrate fell by nearly 50 percent—from 23.0 births per 1,000 in 1954 to 12.3 per 1,000 in 1962 (Goven 1993). Drawing on these data, Hungarian demographers began to warn of an impending disaster and to urge for population policies to reverse the trend (Mód 1961; Klinger 1961).[4]

These demographic changes were not unique to Hungary; they also characterized other East European societies experiencing the effects of industrialization, urbanization, and high rates of female employment. Yet, the pronatalist path taken in Hungary differed from that of other countries in at least two respects. Instead of instituting coercive measures to force women to reproduce, Hungarian demographers proposed population policies based on incentives for mothers (Klinger et al. 1984).[5] The goal was to encourage women to reproduce by securing social conditions conducive to raising children. Moreover, rather than focusing strictly on childbearing, as was done in neighboring countries such as Romania, Hungarian policymakers centered on child rearing (Kligman 1993). They proposed a support system that stretched beyond childbirth and encompassed birth payments, as well as benefits extending through the child-rearing process. Hence, Hungarian demographers advanced a solution to the birthrate problem based on incentives to support both the birth and the rearing of children.

These demographic shifts coincided with the rise of economic problems related to the first wave of Hungarian market reform. As demographers were contemplating the long-term implications of the declining birthrate, Hungarian economic reformers were in the process of designing the New Economic Mechanisms (NEM) introduced in 1968. These reforms provided their own impetus for the rise of a maternalist welfare apparatus. First, by legalizing certain sectors of the second economy and giving enterprises more control in their hiring and firing practices, the reforms spawned new concerns about possible labor surpluses and unemployment. This problem was particularly acute for the regime because much of its legitimacy rested on its ability to secure full employment (Ferge 1992b; Deacon 1993). The Hungarian state therefore had to find a way to siphon off workers from the labor force without provoking mass unemployment. Social policies designed to "encourage" Hungarian mothers to leave the labor force and devote themselves to their children full-time were one way to secure downsizing (Horváth 1986; Goven 1993). In addition to alleviating the side effects of market reform, these policies also facilitated a shift in the responsibility for social reproduction from the enterprise to individual families. Through social policies targeted at Hungarian mothers, the socialist state was able to reduce its investment in the social infrastructure, thereby transferring much of this burden onto Hungarian women.

Whereas these demographic and economic problems presented dilemmas for the socialist state, its distinctly maternalist response in this period
was shaped by the ascendancy of professional psychology. The regime
could have resolved the social and economic problems in a variety of
ways; the fact that it responded by centering on and redefining the role
of mothers resulted largely from the rise of a new cadre of Hungarian
psychologists. After a ten-year hiatus, the psychology department reopened at the University of Budapest in 1957. The first cohort of psychologists focused on the sphere of production and industrial relations. Yet
by the mid-1960s, many had begun to focus on the reproductive sphere
and to develop a new branch of "child-rearing psychology" (*nevelési
pszichológia*). In professional journals and at conferences, they discovered a host of new childhood disorders and neuroses and linked those
disorders to familial breakdown (Lieberman 1964; Gegési 1965). They
then proposed new measures designed by "family experts" to rationalize
the family and ensure the quality control of motherhood—social policies
to give mothers the time and resources to focus on their children, as well
as institutions designed to "scientize" their child-rearing practices.
Hence, in the late 1960s the demographic and economic problems facing
the regime converged with the professional appeals of Hungarian psychologists, paving the way for the emergence of a maternalist welfare
state out of the previous welfare society.

The Maternalist Policy Regime

The centerpiece of this maternalist welfare apparatus was the *Gyermekgondozási Segély* (GYES), a maternity leave grant created in 1967.
When first introduced, the grant provided six months of support equivalent to the recipient's salary and up to two years of additional support at
a fixed rate.[6] In 1969 the grant was extended by six months, thus giving
recipients a total of three years of support. Employers were obliged to
reemploy recipients when the grant was completed. The GYES had two
primary eligibility requirements. First, the grant was offered only to Hungarian mothers; fathers could apply only if the mother was absent or too
sick to care for the children. As Zsuzsa Ferge (1979: 152) put it, the grant
was designed to address the special "biological and psychological needs
of motherhood"—needs Hungarian fathers presumably did not have.
Second, initial GYES regulations stipulated that recipients had to be employed full-time continuously for the twelve months preceding the birth
or for twelve of the last eighteen months prior to the birth.[7] With time,
these requirements were relaxed. By the early 1970s, part-time workers
and students were eligible for the grant. As a result, the percentage of
mothers eligible for the grant increased in its first decade—whereas only

57 percent of mothers were eligible in 1967, that number jumped to 74 percent in 1970, 85 percent in 1974 and over 90 percent in 1978 (Központi Statisztikai Hivatal [KSH] 1981).[8]

Whereas the scholarly literature on GYES has focused on how the grant fulfilled the needs of the regime (Horváth 1986; Ernst 1986; Gal 1994) or on how it solidified a traditional gender division of labor in the workforce and the home (Markus 1970; Ferge 1979; Goven 1993; Adamik 1995), GYES also fostered an important sense of entitlement among Hungarian women.[9] It provided women with a legitimate way to stake a claim in the welfare apparatus. Because the grant was available to a cross-section of Hungarian mothers, it did not become a stigmatized form of assistance. And because the grant was used by diverse groups of women, albeit for different amounts of time, it was never associated with specific classes. One caseworker put it best when I asked about the social connotations of the grant: "GYES was for mothers. I took it, my colleagues took it, and the clients took it. How could I think of it negatively when everyone I knew used it?"

In addition to GYES, a number of shorter child-care leave provisions were established during this period. For instance, the "housework holiday" (*háztartási szabadnap*) allowed mothers with at least two children under age fourteen to take one day of unpaid leave a month. In 1973 a special system of paid leave was established for mothers. Women with one child were entitled to two days of fully paid leave per year, and women with two or more children received five to nine days of leave. The explicit justification for these provisions was "to protect mothers and permit them to fulfill the special responsibilities that accompany child-rearing" (Pongracz 1986: 151). Finally, Hungarian mothers had access to their own system of sick leave benefits (*tappenz*). Women with children under age three received sixty days of paid leave per year, and women with children under age six were entitled to thirty days.[10] As with GYES, Hungarian fathers were eligible for these benefits only if they were single parents.

During this period, the Hungarian system of family allowances (*családi pótlék*) also underwent changes that made assistance more accessible to mothers. First established in the 1930s, family allowances were monthly payments to families to offset the costs of child rearing.[11] Up until the mid-1960s, the payments were intended for large families with three or more children. They were also paid directly to heads of households employed full-time in a state enterprise or cooperative, which meant that in two-parent households the father automatically received the allowance attached to his wages. In 1968 the Ministry of Labor extended the allowance to students, home workers, and part-time employees and also offered it to families with two children. As a result, the number of women eligible for the allowance increased. Then, in 1974 the "head of household" provision was revoked and replaced with a "primary caretaker" clause, which enabled divorced mothers to receive the allowance directly. The new provisions also created an appeal system through which married women could transfer the allowance to their wages, thus bypassing the father altogether. Hence, for the first time Hungarian mothers became entitled to the allowances on their own.

Although no reliable data exist on how many women actually utilized this appeal system, in the two districts of my research I uncovered twenty-five appeals from the 1970s.[12] The justifications on which these women based their appeals were strikingly similar—they were mothers, the ones who cared for children. Many bolstered their claims by raising complaints about their husbands' irresponsible behavior, arguing that the men used the money to finance their "unruly lifestyles" and therefore were not worthy of support. They believed they were *entitled* to support based on their motherhood status, a belief that was confirmed by the caseworkers assessing the appeals. All twenty-five appeals were approved on similar grounds—mothers knew what was best for children and should have the resources to secure their well-being.

This leads to the fourth and final component of the maternalist policy regime of the period—child-rearing assistance programs (*Rendkívuli/ Rendszeres Nevelési Segély*). Created by the Ministry of Education in 1974, these funds were distributed by caseworkers up to six times a year on a per-case basis.[13] Caseworkers had enormous discretion in the allocation of these funds; most lower- and working-class families having trouble raising their children were eligible for the funds provided their difficulties were not the result of their own "mistakes" (Horváth 1982). In practice, caseworkers applied their own eligibility criteria that centered on women's mothering practices. Applicants for the funds were almost exclusively females.[14] The women were put through a battery of tests to prove their domestic competency—tests that included home visits in which caseworkers evaluated their mothering skills. Thus, eligibility decisions were rarely made on the basis of the applicant's material "need." Rather, they were based on their gender performance and presumed domestic competency.

Taken together, these four social provisions formed the core of the maternalist welfare policy regime of the period. These policies trained women on how to stake a claim in the welfare apparatus and on how to emphasize their identities as mothers when couching their appeals. They taught women that as mothers and caretakers, they had "special" needs. What is more, their needs were transformed into social rights through an entitlement system that guaranteed specific resources for mothers. Many Hungarian women learned a similar lesson about their rights as mothers in more direct and immediate ways through contact with the state welfare institutions of the era.

Welfare Practices and the Good Mother Mold

The maternalization of need embedded in the social policies of the last two decades of state socialism filtered down to the institutional level, shaping the practices of Hungarian welfare agencies. Although little scholarly work has been done on state socialist welfare institutions, a fairly extensive network of Hungarian welfare agencies operated during this period.[15] At the center of this structure were local Gyámhatóság offices designed to ensure the well-being of children.[16] Their duties were twofold: they maintained the large bureaucracy surrounding the family and oversaw the upbringing of children in their districts.[17] Also operating at the local level were Child Guidance Centers (*Nevelési Tanácsadók*) that addressed children's educational and psychological problems and drew in Hungarian women for child-rearing counseling. In practice, both institutions focused their work on mothers, thus strengthening and solidifying the maternalist arm of the Hungarian welfare apparatus.

Established in 1952, Gyámhatóság offices employed four to six caseworkers, most of whom were women with limited education.[18] Underlying their understanding of child protection was a vision of motherhood they used to socialize clients. From my archival research of 460 case files from this period, I discovered that caseworkers employed a variety of techniques to evaluate their clients' child-rearing practices. The most common were "domesticity tests," which were administered to an overwhelming majority of clients of the period and had two components. First, clients solicited letters from their children's teachers to verify that they were raising them "properly." Second, caseworkers initiated home visits (*környezeti tanulmányok*) to assess clients' domestic practices firsthand. On these visits, caseworkers meticulously documented clients' family lives; measured the size of their flats; recorded how they furnished their homes, from furniture styles to types of bedding; examined their cleaning skills; tested their cooking ability, checking their cabinets and asking them how to prepare certain dishes;[19] and observed how they interacted with their children. Caseworkers also interrogated neighbors for inside information on clients' lifestyles and child-rearing patterns.

Women's performances on these tests shaped their institutional trajectories. Clients who received high marks fared much better in the agency. These marks were the most important factor in determining who received child-rearing assistance. They overrode all evidence of material need; caseworkers consistently denied aid to women they considered "careless" or "unruly" mothers and spent more time assisting women they believed to be "good mothers." They were more likely to go out of their way to track down a "deadbeat dad" or help to secure an apartment for women who fit their criteria of good mothers. Caseworkers were also more apt to bend the rules for such women—extending their maternity leave grants and waiving deadlines. In this way, these state actors taught women that they could "butter up the bureaucratic machine" by fitting into a particular mold of mother.

These state actors transmitted the same message to women through negative example. During the last two decades of state socialism, the number of Hungarian children placed under state care rose steadily.[20] As with most aspects of their work, caseworkers had discretion in deciding when children should be taken from their homes (Hanák 1983; Domszky 1994). Although the grounds for institutionalization varied, one thread ran through them all—the mother had been deemed "incompetent."[21] Most had alcohol problems, a majority were victims of domestic violence, and many also had mental health problems. Because caseworkers believed these issues fell outside their sphere of influence, they never addressed them. Instead, they labeled these mothers "unfit" and ordered them to become better mothers. As a caseworker said when I asked about a domestic violence case, "This was not my job. It was for the woman to take care of. I protected the child. If the mother didn't do that, I gave the child to someone who did." Once again, the focus was on women's domestic competency—a focus that taught women that their institutional fate depended on their ability to demonstrate "proper" gender practices.

This singular focus on clients' mothering skills had interesting implications for different groups of female clients. One might expect that caseworkers' preoccupation with domestic competency would lead to clear class differences in treatment. But because caseworkers defined domestic competency in terms of a woman's housekeeping, cooking, and decorating skills, their notion of a good mother crosscut class divisions. Because of the absence of labor-saving devices and a domestic service sector, middle-class and professional women did not necessarily have an advantage in the domesticity tests. In fact, caseworkers often commended working-class women for rising above difficult material conditions to take care of their families "properly." They also frequently scolded professional women for devoting too little time to domestic upkeep.[22] Hence, because caseworkers evaluated their female clients' domestic training and competency, the good/bad mother distinction did not fall along clear class lines. Yet, it did correlate rather closely with race. The caseworkers' criteria for evaluating clients had consistently negative effects on Romani clients.[23] Gyámhatóság caseworkers were uniformly intolerant of cultural differences in mothering practices and regularly faulted Romani women for not living up to their standards of cleanliness, decor, and culinary taste.

They were also insensitive to the nonnuclear family models of their Romani clients, frequently exhibiting disgust at households in which numerous extended kin resided or two or more children slept in one bed. As a result, Romani women were far more likely to be pathologized and stigmatized as bad mothers.

Like the Gyámhatóság, the work of Child Guidance Centers of the period also focused on the mothering practices of Hungarian women. Created in 1968 by a new cohort of professional psychologists, these agencies were staffed by three to seven "family experts," most of whom were well-educated women.[24] Guided by child development models and psychoanalytic theories of family life, these psychologists set out to treat childhood disorders and improve child-rearing methods. These offices came in where the Gyámhatóság left off; their approach was less punitive and more educative than the Gyámhatóság's. But like child welfare workers, these state actors also targeted women. They believed in child rearing by design, a scientific mode of raising children with clear prescriptions for Hungarian mothers.

The counseling conducted in these agencies fell into three categories: educational counseling to improve children's school performance, behavior counseling to treat children who acted out, and psychological counseling to guide children toward healthy resolutions of their conflicts (Horányi 1985b). Counselors met with the children a few times a month and updated mothers after each visit. In these briefing sessions, psychologists pulled mothers into the counseling process by linking children's problems to their mothers. Mothers of children who were having educational difficulties were routinely questioned about their involvement in their children's education; those who devoted less than an hour a day to their kids' schooling were scolded. Counselors also regulated the quantity and quality of time mothers spent with children who had behavioral problems, imposing time formulas on their interactions and rules for how they should proceed. No such rules applied to Hungarian fathers; they were absent from the picture.

This focus on the mother was particularly salient in the offices' psychological work with children. To uncover children's psyches, psychologists employed Rorschach tests, thematic apperception tests (TAT), and "world games" (Mérei 1974). Psychologists then analyzed the results to unearth the psychodynamic issues plaguing the children (Tunkli 1975). Because of the strong influence of psychoanalysis on their work, the psychologists' interpretations centered on dilemmas rooted in the Oedipal stage—castration anxiety, penis envy, and gender identity confusion.[25] As a prominent child psychologist explained to me, "Identification was a big problem in Hungary, where we had overprotective mothers and absent fathers. Boys never learned to identify with their fathers, and mothers never let them separate. So we got the boys, years later, with problems related to the unresolved Oedipal stage."[26] So what did they do? They taught the *mothers* how to let go of their sons. "This was a struggle," another psychologist revealed. "Mothers were so wrapped up in their sons, they couldn't break off. I had to convince them it was unhealthy. It took years for some to understand; most never did."[27] Hungarian fathers, who also had not fulfilled their Oedipal expectations, were absent from the equation.

Finally, family experts also initiated counseling with Hungarian mothers. Each agency employed at least one "family caretaker" (*család gondozó*) to conduct home visits. When warranted, psychologists would then instigate counseling with the mothers.[28] Time management was the most common issue addressed in counseling. Psychologists often described mothers as "overworked" and "overburdened" and taught them how to spend more time with their children. For instance, in one 1970 case a woman was sent to a counselor by her son's teacher. After a home visit, the family caretaker reported that the woman "arrived home too exhausted to talk to her son." The counselor instructed her to put a clock on the table every night and speak to the boy for at least an hour. The family caretaker paid follow-up visits to make sure she adjusted her mothering practices accordingly.

As in the Gyámhatóság, the criteria used by family experts had interesting class and racial implications. Again, one might assume that middle-class women had an advantage, given the complex psychological models and formulas adhered to by family experts. Some middle-class women did indeed mobilize their cultural and educational capital to shape counselors' evaluations of their mothering practices. Yet overall, clients were not judged on their ability to speak the language of psychology or time management; rather, they were assessed according to their willingness to devote large amounts of time and energy to their children. In practice, this philosophy undercut the advantages middle-class women may have gained from their higher levels of cultural and educational capital. Family experts regularly complained that middle-class clients refused to make sacrifices for their families and faulted them for being too "careerist" to spend time on GYES or to work part-time. Yet, women with less demanding jobs were frequently applauded for devoting themselves to their families and for taking time off to resolve their children's problems. At the same time, the psychologists' standards had consistently negative effects on Romani women, who were constantly labeled incompetent mothers. Those who spent too little one-on-one quality time with their kids were said to be "uncaring," those who physically reprimanded their kids were deemed "brutal," and those who were illiterate and thus unable to tutor their children were called "ineffective." Hence, although the family experts' model of good mothering crosscut class divisions, it fell neatly along racial lines.

Expanding the Confines of the Maternal: "Mothers Are Wives and Women Too"

The maternalism embedded in the Hungarian welfare apparatus was a mixed blessing for female clients. On the one hand, it offered them financial and institutional resources. It also provided them with a strong sense of entitlement, a channel through which they could secure state assistance. On the other hand, the welfare regime placed their mothering practices under scrutiny and subjected them to new levels of surveillance. For those who did not fit into prescribed models of domesticity, it led to the pathologization of their mothering practices. By positioning them only as mothers, the regime effectively denied women their other identities and obscured their other needs and desires. By reducing women to mothers, the welfare apparatus ignored the multitude of issues impinging on the lives of Hungarian women.

Many female clients seemed aware of these mixed consequences. As a result, they struggled to carve out spaces for themselves within the regime and to use its positive aspects to counteract the negative. One way they did so was to mobilize the resources they accrued from the regime in their domestic power struggles. In doing so, they extended their recognized identities as *mothers* to protect themselves as *wives*. Gyámhatóság clients graced with the "good mother" label were particularly successful at this strategy. Many appropriated the financial resources they received from that office to change their husbands' treatment of them. For instance, in 1974 one female client threatened to transfer the family allowance to her name. She had her caseworker write a letter approving the transfer—a letter she showed her husband when he drank heavily. Other women used the home visits that accompanied child-rearing assistance to achieve this end. In one 1975 case a female client told her caseworker about the obscenities her husband used, that he often called her a "whore" (*kurva*). On subsequent visits, the caseworker scolded the man for his language. In a 1978 case a woman informed her caseworker that she had to apply for assistance because her husband refused to work hard. On later visits, the welfare worker lectured him about his "laziness" and pressured him to work more. Thus, female clients used their caseworkers as instruments to shape and regulate male behavior.

Women who had been deemed "problematic" mothers adhered to a similar strategy. Many tried to neutralize the control their caseworkers and husbands had by playing the two off against each other. These clients attempted to redirect the punitive arm of the state onto their husbands, arguing that they could not fit the good mother mold because of their husbands. One client whose children were institutionalized in 1970 continued to initiate home visits, which she used to provide evidence of domestic violence and to suggest that her husband should be placed in state care instead. Another client who applied for child-rearing assistance in 1974 left wine bottles lined up in front of her door. When her caseworker tripped over the bottles, the client told her about her husband's drinking problem, which prevented her from keeping an "orderly house." Clients also used the coercive arm of the welfare apparatus to control their husbands. Many clients asked for copies of home visit reports to show their spouses. "Look at what the *tanács* said about us," one woman exclaimed to her husband in 1980.[29] Others used the threat of institutionalization to force the men to shape up. In 1969 one client asked that her children be put in state care temporarily to prove to her husband that his abusive behavior had "consequences." In all of these ways, clients tried to use state actors to link their problems to their experiences as wives and to provide help in resolving those problems.

Clients connected to Child Guidance Centers of the period also utilized its educative approach to protect their interests as wives. Some used their involvement in their children's counseling to alter the division of labor in the home; they mobilized the time formulas imposed on them to devote more energy to their children and less to household tasks.[30] Other clients used counselors to make more fundamental changes in their families by linking their children's problems to the *family* environment. "Identification problems," one Romani woman exclaimed in 1970 in response to her counselor's representation of her son's Oedipal issues. "His father is never at home, and when he is, he is drunk." In a 1974 case one mother resisted her counselor's suggestion that she leave work early to take her son to sports programs to vent his aggression. Whenever the idea was raised, she reminded the counselor that her husband was a military man who told their son he was "weak," thus hinting that his hegemonic masculinity was the source of the problem. Still others drew counselors into their family dynamics. Many clients were divorced women who shared flats with their former husbands. These domestic arrangements led to all sorts of conflicts—disputes women often used psychologists to resolve. In one 1972 case a mother had her counselor apply time regulations in her home, determining who could use what room when. And in a 1975 case a woman had her former husband's new wife removed from their flat by convincing the psychologist that her son's bed-wetting and night sweats were caused by the stepmother's disruptive presence.

In addition to expanding the confines of the maternal to protect themselves as wives, female clients also raised needs they had as women. They often drew counselors into their own emotional lives, thus transforming child-rearing counseling into personal therapy. Many spoke of feeling isolated; others revealed serious bouts with depression. These feelings often surfaced in their children's psychological counseling as mothers connected their own loneliness to their children's behaviorial problems. Similar issues arose in time management counseling. Clients frequently shifted the focus of the training to their conflicts between work and home; they spoke of difficulties juggling all of their responsibilities and discussed how that led to feelings of failure. In doing so, clients engaged state actors in the conflicts they experienced as women and created social relationships to mitigate their isolation. By the 1980s, so many women had raised these issues that psychologists gave them a name, appropriately calling them symptoms of the "GYES Syndrome" (Somlai 1994).

In sum, through all of these different tactics female clients used their status as mothers to their advantage. By forcing state actors to acknowledge the larger context in which they mothered, clients advanced a broader definition of their needs as wives. By mobilizing the resources of the welfare apparatus in their domestic struggles, they found ways to meet those needs. And by drawing state actors into their interpersonal lives, they countered the isolation too often associated with mothering. Within this maternalist welfare regime, women developed a repertoire of strategies to secure their well-being and to protect themselves in their everyday lives—a repertoire they soon found themselves defending when the welfare regime changed.

The Liberal Welfare State: Targeting and Treating the "Needy"

The mid-1980s experienced another turning point in the development of the Hungarian welfare state as the welfare apparatus began to shift focus from the maternal to the material. As in the late 1960s, this restructuring was an outgrowth of social, economic, and professional forces. First, beginning in the late 1970s there was a marked increase in social inequality and poverty. As Szelényi and Manchin (1987) argue, a dual system of stratification began to develop—at the top were new entrepreneurial classes with access to second economy goods, incomes, and services, whereas at the bottom were large groups of Hungarians without the skills or resources to secure economy incomes. The latter group, constituting over 30 percent of the population, experienced real pauperization in this period. New social inequalities also began to surface among Hungarian families as female-headed households and urban families with children began slipping into poverty throughout the early 1980s (Ferge 1987; Szalai 1991). These patterns of social differentiation have intensified in the post-1989 period. What was once a widening gap between social classes has become a yawning chasm in the 1990s: official unemployment increased from 0.3 percent in 1987 to over 11 percent in 1993, and the proportion of Hungarians living at or below the subsistence level skyrocketed from 8 percent in 1987 to 16 percent in 1992 to 32 percent in 1994 (Ferge 1996; Andorka 1996).

Hungarian policymakers could have responded to these social problems in a variety of ways. As in the 1960s, the path they took was shaped by the ascendancy of professional groups, this time of sociologists and neoliberal economists. In the early 1980s, sociologists began to exert their "expertise" in this area. Through studies of working-class and Romani communities conducted in the 1970s and 1980s, sociologists became aware of the poverty plaguing large sectors of the population. Moreover, through their practical experiences in poor-relief agencies such as SZETA [Szegényeket Támogató Alap (Fund to Support the Poor)], sociologists uncovered the way these groups were falling through cracks in the system, with their social problems unresolved. Sociologists began to publish articles and research reports that faulted the existing welfare regime for not addressing these problems, and they called for its reform (Ferge 1982, 1987). First and foremost, they proposed more differentiated policies designed to meet the material needs of specific groups (Ferge and Szalai 1985). They also sought to create a network of new institutions, to be staffed from within their ranks, that would treat these needs directly and immediately (Gosztonyi 1993; Révész 1993). In effect, they called for a more discretionary and targeted welfare state—and they did so in the name of the poor, impoverished classes.[31]

Almost paradoxically, these sociologists' appeals resonated with the reform agenda of neoliberal economists. As their counterparts had done in the 1960s, these economists made a direct link between social and economic policy. But whereas earlier reformers used maternalist policies to alleviate economic problems, this new generation of economists saw those policies as economically debilitating. Well versed in liberal economic theory and well aware of International Monetary Fund (IMF) and World Bank demands, neoliberal economists viewed the "needs" of the Hungarian economy as antithetical to the prevailing welfare model. In particular, they claimed this welfare model subjected the state to "grandiose soft budget constraints" (Kornai 1994).[32] The economists pushed to narrow eligibility criteria away from "encompassing" categories such as motherhood to more "exclusive" ones such as the materially needy (Kornai 1994; World Bank 1992). So although neoliberal economists launched their attack in the name of the economy rather than of social class, they joined sociologists to argue that the system "needed" the means-tested policies of a discretionary welfare state.

Hence, in the mid-1980s the social problems facing the state converged with the professional appeals of Hungarian sociologists and economists to pave the way for the emergence of a new welfare regime. As in the 1960s, this convergence prompted a change in the social conception of need, but this time the social architecture of need was etched out on the terrain of class. Once organized around motherhood, the Hungarian welfare apparatus was reconfigured around the poor and needy. As means-tests became the sole method for distributing assistance and welfare institutions were oriented toward poor relief, clients' material needs became the only recognized eligibility criterion. And as eligibility was materialized, the determination of need was individualized and stigmatized. Hungarian women were repositioned in the welfare apparatus; their old set of maternal identities and entitlements was replaced by a new set of class identities and stigmas.

Welfare Policies: From Maternal to Material Need

The first major policy change that marked the shift from the maternal to the material occurred in 1985, five years before the 1990 political regime change. At this time the GYES system was reformed, and maternity leave payments were linked to income. Previously, GYES had consisted of flat-rate payments to all mothers regardless of their income. The flat-rate system was disadvantageous to middle-class and professional women whose salaries were higher than the universal payments; as a result, those women tended to stay on GYES for shorter periods than other classes. In their poverty studies, sociologists linked these use patterns to the rising inequality among Hungarian families, arguing that the patterns widened the social distance between middle-, working-, and lower-class families (Ferge 1987; Szalai 1991). To rectify this situation in 1985 GYES was split into three separate provisions: maternity leave grants (*Gyermekágyi segély*) that ran for six months after childbirth, the child-care grant (*Gyermekgondozási Díj* [GYED]) that extended for eighteen additional months at 75 percent of the mother's previous salary, and child-care assistance (GYES) that ran for another six months at a flat rate. By linking payments to the mother's previous salary, the GYES reforms aimed to entice middle-class women to use the grant and thus to flatten out the class differences associated with it (Szalai 1991; Goven 1993).[33] Hence, for the first time since its creation, income became a central principle in structuring the Hungarian maternity leave system.

Whereas GYES reforms sought to increase middle-class women's usage, all other policy reforms in this period were designed to exclude the middle class and to target needy classes of Hungarians. The first policies to undergo such reform were the local-level child-rearing assistance programs. Beginning in the mid-1980s, these schemes were subjected to stricter income formulas and means-tests. All applicants for funds were required to submit official income documentation from their employers stating the exact amount of their monthly salaries. They also had to report all other assets, including bank statements of their savings and accounts of additional valuable items. Home visitors were deployed to check their accounting and to report any discrepancies to caseworkers. Caseworkers then calculated the overall resources at the applicants' disposal. Only applicants whose monthly income fell below the subsistence level were eligible for the funds. These regulations applied to those seeking occasional (*Rendkívuli Nevelési Segély*) *and* regular assistance (*Rendszeres Nevelési Segély*) and to those applicants caseworkers found "sympathetic," as well as to those they considered "problematic."

Interestingly, the number of Hungarians receiving child-rearing assistance soared during this period. Table 5.1 provides national-level data on the increase. Although these numbers reflect the socioeconomic changes of the period, they also indicate how discretionary the allocation of funds had been during the previous decade. When domesticity tests were replaced by means-tests, caseworkers distributed more of this assistance.

Hungarian welfare policy also took on a more explicitly class character with the decentralization of funding for welfare assistance. The 1990 Local Government Act and the 1992 Social Act restructured the relationship between the national and local governments, effectively shifting much of the burden for welfare funding from the former to the latter. In the new arrangement, the national government would give local governments block grants to cover a portion of their welfare expenditures. The amount of these transfers was to be based on a combination of factors, including the number of inhabitants in a district and the taxes paid by local residents (Szalai and Neményi 1993). This plan bred variation among locales in the level of assistance provided to clients; the smaller, wealthier districts offered their residents more extensive support (Harcsa 1995). In Budapest alone, districts differed in the number of times clients

Table 5.1   Child-Rearing Assistance Cases, 1980–1993

	Regular Assistance	*Occasional Assistance*
1980	11,342	—
1983	19,689	—
1985	27,848	120,309
1987	39,081	194,997
1990	101,033	375,243
1993	289,000	2,341,000

Sources: Müvelodési Minisztérium 1988; Szalai and Neményi 1993; Ferge 1995, 1996

could receive child-rearing assistance and in the types of programs available. Some districts created special funds for poor families with three or more children; others introduced assistance schemes for impoverished families to offset price increases; still others instituted emergency programs for clients who could not afford medicine, clothing, or school meals for their children. These new programs shared one important feature: they were all means-tested and were based exclusively on material need.

This movement toward targeting the needy culminated with the introduction of the *Bokros csomag* in 1995.[34] After almost a year of parliamentary debate and constitutional court review, this plan went into effect in 1996 and dismantled the remaining maternalist social policies. In the form passed by the Hungarian government, the Bokros plan made two major changes to the welfare system. First, it subjected all family allowances to income tests and thus made them available only to certain classes of Hungarian families. In particular, the plan stipulated that only families with monthly incomes below 19,500 forints per person are eligible for an allowance. Since the subsistence level was approximately 14,000 forints per person and the median monthly income was 18,000 to 21,000 forints per person, sectors of the middle class were cut from the allowance.[35]

Second, the plan also restructured the system of child-care grants. These changes were the most contested component of the plan—the Hungarian constitutional court was flooded with appeals from politicians and Hungarian mothers questioning the program's constitutionality. By early 1996 the court had deemed these changes constitutional, and they went into effect on 15 April 1996. The reforms abolished GYED and subjected GYES to income tests. Once entitled to three years of support, Hungarian women were granted twenty-four weeks of maternity leave. Only women whose income fell below the family allowance cutoff of 19,500 forints per person were eligible for an additional year of support at a fixed rate. By subjecting GYES to these means-tests, the plan cut many middle-class mothers from the grant.

Yet, the reform package did more than limit the scope of these policies. It also applied a new definition of need to the national-level policy apparatus—a definition that emphasized income rather than motherhood. This shift was articulated explicitly in the public debate spawned by the reform package. Supporters of the plan frequently used class arguments to justify it. The day the package was announced, Prime Minister Horn stated that Hungary was now divided by class, which necessitated new policies aimed at those in need (Magyar Hirlap 1995). Other government officials made similar claims, drawing on examples of wealthy women who received state assistance. As female member of parliament Szolnoki Andrea put it, "Two well-paid doctors do not deserve a family allowance.

In their budget it is a drop in the ocean. But poor parents should receive more support. This differentiation is necessary" (Kertész 1995: 4). Or as one local government official explained to me, "It is a simple principle. Give to the poor and not to the rich. This is basic. But because of our socialist past, we have a hard time understanding it. We will learn."

In the process, many Hungarian women will also learn their own lesson. The reforms are teaching women that their status as mothers no longer entitles them to state support and that they can no longer stake their claims on the basis of motherhood. The reforms are also socializing women to understand that they will be recognized by the welfare apparatus only as needy individuals. For many female clients this message was not new; it was a message they had received in more direct ways through contact with the state welfare agencies of the period.

Welfare Practices: Testing and Training the Needy

The first institutional outcome of sociologists' attempts to revamp the Hungarian welfare apparatus also appeared five years prior to the 1990 political regime change. In 1985 the Ministry of Education established twelve Family Support Services (*Család Segitő Szogalátok*) to be run on a trial basis. By 1991 over a hundred centers were operating in Hungary, twenty in Budapest alone (Gosztonyi 1993). The presence of these agencies immediately prompted a reorganization of the institutional division of labor. After a series of professional battles, most Child Guidance Centers began to focus only on children. They transferred their family caretakers and clients with domestic problems to Family Support Services or the Gyámhatóság. Thus, the institutional welfare apparatus bifurcated once again, this time between the educative Family Support Centers and the punitive Gyámhatóság. Yet, despite their distinct orientations, both institutions centered on their clients' material lives, thus replacing the earlier maternalization of need with materialization.

Within local-level Gyámhatóság offices, this period was also marked by internal changes in the organization of welfare work. In the late 1980s the number of workers employed in these offices increased by nearly 50 percent (Müvelodési Minisztérium 1988). Local governments then instituted new procedures for the home visits conducted by welfare workers. First, they standardized those visits by setting limits on the number of visits required for different kinds of cases. They also created fixed questionnaires workers used on visits. In doing so, they altered the focus of the investigations. Once designed to assess clients' domestic practices, the investigations became tools for surveying clients' material lives. The questions related to cooking and cleaning skills were removed and replaced with new questions designed to gauge the level of material need. Home visitors were asked to determine the cost and overall "comfort level" of applicants' flats, assess the value of their furniture, list all electronic and household appliances, and note whether they had a telephone or an automobile. The questionnaires were closed-ended, composed of multiple-choice questions and a small space for comments on the applicant; welfare workers thus had less room for their old discretionary practices and reflections on clients' domestic competency.

Like the old domesticity tests, the new poverty tests determined clients' institutional fate. These tests not only shaped *how* clients were treated, they determined *whether* they were dealt with at all by the offices. Caseworkers used the tests to forge their clientele; only women who could demonstrate material need became clients. Women found to be living in stable financial circumstances were routinely shuffled out of the office. "I am sorry, I cannot help you," a caseworker once told a woman seeking advice on her son's delinquent behavior. "You have the resources to deal with the problem, but maybe you can try a probation officer." Others were ignored once they were found to be financially secure. For instance, in 1994 one woman was referred to the office by her son's teacher. On our way to visit the mother, the caseworker told me about the woman's mental problems and her inability to get her son to school regularly. The caseworker was prepared to make a serious intervention—until we reached the home. Although the mother was bedridden and suffering emotionally, she lived in a five-room, well-furnished flat in one of the best areas of the city. After discovering how large her disability pension was, the caseworker dropped the case. When I asked her about this change in attitude, she responded, "I don't have time for that. She can pay someone to take care of her son if she needs to. Please, I have clients who can't even feed their kids."

Caseworkers articulated a similar message through the kinds of assistance offered to women who actually became clients. Overall, these state actors dealt with clients in one of two ways. First, in an overwhelming majority of cases, they distributed financial assistance. Once used as a reward for "good" mothers, child-rearing funds became the main way caseworkers dealt with their clientele—they simply allocated aid to their clients and assumed that would solve the problem. In the two districts of my research, the proportion of clients receiving child-rearing assistance increased dramatically between the mid-1980s and the mid-1990s. Table 5.2 presents the data for one of those districts.[36] As these data show, by 1992 a large majority of clients in this office were recipients of child-rearing assistance. Put another way, three of every four Hungarians connected to this office had been defined as needy or materially deprived.

In addition to distributing child-rearing assistance, caseworkers continued to place large numbers of children in state care. Once used to pun-

Table 5.2   Xth District Assistance Cases, 1985–1992

	Number of Cases	Percentage of All Cases
1985	384	8
1989	1,070	22
1991	3,884	61
1992	5,010	71

Source: KSH 1985, 1989, 1991, 1992.

ish "incompetent" mothers, institutionalization became the central way caseworkers dealt with clients with severe material problems. Although the overall number of Hungarian children placed in state care has remained steady since the mid-1980s, the grounds for institutionalization have changed (Müvelodési Minisztérium 1988). Poverty has become the main justification for removing children from their homes. In the many cases I reviewed from this period, I uncovered very few references to clients' mothering practices. Instead, a new thread ran through the cases—women were deemed incapable of providing basic necessities for their children. This finding is corroborated by statistical data collected by the institutions. In 1984, 29 percent of the children placed in state care were said to be materially (*anyagilag*) endangered; by 1992 that number had increased to 87 percent.[37]

This shift in focus from clients' mothering practices to their material lives gave rise to a new discourse and imagery surrounding the "welfare client." Caseworkers used an extremely condescending tone when speaking or writing about their clientele. Once reserved for Romani women, the image of the "welfare cheat" loomed over all Gyámhatóság clients. "Clients are different today," one older caseworker revealed in an interview. "They lie, cheat, and steal. Even the Hungarians do this now. Terrible![38] The agencies had institutional archives of stories to support this view: home visitors who found electronics and appliances hidden in closets, caseworkers who discovered forged income documents, and clients who came to the office covered with expensive jewelry. Caseworkers also developed a common language to describe their clients, frequently calling them lazy (*lusta*), uncultured (*kulturalátlan*), simple (*egyszeru*), and disorderly (*rendetlen*). They used those defects to explain client poverty. A few caseworkers even used animal metaphors to describe their clients, referring them as cattle and pigs. One office kept air freshener near the entrance to get rid of the "sickening smell" of poverty. In effect, the focus on individual need gave rise to a preoccupation with individual defect; the materialization of need led to the pathologizing of the welfare client.

In many ways, local Family Support Services were designed to counter such practices. Staffed by a new cadre of young, well-educated social workers, these institutions defined themselves in opposition to the Gyám-hatóság. The social workers employed in these offices saw their job as client advocacy; they set out to help clients curb their poverty and navigate through the maze of welfare regulations. Yet, although these social workers did take a less punitive approach, they also adhered to a narrow conception of their clients' needs and constituted them as "needy" individuals.

More specifically, one form of assistance social workers provided to clients was to act as their mediators with other state bodies. All clients came to them voluntarily, often on a walk-in basis. New clients were inevitably greeted with a litany of questions about their income and work history. Social workers then made the necessary calculations to determine whether they were eligible for additional state benefits. If so, they referred clients to the appropriate offices. More typical were clients who had been denied some form of state support. Here, social workers embarked on what can best be termed "client packaging." In effect, they taught clients how to represent themselves to secure state assistance. Many social workers conducted role plays with their clients: "Now pretend I am an assistance officer. How would you explain your problem to me?" In these exercises, social workers critiqued clients' language and tone of voice. "Anger will not work," one social worker told a Romani client. "They don't like that over there." Social workers also told their clients what to emphasize when framing their appeals. "Don't talk about the fights with your husband," one male social worker advised a client. "Just tell them that your husband lost his job and you have no heat." Hence, in their "advocacy" work, social workers taught clients how to couch their appeals in new ways, how to appear sympathetic as well as needy.

Social workers transmitted a similar message through their distribution of the office's resources. Family Services had emergency funds, food, and clothing. Few formal rules guided the allocation of those funds; clients were not *entitled* to any of them (Katona and Szabó 1992). Rather, they had to convince social workers that they needed these resources. In effect, clients had to beg for them. Material deprivation was the most important factor in determining who received benefits. Many female clients staked a claim to the funds on their children's behalf, but they were denied unless they mustered evidence of material need. "I have no money for your son's camp," a social worker told her client. "Ask your ex-husband. My records show that he is still employed." Other women couched their appeals in terms of domestic problems; they, too, were regularly rejected. One woman asked a social worker for money to fix a window through which her husband had thrown a television in a drunken rage. She was denied. Her social worker told me, "Excuse me, but if they can afford a television, they must have the money to fix the window!" Again, only the materially needy were worthy of support.

Although such short-term interactions constituted the bulk of their work, social workers also had small caseloads of clients they met on a regular basis to treat the clients' ongoing, recurrent problems. A number of clients were the beneficiaries of resource management counseling. "Some clients don't realize they are poor," a social worker explained. "They spend money like they had jobs. Then they come in here when they run out [of money]." So social workers taught these clients to economize and budget, showing them how to calculate their monthly expenses and shop for discounted products. Others were counseled about changing their lifestyles. Clients with alcohol problems were routinely lectured about the connection between alcoholism and poverty. "How many forints do you spend on palinka?" a social worker asked a client. "Imagine, if you had that money, you would not be here." Such lifestyle counseling was particularly salient in an office that received funding from the Catholic Church.[39] Here, social workers often tried to instill new "values for living"—such as morality, piety, and frugality—in their clients. As one of them put it, "If more clients lived like this, they would not be in such terrible conditions."

Thus, the approach taken by these social workers echoed that of Gyámhatóság welfare workers. Like their counterparts, social workers materialized their clients' needs. Although their practices lacked the same hostile tone, social workers did locate the source of clients' problems in their behavior and lifestyles. Social workers taught clients that if they represented themselves better or lived more effectively they could improve their situation, thus making a similar connection between individual need and individual defect.

"But We Are Still Mothers"

These changes in the Hungarian welfare apparatus were not carried out on groups of docile, passive female clients. Rather, the women had developed opinions about their needs. They believed the welfare changes were threatening and oppressive, and they criticized the reforms on numerous grounds. First, many female clients mourned the loss of their previous sense of maternal entitlement. They often complained about having to beg for state assistance. When they submitted income documentation, they commented that such information should not be of concern to caseworkers. "Why do you need evidence of my mother's pension?" one young woman asked a caseworker. "Isn't it enough that I am a single mother with two kids?" On home visits, clients frequently demanded that caseworkers justify inquiries into the value of their household items. Others found such investigations degrading. Female clients from the Family Support Services often told me they dreaded coming to the offices because doing so made them feel "embarrassed" and "ashamed." One female client said to a friend as they left the Gyámhatóság, "I always feel dirty here. They are so despising."

A few clients offered politically astute analyses of the long-term effects of the loss of entitlement. These clients viewed the welfare changes negatively because they jeopardized future funding; they claimed the government was more apt to cut programs aimed at the poor. For instance, in 1994 one district reduced the amount of child-rearing assistance. A number of clients immediately interpreted this reduction as proof of the government's disregard for policies supporting the poor. One client made this argument to me the day after the Bokros reforms were introduced. When she learned I was from the United States she asked about the welfare reforms underway there, which she had heard were similar to the Bokros plan. I explained that they were different—that they were cuts in the already targeted AFDC (Aid to Families with Dependent Children) program that paled in comparison with those under attack in Hungary. She quickly corrected me: "You pay attention. This was the first step. Then they will cut more. It will not be so different."

Other female clients seemed most troubled by their loss of institutional resources. This was particularly true of Gyámhatóság clients who had come to rely on caseworkers in their domestic struggles. On home visits, clients often became disgruntled at welfare workers' indifference to their familial problems. As they told stories of domestic turmoil to the blank, uninterested faces of caseworkers, they became frustrated. "Did you hear me?" one Romani woman exclaimed as her caseworker measured the size of her flat. "I said that he goes to those prostitutes on Rákóczi square. This is dangerous for the little one, with all the diseases. Are you writing this down?" In another case, a female client became furious when she received no response to accounts of her husband's abuse. When we arrived at her flat, she was cleaning and her husband was sleeping. As the welfare worker made her usual calculations, the client whispered stories about the man's heavy drinking and violence. When the caseworker interrupted to ask if she had a car, the woman began yelling about how no one cared and the Gyámhatóság was no good. The caseworker responded that she was assessing the woman's eligibility for child-rearing support, not the quality of her marriage. As we left, the woman returned to her sweeping with a defeated look on her face.

Because of their loss of entitlement and institutional resources, many female clients deemed the welfare regime as dangerous and threatening; they experienced it as narrowing their room to maneuver in their everyday lives. In response, they reasserted the one sense of entitlement they knew—a sense of entitlement based on motherhood. Although this positioning had limitations, they had learned to use it to their advantage and to expand their identities as mothers to protect their interests as wives and women. In the postsocialist period, then, they tried to salvage that identity. Women had numerous ways of doing so. Prior to the Bokros plan, one common tactic had been to extend the entitlement accrued from GYES to other areas. Many tried to use GYES to become eligible for other forms of state support. For instance, when they applied for child-rearing assistance, clients who were on GYES often made a big fuss about it. They repeated it over and over to caseworkers in hopes that it would help their applications. Others grounded their appeals in terms of GYES, arguing that they needed support because of lost wages. When one client's application was rejected, she argued that women on GYES should not be subjected to the same means-tests since they had chosen not to work, on their "children's behalf." This use of GYES was particularly salient in Family Support Centers, where many women pleaded for help on the basis of GYES—if the government was willing to support them to care for their children, couldn't social workers help out, too?

Interestingly, some clients used GYES to counter the condescending approach of caseworkers; they appropriated GYES as a shield to defend themselves against stigmatization. Clients often claimed their poverty was temporary, the result of GYES. "We were in a good material situation before the baby," one client remarked, "but since then we have fallen." They were not lazy, simple, or disorderly; they were committed mothers willing to live in difficult conditions to be with their children. Female clients used a different tone of voice when speaking of GYES. When caseworkers quizzed them about their material lives in the large collective offices, clients tended to whisper as they listed the types of poor relief they received. But when they mentioned GYES, they spoke up. "Oh, and of course I am on GYES," a previously quiet woman shouted. Clients also mobilized GYES to connect with caseworkers and to close the social distance separating them. For instance, two caseworkers in one of the offices were pregnant. Female clients often asked them about their pregnancies and their plans for child-care leave. They discussed their experiences with the grant, prompting a conversation about something shared. A client joked about one of these caseworkers after she went on leave, "I hope her husband is well paid. Maybe she will come in after me, sitting on my side of the desk this time." Hence, in these ways female clients appropriated GYES to counteract the pathologizing of their needs.

Other women mobilized the products of GYES to reassert a sense of entitlement, trying to stake a claim to state support in the name of their children. Clients brought children of all ages to the offices. Waiting rooms seemed like playgrounds, with children running around and screaming. Mothers warned them not to get dirty before they saw the caseworkers. Once inside the office, mothers drew on their children to win support, some pointing out how well behaved their children were. Others brought school records to prove they were responsible mothers. "Look how my son writes his name," said one client whose income was just above the cutoff for assistance. "I taught him this." A few had their kids sing and dance to impress social workers. In effect, clients tried to butter up the bureaucratic machine by illustrating that they were good mothers with good kids. Whereas this strategy may have worked for them in the past, it was futile in this context. Social workers just looked at them, perplexed by the "strange" things clients did to get assistance.

Clients whose children had been placed in state care used similar strategies. Many appealed the decisions by arguing that material neglect was not maternal neglect. They tried to convince caseworkers that they were competent mothers despite their poverty. On home visits, they tried to exhibit good mothering skills in attempts to get their children back. In one case, a woman who lived in a dark, humid basement flat put out a plate of cookies when we arrived. They were her son's favorite cookies, and she took them to him when she visited the children's home. One single mother who lived in a small flat with two other families showed us where her daughter had slept before she was taken away—a small old cot with a worn-out teddy bear on it. She paid extra rent for the cot but always did what was best for the "little one." Yet, caseworkers seldom budged; they rarely let clients distract them from a narrow focus on their material lives.

Finally, a few clients protested the materialization of their needs in a more direct fashion by engaging in shouting matches with caseworkers, and refusing to accept the new rules. They overtly challenged the limited focus on their material lives and forced social workers to explain why their needs as mothers no longer mattered. In these exchanges, female clients asked some penetrating questions: Why was it important if they had televisions or VCRs? And why wasn't it important that they raised their kids "properly"? Why was it relevant if they knew how to economize? And why wasn't it relevant that their husbands beat them? Who made these decisions? Few clients received answers to these questions. The needy ones were given a little money and shuffled out of the office; the others were just shuffled out.

Conclusion

The conceptualization of the changing Hungarian welfare regime presented in this chapter differs from prevailing models of the East European welfare state transition. First, rather than compare the Hungarian welfare state to a Western mythology of how welfare states "should" operate, I traced the dynamics of welfare state transformation within Hungary over time. Second, rather than utilize the quantitative categories of size or scope to guide my comparison, I approached it through the lens of social architectures of need. This conceptual lens drew into focus parallel changes on three terrains of the Hungarian welfare state—regime policies, practices, and client strategies—thereby illuminating how the transition in the welfare state marks a fundamental change in the meaning of welfare itself.

During the last two decades of state socialism, most "needs talk" revolved around motherhood. Social policies extended special support to mothers, state caseworkers employed domesticity tests to survey mothering practices, and state psychologists mobilized family models to rationalize child rearing. Thus, the policies drew on women's identities as mothers. In the postsocialist period, maternal needs talk has been dislodged by a new language of welfare. As social provisions are means-tested, state assistance is extended to the impoverished. As poverty tests replace domesticity tests and poor relief substitutes for child-rearing counseling, state support is targeting the needy. In the process, women's identities as mothers are being reconfigured and displaced by a new set of identities based on income. Hence, the conceptual lens of architectures of need revealed how historical shifts in conceptions of need drew upon and defined women's identities in divergent ways.

The conceptual framework developed in this chapter also enables us to assess the effects of these conceptions of need on women. Through a parallel analysis of the policies and practices of past and present Hungarian welfare regimes, I revealed variations in their levels of discursive penetrability and in the institutional resources offered to women. Although the state socialist welfare regime confined most needs talk to the maternal, female clients expanded it to include their needs as wives. Likewise, although the regime scrutinized women's mothering practices, it also gave them the resources to scrutinize with—caseworkers to scold their husbands, counselors to set household rules, and welfare funds to serve as domestic collateral. The postsocialist welfare regime accords women less room to maneuver. It hears the appeals of certain classes of women and only appeals connected to their material lives. Moreover, state actors read new meanings into those appeals, interpreting them for evidence of individual defect and pathology. Although state actors continue to scrutinize, they no longer offer women the resources to scrutinize with. When clients used their children and domestic skills to resist, they were responding to that contraction in space. As they tried to salvage their past identities as mothers, they sent a message about the discursive and practical losses they are suffering in the present.

Whereas these clients' strategies reveal much about the relationship between the past and present in Hungary, they also have significance for the future. Women's contests with the system raise questions about the limitations of a welfare apparatus that restricts itself to the material. In particular, their experience forces us to contemplate the ease with which a materialization of need breeds an individualization of need and the speed with which an individualization of need leads to the stigmatization of the needy. It also forces us to think about how this kind of needs talk closes off channels through which women can define and advance their own interests. When these Hungarian clients went to battle against the postsocialist welfare regime, they struggled to develop a more responsive welfare structure and more participatory needs talk. Through their resistance they raised fundamental questions about how welfare policies and institutions can be structured to give women discursive and practical resources—questions that will remain at the center of the politics of need for decades of welfare regimes to come.

Notes

Acknowledgments: Research for this chapter was supported by grants from the International Research and Exchanges Board (IREX), the Joint Committee on Eastern Europe of the American Council of Learned Societies and the Social Science Research Council, and the Office of the Chancellor at the University of California, Berkeley.

1. The data in this chapter are drawn from research carried out in Budapest from October 1993 to April 1995. During this period I conducted research on the development of the welfare apparatus in two Budapest districts. To protect the identities of my subjects, I am forced to keep the districts of my research anonymous. I will use X and XX to identify them. These districts were chosen on the basis of various demographic criteria—they were similar in size but with varied class and ethnicity of their inhabitants. District X was a historically impoverished area with an ethnically diverse population, whereas District XX had working-class, middle-class, and bourgeois pockets with relative ethnic homogeneity. This mixture allowed me to examine the practices of welfare offices working with different populations and hence to ensure the generalizability of my research findings. In my research, I collected four types of data. First, I conducted eighteen months of fieldwork in the three social welfare institutions of these districts: Child Protective Services (Gyámhatóságok), Child Guidance Centers (Nevelési Tanácsadók), and Family Support Centers (Család Segítő Szogálatok). I had access to all areas of their work—I attended staff meetings, observed social worker–client interactions, and accompanied caseworkers on home visits. Second, I completed thirty-five in-depth, open-ended interviews with Hungarians affiliated with

the social welfare apparatus from 1952 to 1994. My respondents included former caseworkers, psychologists, local government officials, and politicians. Third, I carried out primary source research in the local government archives of both districts. In particular, I analyzed a random sample of case files from the Gyámhatóság (1952–1994) and the Nevelési Tanácsadok (1969–1994). I sampled 100 cases from each institution for each decade under examination, bringing my total sample to over 1,000 cases. Finally, I collected primary and secondary source materials on the social policies, laws, and provisions produced at the national level in the state socialist and postcommunist periods.

2. For insightful discussions of the relationship between the state and the family under state socialism, see Verdery (1994) and Goven (1993).

3. Prior to this point, eligibility had been *informally* linked to other social characteristics, the most important of which was bureaucratic privilege. As many Hungarians have shown, the Hungarian "welfare society" bred its own forms of inequality (Szelényi 1978, 1983; Szelényi and Manchin 1987; Ladányi 1975; Szalai 1984). My point here is that by the mid-1960s eligibility had become *formally* tied to other characteristics, including age, family structure, and, to some extent, ethnicity. In terms of the latter, in the early 1970s the Hungarian Romani population was given limited preferential treatment in state policy, especially in the sphere of housing. For more on this, see Kemény (1974) and Hooz (1975).

4. For an excellent discussion of how these demographic changes were appropriated by the political opposition of the period to oppose the regime and to challenge existing gender relations, see Goven (1993), especially chapter 3.

5. More specifically, countries such as Romania and Poland dealt with similar demographic shifts by outlawing abortion and restricting access to birth control rather than instituting an incentive structure for mothers (Kligman 1993). Thus, their population policies were centered more on childbearing than on child rearing. I thank Gail Kligman and Katherine Verdery for drawing this comparative point to my attention.

6. The fixed rates varied over time but generally hovered at around 50 percent to 65 percent of the average Hungarian wage. For data on this, see KSH (1981).

7. Agricultural workers had to participate in at least 120 days of collective work in the twelve months prior to the birth.

8. A similar increase characterized women's use patterns. The percentage of Hungarian mothers using the grant rose steadily over this period. By the mid-1970s, over 15 percent of female workers were on GYES at any given moment. At the same time, significant class differences were found in use patterns. These differences surfaced in the amount of time different groups of mothers spent on the grant. Whereas an overwhelming majority of women from all classes used the grant, well-educated, better-paid professionals tended to stay on it for shorter periods. In 1985 the Hungarian government tried to alter that pattern by giving recipients the option to take 75 percent of their previous salary for the grant's tenure. This transition from GYES to GYED and its class implications are discussed in the following section. For more data on women's use patterns and the ways they varied by class and economic sector, see KSH (1981, 1988).

9. This sense of entitlement can be seen in the appeals submitted to the Ministry of Labor by women who had been denied GYES. As Forgó (1987) revealed, the two largest groups of women denied GYES were those who failed to meet the work requirements and those who wanted to use the grant for more than one child. Their appeals exhibited an incredible sense of entitlement—they couched the appeals in terms of their *rights* as mothers and argued that motherhood entitled them to the benefits. Since the appeals were transferred to local governments for review, no reliable national-level data exist on how many were actually granted.

10. The amount of the benefits varied by economic sector and enterprise, but most hovered around 50 percent to 70 percent of the recipient's salary. See Ferge (1979), Gal (1969), and Pongrácz (1986) for more on Hungary's sick leave regulations.

11. Initially, these allowances were designed for civil servants. Just prior to World War II they were extended to those employed in enterprises with more than twenty workers. After 1948 the system was extended to industrial workers with three or more children. In 1959 it was extended to single mothers and agricultural workers; in 1966 workers with two children became eligible. It was not until 1975 that families with one child could receive the allowance. For more on the different shifts in the focus of these allowances, see Gal (1969), Pongrácz (1986), and Gyáni (1994).

12. That is, from my sample of 223 Gyámhatóság cases in the 1970s, roughly 10 percent of the cases involved appeals to switch the family allowance to the mother's name. Without reliable national-level data I cannot assess whether this finding is representative of other districts.

13. The use of the funds varied by district. In the two districts of my research, 200 to 300 assistance cases of some sort were initiated each year throughout the late 1970s and early 1980s. The number increased dramatically in the mid-1980s. See Tables 5.1 and 5.2 for these data.

14. Although no national-level data exist on the gender of the recipients, in the 170 assistance applications I reviewed in my archival research, only two were initiated by Hungarian fathers.

15. What is more, the few existing analyses of Hungarian welfare work in this period are completely gender blind (Konrád 1974; Hanak 1983; Horváth 1982; Domszky 1994). For instance, whereas Konrád (1974) provides a powerful (albeit literary) analysis of these institutions, he fails to mention that the overwhelming majority of state actors and clients connected to them were women. Further, he does not even attempt to unearth the gender regime underlying their institutional practices.

16. All Hungarian families had some contact with the Gyámhatóság since parents were required to register with these offices after the birth of each child. The two institutions I studied averaged 8,000 to 12,000 cases per year throughout the period; of this number, approximately half were ongoing cases that involved regular contact. Thus, approximately 10 to 15 percent of Hungarians in these districts had some contact with these offices on a yearly basis, with 5 to 7 percent of Hungarians maintaining regular contact with the Gyámhatóság.

17. In addition to registering children, the Gyámhatóság's other bureaucratic duties included making recommendations in child custody cases, setting and enforcing child support payments, solving housing problems, providing permission for minors to get married, and ruling on all GYES and family allowance appeals. This bureaucratic work constituted approximately 30 to 40 percent of the caseload; the rest was devoted to child protection work.

18. An overwhelming majority of these state workers had only secondary school degrees. A few also had degrees in law or legal administration from technical colleges (*szakfőiskola*). See Művelősi Minisztérium (1988) for these data.

19. For instance, consider a 1970 comment by a caseworker on a home visit to resolve a custody dispute: "The woman seemed like she cooked. But when I asked her how she did stuffed cabbage, she hesitated. I do not think she cooks regularly for the children."

20. More specifically, from 1965 to 1985 the number of children placed in some kind of state care (including temporary institutions) nearly doubled— jumping from 33,480 in 1965 to 38,353 in 1975 to 60,949 in 1985. Put another way, whereas 1 percent of Hungarian children under age seventeen were in state care in 1965, 2.3 percent were in such institutions by 1985. See Művelődési Minisztérium (1988) for these data.

21. In the two districts of my research I uncovered 117 cases of institutionalization during this period, 98 of which involved such "mother blame."

22. This was particularly true in divorce cases. That is, most middle-class and professional women became Gyámhatóság clients through divorce and custody disputes. Such cases constituted a large part of the agency's caseload. Hence, many caseworkers were deployed to assess the home environment of middle-class women to determine custody arrangements. And it was through these visits that such women were regularly blamed for being too careerist and uncommitted to their children and their families.

23. Unfortunately, I cannot give precise data on how many Romani clients were deemed "bad mothers" because caseworkers were not permitted to state clients' race. They were forbidden to note whether a client was Romani. Yet, caseworkers frequently allowed racism to slip into their case reports by calling clients "un-Hungarian" or even "dirty Gypsies." These slips enabled me to uncover the racialized undercurrents of their work.

24. In contrast to Gyámhatóság workers, almost all state psychologists had advanced degrees. In the districts of my research, they were evenly split between those with university degrees and those with degrees from technical colleges in teaching, pedagogy, or psychology.

25. One 1973 case beautifully illustrates their interpretive biases. In this case, a five-year-old boy was brought into the office by his mother who was concerned about his bed-wetting. A psychologist conducted a world game with the boy in which she asked him to build his own world using small figures. In the midst of the game, the boy retreated to the bathroom three times. The psychologist fixated on this, writing that it signified castration anxiety. She wrote in her notes on the case: "The boy repeatedly went to the bathroom during our session to check if his penis was still there. He fears that it will disappear. This is obviously the source of the bed-wetting."

26. Caseworker interview, 6 April 1994.

27. Caseworker interview, 9 May 1994.

28. In the hundreds of cases I reviewed, I did not uncover a single example of a father receiving therapy—even in cases in which the father was clearly the root of the problem. One example comes to mind. In 1976 two boys were referred to the office because they had been acting out in school. In an initial discussion with their mother, the counselor learned that their father was a serious alcoholic who often climbed to the top of their high-rise apartment building (*lakótelep*) and threatened to jump. Instead of calling the father in, the counselor initiated sessions with the mother to advise her on how to control her husband's drinking, how to hide the alcohol or water down his wine. In one session she even advised the woman to make larger dinners as a way to fill her husband up so the alcohol would not dramatically affect him.

29. This incident was reported by a Gyámhatóság family visitor and was used as an argument not to institutionalize the woman's children.

30. For instance, in one 1975 case a mother demanded that her husband participate more in the household while she addressed their children's behaviorial problems. As a family caretaker recounted after a home visit, "I arrived at the home at 6:30. The mother was in the back working with the boys while the father was heating up the food. When I asked her about it, she smiled and said he did this since the therapy started."

31. Herein lies an interesting irony. In the beginning, poverty work was an oppositional move by sociologists. Many were closely connected to dissident circles and saw a focus on poverty as an attempt to use social democratic politics to critique actually existing socialism. At the same time, sociologists had an interest in framing the problem in class terms, which allowed them to carve out places for themselves in the welfare apparatus as both policymakers and state actors. In a sense, many were sociological "intellectuals on the road to state power" (Szelényi and Konrád 1979). And in the post-1989 period, many did reach that goal. The new Hungarian welfare state became a profitable venture for them; sociologists have found new jobs in this welfare apparatus and have created new journals, educational institutions, and publishing companies with which to analyze it.

32. One common way neoliberal economists do this is through international comparisons that show Hungarian welfare expenditures to be greater than those of "advanced" Western welfare states. These greater welfare expenditures, neoliberal economists argue, are economically infeasible and will lead to a rapid decline in economic growth. For the best examples of this argument, see Kornai (1994) and Tóth (1994).

33. There was also a racialized undercurrent in this move from GYES to GYED. That is, in addition to differing by class, GYES use patterns varied by race, with Romani women using the grant for longer periods. The shift to GYED was also an attempt to convince more white, non-Romani Hungarians to have children and stay on the grant longer.

34. Despite the significant political regime change in 1990, very few policy reforms were carried out on national-level maternalist programs from 1985 to 1995. Instead, most of the key shifts occurred at the local level. Interestingly, it

may have been the conservative Christian ideology ascribed to by the MDF [Magyar Demokrata Forum (Hungarian Democratic Forum)] government that "saved" these programs—the government's ideological commitment to the "Hungarian family" and "traditional gender roles" may have inhibited it from scaling back the programs. In contrast, the MSzP [Magyar Szocialista Part (Hungarian Socialist Party)] is less encumbered by such ideological baggage and is more committed to pleasing the IMF and the World Bank—a commitment that may have led the MSzP to acquiesce to the agencies' demands to cut social spending. See Kornai (1994) and Ferge (1995) for two different versions of this explanation.

35. These numbers were compiled from 1993 data collected by Ferge (1995) and adjusted for the rate of inflation. The median monthly income was calculated only for active earners; had pensioners and the unemployed been included, the rate would have been significantly lower. The new cutoff is higher for single parents, at 23,400 forints per person.

36. As these data also reveal, the number of clients connected to these offices increased during this period. For instance, in the district described here, the total number of ongoing cases handled by the office jumped from approximately 4,700 in 1985 to over 7,000 in 1992.

37. These data were drawn from the case summaries collected by the welfare institutions in the two districts of my research.

38. The caseworker distinguished between Romani and non-Romani clients and meant that non-Romani clients now cheat and steal. Since Romani clients are also Hungarians, her comment had racist overtones.

39. A few Family Support Services received funds from different nongovernment bodies such as the Soros Foundation, the Red Cross, and the European Council. These funds were usually connected to specific programs run by social workers. To my knowledge, this center was the only one in Budapest to receive ongoing support from the Catholic Church.

References

Adamik, Mária. 1995. How Can Hungarian Women Lose What They Never Had? Paper presented at the conference "Gender in Transition." Collegium Budapest, 23 January.

Andorka, Rudolf. 1996. A Társadalmi Egyenlőtlenségek Növekedése A Rendszerváltás Óta. *Szociológiai Szemle* 1: 70–92.

Andorka, Rudolf, and István Tóth. 1995. A Jóléti Rendszer Jellemzői és Reformjának Lehetőségei. *Közgazdasági Szemle* 1: 1–29.

Deacon, Robert. 1992a. East European Welfare: Past, Present and Future in Comparative Context. In *The New Eastern Europe: Social Policy Past, Present and Future,* ed. R. Deacon. London: Sage.

———. 1992b. Social Policy, Social Justice and Citizenship in Eastern Europe. In *Social Policy, Social Justice and Citizenship in Eastern Europe,* ed. R. Deacon. Aldershot: Avebury.

Domszky, András. 1994. A Gyermek és Ifjúságvédelem Magyarországon. In *A*

Gyermekvédelem Nemzetközi Gyakorlata, eds. L. Csokay, A. Domszky, V. Hazsai, and M. Herczog. Budapest: Pont Kiadó, 270–328.

Ernst, Gabriella. 1986. A Munka, A Nő és a GYES Rendszere. *Munkaügyi Szemle* 3: 182–198.

Ferge, Zsuzsa. 1979. *A Society in the Making: Hungarian Social and Societal Policy 1945–1975.* New York: M. E. Sharpe.

———. 1982. *Javaslat a Szociálpolitikai Rendszer Módosítására.* Budapest: MTA.

———. 1987. *Szociálpolitika Ma és Holnap.* Budapest: MTA.

———. 1991. Recent Trends in Social Policy in Hungary. In *Economic Reforms and Welfare Systems in the USSR, Poland and Hungary*, ed. J. Adam. New York: St. Martin's.

———. 1992a. Social Policy Regimes and Social Structure. In *Social Policy in a Changing Europe*, ed. J. Kohlberg and Zs. Ferge. Boulder: Westview.

———. 1992b. Unemployment in Hungary: The Need for a New Ideology. In *Social Policy, Social Justice and Citizenship in Eastern Europe*, ed. B. Deacon. Aldershot: Avebury.

———. 1995. A Célzott Szociálpolitika Lehetőségei. Paper presented at the conference "A Jóléti Rendszer Reformja." ELTE [Eötvös Lóránd Tudományegyetem] Szociálpolitika Tanszék, 24 March.

———. 1996. A Magyar Segélyezési Rendszer Reformja II. *Esély* 1.

Ferge, Zsuzsa, and Júlia Szalai. 1985. *Fordulat és Reform.* Budapest: MTA.

Forgó, Györgyné. 1987. A Gyermekgondozási Segély Méltanyossági Ügyek Elbírálása Szerzett Tapasztalatok. *Szociálpolitikai Értesítő* 4.

Fraser, Nancy. 1989. *Unruly Practices.* Minneapolis: University of Minnesota Press.

Fraser, Nancy, and Linda Gordon. 1994. A Genealogy of Dependency: Tracing a Keyword of the U.S. Welfare State. *Signs* 19: 21.

Gál, László. 1969. *Szociálpolitikánk Két Évtizede.* Budapest: Kossuth Könyvkiadó.

Gal, Susan. 1994. Gender in the Post-Socialist Transition: The Abortion Debate in Hungary. *East European Politics and Societies* 8: 2.

Gégési, Pal. 1965. Pszichológiai Tanulmányok: Nevelési Pszichológia. Budapest: Akadémiai Kiadó.

Gosztonyi, Géza. 1993. Hatóság + Szolgálat. *Esély* 4: 14–35.

Goven, Joanna. 1993. *The Gendered Foundations of Hungarian State Socialism: State, Society and the Anti-Politics of Anti-Feminism.* Ph.D. dissertation in Political Science, University of California, Berkeley.

Gyáni, Gábor. 1994. *A Szociálpolitika Múltja Magyarországon.* Budapest: MTA Történettudományi Intézete.

Hanák, Katalin. 1983. *Társadalom és Gyermekvédelem.* Budapest: Kiadó.

Harcsa, István. 1995. *Szociális Ellátás az Önkormányzatoknál (A Kísérleti Adatgyűjtés Tapasztalata).* Budapest: Központi Statisztikai Hivatal.

Hooz, Istvan. 1975. A Cigány és a nem Cigány Népesség Társadalmi és Kulturális Helyzetében Lévő Fontosabb Különbségekről. *Állam és Jogtudomány* 4: 49–66.

Horányi, Annabella. 1985. A Fővárosi Nevelési Tanácsadók Tevékenységéről. In *Nevelési Tanácsadás Elmélete és Gyakorlata,* ed. A. Horanyi. Budapest: Tankönyvkiadó, 237–249.

Horváth, Ágota. 1982. Egy Segély Anatómiája. In *Oktatásról és Társadalompolitikáról.* Budapest: Szociológiai Kutató Intézete.

Horváth, Erika. 1986. *A GYEStól a GYEDig.* Budapest: Kiadó.

Katona, László, and Judit Szabó. 1992. Temetés, Tüzelő, Napközi: Diszkrecionális Segélyezés A Családsegitő Központokban. *Esély* 5: 52–57.

Kemény, Istvan. 1974. A Magyarországi Cigány Lakosság. *Valóság* 11: 63–72.

Kertész, Péter. 1995. Vélemények a Szociális Ellátórendszer Átalakításaról. *Magyar Hírlap,* March 21.

Kligman, Gail. 1993. The Politics of Reproduction in Ceauşescu's Romania. *East European Politics and Societies* 6: 364–418.

Klinger, András. 1961. A Társadalmi Rétegenként Differenciált Termékenység Alakulása Magyarországon. *Demográfia* 4: 4.

Klinger, András, B. Barta, and G. Vukovich. 1984. *Fertility and Female Employment in Hungary.* Geneva: International Labor Organization.

Konrád, György. 1974. *The Caseworker.* New York: Harcourt, Brace, and Jovanovich.

Kornai, János. 1994. Lasting Growth as the Top Priority. Collegium Budapest, Discussion Paper no. 7.

———. 1993. *Útkeresés.* Budapest: Századvég Kiadó.

Központi Statisztikai Hivatal (KSH). 1981. *A Gyermekgondozási Segély Igénybevétele és Hatásai.* Budapest: Társadalmi Statisztikai Főosztály.

———. 1988. *A Gyermekgondozási Díj Igénybevétele és Hatásai.* Budapest: Társadalmi Statisztikai Főosztály.

———. 1968–1995. "A Gyámhatóság Tevékenységéről." Budapest: Társadalmi Főosztály.

Ladányi, János. 1975. Fogyasztói Árak és Szociálpolitika. *Valóság* 12: 16–19.

Lieberman, Lucy. 1964. A Nevelési Tanácsadás Problémai Hazánkban. *Magyar Pszichológiai Szemle* 21: 579–586.

Magyar Hírlap. 1995. "Horn: Ez még csak a kezdet," 15 March: 1.

Márkus, Mária. 1970. A Nő Helyzete A Munka világában," *Kortárs* Vol. 14, no. 2: 126–42.

Mérei, Ferenc. 1974. *Klinikai Pszichodiagnosztikai Módszerek.* Budapest: Medicina Könyvkiadó.

Mód, Aladárné. 1961. Születésszám és Életszínvonal. *Demográfia* 4: 3.

Művelődési Minisztérium. 1988. *Statisztikai Tájekoztató: Gyermekvédelem.* Budapest: Tudományszervezési és Informatikai Intézet.

Pongrácz, László. 1986. *Szociálpolitikai Ismeretek.* Budapest: Munkügyi Kutató Intézet.

Révész, Magda. 1993. Hungarian Family Helping Centers: Theory and Practice. Paper presented at the National Association of Social Workers Annual Conference, Orlando, Florida.

Somlai, Péter. 1994. Kötelékek—Széltörésben. *Család, Gyermek, Ifjúság* 8, no. 2: 3–4.

Szalai, Júlia. 1984. *Az Egészségügy Betegségei.* Budapest: MTA.

———. 1991. Some Aspects of the Changing Situation of Women in Hungary. *Signs* 17: 1.

———. 1994. *Urban Poverty and Social Policy in the Context of Adjustment: The Case of Hungary.* Budapest: MTA.

Szalai, Júlia, and Mária Neményi. 1993. *Hungary in the 1980s: A Historic Review of Social Policy and Urban Level Interventions.* Washington, D.C.: World Bank.

Szelényi, Iván. 1978. Urban Inequalities Under State Socialist Redistributive Economies. *International Journal of Comparative Sociology* 1: 61–87.

———. 1983. *Urban Inequalities Under State Socialism.* Oxford: Oxford University Press.

Szelényi, Iván, and György Konrád. 1979. *Intellectuals on the Road to Class Power.* New York: Harcourt, Brace, and Jovanovich.

Szelényi, Iván and János Ladanyi. 1996. Egy Posztkommunista New Deal Esélyei Kelet Közép Európában, *Kritika,* January.

Szelényi, Iván, and Róbert Manchin. 1987. Social Policy Under State Socialism: Market Redistribution and Social Inequalities in East European Socialist Societies. In *Stagnation and Renewal in Social Policy,* ed. G. Esping-Andersen. New York: M. E. Sharpe.

Tímár, János. 1991. Economic Reform and New Employment Problems in Hungary. In *Economic Reforms and Welfare Systems in the USSR, Poland and Hungary,* ed. J. Adam. New York: St. Martin's.

Tóth, György. 1994. A Jóléti Rendszer az Átmeneti Időszakban. *Közgazdasági Szemle* 4(4): 313–340.

Tunkli, László. 1975. Pszichológiai Munka a Fővárosi Nevelési Tanácsadókban. *Pszichológiai Tanulmányok* 18: 269–275.

Verdery, Katherine. 1994. From Parent-State to Family Patriarchs: Gender and Nation in Contemporary Eastern Europe. *EEPS* 8: 2.

World Bank. 1992. *Hungary: Reform of Social Policy and Expenditures.* Washington, D.C.: World Bank.

6

Polish Peasants in the "Valley of Transition": Responses to Postsocialist Reforms

Slawomira Zbierski-Salameh

Theorists and reform strategies of the postsocialist transition have underlined the problem of introducing capitalist institutions in the absence of a bourgeoisie (Staniszkis 1991; Ekiert 1990; Lewandowski and Szomburg 1990). With no historical subjects invested in such changes, the transformation of Eastern Europe would have to be guided by theoretical rather than real interests. In this view, which takes the patterns of capitalist development in the West as a point of reference for Eastern Europe, Polish agriculture appeared to be in a particularly advantageous position. Its unique historical development under state socialism meant the vast majority of agricultural land in Poland was already held privately as postsocialist reforms began. The neoliberal postsocialist reform program seemed to be in harmony, then, with the peasants' ongoing struggle against administrative control and the systematic abrogation of their property rights under state socialism. Thus, at its outset, agriculture already contained historical subjects who potentially had a real interest in the objectives of reform. In consequence, the Polish transition might be fueled from below through a process of the *embourgeoisement of the peasantry*.

Whereas the rest of the economy faced the daunting project of fundamental restructuring, agriculturalists were expected to move into a capitalist type of production, prompted by reform-induced incentives. Neoliberal reform strategists saw the end of state regulation as synonymous with market regulation and guarantees of private ownership rights. With the full liberalization of prices and trade, individual agricultural producers were expected to find it in their rational self-interest to increase efficiency and volume and to commodify production. The reform strategists sought to restore peasants' ownership rights through unrestricted access to productive resources and to enhance them with liberalized trade. Furthermore, they expected liberalized trade to bring competition to the state-owned and pseudocooperative monopolistic outlets that surrounded individual agricultural production at both input and output levels. Reformers also anticipated that rationalized private landholdings and a progressively transformed ownership structure would increase economic rationality on the micro level. By shifting to capital-intensive farming methods, they projected, successful peasants would consolidate and expand their holdings, thus reversing the tendency toward fragmentation that had occurred under state socialism; moreover, the most prosperous peasants would absorb the approximately 20 percent of agricultural land held in state farms. Consistent with their proclamations of the economic and ideological superiority of private property, the reformers favored breaking up the land in the state farms and auctioning it off to local peasants.

The postsocialist reformers' reliance on peasants as a social base was not limited to peasants' economic behavior but also applied to their social ethos, thought to permeate all of society. Seeing the peasants' distinctive "ethos of labor" (the supposed result of their direct contact with nature) as a legitimizing force in the transition, reformers argued that peasants would help to chart the social agenda for the transition and would accept its unavoidable hardships. As Staniszkis (1991: 133) put it, they drew on peasants' "tenacity, patience, and resistance to setbacks" and argued that peasant "pragmatism" was essential to the success of the reforms.

Whereas the postsocialist strategists foresaw the reforms resulting in the embourgeoisement of the peasantry, some scholars claimed instead that a rural bourgeoisie had already emerged in the late socialist period. Nagengast (1990, 1991), for example, argued that state socialist agricultural policies precipitated the gradual capitalization of farming and marketing and with it the economic polarization of the peasantry. In the 1980s, as agrarian policies to combat food shortages furthered the differentiation of the once relatively homogeneous Polish peasantry, changing rural ideas about inequality also helped to legitimize that polarization.[2] Szelényi (1988) advanced a similar thesis regarding the nascent rural bourgeoisie of late socialist Hungary. Through his notion of "interrupted embourgeoisement," however, Szelényi gave cultural traits primary importance in the rise of agricultural capitalism. He argued that only the heirs of presocialist entrepreneurs, through their cultural capital, took advantage of the incentives offered by Hungary's market-oriented policies in the 1970s and 1980s. Hence, both Nagengast and Szelényi presupposed the existence of not potential but *actual* and *real* interests. Although the interests of a rural bourgeoisie were formed within socialism, they were expected to carry over into the postsocialist transition and to be congruent with the objectives of the post-1989 reforms.

Yet, the Polish reality has been far from both the reformers' expectations and these scholarly accounts. Instead of pursuing greater productive efficiency and growth, peasants have "involuted" their production and retreated from markets. Rather than simply accepting the hardships of the transition or promoting economic individualism and the independence of economic enterprises, peasants were among the first social groups to stage massive opposition to the reforms. Within a few months of the inauguration of the Balcerowicz program, peasants of varying levels of wealth united to call for reformulating the program, and they elicited great support from the general populace. Once thought to be allies of the postsocialist transition, peasants turned out to be among its main foes.[3]

In this chapter I will explain this unanticipated turnaround by comparing peasant behavior not with an ahistorical image of capitalism in the West but with Poland's immediate past. Rather than directly extrapolating from peasants' context-specific past behaviors to project their responses to the postsocialist reforms, however, I will demonstrate how the past is mediated by the realities of the transition. My approach is thus similar to that of Creed (chapter 7, this volume), in which the meanings of the past are transformed as they enter into the new context.

For these purposes I draw on the work of Przeworski (1985). In his theory of transition, Przeworski problematizes Marx's thesis that workers' economic interest under capitalism inevitably leads them to embrace socialism.[4] Przeworski challenges this thesis because it fails to acknowledge the historical alternatives available to workers, in particular the possibility of reforming capitalism to improve their welfare. He also rejects the thesis on the grounds that it leaves unexamined the economic deprivations entailed in the change to a socialist alternative—what he calls the "valley of transition." By advancing their economic interests along the capitalist path through a compromise with capitalists, workers could avoid the transitional valley to socialism and safeguard their material welfare. According to Przeworski, if suitable historical conditions exist to allow such compromise, those conditions could deter workers from pursuing a socialist path even if they perceived socialism as superior. Hence, Przeworski's valley of transition focuses on the relative cost of transition as compared with historical alternatives and points to the necessity of examining the absolute and relative deprivations economic agents experience as the essential components that shape their responses to reform measures.

Przeworski's work deals with the workers' valley of transition from capitalism to socialism. I would claim that Polish peasants in the transition from socialism to capitalism can be understood in similar terms. The peasants' responses to the postsocialist reform measures must be filtered through the historical possibilities that opened up to them under state socialism; the economic deprivation experienced under the reform program must be compared to the costs and benefits of previous reforms. During the 1980s, compatibility between private property and economic egalitarianism became a historical possibility *within* state socialism.[5] Although the Jaruzelski government crushed the Solidarity movement when it imposed martial law in 1981, it also introduced fundamental economic changes in an effort to preserve the socialist system. Food shortages in 1980–1981 forced the regime to recognize the demands of Rural Solidarity and to grant constitutional guarantees to private landownership. Unprecedented in the history of state socialism, these constitutional guarantees affirmed the permanent and equal standing of private property with other forms of ownership. The deepening of the food crisis in the late 1980s pushed the socialist government to move beyond the formal *legal* recognition of private property rights toward the realization of the socialist promise of *economic* equality for private property owners. In 1988 the government institutionalized protectionist measures that set minimal prices for agricultural goods based not on actual production costs but on bringing rural and urban incomes into parity.

The responses of Polish peasants to the market transition must be seen through the prism of these historical possibilities, which state socialism created. In addition to this historical comparison, peasants' experiences of the transition must also be related to the deprivations endured by economic agents from other agricultural subsectors. Thus, given the reform pronouncements about the superiority of private property, the peasants might expect different "bottoms" of the transitional valley for different ownership subsectors within agriculture; they might assume that the transition costs for private owners would be less than those for firms in the state and cooperative agricultural subsectors. But in practice, peasants faced higher transition costs. Hence, their response to reforms must also be viewed in relation to the deprivations of other economic agents within agriculture. With these terms clarified, we can better grasp why peasants' threshold of tolerance was much lower than the reformers had anticipated.

My discussion is based on ethnographic research conducted in a rural community in the Wielkopolska (Greater Poland) region in west-central Poland between 1991 and 1993. A cluster of sixteen villages, integrated administratively under a local government into one community (*gmina*) I have called "Rolnicy," offered a best-case scenario for the postsocialist goal of a swift transition to capitalist agriculture. The community had a long tradition of commodity relations dating back to the several decades of Prussian domination over western Poland in the nineteenth century (Kochanowicz 1989; Topolski 1977) and reinforced by specific agrarian policies of the 1970s and 1980s (Kolankiewicz and Lewis 1988). Its farms were highly capitalized and its infrastructure relatively well developed, and it was near a major urban and industrial center. The community also contained all three agricultural subsectors—private, cooperative, and state farms—thus allowing me to assess the different impacts of reforms on changes in each subsector, on economic relations among them, and on the agrarian ownership structure.[6] I conducted multiple interviews with sixty-eight peasant families and representatives of local economic, political, and government institutions of the *gmina*.

From Neoliberal Myth to Polish Reality: The Outcomes of Postsocialist Agricultural Policy

The postsocialist stabilization package introduced in Poland had profound effects on peasants' capacity to exercise private ownership. First, the reforms restricted their access to productive resources through price destabilization and the selective allocation of financial credits. Second, new institutional constraints attendant upon the reforms curtailed peasants' ability to accrue profits from production. Finally, the reforms undermined peasants' capacity to transfer their ownership and move into new agricultural markets. In short, far from the neoliberal expectations, postsocialist agrarian policy ended up undercutting key components of the agricultural economy.

Price Liberalization or Destabilization?

The rapid and comprehensive liberalization of prices under the Balcerowicz stabilization plan fundamentally reshaped the structure of agricultural prices and, consequently, the profitability of agricultural production. Because Wojciech Jaruzelski's partial price reform in mid-1980 had commercialized retail food prices, price liberalization in the 1990s primarily affected the prices of agricultural inputs (previously administratively controlled and state subsidized), which rose to astronomical heights. Prior to the Balcerowicz plan, hyperinflation had pushed up the prices of agricultural inputs by an average of 800 percent; the immediate result of instituting the plan was that those prices soared by 1,800 percent, quickly approaching the level of world prices.[7] Retail food prices, however, rose at the slower pace of approximately 250 percent, hence lagging behind world prices.[8] Although fairly modest in comparison to

the jump in input prices, this increase in food prices was at the high end
of what was economically and politically tolerable for Polish society. To
cool the hyperinflation plaguing the Polish economy, the Balcerowicz
plan coupled price liberalization with control over the population's disposable incomes. However much wages increased, they were drastically
outpaced by the cost of food products. Far exceeding Sachs's predictions,
some estimates indicated that in 1990 Polish people's purchasing capacity fell by 40 to 60 percent for both agricultural and nonagricultural
goods.[9] In their combined effect, price liberalization and simultaneous
wage controls significantly constrained domestic food demand. Hence,
agricultural producers faced sharp increases in agricultural resource costs
and a reduction in domestic demand for their products.

Given the previous socialist experience of chronic excess food demand
and shortages on the supply side, the unprecedented drop in demand trig-
gered by the stabilization program was not fully anticipated. Policymakers did not recognize the program's implications for agricultural production. At that time, in an attempt to curtail food demand that consistently
and increasingly outpaced the food production capacity of domestic agriculture, Jaruzelski had freed agricultural product prices while holding agricultural input prices at low, state-subsidized levels. This partial price reform brought the peasants windfall profits. As an outcome of Jaruzelski's
reform, by 1988 the average peasant income exceeded that of urban
workers by 17 percent. By the first quarter of 1990, however, that gain
had been reversed, with peasant incomes dropping to 86 percent of
workers' incomes. The stabilization program further amplified the dramatic reversal of the price structure, as a clear correlation between the
procurement prices paid for agricultural goods and the increased retail
food prices ceased to exist.

Peasants' Access to Productive Resources

From the outset, previous agrarian policies created problems for Poland's fiscal policies with regard to agriculture. To ensure the balanced
development of that sector—a sector that had suffered chronic underin-
vestment during the socialist period—the plan called for a substantial in-
fusion of capital into agriculture as a whole and into its specific branches
(most notably the production of agricultural inputs and food processing).[11] Simultaneously, the plan aimed to reduce expenditures drastically
to redress the deep fiscal crisis of the postsocialist state. In consequence
of these two contradictory objectives, the actual funds advanced for agriculture fell far below estimated needs.[12]

The allocation of credits for individual peasants increased by nearly 50
percent from 1989 to 1992, which appeared to be in line with the pro-

grammatic commitment to developing individual agricultural production. The allocation, however, represented a negligible—indeed, a declining—proportion of the credits allocated to all economic units within this period.[13] Immediately prior to the inauguration of the program, peasants received roughly 40 percent of all credits designated for private initiative. From 1990 to 1992, the average per year dropped to about 20 percent.[14]

In addition to the scarcity of available financial resources, local-level implementation of credit allocation guidelines also limited the individual peasant's access to financial capital. Starting in 1991–1992, the majority of peasants in Rolnicy reported having no information about funds available for agriculture. Many complained about discrepancies in the information disseminated at national and local levels. Following mass media announcements of new financial assistance for private agriculture, local financial institutions would frequently deny to inquiring and frustrated peasants that such funds existed. Overall, very few peasants reported obtaining preferential credit for the purchase of agricultural inputs such as fertilizers and pesticides. The small group that did received negligible amounts in comparison to production needs. The peasants also alleged that timely notification and acceptance of preferential credit petitions by the local cooperative bank were extended only to a selected few who had preexisting personal connections with local and regional financial institutions dating back to state socialism.

When the local cooperative bank received its limited allotment of preferential agricultural credits, it extended a total of 18 billion zloty for the construction of two new food processing sites within the borders of Rolnicy.[15] Meat and dairy processing plants were started by former directors of regional state processing enterprises. Initially, peasants viewed these sites as potential markets for their goods, but that perception was short-lived. Both projects far exceeded the original projections of necessary capital investment. Short of funds, neither facility reached the completion stage. The servicing of advanced investment loans on these sites led the local cooperative bank to declare bankruptcy in early 1994. Uncertain about the fate of their deposits, peasants (as cooperative members of the bank) voiced deep resentment over the bank's loan allocation policies—particularly its support of two outsiders who had undeniable ties to the former ruling elites and its lack of funds for cooperative members.

In addition, the requirements attached to these preferential credits artificially reduced the demand for them, despite the fact that production needs far exceeded the level of financial assistance available. In 1991 the bank received 1 billion zloty from the European Fund for the Development of Polish Agriculture toward preferential credits for fertilizers and pesticides. Because the fund made the money available in April, too late in the agricultural production cycle for fertilizers and pesticides to be applied, and would not consider petitions retrospectively, only half of the available funds were utilized. The situation was repeated in 1992. Furthermore, the European Community (EC) advanced funds through the local cooperative bank for the purpose of modernizing Polish agriculture; for these funds a sophisticated business plan had to be submitted with the credit application. With no such skills of their own and no services available to assist them, peasants in Rolnicy generated no demand for these funds.

Hence, the tightening of the money supply consistent with the stabilization program produced a shift in credit preferences. Despite the government's programmatic commitment to modernize and restructure agriculture—specifically its preferred private subsector—few financial resources were extended to peasants for renewal of their production cycle, and none were offered for expanding and modernizing their farms.[16] For expansion and modernization, peasants were expected to generate their own funds through increased productivity (which the other constraints precluded).

The absolute deprivation peasants were experiencing in their access to financial resources was compounded by their sense of relative deprivation vis-à-vis economic agents in state agricultural sectors, which the reforms had claimed to eliminate.[17] Fearing temporary imbalances in the grain market, the government provided the monopolistic procurement centers with preferential credits for storing and drying grain. The government justified such measures as indirect support for individual producers, who would now face less uncertainty in demand for their crops. Peasants saw, however, that contrary to government promises they carried disproportionately the transition's high costs.

In addition to limited access to credits, peasants also experienced restricted access to agricultural machinery. Defying conventional economic measures, the private subsector in agriculture emerged from state socialism with a curious mixture of both undercapitalization and overcapitalization (Brooks 1991a). Having failed to collectivize agriculture, successive socialist regimes adopted various measures aimed at denying peasants productive autonomy, particularly the right to own agricultural implements. A vast network of agricultural circles was designed to provide machinery services for private farms. The prohibition on private ownership of agricultural machinery was partially liberalized in the mid-1970s, allowing individual agricultural producers to acquire used machines from state and cooperative agricultural enterprises. Increased mechanization resulted from the peasants' strong drive to reduce their dependence on the ever-capricious agricultural circles. Hence, secondhand machines designed and produced for agricultural economies of scale steadily found their way to the individual subsector, with its highly fragmented landowning structure.[18] This progressive mechanization of the private subsector was unsuitable for relatively small plots and also involved increasingly outdated stock.

The liberalization of trade was designed to rationalize and renew the mechanization of agriculture by opening Polish markets to foreign suppliers of agricultural implements suitable for small-scale agricultural production, which would introduce competition to the highly concentrated domestic agricultural industry. In Rolnicy the agricultural machinery dealer enlarged his operations in a way that seemed to attest to the dynamic mechanization of Polish agriculture sparked by the reforms. This one-man parts-exchange shop, which opened in the late 1980s, grew explosively during the first two years of the postsocialist reforms. It became a modern company of impressive size in terms of employment, revenues, and its market, which stretched to several *voyevodships* in west-central Poland. The owner's ever-expanding lot displayed countless new tractors and other domestic and imported machinery that gave the impression of a thriving machinery dealership.

Yet, people rarely came to buy the new machinery. The owner's clients, primarily from the state farms and agricultural cooperatives, were mainly interested in the replacement or repair of parts for their existing equipment. Few of the peasants I interviewed had purchased any new machines during the three years of the postsocialist transition, and they did not foresee being able to do so in the near future. The new structure of agricultural prices did not allow them to put aside any funds for amortizing their equipment. A few young peasants in the *gmina* who had desperately needed equipment at the onset of the reforms had tried to increase their productive efficiency by investing in higher-quality imported machinery; they were threatened imminently with losing their farms because of the mounting debt on their loans.

Just as access to new agricultural machinery had failed to materialize, reform narrowed peasants' ability to hire machinery services. The liberalization of prices for energy and fuel greatly increased the fees agricultural circles charged for those services. Although fees had become a significant part of the overall cost of private agricultural production in the 1980s, the new rates proved prohibitive for many peasants who, unable to meet them, reverted to the use of outdated and barely operative equipment.[19] Two families proudly reported that they had assembled a grain harvester out of three dilapidated combines purchased from a liquidated state farm for a sum equivalent to the harvesting fee charged by the agricultural circles. These peasants-turned-mechanics jointly harvested their individual crops and those of their neighbors.[20]

Hence, in the new market-oriented economic environment, peasants found it increasingly difficult to gain access to agricultural machinery. The equipment available through agricultural circles came with ever-higher fees, and acquiring one's own machinery was increasingly difficult because of its cost relative to peasants' incomes. This situation resulted in a steady decapitalization and aging of the machinery, as well as in diminished quality of the work performed.

Peasants Face Monopsonistic Buyers

Constant shortages in the domestic food supply and the socialist legacy of underdevelopment in agriculture-related industry led postsocialist reformers to identify the supply of agricultural inputs as potentially the most uncertain point in the transition period's system of food production and distribution. Yet, what turned out to be the most critical and uncertain point was the *disposal* of agricultural products. Uncertainty about markets was caused indirectly by the decline in consumer purchasing power and shifting preferences (toward foreign food products); its more immediate cause, however, was the procurement centers' strategy of adjusting to reforms.

At first, the procurement of crop and animal commodities was handled almost exclusively by state-controlled agricultural trade cooperatives.[21] Policymakers' commitment to a comprehensive reduction or removal of subsidies threw procurement cooperatives and state-owned agricultural processing enterprises into hard budget constraints almost overnight.[22] To adjust, procurement centers cut their operations to the level of their sales and reduced the costs of operation.[23] Both strategies directly affected their economic relations with individual agricultural producers.

Shortly after the introduction of reforms, peasants reported frequent difficulties in selling their output.[24] Procurement centers purchased agricultural goods on a first-come-first-served basis—without prior notice to their agricultural suppliers about the size or type of procurement for a specific day. By the first postsocialist harvest, peasants were standing in line for several hours or even days with containers full of grain, only to be told that the procurement was finished for an undetermined period. Several factors limited peasants' ability to gather accurate and updated information about open sites of agricultural procurements: the lack of advance information from procurement centers; the shortage of phones in the countryside, especially in peasant households; an inadequate road network; and the increased cost of gasoline and thus of transportation. In several instances, peasants reported that by the time they had located and reached an open procurement center, they were turned away again. Furthermore, because working with larger agricultural suppliers was more cost-effective for the centers, they tended to prefer dealing with agricultural cooperatives and state farms rather than individual farmers.[25]

The procurement centers adopted various measures to lower the cost of their operations and to transfer some of those costs to agricultural producers. The peasants I interviewed often pointed out that given the prohibitive cost of commercial credits, procurement centers dealt with their cash flow problems by delaying payments to their suppliers for indeterminate periods—often three months or more. Uncertainties about the schedule and level of payment extended even to crops such as rapeseed that were under delivery contracts. The centers would unilaterally modify those contracts, which specified various elements of the transaction including the size, price, and quality of the procurement. Hence, the centers were obliged to absorb only specified amounts of output, leaving the issues of price and quality open to current market fluctuations. In addition to postponing payments for grain and animal deliveries, the centers began to charge individual agricultural producers for the storage of grains procured from them.

The procurement centers' adjustment strategy also affected the way they determined the quality of agricultural output. The peasants I interviewed claimed the procurement centers raised quality standards artificially to pay lower prices for their output; moreover, they questioned the validity and accuracy of the center-administered tests that determined output prices. Unlike the agricultural cooperatives or state farms, peasants did not possess the equipment to verify test results independently.[26] A good example of this problem can be seen in procurement centers' milk classification practices. Because milk production provides the only steady source of yearly income for over a million agricultural households, reductions in this income caused great difficulty. The drop in procurement prices, consequent upon the removal of milk subsidies, was one source of difficulty, but for peasants the classification system was an even greater problem; they repeatedly challenged its validity with procurement centers. Such conflicts were not new: aspects of the system (such as bimonthly retroactive notification and payment) had been in place during the socialist period. Peasants had complained, for example, that notifying them of milk quality retroactively was both costly and unfair to milk suppliers, for learning on the last day of a bimonthly pay period that one's milk was contaminated led to a significant loss of income. These dissatisfactions had contributed to a withdrawal from milk cattle production in both the studied region and nationwide.[27]

Ironically, the reforms perpetuated these contested classification practices. In the face of milk shortages, monopolistic procurement centers were unable to lower their operating costs based on arbitrarily restricting procurement, as was the case with grain. Instead, the centers attempted to maintain their profits by manipulating milk classification. All of the peasants I interviewed complained about having to submit to an increas-

ingly complicated classification system tied to different payment levels;
meanwhile, the procurement centers sold the milk to retail distributors
under a single price tag. Peasants also suspected that the centers cheated:
suspecting unfair milk testing, many used amateur verification methods.
They reported submitting identical milk samples in two batches under
two separate names or resubmitting the same milk sample on separate
days, only to have the samples classified into two distinct categories and
levels of payment.[28]

All of these measures heightened antagonistic relations with milk suppliers that dated back to the socialist period.[29] Although one of the first
legislative initiatives of the postsocialist government was to restructure
the local cooperatives in a spirit of genuinely cooperative ownership, as
formal collective co-owners of the milk procurement centers peasants felt
increasingly alienated from these local organizations. They did not feel
the increased membership fee they paid for guaranteed milk procurement
enhanced their cooperative ownership within the centers. Rather, they
saw the fee as an abrogation of their individual ownership right to income—as a way further to expropriate their milk profits. As private
property owners and agricultural suppliers of the procurement centers,
peasants saw simply the replacement of large national monopsonies with
local-level ones.

This situation resulted in the development of spontaneous private competition in specific agricultural markets. In the case of pork distribution,
peasants began to bypass the monopsonistic centers altogether, slaughtering the swine themselves and selling the meat directly to consumers on
the open market. A number of obstacles prevented these alternative practices (begun prior to the 1990 reforms) from effectively challenging the
monopsonistic control of state procurement centers. Specifically, the previous system of selling meat on the street was supplanted by a more organized meat market. After obtaining special permits, peasants who were
able to provide a substantial down payment received permanent stands
in the open market in a nearby major urban center. These sales often exceeded those of their domestic production, prompting them to purchase
meat directly from other local peasants. Tax disincentives and an awareness of the risks involved in a complete specialization in retail, however,
led these independent distributors to maintain agricultural production as
primary and to treat distribution as a sideline, which limited the potential
scope of their sales operations. The lack of investment capital and an
underdeveloped transport system also prevented the nascent distribution
network from expanding into areas where market demand was relatively
high, such as the industrial mining region of Silesia in southwest Poland.
In the end, these systemic constraints kept individual distributors from
expanding and thus left local procurement centers under monopsonistic

control. The weak competition of the private sector was insufficient to instill market regulation of meat prices. Eventually, the higher prices private meat distributors paid to producers in 1990–1991 fell to match the lower price level dictated by procurement centers.

The creation of private food processing enterprises faced multiple constraints similar to those that worked against the expansion of spontaneous private distribution. The experiences of one young peasant, Robert S., embody the difficulties of venturing into private agricultural processing. For several years Robert ran a specialized poultry farm in Rolnicy, producing annually in the late 1980s 60,000 to 80,000 poultry on two hectares. In the wake of the reforms, Robert was almost immediately squeezed to the breaking point by increasingly unfavorable prices and an uncertain demand for his product. His farm's small size and specialized equipment precluded him from simply exiting into subsistence production. Thus, he decided to establish a medium-sized poultry slaughtering and processing plant.[30]

Robert seemed to symbolize the kind of entrepreneur postsocialist agricultural policy sought to nurture. His strongest and most unique asset was his extensive knowledge of the field he was about to enter. At the time of my first contact with him in 1991, he had already invested over a year of his time and 500 million zloty in processing fees.[31] Given the impoverished population, Robert saw the potential for a vast market for cheaper poultry products. He also understood the state processing plants' limited flexibility to restructure themselves in the face of new economic requirements. Therefore, he aimed to give state poultry processing enterprises competition by developing new lines of production and bringing down the cost per unit.[32] Based on a genetically improved chicken that required 20 percent less feed and a shorter production cycle, he planned to produce inexpensive chicken burgers and nuggets, as well as higher-priced fillets. All products would be handled in modern vacuum packaging, something not offered by state processing enterprises. Robert's plan called for installing imported equipment, which, although it would be 50 percent more costly than the domestic equivalent, would have higher energy efficiency and lower labor costs; these savings would enable him to recoup the higher cost more quickly.

Robert also had partial access to input and output markets. As he developed his business plan, he opened a small fodder outlet for local poultry production. The outlet allowed him to stay afloat financially while locating poultry producers and identifying the local potential for his projected plant. Through his contacts with poultry producers he determined that local poultry production would be sufficient to meet his processing plant's capacity of 2 million chickens annually. He envisioned organizing the existing fragmented poultry food chain into a horizontally

integrated network of contract-bound fodder suppliers, chicken producers, medical and veterinary services, and a poultry processing plant,
which would eliminate the uncertainty of transactions with state procurement plants and would also reduce costs.

In researching his alternatives, Robert established contacts with a
Dutch poultry production and processing enterprise. Based on credit issued by the Dutch company, he had secured funds for all of his poultry
processing and packaging machinery. He had also obtained access to the
Dutch market for the first three years of production output, contingent
on his obtaining government permits for start-up and domestic credits to
build housing for the processing equipment.

The Ministry of Agriculture in Warsaw repeatedly encouraged Robert
but provided no actual support. He was told the ministry could not fur-
nish him with the necessary authorizations or refer him to the officials
who could. At length Robert was sent to the central cooperative bank to
obtain financial backing for his foreign credit.[33] There he was told he
could apply for funds under a World Bank program that had a processing
time of five months. The application required a detailed business plan,
but the bank gave applicants no assistance with that plan.[34] Eventually,
Robert's application was denied without adequate explanation. Furthermore, because of an insufficient number of independent sanitary inspec-
tors, the *voyevodship* authority required that Robert obtain authoriza-
tion for the location of his future processing plant from a qualified staff
member at the state poultry processing plant—Robert's direct competitor. After three years of continual attempts to obtain authorizations and
permits to take out foreign loans for specialized equipment and domestic
loans for erecting buildings, Robert's construction site remained unfinished.

Involution of Production and Evolution of
Peasants' Political Resistance

In an attempt to free private property owners from the state, postsocialist
price and trade liberalization reforms subjected peasants to a new set of
constraints—higher costs of production resources, uncertain demand for
agricultural outputs, and heightened arbitrariness of business transactions. In contrast to reformers' expectations that peasants would remain
patient with and tolerant of these hardships, peasants reacted strongly
against them. Economically, they responded through an involution of
production and a retreat from markets. Politically, they responded by
waging protests that challenged the postsocialist reforms at their foundation.

Economic Adjustment: Involution and the Closed-Cycle Production System

In the new economic environment, peasants were motivated not to increase productivity, as the reformers would have it, but to reduce their production costs and minimize their exposure to procurement centers. These considerations led peasants to an overall involution of production and to a *closed-cycle production system*; that is, they increasingly relied on themselves to generate the resources necessary for the renewal of their production cycles. All production lines became interdependent. Peasants selected field crops to enhance their animal husbandry, whose by-products (mainly manure) became the input for renewing crop production. With the exception of wheat, rapeseed, and sugar beets, for which they actively sought markets, peasants diverted almost all other field crops away from the market into animal husbandry.

In switching to closed-cycle production, peasants drastically limited their demand for chemical fertilizers, pesticides, and improved seed strains. Regardless of their past practices of input utilization or the size of their holdings, all of my respondents had reduced fertilizer use by 50 to 70 percent in 1990. They maintained that level through 1991 and 1992[35]—some reported abandoning chemical fertilizers altogether on selected grains. They also reported an approximately 30 percent reduction in the application of pesticides, herbicides, and the like. In avoiding the purchase of genetically improved grain seeds, peasants began to rely on neighborhood seed exchanges to renew crop production. Similarly, they curtailed or eliminated purchases of mineral and high protein feed supplements that had previously been considered indispensable to animal husbandry.

The new emphasis in animal production was selective. The rapid withdrawal of milk subsidies in the Balcerowicz reform package only accelerated a clear trend toward decreasing milk cattle herds in the private agricultural subsector.[36] Instead, all peasants in Rolnicy concentrated on starting or expanding production of swine. The swine production cycle was five or six times shorter than that of cattle and hence provided relatively frequent and steady income for peasants with limited financial reserves. Production costs dictated the scale of swine farming; all farmers I interviewed increased their production only within the limits of existing facilities, refraining from any new investments. Sporadically, they might devote substantial labor to adapt existing cattle production facilities to enlarge the swine stock.[37]

These cost-cutting measures and the shift to closed-cycle production had a ripple effect in the agricultural sector. The piglet market virtually collapsed as peasants started to rely on their own stock for reproduction rather than buying piglets from specialized breeders. Also, the high cost of feed almost completely eradicated the market for partially grown swine, which had flourished during the socialist period. In the new circumstances, peasants returned to the market only when their swine were fully fattened. The market they returned to, however, was persistently dominated by monopolistic procurement centers.

Likewise, the logic of closed-cycle production not only implied a purposeful retreat from specific markets but also affected those into which peasants might expand. In 1990, when a modern vegetable oil plant was built near Rolnicy, peasants saw real prospects for a significant and stable demand for rapeseed. Yet, the peasants I interviewed who had previously cultivated rapeseed planned to increase their production only marginally, if at all. Adopting closed-cycle production as a way of surviving the reform period meant keeping a relative balance among lines of production, which might mean restricting pursuit of favorable market opportunities.

For the majority of peasants I interviewed who were engaged in polyculture, adopting a closed-cycle system involved at most a shift in emphasis among existing lines of production. Those peasants whose farming patterns were already specialized, however, found adapting to the rapidly changing economic environment in 1990 far more difficult. The high cost of quality fodder and the fall in procurement prices for swine led those who had specialized in swine production under state socialism, for example, to reduce their output. A retreat to closed-cycle production implied radically scaling back the numbers of animals proportional to the amount of arable land from which those animals could be fed. Thus, eight people I interviewed had reduced their output to merely 10 percent of their production level in the mid-1980s.[38]

For peasants previously involved in other specialties, the process of switching to closed-cycle production was equally difficult. Those who had established multiyear contracts with the state trading agency to develop genetically improved seed, based on specialized equipment and seasonal employment of hired labor, faced few alternatives when their production contracts were eliminated following drastic cuts in state funds. The specialized profile of their farms left those peasants without ownership of even the most rudimentary machinery or utility buildings necessary for polycultural crop and animal production. Thus, previously specialized and commercially oriented peasants who sought to switch to closed-cycle production had to generate substantial funds. Fearful of commercial loans, peasants in Rolnicy pursued two avenues: they sold portions of their land and took up supplemental employment outside agriculture. Whereas state socialism had created a stratum of peasant workers drawn primarily from the ranks of smallholders (0.5 to 2 hectares), the postsocialist environment pushed middle-sized owners (7 to 15 hectares) with specialized, commodified production profiles into this stratum.[39]

Although the Balcerowicz program liberalized land transactions in an unprecedented way, land sales in Rolnicy were limited in number and scope through the period of my research. Middle-sized agricultural producers were the most active in selling their land—their last resort for generating cash to renew the production cycle and thus save their farms. These survival strategies were reflected in local statistics. In the area I studied, during the years 1990–1994 the number of farms within the 7- to 10-hectare range declined (from 110 to 99). There was a parallel decrease in the total land area occupied by 7-to-10 hectare farms in the community, from 888 hectares to 800 hectares. Simultaneously, smaller farms—those within the range of 5 to 7 hectares—grew in terms of numbers of farms (from 40 to 53) and share of total land area occupied by this category (from 266 to 328 hectares).[40] These same processes also appear in national-level statistics and point to continued fragmentation of the private landholding structure rather than to the rationalization for which reformers had hoped.[41]

In short, the reform initiatives led to an overall involution within agriculture. The shift to a closed-cycle production system implied an extensive type of production that resulted in lower yields and withdrawal from market exchanges.[42] This shift forced already specialized peasants to reduce their farm sizes and take on second jobs.

Evolution of Peasant Political Resistance to Reforms

In addition to these economic responses, peasants also engaged in collective protest against postsocialist agrarian policy. To preserve the integrity of its plan (i.e., the comprehensive introduction of markets as exclusive regulators of economic transactions), the government insisted on withholding direct state support both for individual producers and for the agricultural sector as a whole (Balcerowicz 1992: 92, 1995: 423). Yet, peasants perceived the subsequent results of reform not as the invisible hand of the market but rather as antipeasant measures deliberately inflicted on them by the government. Those perceptions were potent in mobilizing peasants against the terms of state-imposed economic transactions.[43] The network of preexisting peasant political organizations, formed in the 1980s to challenge state socialism, facilitated peasants' efforts to thrust economic negotiations into the political arena (Friszke 1990). Those efforts coincided with the political opposition to the Balcerowicz program articulated during the 1990 presidential campaign.[44] In effect, the postsocialist state was diverted from its long-term goals and toward damage control and the pursuit of short-term political and economic stability.[45]

The peasants' collective action underwent three stages within the first three years of the transition. In the first phase, disputes were regional, centered on specific economic transactions; they led to corporate concessions. In early 1992, with the rise of Self-Defense, a splinter group of Rural Solidarity, political resistance became nationwide. No longer focused on the terms of specific transactions, resistance challenged the overall market logic of the economic transactions the government was imposing. In the third stage, peasants successfully reformulated their class-based economic demands into national and societal grievances against the postsocialist state and its program.

An early incident of collective action took place in fall 1990. The acute uncertainty private cultivators had experienced concerning demand for the summer 1990 grain harvest was renewed in the fall during the harvest of the two most important industrial crops in Poland—sugar beets and potatoes. Across the country, production contracts between the sugar processing plants and sugar beet producers had been signed in spring 1990. When it came time to pay, some sugar processing plants reneged on the price levels stipulated in the contract, thus precipitating a blockade of the processing plants in the affected regions that induced national-level negotiations between the central committee of Rural Solidarity and representatives of the sugar industry. The government was drawn into the conflict early on, initially as a mediating party in the negotiations. As multilevel talks continued, the blockade of selected roads and individual processing plants spread. To avert national-level social unrest, the government agreed to purchase the excess sugar beets the processing plants did not take.[46]

This precedent established by direct government action in resolving the sugar beet crisis was soon repeated in a regional conflict between peasants and local milk procurement centers. The local units of Rural Solidarity organized a prompt and efficient peasant strike that was met with an equally prompt intervention from the Ministry of Agriculture. The ministry advanced guaranteed preferential loans to the procurement centers, hence covering delinquent payments to milk producers.[47]

Although the state was implicated in the sugar beet and milk crises, these conflicts were played out primarily between representatives of the industrial buyers and agricultural producers. The 1990 potato crisis, by contrast, brought the state directly to the center of agricultural conflict. In 1990 the processing industries in potato flour, starch, and cereal reduced their purchases by one-third. The most significant factor in the drop in potato demand was a depression in domestic alcohol production prompted by cheap imported alcohol. Liberalized international trade regulations brought a massive influx of alcohol from Germany in the second half of 1989 through early 1990. An investigation conducted by an independent government accounting agency, NIK [Najwyzsza Izba Kontroli (Supreme Assessor's Office)] estimated that state-owned and private enterprises together imported over 18 million liters of alcohol at the end of 1989. In early 1990 imports expanded further, with private enterprises at the forefront. The comprehensive and swift liberalization of trade resulted in insufficient guidelines and controls over tariffs and licensing. Alcohol was smuggled into Poland at great profit and without limit.

"Alcohol-gate" became a major liability for the Balcerowicz program, which was linked to the promotion of shady deals and the undermining of legitimate private agriculture. Instead of having an antimonopolistic effect on the domestic alcohol industry, the program narrowed the scale of domestic production within alcohol plants and shrank the suppliers' base, now drawn almost exclusively from the state farms. Further, although intended as part of a stabilization package to alleviate the staggering deficit, the program inflicted significant losses (estimated as billions of zlotys) on the state budget.[48] The massive influx of imported alcohol not only called into question the credibility of the Balcerowicz program but also violated the objectives of a social program inherited from the socialist government that was still validated by law, as well as in the public consciousness.[49]

In fall 1990, in protest of the government's role in the potato crisis, peasants marched on the capital, dropped loads of potatoes at the Ministry of Agriculture building, and occupied government buildings. They cast the trade liberalization policies as not simply antipeasant but also anti-Polish, as destroying the domestic economy and undermining societal values.

Hence, by fall 1990 the sugar beet and potato crises had produced a collective antigovernment reaction that went beyond the question of ownership rights. By incorporating nationalist and social accents into their protests, peasants gained broader social support.[50] Political organizations representing agricultural producers articulated three basic demands for the reformulation of agrarian policy: guaranteed minimum prices for agricultural goods, aid for agricultural production through preferential credits, and protection of domestic production through steep tariffs on foreign agricultural goods. These three demands set the stage for numerous negotiations between peasants' representatives from different political parties and government representatives over the scope and nature of state intervention. The negotiations were bogged down by conflicting demands for sector-specific versus general intervention.[51] Participants also clashed over the locus of state intervention, whether it should occur at the point of production or at the points of distribution and processing.[52] Dismayed at its inability to realize its demands, on 16 March 1991 Rural Solidarity called for a national strike. One week later, over

500 road blockades had been organized in forty-seven provinces throughout Poland.[53] Peasants renewed their key demands to the government: the restoration of profits through minimal price setting, provision of preferential credits, and the imposition of effective tariffs for imported food.

In early 1992 the Jan Olszewski government was further challenged by a newly formed radical-populist peasant union organization, Samoobrona (Self-Defense), a splinter group of Rural Solidarity.[54] At first, the group attracted commercially oriented agricultural producers with high debt liabilities.[55] It quickly broadened its membership to an estimated quarter of a million people, including a segment of its former parent organization, Rural Solidarity. Samoobrona showed its strongest presence in *voyevodships* with long traditions of commercialized agricultural production.[56]

By the end of 1991, when a growing number of enterprises with tax and loan arrears were testing the government's commitment to the program, it was Samoobrona that turned debt payments into a political platform.[51] Under the motto "That is not what we agreed with Balcerowicz," Samoobrona's members refused responsibility for loan repayments. They branded the interest rates as "criminal" and demanded that the government stop liquidating farms in default and that it sponsor the creation of a new Debt Restructuring Fund. Moreover, Samoobrona promulgated a conspiracy theory as its ideological platform. It branded all reformers and officials implementing agricultural policies as "criminals and thieves" who were acting on the directives of "foreign interests," particularly those of the International Monetary Fund (IMF) and the World Bank. Based on this denunciation of reforms as "anti-Polish" and "anti-peasant," Samoobrona members resorted to paramilitary, law-breaking activities. They disrupted numerous liquidation sales of indebted agricultural enterprises in the name of preserving individual peasant work stations and domestic production endangered by the influx of foreign foods. They engaged in a campaign of physical and mental intimidation toward government officials who were implementing reforms on local and regional levels.[58] To exert pressure on the central government, in mid-1992 Samoobrona occupied the Agricultural Ministry building. It further mobilized its members from six *voyevodships*, staging a highly publicized blockade of the roads and a "tractor march on the capital."

The main political parties appealing to agricultural constituencies (Polish Peasant Movement and Rural Solidarity) quickly distanced themselves from Samoobrona, particularly from its tactics. Its methods of operation did not find approval among the wider society or the peasants. The majority of peasants I interviewed did not condone taking out and then defaulting on loans, even though they supported Samoobrona's negative assessment of the agricultural and monetary policies. With pride, they contrasted their own responses to those of Samoobrona's indebted members; instead of irresponsibly accepting loans they could not repay, they preserved their farms by refraining from taking such loans. They also worried that Samoobrona might create a backlash against peasants' image in the wider society, constructing them as conservative promoters of lawlessness.

Although Samoobrona's formulations and tactics were radical, they did reverberate with the broader demands of a majority of peasants and their political parties. Particularly popular were the group's demands for preferential credits for agriculture and for government protection of domestic food production. Further, in characterizing government officials at all levels as highly opportunistic and corrupt, Samoobrona echoed and reinforced a growing perception among peasants that their hardships were not inevitable but were deliberately imposed by incompetent and dishonest officials. This mixed perception of Samoobrona, combined with its growing numbers, caused government officials, the police, and the courts to confront the group's illegal activities in a cautious, protracted, and inconsistent manner.[59] As Samoobrona prided itself on breaking laws it considered unjust, the government grew hesitant to enforce the rule of law.

In early 1993 Samoobrona's political platform shifted from the defense of indebted peasants and embattled agriculture. Envisioning itself as a future electoral bloc, a newly formed offshoot of Samoobrona, the Committee for the National Self-Defense, spoke for preservation not only of individual peasant farms but of all individual work stations. On a more global level, it also proclaimed opposition to the reform program's social consequences. The group's leadership included World War II heroes, literary intelligentsia, and former party activists. Its ranks were open to all social groups experiencing adverse social consequences as a result of the new economic program: the homeless, the unemployed, pensioners, and veterans. In short, the group's specific grievances broadened into a conflict between the dispossessed and the state. As its membership diversified, the committee's identity rested increasingly on collective opposition to the state, evident in the increased use of general identities such as "nation" and "society."

Collective opposition to the government and its program led to dramatic results in the September 1993 parliamentary election, as stunning as the 1989 election that unexpectedly ended the socialist era. The 1993 election effectively ended the 1989–1993 regime that had dislodged state socialism from power. Dominating the elections were the Polish Peasant Movement and the postcommunist Union of the Democratic Left, which together received 36 percent of the vote—and 66 percent of the parliamentary seats. Although acknowledging the need to continue with reforms, the coalition formed by these parties criticized the previous government for its excessively harsh measures and its unfounded faith in the free market. By contrast, the coalition called for slower privatization, pay hikes, unemployment measures, and the pursuit of "capitalism with a human face."

Conclusion: The Polish Advantage Thwarts the Transition

The architects—both Western and Polish—of the postsocialist reforms presented their program as modeled on proven "Western" patterns. For many of its critics, the program was tailored to an obsolete nineteenth-century laissez-fare capitalism. I would argue that the model was *postsocialist* and that its neoliberal underpinnings were derived from an overemphasis on the economic failures of previous efforts to reform state socialism. The critical assessment of past efforts led to an assumption that the comprehensive and swift removal of all state intervention would spontaneously release economic initiatives among private property owners. This narrow preoccupation with the removal of past barriers obstructed the reformers' vision; they failed to see how the withering away of the state posed insurmountable barriers to market entry for newly "liberalized" private property owners and left the postsocialist state with inadequate institutional and technical capacity to guide the transition. The economic and legislative environment thus constrained the ownership rights of private owners. Despite formal liberalization, peasants experienced more restricted access to productive resources than they had during the socialist period. The scope of their control over production shrank, pushing even previously specialized peasants into involuted, intensive agricultural production. They endured systematic and—to them—transparent drains on their profits. Their high transition costs compared unfavorably not only with their position in late socialism but also with those of other agricultural subsectors (such as state farms and cooperatives).

Some scholars have argued that the involution of production and the instability of the markets were inevitable yet transient elements of any change of this scale (Winiecki 1991). I would argue that these economic and political outcomes have more *fundamental* and *lasting* effects on the overall course of postsocialist transformation. The reform measures stood in stark contrast to the progressive consolidation of peasants' ownership rights in the late phase of state socialism. By reversing the agrarian price structure that was favorable to peasants, the stabilization package immediately took away the individual benefits won at the end of state socialism and undermined future economic development. When subjected to arbitrary socialist state encroachment on their ownership rights, peasants fought hard (through Rural Solidarity) for constitutional guarantees of their civil and property rights. In dismantling authoritarianism and state regulation, the postsocialist reform stabilization package did not establish a rule of law (Litwack 1991; Cooter 1992).[60] Rather, it subjected peasants to heightened uncertainty in access to markets. Accordingly, the reform package increased the arbitrariness and instability of their economic transactions.

In concluding his analysis of the transition from capitalism to socialism, Przeworski posits that given the alternatives available within capitalism for improving workers' economic welfare and given the costly valley of transition, workers cannot be expected to opt for socialism based merely on their narrow economic interests. Their reorientation from one system to another could be guided not by their belief in the *economic* superiority of socialism but rather by its promise of *social* superiority. They will embark on this historical progression only if it leads to a society that promises higher production capacity, as well as more egalitarian principles of redistribution (Przeworski 1985: 235–238).[61] The postsocialist reformers' quest for increased economic efficiency rested on the assumption that allocative decisions could be separated from redistributive ones (Murrell 1991; Przeworski 1991). In their self-definition and in their vision of the future affluent society, the reformers unconditionally rejected socialism as a shortage economy marked by economic wastefulness and arbitrariness. The early reality of the transition challenged that vision. Not only did the stabilization package push peasants into a deep valley of high individual transition costs, but it also undermined their confidence in the system's capacity to realize its aim of increasing economic efficiency. Peasants viewed the package as promoting the mismanagement of resources and shady opportunities for the enrichment of old political and economic elites.

Moreover, peasants evaluated their present position and projected the future based on an assessment of state socialism that differed from that of the reformers'. While many Poles had criticized state socialism not for its basic principles but rather for their disjuncture from reality (Burawoy and Lukács 1992), Poland's peasants did not experience that disjuncture as acutely as others. The unique historical possibility that opened up for peasants during the last period of socialism provided them with individual economic gains that benefited society and advanced the central promises of socialism—economic equality and economic security. Through this prism, the peasants saw themselves in the transition not only as separated from the far side of the valley (capitalism) by unavoidable transitional costs. In their eyes, the far side also failed to *improve upon* state socialism and hence did not legitimate these individual and collective costs.[62]

Rejecting the idea that historical development is inherently progressive, Balcerowicz defended economic liberalism and promoted the model of nineteenth century competitive capitalism as more dynamic in its economic growth than that of late capitalism, and thus as a better guide for the postsocialist transition.[63] Przeworski's theory of transition suggests a quite different conclusion. Neither the model of competitive capitalism nor that of late capitalism can be a relevant comparative base for understanding the direction of postsocialist change. Rather, one must look to state socialism to see how it conditioned the subsequent trajectory of Polish society. A historical experience under socialism in which peasants' individual gains were integrally connected to the advancement of collective benefits became their "ethical imperative" to reject a historical alternative aimed at narrowly individual economic benefits. The peasants' early rejection of the reforms was not merely an attempt to avoid temporary material deprivation, it was also a challenge to the foundation of the neoliberal program. Thus, the ascendant Polish peasant bourgeoisie was unlike their counterparts in the West's transition to capitalism. The peasants were promoting *actual* "people's capitalism," not advancing *potentially* universal individual economic interests. Hence, the first "free private owners" denounced the postsocialist system by effectively translating their particularistic economic demands into the language of collective struggle that united all those dispossessed by the reform. The casualty of this struggle was the state's capacity to carry out its program.

Notes

1. The private sector within Polish agriculture remained almost unchanged in the excessive fragmentation of private landholdings from the onset and throughout the duration of state socialism. Fragmentation resulted from continual abrogation of the peasants' rights of access to productive resources and to exchange, acquire, or transfer land. See Korbonski (1965); Magyar (1984).

2. Nagengast found in Polish populism what Weber found in Protestantism in relation to the rise of capitalism. As she pointed out, the populism dating back to the nineteenth century, which centered around the values of freedom, independence of the private producer, and economic individualism, encouraged the allocation of a disproportional share of economic resources to the top layer of the peasantry and cast moral disapproval on the impoverished bottom. Thus, populism legitimated economic polarization within the peasantry. The same populist ideology, with the value it placed on the independence of individual enterprises, legitimated peasant opposition to socialism with its abrogation of individual property rights (Nagengast 1991).

3. In this chapter I will refer to peasants as a social category distinguishable

both from farmers in developed capitalist economies and from rural dwellers involved in part in agricultural production and incorporated into the national labor market of a socialist state. Although socialist agrarian policies promoted some economic differentiation within the peasantry (seen by some as its "farmerization"), they also generated peasant resistance to state interference, cemented peasant loyalty to traditional ideals, and thus preserved a certain degree of rural homogeneity. Hann (1985: 13) eloquently articulates the significance of this homogeneity when he states: "Peasantry survives *in spite of* certain objective economic possibilities—concessions by the authorities, necessary to avoid shortfalls but taken up only by small numbers of well-placed individuals. The majority has resisted, not because of any inherent peasant opposition to progress and commercialisation . . . but because this was a natural response to discriminatory policies against the private sector and agriculture as a whole."

4. In his reformulation of Marx's theory, Przeworski upholds the Marxist premises of the rationality of workers' behavior, workers' interests in continual improvement of their material conditions, and the potential superiority of socialism's economic capacity over capitalism.

5. I perceive this historical possibility as a direct outcome of a specific crisis of socialism in Poland. In my dissertation, I develop the concept of an *asynchronic* crisis of socialism wherein prior to the political collapse of the system in 1989, the economic and property relations of the socialist system were transcended. This led to a simultaneous advancement of private property rights and of economic egalitarianism between urban and rural segments of society.

6. For clarity, I focused this article on the category of private agricultural producers who under state socialism derived their livelihood from full-time agricultural production. Their farms ranged in size from 7 to 25 hectares.

7. For more data on these increases, see *Tygodnik Rolnikow,* nos. 45–46 (November 1990): 11–18; nos. 3–4 (January 1991): 20–22; *Polityka* 2 (1706) (13 January 1990): 6; 3 (1707) (20 January 1990): 1, 6.

8. For more on this point, see *Polityka,* no. 5 (2 February 1991): 8.

9. Ibid.

10. For example, whereas prices for dairy products increased significantly during 1990 (especially for butter and cheese), milk procurement prices remained practically unchanged at the level of 500–600 złoty/liter. See *Tygodnik Rolnikow,* nos. 51–52 (30 December 1990): 6; 43–44 (28 October–4 November 1990): 8.

11. In government estimates, the needs for capital investment in agriculture far exceeded 600 billion zloty as of 1990. The investment needs in rural infrastructure amounted to 178 billion złoty; in the food processing industry, 158 billion; in creating small rural businesses to absorb superfluous labor from restructured agricultural production units, about 240 billion. Restructuring the small family-based agricultural enterprises was expected to cost 60 billion złoty (MRGZ 1993).

12. Hence, financial investments in the agricultural sector in the second year of the transition amounted to 30 billion złoty, a fraction of an estimated need of 610 billion złoty. Almost half came for the financial resources of the peasants

themselves; only about a fifth of the sum was covered by the state budget. State expenditures for agriculture decreased steadily; in 1990 the amount spent on agriculture was only half that of the preceding year. For 1991, investments were 20 percent of the 1989 level, and for 1992 they were only 16 percent (ibid., table 4).

13. In 1989 the proportion of credits allocated to private agriculture was only 1.6 percent. In 1990 the figure rose to 2.2 percent, in 1991 to 3.3 percent, and in 1992 to 3.7 percent. See statistical data of Professor J. Weclawski in ibid. (table 6).

14. Ibid.

15. The bank received funds for preferential fertilizer and pesticide credits twice in 1990, in the amount of 250 million zloty each. In the following years the amount was doubled. Loans for processing plants were channeled to local banks by the regional cooperative bank, which administered the modernization funds of the European Foundation for the Development of Polish Agriculture.

16. Compared with 1985, when credits for investments constituted over 75 percent of all credits advanced for agricultural purposes, the ratio decreased to 62 percent in 1989 and to 20 percent in 1991 and 1992 (GUS 1992, 1993). Proportional with this declining ratio of investment credits was a dramatic decline in the construction of new utility buildings for agriculture, especially in its private sector. Construction of buildings for fattening swine, for milk and meat cattle production, and for grain storage was cut by half (from 30 thousand to 15 thousand buildings) between 1989 and 1992. By comparison, in 1985, 38,655 new units were constructed (GUS 1993, p. 342).

17. Nostalgic and bitter, many peasants compared these postsocialist credit policies with those from the golden era of the 1970s and 1980s under Edward Gierek's and Wojciech Jaruzelski's regimes when investment credits had single-digit interest rates. Additionally, significant portions of the investment credits were customarily forgiven as long as a credit recipient maintained his or her production at a specified level.

18. From 1980 to 1992, the number of tractors within the individual peasant subsector tripled. By 1985 the private agricultural subsector was outpacing the state farm sector in terms of the units of mechanical drafting power per 100 hectares of arable lands. In 1980 the private subsector was trailing both the cooperative and state farm subsectors with 21.6 units of draught power/100 hectares compared with 30.7 and 25.7 units/100 hectares, respectively. A decade later the trend had reversed. By 1990 private peasants had 48.9 units/100 hectares, the cooperative sector 36/100 hectares, and the state sector only 27/100 hectares. The next two years widened the gap between the sectors in terms of mechanized draught power: the private subsector rose continuously to 49.1 units/100 hectares, whereas the cooperative and state subsectors declined to 32.0/100 hectares and 23.9/100 hectares, respectively.

19. The practices observed in the villages under study reflect more general trends. The course of aging machinery stock in Polish agriculture was not reversed in 1990 but, rather, was deepened. In 1990 the coefficient of agricultural machinery renewal fell to 3.8 percent from the preceding year's level of 5.2 percent. In 1992 it dropped further to 1.4 percent (GUS 1993, p. 342).

20. With the opening of the Polish-German border, large numbers of old un-documented agricultural machinery from Germany found their was to the Polish countryside. These machines came without spare parts. New foreign machinery far exceeded the purchasing power of Polish peasants.

21. Under state socialism, the local agricultural trade cooperatives had sec-ondary and tertiary cooperative structures that were integrated into a command economy. The delivery of foods was based on directives and was subject to the manipulation of input and output prices by a complex system of state subsidies. The price for agricultural outputs was determined by administratively balancing the subsidies on agricultural production, distribution, processing and consump-tion. Although a small private market for agricultural goods existed, it was resid-ual to the state-controlled cooperative system and handled selected produce such as vegetables, fruits, flowers, and eggs. In light of a persistent and growing gap between demand for food and the agricultural sector's capacity throughout state socialism, subsidies were set to maximize state procurement of agricultural out-put. The monopolistic procurement position of the state-controlled trade system was assured by making producers' access to agricultural inputs and services con-tingent on their channeling agricultural output through state procurement coop-eratives.

22. In the 1980s milk and meat were subsidized at 60 to 80 percent. In the aftermath of the macrostabilization program and the reduction of state expendi-tures, the postsocialist state budgeted 0.2 percent of gross domestic product (GDP) for agricultural input subsidies, down from 3.4 percent to 4.8 percent of GDP in the period 1986–1989 and 1.3 percent in 1989 (World Bank 1990: 32–33; *Zielony Sztandar* 44 (3 November 1991: 6).

23. Initially, the drop in the consumer aggregate and relative demand for food led to a buildup of procurement center inventories. Yet, the centers soon geared their efforts toward decreasing their reserves by purchasing from agricultural producers below the level of their sales to retail redistributors. As a result, they maintained inventories proportional to the level of reduced sales.

24. Whereas in 1990 overall procurement of all grains stood at 6,385 million tons, it was slashed to 4,598 million tons in 1991 and further reduced to 3,769 million tons in 1992 (GUS 1993, p. 387).

25. National statistics confirm the preferential access of state farms and ag-ricultural production cooperatives to output markets compared with that of peasants in my research area. Thus, in 1990 grain purchase from state farms in-creased by 13 percent from the previous year. At the same time, purchases from individual producers decreased by almost 10 percent, dropping further in the sub-sequent year to only 75 percent of the 1989 level. Although the decline was slowed in 1992, the recovery of demand for grain output was faster for the ag-ricultural state farms and cooperatives than for individual producers. The latter recovered 90 percent of sales in 1992 compared with sales the preceding year. The disparity in the rates of procurement by agricultural subsector becomes even more visible in relation to the different rates of output: the 13 percent increase in grain procurement rates from state farms between 1990 and 1991 occurred against a slight decline in grain production (GUS 1994, tables 44 [446], p. 385, 45 [447], p. 386, and 47 [449], p. 387; also GUS 1993, table 1 [413], p. 319).

26. Concerning grain humidity tests, peasants did not have the means to retest or the facilities to reduce the grain water content if requested by the centers.

27. In 1980 there were over 5 million milk cattle in Poland; the number fell to 4.8 million in 1985. When reforms began in 1990, the numbers fell further, to 4.3 million. From 1990 to 1993 another dramatic drop occurred of 0.7 million, to 3.6 million head of cattle. The decreasing herd size corresponded with a drop in global milk production. In 1980 production was 16 billion liters, falling in 1990 to just over 15.3 billion liters. Within the first three years of the postsocialist economy, production declined to 12.2 billion liters (GUS 1994, table 30 [432], p. 380, and table 22 [424], p. 76).

28. The peasants' battles with the milk procurement center in Rolnicy were very representative of the relations between peasants and milk centers nationwide. See *Tygodnik Rolnikow* March (3–10 1991): nos. 9–10, 5.

29. From the date of their creation in state socialism, peasants viewed the milk procurement centers with deep suspicion—as local organizations integrated into the complex system of a redistributive economy and designed to exercise state control over private agricultural owners.

30. As Robert recounted the reasons for closing his poultry production, he told me of his last negotiations with a director of the state poultry procurement and processing plant. This plant, built in the 1970s, had a production capacity of 50,000 poultry a day and served all of the *voyevodship*. The plant had an extensive administration network of 2,000 employees. Its machinery and freezers, designed for handling large amounts of poultry feed, were effectively impossible to subdivide and reorganize, as a new economic environment demanded. As the enterprise cut production by 60 to 70 percent, reflecting the decline in consumer demand and the collapse of specialized poultry farms, its costs of production increased dramatically per unit of output. With no existing private competition in procuring poultry, the enterprise began reducing its costs by lowering the procurement poultry prices it offered suppliers. A week before scheduled delivery of 20,000 contracted poultry, Robert negotiated the procurement price with the plant's director, who offered him 4,000 zloty when the average price nationwide was 6000 to 7,000 zloty per chicken. For three days Robert hesitated. Each day's deliberation cost him an additional 1 million zloty in feed. On the fourth day, feeling outraged and defeated, he delivered 20,000 chickens at the price the director had originally offered. He closed his poultry production and threw himself feverishly into competition with the state poultry processing plant.

31. This amount was equivalent to $110,000. He generated this money from cash savings and by selling his car and specialized equipment.

32. The type of chicken raised in Poland (Astra) had proven to be very expensive in production; every kilogram of chicken weight required 2.6 kilograms of feed. Polish chicken also had a relatively low meat-to-bone ratio compared with, for example, its Dutch counterpart.

33. Applicants for foreign credit were charged 2.5 percent of the loan's value and had to put down collateral equal to the amount of the loan plus 20 percent.

34. Unlike the majority of other foreign aid, the 1990 funds available from the World Bank were uniquely designated for the development of agriculture in gen-

eral and of the food processing industry in particular. The funds were allocated through Polish commercial banks and were greatly underutilized because of the processing fees and the unattractive interest rates.

35. Cuts in fertilizer use in the villages studied reflected more general tendencies in Polish agriculture. In 1989–1990 fertilizer use had already been reduced by 20 percent, yet after the Balcerowicz price liberalization even greater drops occurred of 50 percent in 1990–1991 and 80 percent in 1991–1992. The reduction rates varied across agricultural subsectors, with deeper cuts in fertilizer application by individual peasants compared with the agricultural production cooperatives or state farms (GUS 1993, p. 343, table 37 [449]). Brooks (1991b) pointed out already low fertilization rates in Poland at the onset of the reforms compared with the advanced countries.

36. Even those few peasants in the *gmina* who had successfully engaged in specialized milk cattle production for over twenty years had reduced their production to a self-sufficiency level.

37. The *gmina* studied reflected national trends in that respect. In 1990 approximately 11,000 new facilities were built for animal production, half the number built in 1985. This number decreased further from 8,500 in 1991 to 5,500 in 1993. The threefold decrease in construction of new facilities for swine production was still slower than the sixfold reduction in new facilities for cattle production (GUS 1994, p. 381, tables 32 [434] and 33 [435]).

38. This involution of production was compounded further by reductions in land area farmed. Throughout the 1980s, state preferential credits (at 3 percent interest) supported the extensive modernization of farms in terms of utility buildings, machinery, and expanded production. Fearful that the unpaid remainder of those loans would be refinanced at postliberalization interest levels, many peasants sold small portions of their lands to generate the cash needed to repay the loans quickly and fully.

39. For further discussion of peasant workers, see Szelényi (1988); Szemberg (1980); Turski (1965).

40. These changes are reflected in data compiled by the *gmina* local government assessor's office. Plots of 2 to 5 hectares grew even more rapidly (both in number and in the overall land share within that category), thus solidifying the base of peasant workers in the postsocialist period.

41. On the national level, the slow process of consolidating lands by larger landholders (farms 10 to 15 hectares and above), as occurred in the last decade of socialism, has been halted or even reversed throughout the postsocialist period. Thus, the shares of farms within the ranges of 7.0 to 9.9 hectares, 10.0 to 14.9 hectares, and above 15 hectares all slightly decreased, whereas the percentage of small farms—2.0 to 4.9 hectares and 5.0 to 6.7 hectares—increased. In 1989 the average private farm was 7.2 hectares; by 1993 it had dropped to 7.1 hectares (GUS 1994, p. 361, table 6).

42. Average crop yields during the last five years of socialism were approximately 3,100 kilograms/hectare. Within the first four years of postsocialist transition yields decreased to an average of approximately 2,500 kilograms/hectare. During the same period there was a parallel decrease in the average number of

cattle produced per hectare of agricultural land—from 56 to 46 (*Maly Rocznik Statystyczny* 1995, pp. 228, 232, tables 8, 11).

43. An early sign of peasants' rejection of the Balcerowicz program was their clash with police in Mlawa near Warsaw in spring 1990.

44. Lech Walesa, with the Center Union (a political party that broke away from the Solidarity coalition), had proposed an alternative to the Balcerowicz plan. In what he called a "war at the top," Walesa attacked the postsocialist government over unemployment and declining demand, output, and real incomes. He affirmed a modern market capitalist economy "as the only economic order assuring civilized development" and pointed to the necessity of "including a system of social security appropriate to the level of our economic development." His proposed remedy was the acceleration of reforms (*przyspieszenie*) to shorten transition costs. To reactivate the economy, he called for eliminating wage restrictions, reducing taxes, and introducing guaranteed prices for agriculture. See text in *Gazeta Wyborcza* [Warsaw], June 1990.

45. In early summer 1990, the Tadeusz Mazowiecki government showed visible signs of internal factions and of deviating from its original program. In May the Economic Council within the Council of Ministers proposed loosening fiscal discipline and some state intervention. In particular, it proposed instituting preferential loans and minimum prices for agriculture. Those changes provoked the resignation of the first vice minister on the Balcerowicz team, Marek Dabrowksi. For more details on the economic program debates, see Balcerowicz (1992); Przeworski (1993); Mack (1993).

46. In principle, the corporate resolution of the sugar beet crisis also included a demand that the government immediately establish trade tariffs to prevent the dumping practiced by the West, perceived by otherwise opposing sides as effectively destroying domestic sugar beet production and processing.

47. The government also offered preferential loans to stimulate high-quality milk production within the individual farming sector. Petitions for these loans were to be sponsored by local boards of milk procurement cooperatives, as well as by the chapters of the Cattle Breeders and Producers (for more details, see *Tygodnik Rolnikow* nos. 45–46. (November 14–21 1990): 9.) The peasants in Rolnicy, however, found the loans were totally unavailable. Given their antagonistic relations with the cooperatives, they also considered the procedure of applying for the loans to be misguided and unfair to peasants.

48. See *Polityka* 32 (1736) (11 August 1990); 20 (1776) (8 May 1991).

49. The 1982 Bill on Alcoholic Abstinence aimed to preserve and enforce a state monopoly over the production, sale, and consumption of alcohol as a means to combat rampant alcoholism in Polish society.

50. A survey conducted by CBOS [Centrum Badania Opinii Spolecznych (Center for Analysis of Social Opinion)] in the aftermath of road blockades and the occupation of government buildings in 1990 found that 33 percent of society saw the demands of the peasants as fully justified and another 38 percent recognized the majority of the demands as justified; only 5.5 percent responded negatively to the peasants' demands, whereas 16.7 percent supported some of the demands but generally found them unjustified. Over 66.6 percent of respondents

proposed that the government change its economic plan along the lines of peasant demands. See *Polityka* 31 (1735) (4 August 1990): 6.

51. Since all peasants insisted that the specific nature of agriculture justified state intervention, the issue provoked deep divisions within the government ministries. The Ministries of Finance and Cooperation with Abroad opposed the Ministry of Agriculture on the issue of curtailing trade liberalization to protect domestic food production.

52. The neoliberal premises guiding the reform program, reinforced by the immediate pressures of the potato and sugar beet crises, had inclined the government to gear its interventionist measures primarily toward stabilizing distribution and agricultural processing. The government avoided assisting individual producers financially since such intervention was considered a form of state subsidy obstructing market regulation of production. In handling the negotiations with peasants, government officials emphasized that they had to help existing procurement centers and processing plants sustain their operations so peasants might preserve and enlarge their demand base.

53. *Gazeta Rolnicza,* nos. 13–14 (31 March–7 April 1991): 2.

54. The Samoobrona was formed by A. Lepper, an individual producer with 120 hectares from the Northeastern province of Poland who amassed interest arrears of close to 1 billion zloty on a loan of 280 million złoty.

55. Of 2.5 million individual agricultural enterprises, 183,000 took out loans, 23,000 were in debt, and 4,000 were facing liquidation. People closely associated with Lepper in Samoobrona claimed to be peasants who had been burned in their efforts to take economic initiative in the new postsocialist system. See *Rzeczpospolita* 157 (6 July 1992): 3.

56. The strongest centers of Samoobrona were in agricultural regions— Poznanskie, Koszalinskie (where Samoobrona originated), Leszczynskie, Kaliskie, and Bydgoskie *voyevodships.* Only three *voyevodships* had no regional representation in Samoobrona—Krakowskie, Nowosadeckie, and Bialostockie. See *Rzeczpospolita* 157 (6 July 1992): 3; *Polityka,* no. 14 (3 April 1993): 3; no. 34 (21 August 1993): 3.

57. By the end of 1991, about a third of the loans made by commercial banks were nonperforming. Interest arrears were up by 35 percent in nominal terms during the second half of 1991, and interest payments were increasingly capitalized. In addition, enterprises were accumulating tax arrears. At the end of 1991, 12 percent of total tax revenues for 1991 constituted tax arrears. For specific taxes such as the penalty tax for exceeding the government limit for wages, arrears were substantially higher, reaching almost half of tax payments. See Blanchard, Oliver and Dabrowski, Marek et al. (1993: 109–149).

58. For details on the Samoobrona campaign to remove officials from their posts, see *Wprost,* no. 35 (29 August 1992); *Polityka,* no. 14 (1874) (3 April 1993).

59. *Polityka,* no. 14 (1874) (3 April 1993).

60. Litwack (1991) views economic legality as a prerequisite for creating incentives that could support a healthy market. He defines such legality as a mutually consistent set of economic laws *and* beliefs by the population in the stability

and enforcement of these laws. Both elements were undermined in the early stages of Poland's agrarian transition.

61. Przeworski concludes that "an 'ethical imperative' will have to guide workers in the transition from capitalism to socialism . . . I am now prepared to claim that socialism would be superior because it would permit the society as a whole, by which I mean all individuals through democratic process, to decide collectively which needs should be satisfied in the process of accumulation. This choice is not available under capitalism, where the economic mechanism can only maximize the production of commodities, independently of anyone's will" (1985: 237–238).

62. Reflecting this perception are the outcomes of the 1995 presidential elections in the community I studied. Consistently, peasants voted against Walesa and for the new Social Democratic candidate Aleksander Kwasniewski, a former member of the state socialist regime.

63. See his article "Panstwo—Sila Nadprzyrodzona?" (The State—A Supernatural Power?) (Balcerowicz 1993).

References

Balcerowicz, Leszek. 1992. *800 Dni. Szok Kontrolowany.* Warsaw: Polska Oficyna Wydawnicza BGW.

———. 1993. Panstwo—Sila Nadprzyrodzona? (The State—A Supernatural Power?) *Wprost* 25 (20 June): 22.

———. 1995. *Wolnosc i Rozwoj. Ekonomia Wolnego Rynku.* Krakow: Znak.

Blanchard, Oliver, and Marek Dabrowski. 1993. The Progress of Restructuring in Poland. In *Post-Communist Reform: Pain and Progress,* ed. Oliver Blanchard, Maxim Boycko, Marek Dabrowski, Rudiger Dornbusch, Richard Layard, and Andrei Shleifer. Cambridge: MIT Press.

Brooks, Karen. 1991a. *Decollectivization and the Agricultural Transition in Eastern and Central Europe.* Washington, D.C.: World Bank, October. WPS 793.

———. 1991b. *Agriculture and the Transition to the Market.* Washington, D.C.: World Bank, October. WPS 666.

Burawoy, Michael, and János Lukács. 1992. *The Radiant Past: Ideology and Reality in Hungary's Road to Capitalism.* Chicago: University of Chicago Press.

Cooter, Robert. 1992. Organization as Property: An Economic Analysis of Property Law Applied to Privatization. In *The Emergence of Market Economies in Eastern Europe,* ed. Christopher Clague and Gordon C. Rausser. Oxford: Blackwell.

Ekiert, Grzegorz. 1990. Democratisation Processes in East Central Europe: A Theoretical Reconsideration. *British Journal of Political Science* 21 (3 July 1991): 285–313.

Friszke, Andrzej. 1990. The Polish Political Scene (1989). *East European Politics and Societies* 4 (2): 305–341.

Glowny Urzad Statystyczny (GUS). 1992, 1993, 1994, 1995. *Roczniki Statystyczne.* Warsaw.

Hann, C. 1985. *A Village Without Solidarity: Polish Peasants in Years of Crisis.* New Haven: Yale University Press.

Kochanowicz, Jacek. 1989. The Polish Economy and the Evolution of Dependency. In *The Origins of Backwardness in Eastern Europe: Economics and Politics from the Middle Ages Until the Early Twentieth Century,* ed. Daniel Chirot. Berkeley: University of California Press.

Kolankiewicz, George, and Paul Lewis. 1988. *Poland: Politics, Economics and Society.* London: Pinter.

Korbonski, Andrzej. 1965. *The Politics of Socialist Agriculture in Poland: 1945–1960.* New York: Columbia University Press.

Lewandowski, J., and J. Szomburg. 1990. Strategia Prywatizacji. In *Transformacja Gospodarki.* Gdansk: Instytut Badan nad Gospodarka Rynkowa, no. 7.

Litwack, John M. 1991. Discretionary Behavior and Soviet Economic Reform. *Soviet Studies,* vol. 43, no. 2 (April): 255–279.

Mack, Wales. 1993. *Rethinking the Market, Reconfiguring Institutions: The Case of Polish Agriculture.* Ph.D. dissertation in Political Science, University of California, Berkeley.

Magyar, M. 1984. *Peasantry and Agrarian Policy in Poland, 1944–1982.* Unpublished Ms.

Maly Rocznik Statystyczny. 1995. Warszawa: Glowny Urzad Statystyczny.

Ministerstwo Rolnictwa i Gospodarki Zywnosciowej (MRGZ). 1993. *Raport o stanie rolnictwa i gospodarki zywnosciowej.* Warszawa: December 7.

Murrell, Peter. 1991. Can Neoclassical Economics Underpin the Reform of Centrally Planned Economies? *Journal of Economic Perspectives* 5(4): 59–76.

Nagengast, Carole. 1990. Populism and the Polish State. *Socialist Review* 2: 80–101.

———. 1991. *Reluctant Socialists, Rural Entrepreneurs: Class, Culture, and the Polish State.* Boulder: Westview.

Przeworski, Adam. 1985. *Capitalism and Social Democracy.* Cambridge: Cambridge University Press.

———. 1991. *Democracy and the Market: Political and Economic Reforms in Eastern Europe and Latin America.* Cambridge: Cambridge University Press.

———. 1993. Economic Reforms, Public Opinion, and Political Institutions: Poland in the Eastern European Perspective. In *Economic Reforms in New Democracies: A Social-Democratic Approach,* ed. Louiz Carlos Bresser Pereira Jose Maria Maravall, and Adam Przeworski, Cambridge: Cambridge University Press.

Staniszkis, Jadwiga. 1991. *The Dynamics of the Breakthrough in Eastern Europe.* Berkeley: University of California Press.

Szelényi, Iván. 1988. *Socialist Entrepreneurs: Embourgeoisement in Rural Hungary.* Madison: University of Wisconsin Press.

Szemberg, Anna. 1980. *Przeobrazenia spoleczno-ekonomiczne indywidualnych gospodarstw rolnych.* Warsaw: Zaklad Wydawnictw CZSR.

Topolski, Jerzy. 1977. *Gospodarka polska a europejska w XVI–XVIII wieku.* Poznan: Wydawnictwo Poznanskie.

Turski, Richard. 1965. *Miedzy miastem a wsia. Struktura spoleczno-zawodowa chlopow-robotnikow w Polsce.* Warszawa: Panstwowe Wydawnictwo Naukowe.

Winiecki, Jan. 1991. The Inevitability of a Fall in Output in the Early Stages of Transition to the Market: Theoretical Underpinnings. *Soviet Studies* 43, (4 October): 669–676.

World Bank. 1990. *An Agricultural Strategy for Poland.* Washington, D.C.: World Bank.

7

Deconstructing Socialism in Bulgaria

Gerald W. Creed

The title of this chapter carries a double meaning. Most obviously, it refers to the attempt, begun in 1989, to dismantle the socialist edifice. Although citizens throughout Eastern Europe and the West enthusiastically joined this project, by the mid-1990s they still had not accomplished their objective. Privatization of state resources remained incomplete, and most of the new democracies retained functions characteristics of state socialism. More telling, socialist parties continued to garner significant electoral support in the context of free elections, periodically acquiring leadership positions (Perlez 1994). In Bulgaria the socialist successor to the Communist Party won the first free parliamentary election in 1990. It was defeated in the subsequent election in 1991, only to emerge victorious again in the third national contest in 1994. The party later lost considerable support in the wake of worsening economic conditions and was overwhelmed in the general election of 1997. Still, significant allegiance to the Socialist Party remains. Indeed, various socialist and communist parties collectively received over 25 percent of the 1997 vote. How could such attitudes develop/persist given the abject and deplorable status of the communist project after 1989 (Stokes 1993: 3)? Can they be expected to continue, and, if so, to what effect?

This chapter contributes to answering these questions by deconstructing socialist support in a critical sense. Drawing upon ethnographic research in a Bulgarian village, I attempt to break down the political category of "socialism" to expose diverse and even divergent local meanings and motivations. By critically deconstructing socialist support in this way, we gain insight into why it has been so difficult to deconstruct socialist practice. In previous work (Creed 1995), I traced socialist support to the myriad roles of agriculture under socialism and to the threat transition poses to crucial agrarian arrangements and associated identities. Here I expand on that earlier analysis, probing in the same vein for additional considerations underlying socialist "survivals" and "revivals."

Specialists on the process of change in the former Soviet bloc have already provided a litany of explanations for sluggish change and continuing socialist sentiment, from the pain occasioned by the transition to the continuing control of entrenched power holders and the near impossibility of coordinating political, economic, and social transitions.[1] As this volume's introduction points out, most of these explanations jump between the past and the future, conceptually linking would-be capitalist institutions to the socialist legacies that obstruct their installation. Although logically valid, these arguments fail to capture fully the nuances and dynamics of socialist sentiment conveyed to me by Bulgarian villagers. Their socialist support was increasingly a product of their participation in the transition rather than a holdover from the past or a new utopian vision. Whereas early responses to the transition reflected inherited models of capitalism and socialism, this was less true by the mid-1990s; the unfolding of the transition itself became the central consideration. For example, the pain of transition became a major problem not simply because it was painful but because as the transition proceeded, it moved from being a temporary inconvenience on the road to capitalism to a seemingly permanent discomfort. Similarly, as Bunce and Csanádi (1993) point out, the continuing uncertainty of the transition transformed the very nature of strategic behavior.

The focus on such dynamics need not deny the past or ignore the future. In social processes there is no such thing as a clean sltate (Millar and Wolchik 1994: 28), and even if we accept capitalism as the inevitable outcome, "real capitalisms," as Corrigan and Sayer (1985: 189) point out, can only be constructed from the transformation of preexisting social forms that inevitably influence the result. The important point is to see both legacies and objectives, inputs and outcomes, as mediated by people's experiences in the present. People can be influenced and even constrained by history without being its prisoners. The Bulgarian villagers I knew were weighed down by their socialist background, but they were not crushed under it; they struggled with it toward new objectives. Then, as their destination grew more distant and the terrain more rugged, they had to take their eyes off the prize and concentrate on their immediate circumstances—the journey itself became the focus of their interest and concern.

In the context of such shifting perspectives, the past can take on different meanings and significance so that legacies themselves are not unambiguous. This reality constitutes a serious challenge to "legacy" theories of transition. People have multiple images of the past—as both positive and negative, difficult and improving (Pine 1995; Creed 1998)—and the synthesis that results is very much a contemporary product. In other words, villagers view the past differently in response to the unfolding of the transition. To appeal to the socialist legacy to explain the present, then, is to invoke yet another *variable* that must be understood ethnographically and dynamically. We must look at the dynamics of transition to understand why particular aspects of the past resonate more than others, why they come to the fore in particular times, and what they mean in new contexts (cf. Dunn, chapter 4, this volume).

As postmodern insights suggest, it is difficult to achieve this perspective; we are restricted by the very parameters of our discourse. Because some of the same political actors in Eastern Europe use the same terms as before, we are wont to see current support for socialist parties as a revival or reversal and thus as a conservative or even reactionary moment.[2] But if we begin instead with the idea that political categories are themselves dynamic, taking on different meanings and functions as they are embraced and deployed, we can see something different hapening. Old forms and symbols are being redefined as they are mobilized for new objectives in new political and economic contexts.

This perspective was forced on me by ethnographic experience in the northwestern Bulgarian village of Zamfirovo, where I conducted fieldwork regularly between 1987 and 1997. The village is not necessarily typical of the Bulgarian countryside; it had a history of socialist activism prior to World War II and an especially successful experience with socialist industrialization. The latter may have amplified the negative economic consequences of the early transition, while the former rendered socialism a more likely response. Still, during my fieldwork since 1989 I realized that villagers were supporting the Socialist Party for myriad reasons, many of which diverged from Western stereotypes of conservatism or nostalgia. Thus, I came to see that not all contemporary socialist sentiment is conservative or reactionary but that it includes elements of post-communist resistance and even civic empowerment—it is not only resistant socialism but a form of socialist resistance.

Moreover, this resistance can be nuanced ethnographically in multiple ways. Socialism provides a means of resistance, but the motivation of that resistance may vary across populations and can shift with time. By talking to villagers over the years since 1989, I discovered numerous, even contradictory motivations for socialist support. I was also able to trace changes in political sentiment. In some cases villagers altered their party allegiance, especially after the abysmal performance of the socialist government in 1996.[3] Other villagers I interviewed had voted socialist in every election since 1990, but the reasons they gave for doing so shifted in response to the way the transition unfolded. As a result, socialism meant something different to them in 1997 than it had in 1988 and 1995.

In the following analysis I attempt to demonstrate three points: that Bulgarian support for socialism in the mid-1990s was not merely a holdover from the past but was also a form of resistance in the present, that the target of resistance was not democratic capitalism per se but rather a variety of foci reflecting diverse concerns associated with the transition, and that the motivations behind socialist support shifted in response to the fortunes of transition. Together, these insights allow us to invert the common interpretation of socialist allegiance—it is not a communist legacy obstructing democratization but a manifestation of popular democratic participation. I begin with a sample of political opinions from a few villagers who have shared their feelings with me in some detail over the years. Based on these and other comments, I attempt to summarize some of the concerns I detected repeatedly underlying expressions of socialist support. I conclude with a brief discussion of what these factors may portend for the future of socialist ideas and parties. My aim is to contribute ethnographically to a better understanding of the dynamics of transition and to nuance how we think about the "legacies" of the communist era.

Village Socialists

During my first fieldwork in Zamfirovo in 1987–1988, Bulgaria initiated its own version of perestroika, providing a brief preview of post socialist political debates. Village responses to reforms often reflected prior ideological commitments, but they were mediated by villagers' assessments of their future prospects (Creed 1991). In other words, opinions were shaped strongly by one's perception of personal benefits in the promised reforms. Interestingly, some of those who determined they could not profit began using socialist ideological arguments against the new reforms even though they had previously been critical of Communist Party policy. This observation was my first indication that Marxist-Leninist ideas were not merely the ideological muscle of a hegemonic political system but a political resource villagers could deploy strategically for their own purposes. Although such actions originally struck me as hypocritical, I came to feel otherwise as these villagers' attitudes toward socialism began to shift in tandem with its political and economic utility. As socialism became more useful, they not only utilized it but reassessed their attitude toward the socialist system.

Since perestroika was just the latest reform in a seemingly perpetual reform process, few villagers thought it would amount to much, so the extent of such political manipulation was limited. Still, this experience kept me from assuming that postcommunist support for the Socialist Party was merely a carryover from the past. Instead, I began to wonder who was using socialism this time and why. Villagers' comments and predictions around perestroika, which they clearly saw as a reform in the direction of capitalism, also gave me insight into how they were likely to interpret the more explicit movement to capitalism associated with the transition.[4] Thus, my ethnographic experience with state socialism helped me to recognize diverse political possibilities in the 1990s. Between 1992 and 1997 I spoke regularly with the same villagers about their political attitudes, tracing different motivations and concerns. The following three examples provide a small sample of that diversity from 1995.[5]

Dimitur was a seventy-one-year-old retired village administrator. His employment history included a short stint as the assistant mayor, but he had spent the bulk of his working years as the director of a collection of village commercial enterprises, including a sewing workshop and a workshop that made plastic lids. He lived with his wife, who was also retired, having worked several years in a rug-weaving enterprise before finishing her career in a workshop that mechanically transferred thread for knitting machines. They had a daughter and a son. The former lived with her husband's family on the other side of the village; the son lived in Sofia and rarely visited Zamfirovo except during the summer when there was agricultural work to be done and produce available to take back to town.

Dimitur was a member of the Communist Party and continued to support its socialist successor after 1989, but he was articulate about the difference: "There had to be a change. They [Communist leaders] did not pay attention to the things that needed doing. They were not concerned about economic development or improving life for the people but rather with their own privileges and advantages. That had to change." This feeling was not entirely novel for Dimitur. Following his retirement in the mid-1980s he became increasingly critical of the village administration and the party leadership. Still, he maintained that changes should build on socialist achievements. For example, he supported competition but thought the state should subsidize cooperative farms and state enterprises to *make* them competitive. He believed people who wanted to farm privately should be permitted to do so, although he insisted that the cooperative farms should decide which land they got. He advocated differential wages according to worker ability and performance, but he did not think the difference should be too big: "some difference, of course, but not such a large one." Those who could not get jobs should be put to work by the state cleaning streets or doing other civic work (i.e., "workfare").

Clearly, Dimitur does not fit the stereotype of an old-guard socialist, at least not well enough to explain his avid support of the Socialist Party. In explaining his politics, he focused less on the Socialist Party platform and more on the opposition's radical rejection of the old system: "They want to destroy everything and start over from scratch. Well, if you destroy what we have, then we will have nothing, and from nothing you get nothing." At the same time he acknowledged that it may already be too late to salvage anything, given the havoc of the past few years. Despite being part of the village's old guard, Dimitur saw the transition as an opportunity to redefine socialism. In many ways his vision revived failed reform objectives of the past and moved toward social democratic models.

Maria was a fifty-year-old schoolteacher. She served a stint in village administration and, like most people who achieved such positions, was also a Communist Party member. She lived with her husband, his retired parents, and her two teenage daughters. As a teacher, her job was fairly secure, although she complained about the meager salary. Her husband's job in a village factory that made electrical motor parts was tenuous. The factory was a branch assembly plant for a large Sofia enterprise that, like other socialist "dinosaurs" (Ickes and Ryterman 1992), operated erratically and paid workers even more erratically. Both children were away in school (one in high school, the other at a technical school), so they provided little help outside of summer vacation. Maria worried about having enough cash to pay the rent for the rooms they had in town.

Maria insisted she was "not one of those who are party members one day and then against the party the next. The biggest UDF[6] supporters were all members of the [Communist] party. They change colors according to whichever way the wind blows. They have no principles." Her principles were unambiguous: she was an ardent supporter of the Socialist Party. In fact, she saw little need to change the old system. She blamed corrupt leaders for past problems and for the collapse. In her view, Mikhail Gorbachev was ultimately responsible and was just like the corrupt UDF officials who at first benefited from socialism and then saw a bigger personal payoff in its destruction. What was needed, according to Maria, was to reestablish the old system with conscientious leaders. When I asked her what was going to prevent those leaders from again descending into corruption and selfishness, she said she believed the lesson of the collapse would keep them diligent.

Maria saw only decine in the changes since 1989: increased crime, a collective "psychological crisis," and community divisiveness. "You might not notice just during the summer, but if you could stay longer you would recognize the psychological consequences. People are insecure, and there is so much conflict about every little thing: over land, over anything that a person gets—there are accusations about how he got it, and then he gets mad at the accusers and soon whole families are not speaking to each other," she explained. I told her I knew of many such conflicts from the 1980s, but she insisted they had increased. She trivialized democratic inroads, saying most older villagers did not even understand what they were voting for. I suggested that her very vocal criticism was in some sense a privilege of democratization, but she countered that for people like her it was meaningless since no one listened to what they had to say. She also questioned the interests of "Western countries," claiming they were interested only in a new market for their goods. She was extremely critical of the general breakdown of authority and insisted that life was dangerous now: "Don't bother to call the police, they are afraid to do anything. Freedom? I don't know, but I'm not free to do a lot of things because I'm scared to travel by myself or I don't have the money."

Maria comes close to the stereotype of an unrepentant communist. But she was hardly typical. Many villagers, in fact, relished her discontinent as appropriate retribution for her past privileges as a party functionary. Nevertheless, some of those same detractors joined her in voting for the Socialist Party.

One of those villagers was Ivan, a thirty-nine-year-old unemployed factory worker who gave up his job in the same factory in which Maria's husband worked. Ivan's wife was also unemployed, having lost her job in the village cookie enterprise when it closed in 1994. They lived with their son and daughter, both adolescents. Ivan's mother had shared the house with them during the 1980s, but she had died in 1992. With no other income or pension and two offspring to support, Ivan could not wait around for the insecure work at the factory (as Maria's husband did); he opted instead for temporary construction jobs in nearby towns. He said jobs could be found, at least more often than he worked in the factory, but it was hard work, and one had to be careful since some contractors absconded with investors' money before paying their workers. He had no nostalgia for socialism and, in fact, voted for the opposition in the first two elections. But he voted for the socialists in the third election and had become increasingly cynical about the transition.

> I'm not going to vote in the next election. What is the point? Whoever wins, it's the same mess. I thought it would be better, but things have gotten worse. At first, I thought the difficulties were just temporary adjustments, but they keep getting worse. My wife is unemployed because the cookie factory couldn't sell any of its production. We can't compete with goods from everywhere else. We're too far behind, and even when the imports are junk, people prefer foreign junk to Bulgarian goods. The government has to protect its own market and production, otherwise we will never be able to develop.

Ivan wanted to leave the village altogether, but he could not find reliable (or adequately remunerative) work in town. Furthermore, as he put it, his family was "bound to the land" by its subsistence needs. His wife worked full-time tending more than a hectare of land and canned enough food for the family to live on for a year. Ivan and the children helped out when they were not at work or at school.

Ivan was only thirty-nine years old, but he worried about a future when he and his wife would be too old to farm, especially since he expected agriculture to become increasingly difficult. He was particularly concerned about the lack of money for herbicides and pesticides, insisting that without them the wilderness would reclaim the fields (an observation provoked in part by an infestation of field mice in 1995 that contributed to low wheat yields): "Of course, there are a lot of mice, and there will be more. We used to go out in large brigades, forming a human chain across an entire block of wheat and putting down pesticides every several meters. Now they put down a little every decare if they put down any at all, and look at the results." He made a similar argument about the growth of weeds in the absence of herbicides: "Look at what they harvested this year—the wheat is full of trash and weeds. Sometimes even the goats won't eat it. If you think the yield is bad, deduct the weight of the garbage from the harvest and you will see how bad it really is." He blamed the state: "Most villagers don't have the resources to buy herbicides and pesticides now that they are so expensive. If the state doesn't help, we can't continue; the wilderness will take over." His prediction seemed to be coming true, as the 1996 wheat harvest was even lower than that of 1995, provoking a grain crisis throughout the country and forcing some municipalities to ration bread.

Ivan complained about the Socialist Party and described its power as a continuation of authoritarianism. Yet, he voted for the party (at least once) because of one issue traditionally associated with state socialism—economic regulation and control.

Socialist Resistance

The political opinions of Ivan, Maria, and Dimitur do not convey the full diversity of socialist motivations in Zamfirovo, but by attending to many such stories—each unique in its own way—we can discern some recurrent themes. Clearly, one of the central issues driving village support for socialism in the 1990s was the threat to economic well-being. Village unemployment was extensive by 1992 and became worse each subsequent year. Many of the village's nonagricultural enterprises had closed, and those that remained worked erratically. A few private enterprises opened, including a small cheese plant, but they survived only a few months, thus confirming the limited possibilities for new businesses. The one successful entrepreneur in the village, an exporter who returned from Sofia to purchase wild products from villagers, had to keep shifting his product base as villagers depleted the region first of mushrooms and then of snails. Obviously, this strategy was finite. Small private shops with low overhead sprang up and survived, but their profits were limited by village customers' unemployment. Inflation simultaneously exacerbated the loss of income and diminished the value of pensions (which failed to keep pace). Most villagers were clearly experiencing a decline in their standard of living. To the degree that they perceived transition as a move away from socialism, the economic difficulties associated with transition became reasons for supporting socialism.

Villagers had anticipated some of these negative developments on the basis of folk models of capitalism, which generated early socialist support in 1990. They cobbled together their expectations and images of a capitalist future from a variety of sources, including their experience with "market" reforms under socialism, negative socialist propaganda about capitalist societies, contrary utopian images of capitalism provoked by the automatic disbelief of state propaganda, information from contacts or relatives abroad, Western popular culture allowed in by the state or acquired informally, a general inversion of socialist experiences reflecting the Cold War opposition between the two systems, and the profile of the early opposition leadership. Although I was not in the village for the 1990 and 1991 elections, villagers peppered their discussions in 1992 with "I told you so," indicating that they had projected dire consequences from the start. Troxel (1993) suggests the same in attributing socialist support in the early 1990s to fear.

Still, when the freely elected socialist government took over in 1990, it actually brought on some of the (perhaps unavoidable) difficulties Bulgarians had hoped to avoid by voting socialist. Predictably, the Socialist Party lost some support. This loss was somewhat reversed by the even worse performance of the UDF government after the 1991 election, but the socialists reconfirmed their incompetence when they were reelected in 1994. What became increasingly clear to villagers was that neither party could sustain socialist economic developments or protect economic well-being in the "new world disorder" (Jowitt 1992). As the Socialist Party participated increasingly in the economic transition, its popularity as a steward of socialist achievements dissipated. This is clear in Ivan's comment earlier, that he had lost faith in the economic abilities of both parties. Villagers who had supported the Socialist Party all along made similar comments. Maria's remarks are particularly revealing in this regard. Her major support for the Socialist Party in 1992 and 1993 hinged on the need to protect socialist economic achievements. In 1995, with many socialist economic structures and institutions already in ruins, she still advocated a "return" to the old system, but the grounds of her argument had shifted to other considerations—notably the pyschological disorientation and increased criminality accompanying the new arrangements.

The economic failures of the first postcommunist socialist government might have completely eroded rural support for socialism had it not been for the special case of agriculture.[7] The concern over agriculture reflected both its contribution to villagers' livelihood and its centrality in the prior socialist system, which had granted local producers significant influence in manipulating state regulations to maximize household economic prosperity. Before 1989, villagers depended on subsistence farming to augment their wages or pensions, allowing them to concentrate cash resources on more significant purchases such as building materials, household appliances, cars, and fashion. Shortages and poor distribution networks made subsistence production even more essential. Consequently, villagers produced most of their own vegetables, meat, dairy products, and alcohol (wine and brandy).

Although transition to capitalism would not seem to pose a threat to such "private" activity, subsistence farming had actually been dependent on the cooperative farm system, which despite its appellation operated much like a socialist state institution. The Zamfirovo cooperative farm and machine tractor station had provided machinery and labor to plow, sow, and even harvest villagers' personal grain plots. Grain products, in turn, fed the private livestock of villagers, which provided milk and meat as well as manure for fertilizing vegetable plots. Some of these household products had made their way back into the state sector through sale to state procurement agencies. In return, villagers had received part of the purchase price in concentrated feed for their other animals. Clearly, subsistence production had been intertwined with the cooperative-state sector.

Given the historical and ideological link between communism and collectivization, in the early years after 1989 Zamfirovo villagers commonly attributed anticooperative attitudes to the anticommunist opposition and equated the transition in general with decollectivization. Since their subsistence production had depended on the socialist cooperative structure, villagers worried about their sustenance in a postsocialist context. This threat materialized soon after the opposition gained power; one of its first major parliamentary actions was the passage of legislation to "liquidate" existing cooperative farms. Liquidation committees took over each farm in spring 1992 to liquidate all cooperative assets through either restitution to former owners or sale.

In response, incensed villagers turned again to the Socialist Party, just at a time when the party's prior economic and political incompetence had led many to question such support. Socialist Party leaders apparently recognized the popularity of the cooperative farm system and aligned themselves closely with it, passing legislation each time they were in power to facilitate the continuation of supposedly "reformed" cooperatives. As the champions of cooperativism, the leaders retained support in parts of the countryside where cooperatives remained essential to household econo-mies. Thus, rural support for the Socialist Party in the mid-1990s contin-ued to reflect an economic motivation even though socialist leaders were responsible for the worsening economic conditions at the national level after 1994. In fact, since economic difficulties such as unemployment and inflation actually increased villagers' dependence on subsistence produc-tion (and thus on cooperative supports), economic decline could strengthen their allegiance to the Socialist Party *for economic reasons* even though the economic decline occurred under socialist guidance. This situation is especially likely if villagers doubt the ability of any party to solve the national economic crisis, as Ivan expressed clearly in his earlier comments. Under such circumstances villagers may support the party most likely to maintain optimal conditions for their survival strategies. So although they may have voted for the socialists in early elections out of fear of the economic alternatives, I believe the nature of the transition itself kept some of them voting socialist even as the Socialist Party proved economically ineffectual. If so, the economic value (and meaning) of so-cialism shifted further toward subsistence.

Under state socialism cooperative farms had carried more than strictly economic significance. In helping villagers with subsistence production, the cooperative farm had reduced the amount of manual field labor, and since the farm had also carried out all large-scale cultivation it collec-tively relieved villagers of much of the agricultural labor associated with rural life. All of this combined with the developoment of alternative ser-vice, administrative, and industrial jobs to transform village identities. Villagers ceased to think of themselves as peasants and identified instead with their nonagricultural occupations. Just as the state was central to life under communism, one's connection to the state became increasingly elemental to identity; for most citizens, their formal occupation provided their main connection to the state. Village workers and even pensioners ceased to think of themselves as peasants even though they continued to produce much of their own food. Their wage labor allowed them to iden-tify instead with the celebrated socialist proletariat. Subsistence farming became a secondary part of identity, just as it was supposedly a second-ary contributor to the state socialist economy. After 1989, industrial un(-der)employment, the dismantling of the cooperative farms, and the in-creasing dependence on subsistence production threatened all of these notions and seemed to be turning villagers back into peasants. Villagers resisted this threat to their modernity by supporting the original archi-

tects of agricultural modernization and rurual industrialization—the socialists, at least until prove unhelpful.

The fear of being returned to peasant status revealed a broader issue
fueling rural socialist sentiment after 1989: distaste for urban cultural superiority. Villagers' aversion to peasant status reflected the cultural hierarchy that had accompanied economic development in Bulgaria (indeed,
the world), whereby rustic people were devalued vis-à-vis urban(e) citizens (Creed and Ching 1997). Villagers tried to restrain such attitudes by
voting for the Socialist Party. This may seem paradoxical, for it was *socialist* development that had culturally devalued country people in the
first place. Indeed, villagers in the 1980s had complained about being ignored by the Communist Party elite and being looked down on by urbanites, including relatives who came to pick up farm produce. They laughed
off state propaganda lauding the worker-peasant alliance and the victory
of socialism in the countryside. Even when they praised rural life, their
comments were usually phrased defensively (e.g., "You can't get this in
the city"), revealing the slight they felt as villagers.

Still, villagers took consolation from the ideological association between socialism and the cooperative village, which had been missing
from the early platforms of the UDF. In fact, in the early 1990s the Socialist Party came to be seen as a guardian of rural concerns because the
opposition was so strongly associated with urban intellectuals. For villagers already worried about being repeasantized and thus economically and
culturally devalued, the opposition's urban profile was a default argument *for* the Socialist Party. Previously suspect socialism thus became relatively more attractive in light of new alternatives. Far from being a carryover from the past, this dimension of socialist support was in part a
reversal of former political associations in response to the particulars of
the Bulgarian transition. The politics and personalities of the early transition established the Socialist Party as a relative protector of rural people
and culture.

The previously cited economic difficulties contributed further to the
political differentiation of rural and urban populations. As mentioned repeatedly, under state socialism most urbanites came to depend on the
subsistence production of their rural relatives for food, wine, and brandy.
In the 1990s, inflation and urban unemployment increased that dependence. Still, such a safety net made it easier for urbanites to continue to
support radical reformers even in the face of increasing economic difficulties. Their rural relatives who had to do most of the work, however,
had difficulty meeting the increasing demands, so the transition became
a physical drain. Thus, the economic interdependence of urbanites and
villagers under state socialism drove the two groups further apart politically after 1989. The economic crises and political pluralism of the transi-

tion rendered what had been a means of informal integration into a force for political differentiation. Rural-urban relations had not been idyllic before 1989, but the transition exacerbated the tensions and transformed them into political differences. Political competition then increased.

The Socialist Party not only offered villagers a means to assert their value in Bulgarian society, but it also helped them reclaim a protected space within the new world order after 1989. During the 1980s villagers had felt disadvantaged compared to Westerners and they often attributed such differences to socialism—sometimes as a form of dissent but at other times without any evident criticism, as if it were a statement of (natural) fact. The naturalization of the communist-capitalist division evident in such statements had allowed villagers to rationalize their marginal position in the world. They were socialists by residence even if they were not members of the Communist Party, and that designation accounted for their economic and cultural situation—it exempted them from evaluation by the hegemonic criteria of Western capitalism. In other words, their identity as socialist citizens (not necessarily supporters) had assuaged their sense of global marginality in the late twentieth century. The disintegration of the communist bloc removed that distinction, and many of those who celebrated the collapse soon felt the brunt of global devaluation (especially those anticipating that they would be repeasantized). In the 1990s villager talked constantly about their place in the world, questioning whether they were indeed "European" and "Western" or rather "wild," "oriental," "aboriginal," or "mixed," to name some of the recurrent alternatives. They often elaborated on how these identities impeded or foreclosed the possibility of transformation. Supporting the Socialist Party was a way to resist the political, economic, and cultural hierarchies defined by global capitalism or, more precisely, to claim exemption from those rankings even while participating in the capitalist world.

For similar reasons, villagers saw the changes as a threat to their political influence. This was truly ironic given the stereotypical association of socialism with repression and of postsocialism with democracy. Even if village members of the Communist Party had stood on the lowest rung of the political ladder during state socialism, they were at least integrated into a national structure. By contrast, early village supporters of the opposition had little, if any, input into the UDF, and opposition leaders of the early 1990s made little effort to court them. At the same time, the dismantling of socialism undermined the conflicting complementarity (the systemic integration of all social processes within a totalizing state) that had granted villagers some, albeit limited, political influence (Creed 1998). For example, the importance of subsistence production for the economy as a whole had kept life in the minds of central planners, whereas ideological tenets of equality limited the extent of rural marginality. Clearly, the official elimination of these policies and the destruction of the integrated system jeopardized villagers' *informal* influence on politics. At the same time, they were not convinced that they would acquire more *formal* influence: democratization promised everyone a voice, but villagers saw themselves as a weak minority likely to be overwhelmed by other constituencies.

The resistance to new marginalities and concern about village identities fused in one of the major factors driving socialist support: the concern for equality. Back in the 1980s, villagers had commonly cited equality as an aspect of both national and local identity. They recognized variation in wealth, but its extent and impact were minimal. By the 1990s, with rumors flying about the new millionaire "businessmen" (they use the English word), I was constantly asked why equality had to be so extensive under capitalism. To the degree that most villagers saw themselves getting poorer, their discomfort was just another of their general fears, but it also reflected concern about the impact of differentiation on the village community. In the Bulgarian countryside, with its presocialist history of relatively equal smallholdings and its subsequent communist egalitarianism, the differentiation that followed 1989 suggested a major restructuring of village community relations. Amid the density of social life, such a restructuring affected one's very sense of self. This multifaceted transformation underlies the crisis Maria (in the previous section) saw as "psychological." The threat to villagers' cultural identity, their sense of community, and their economic fortunes all intersected in the anxiety over increasing inequality; the socialist ideological commitment to equality served as a lightning rod for this political energy.

The concern about equality was the consequence of a more general dislocation after 1989—a shift in the meaning and role of money (cf. Verdery 1995). Although commodification had occurred in Bulgaria during the socialist period (cf. Lampland 1995), many villagers were shocked at the results of cutting money loose from state financial control. Under socialism, money could usually be accumulated in the quantities needed. Major purchases such as automobiles required advance planning and tapping numerous relatives and friends, but a village household could generally obtain enough money for the limited consumer goods it considered desirable. By 1992 that was no longer the case. Just as the consumer market expanded, money became much harder to acquire. Furthermore, getting it was no longer enough, as money's value evaporated mysteriously in the face of inflation and plummeting exchange rates. This situation led to the popularity of extraordinary solutions to money's devaluation, such as pyramid schemes (Verdery 1995). Voting socialist was perhaps an alternative way of dealing with the same problem (although the two solutions were not mutually exclusive): by reintroducing rationality into the seeming chaos of formal financial institutions, socialism might obviate the need for such extraordinary measures. Indeed, what does an economy that is out of control need if not some planning and commanding—socialist specialties. The Socialist Party also promised to inject morality into the seemingly amoral world of the dollar. Rampant corruption and criminality after 1989 confirmed stereotypes of capitalism as unrestrained greed, whereas socialists offered moral restraints through their ideological commitment (albeit compromised in practice) to social welfare and equality.

The changing role and meaning of money also help us to account for the strength of socialist sentiment among older villagers, who expressed incomprehension at the new fiscal logic. Since young people seemed the only ones with a chance to master the new "secrets," the changes inverted social expectations of parents helping and supporting children. Both sides resented this shift but especially parents, who were thrown back on subsistence production as their only way to reciprocate, further exacerbating the discontent associated with farming.

Whereas new economic forces threatened to reconfigure social relations, the continuing density of those relations in the village made it difficult for people like Maria, who had been members of the Communist Party before 1989, to abandon their views. Villagers knew each other's political history; former Communist Party members who tried to shift allegiance after 1989 were ridiculed as hypocrites by supporters of both the opposition and the Socialist Party, as is evident in Maria's defense of her continuing commitment to socialism. Even the motives of villagers who had left the party (or been purged from it) prior to 1989 were suspect since they had once joined it. Such community knowledge and judgment encouraged several villagers who had been party members to continue to support its successor or to avoid political statements altogether.

As implied previously, socialism's association with strict law enforcement constituted further grounds for reevaluating the past. An increasing number of villagers expressed support for socialism as a remedy for criminality and the apparent breakdown of authority, perhaps most evident in the problem of theft. Reports of village theft multiplied each summer during the 1990s, becoming grander and more brazen. One woman tried to start a photocopying service in the town hall, but someone stole the machine the day it arrived. After the village livestock had been returned or sold, looters leveled the cooperative building for bricks and other construction materials. One man reported watching villagers clean a cooperative field of newly baled hay before the truck could arrive to pick up the bales. These very visible and irrevocable losses made strong impressions. Theft had occurred under socialism, especially from state property, but it was virtually institutionalized—and more discreet (Creed 1998: 197–

200). Indeed, with the prospect of restitution the meaning of theft shifted from a regular and somewhat benign reappropriation of state resources to a feeding frenzy on cooperative and potentially private property. Therefore, theft not only increased and became more public, but its cultural valence shifted to a more negative and dangerous one.

Other forms of criminality complemented the new image of theft. Whereas the state-controlled media of socialism had reported only selectively on criminality, crime became a major media obsession in the 1990s, thus aggravating perceptions of its frequency. People also acquired more personal experience as the transition and the Serbian embargo "democratized" possibilities for trafficking in contraband. People saw "mafias" everywhere. Previously, the term had been restricted to cliques of communist leaders, but by the mid-1990s villagers applied it to almost any criminal activity, organized or not. Villagers assured me that it was pointless to start a business in town because you would be shaken down by strongmen demanding protection money. By 1996 the English word *bodyguard* had entered common parlance as the term for security personnel. Its village use clearly implied a degree of suspicion not conveyed by the Bulgarian word *pazach*.

Nostalgia for law and order was part of a broader desire for stability, which people associated with the pre-1989 socialist period. By the 1990s socialism represented not simply security but something solid in the constantly shifting terrain (which many villager professed not to understand). Unfortunately, for a few the concern for order and stability bled into a more disturbing desire for authoritarianism. These villagers approached the stereotype of unreformed, unrepentant communists described by the opposition. They advocated a wholesale return to the old system, sometimes in language more extreme than that I recalled from the 1980s. This possibility emerges from Maria's claim that she is not one of those to shift political allegiances—a claim that makes sense only if one sees the Socialist Party as a clear continuation of the communist one rather than as a reformed social democratic party, as Dimitur seemed to think. For Maria and others, the havoc of the transition proved first and foremost that rigid control was the only way to promote and maintain social welfare and economic stability. Some blamed this unfortunate conclusion on weaknesses in the Bulgarian national character, whereas others targeted interference from external forces such as the World Bank and the International Monetary Fund. The latter explanation provided a point of convergence with more explicit nationalists.

Although such neo-Stalinists were among the most vocal village commentators in the early 1990s, they constituted only a fraction of those who voiced support for the idea of socialism or the Socialist Party. There were a plethora of reasons others voted for the socialists and a variety of views as to what they thought socialism should actually be. Whereas one person supported socialism to stave off economic decline, his neighbor voted socialist in defense of her village identity. For most villagers no single issue was determinant; rather, a combination of reasons led them to side with the socialists. Regardless, for many villagers support for the Socialist Party did not represent a nostalgic desire to return to the past but rather an attempt to use ideas associated with socialism to influence the future. This conclusion is supported by survey data that found only 5.5 percent of Bulgarians in favor of restoring the old socialist system (Mason 1995: 405). The remaining majority of the Socialist Party's supporters must be tapping socialism for other reasons. The Communist Party provided them with the political and rhetorical resources they are now using to defend their interests in ways the prior socialist state never intended or allowed. In this sense, the so-called socialist resurgence is perhaps the strongest evidence to date of a successful shift to democratic practices, at least in the village context.

The Future of Socialist Support

Several younger villagers predicted to me that socialist support would eventually disappear altogether because it was concentrated among the elderly and would therefore die off with them. Similar arguments undergird the view that it will take "a generation" to turn things around in Eastern Europe (Mason 1995: 402, 406). At the same time, the Socialist Party is restrained from courting new and different constituencies by the double bind Phillips (1994: 530) noted for the German Party of Democratic Socialism: the party needs to change to expand, but too much change risks alienating its core constituencies. Some of the same concerns that convinced elderly villagers to support the socialists, however, may lead the subsequent generation to do likewise. Concerns over agriculture and repeasantization may be passed on to urban relatives when parents die and children have to take up subsistence farming to survive or prosper. Because few have prospects for building up nest eggs, they will also eventually inherit their parents' concern about pensions—an important reason to support the socialists.

Indeed, I have already seen changes in villagers' politics as their households move through the developmental cycle. One early UDF supporter was enthusiastic about private agriculture in 1992, but when his son got a job in town and moved away with the grandchildren (also of working ages), he changed his tune. When we see socialist support among the elderly not just as a conservative holdover but as a response to specific problems, we can better assess the degree to which socialism may resonate for the next generation of grandparents. Furthermore, a reforming Socialist Party does not necessarily risk losing its core supporters, as Phillips (1994) suggests, if they are rethinking their own prospects and possibilities in continually shifting contexts.

The lesson of this chapter is that the future of socialist parties in Bulgaria is impossible to predict, for the meanings and functions of socialism shift in relation to new developments. In the early 1990s the ongoing need for subsistence production and the differential impact of such activity on rural and urban populations differentiated them politically, therby perpetuating a rural socialist sentiment associated with sustaining agriculture. The 1996 Bulgarian economic crisis, however, underminded this association.[8] In 1995 and 1996 severe bread and wheat storages resulted from poor harvests, both under socialist watch. This crisis jeopardized villagers' continuing commitment to socialism as the 1997 election revealed, but the ultimate fate of socialist parties will depend on the evolving links between agriculture and other activities, as well as on the degree to which other parties offer viable and attractive alternatives.

In this chapter I have shown that rural socialist sentiment in the mid-1990s was as much a product of the Bulgarian transition as it was a legacy of the socialist past and, moreover, that it was largely a democratic response to new circumstances, rather than a throwback. Socialism offered villagers a political vocabulary and a vehicle for resistance, but the dynamics of transformation produced the targets. The evidence for this ironic conclusion came from the variety of political, economic, and cultural motives I discovered among village socialist supporters in the 1990s—a diversity that revealed multiple meanings for socialism itself. I was further convinced by watching these motives and meanings change as the transition unfolded.

My response is not to deny the relevance of socialist legacies but to recast them as *contemporary questions* instead of historical answers. When we try to explain these legacies—probing what they mean to the people involved and why they are more robust than other aspects of prior socialist practice—we begin to see the transformation of socialist systems as a distinctive social process in and of itself. The utility of socialism as a vehicle for protest in a supposedly postsocialist context gave it a new purpose and a new lease on political life. Its use, however, nourishes *old* oppositions, so observers may fail to recognize the novel motivations behind that use. Thus, many UDF supporters saw socialist support as threatening to restore the past, when, in fact, many socialist supporters had no such ambitions. Indeed, the socialists' role in directing the transition since 1994 has imperiled their ability to capitalize automatically on antitransition sentiment. For some disgruntled villagers, the opposition between socialism and postsocialism is part of the Socialist Party's appeal, but as the party participates increasingly in the process of change, that appeal may dissipate; even these supporters may lose confidence in socialism generally. Their commitment might be sustained, however, if alternative socialist parties emerge to challege the current one's near monopoly over socialist ideas. Here, the continuation of neo-Stalinist models is dangerous, as they could provide an alternative venue for socialist commitments—especially if people feel betrayed by more social democratic models. As I noted at the start, our discursive categories can exercise their own determinancy. For this reason we should engage actively in deconstructing them.

Notes

Acknowledgments: The research for this chapter was funded by the Joint Committee on Eastern Europe of the Social Science Research Council and the American Council of Learned Societies, the Wenner-Gren Foundation for Anthropological Research, and the PSC-CUNY Research Awards Program of the City University of New York. I am grateful to them and also to the participants in the Ethnographies of Transition conference who inspired many of my ideas, especially Michael Burawoy, Caroline Humphrey, Martha Lampland, and Katherine Verdery.

1. This literature is too extensive and rich to summarize (or even characterize). For a sample see the articles submitted to the Joint Economic Committee of Congress (1994).

2. Conversely, we sometimes fail to see similarities where they exist. For example, analysts of Romania (Verdery and Kligman 1992; Tismaneanu 1993) have documented the communist continuities sometimes obscured by the government's anticommunist rhetoric.

3. The outcome of the first two parliamentary elections remained fairly consistent for the village, with the Socialist Party winning by approximately a two-to-one margin. The 1994 election revealed a relative increase in socialist support, but it had more than eroded by 1997 when the Socialist Party managed only a slim village victory.

4. I do not assume that "capitalism" is the best way to characterize what is actually going on in Bulgaria now or that it will be, but people view the transition and the contemporary period as a move toward that objective; thus, capitalist models strongly inform and influence their actions and responses.

5. Names and identifying details have been altered to ensure informant anonymity.

6. The UDF stands for the Union of Democratic Forces, the primary competitor of the Socialist Party. The UDF began as a broad coalition that included most of the antisocialist parties in the country except for the Movement for Rights and Freedom, which was identified with the Turkish minority. The UDF has since splintered, divided, and partially reunited, but it remains the primary opposition force.

7. The following discussion of agriculture and identity is summarized from Creed (1995). For more extended treatment of these topics, see the original.

8. The economy nearly collapsed in late spring 1996 when the state bank was unable to maintain the value of the Bulgarian currency as a result of dwindling foreign reserves and an impending debt payment.

References

Bunce, Valerie, and Mária Csanádi. 1993. Uncertainty in the Transition: Post-Communism in Hungary. *East European Politics and Societies* 7(2): 240–275.

Corrigan, Philip, and Derek Sayer. 1985. *The Great Arch: English State Formation as Cultural Revolution.* Oxford: Basil Blackwell.

Creed, Gerald W. 1991. Between Economy and Ideology: Local Level Perspectives on Political and Economic Reform in Bulgaria. *Socialism and Democracy* 13: 45–65.

———. 1995. The Politics of Agriculture: Identity and Socialist Sentiment in Bulgaria. *Slavic Review* 54(4): 843–868.

———. 1998. *Domesticating Revolution: From Socialist Reform to Ambivalent Transition in a Bulgarian Village.* University Park: Pennsylvania State University Press.

Creed, Gerald W., and Barbara Ching. 1997. Recognizing Rusticity: Identity and the Power of Place. In *Knowing Your Place: Rural Identity and Cultural Hierarchy,* Barbara Ching and Gerald W. Creed, eds. New York: Routledge.

Ickes, Barry, and Randi Ryterman. 1992. Credit for Small Firms, Not Dinosaurs. *Orbis* 36(3): 333–348.

Joint Economic Committee. 1994. *East-Central European Economies in Transition.* Washington, D.C.: U.S. Government Printing Office.

Jowitt, Ken. 1992. *New World Disorder: The Leninist Extinction.* Berkeley: University of California Press.

Lampland, Martha. 1995. *The Object of Labor: Commodification in Socialist Hungary.* Chicago: University of Chicago Press.

Mason, David. 1995. Attitudes Toward the Market and Political Participation in the Postcommunist States. *Slavic Review* 54(2): 385–406.

Millar, James R., and Sharon L. Wolchik. 1994. Introduction: The Social Legacies and the Aftermath of Communism. In *The Social Legacy of Communism,* eds. James R. Millar and Sharon L. Wolchick. New York: Woodrow Wilson Center Press and Cambridge University Press.

Perlez, Jane. 1994. Welcome Back, Lenin. *New York Times,* 31 May: A1, A9.

Phillips, Ann L. 1994. Socialism with a New Face? The PDS in Search of Reform. *East European Politics and Societies* 8(3): 495–530.

Pine, Frances. 1995. Dealing with Fragmentation: Women and Work in Post-Socialist Poland. Paper presented at the Fifth World Congress of Central and East European Studies, Warsaw, Poland, 6–11 August.

Stokes, Gale. 1993. *The Walls Came Tumbling Down: The Collapse of Communism in Eastern Europe.* New York: Oxford University Press.

Tismaneanu, Vladimir. 1993. The Quasi-Revolution and Its Discontents: Emerging Political Pluralism in Post-Ceauşescu Romania. *East European Politics and Societies* 7(2): 309–348.

Troxel, Luan. 1993. Socialist Persistence in the Bulgarian Elections of 1990–1991. *East European Quarterly* 26(4): 407–430.

Verdery, Katherine. 1995. Faith, Hope and *Caritas* in the Land of the Pyramids: Romania, 1990 to 1994. *Comparative Studies in Society and History* 37(4): 625–669.

Verdery, Katherine, and Gail Kligman. 1992. Romania After Ceauşescu: Post-Communist Communism?" In *Eastern Europe in Revolution,* ed. Ivo Banac, Ithaca: Cornell University Press.

8

Redefining the Collective: Russian Mineworkers in Transition

Sarah Ashwin

In the years 1989–1993 mineworkers constituted a key element of the "democratic" movement in Russia. Mineworkers' strikes in 1989 and 1991 played a crucial role in the destruction of the Soviet system; thereafter, the leaders of the independent miners' movement that grew out of those strikes never failed to offer support to Boris Yeltsin at vital moments in his struggle with the conservatives. Since 1993, however, support for the communists and nationalists has been growing in mining regions; by the 1995 election the once reformist Kuzbass coal basin in western Siberia had become renowned as a communist stronghold, while the polar coalfield of Vorkuta, with its strong anticommunist traditions deriving from its gulag past, voted heavily for Vladimir Zhirinovsky. Why have the mineworkers, once in the vanguard of democratization, turned to authoritarian politics? This dramatic transformation cannot merely be explained away as a reaction to falling living standards, because even those in Kuzbass who have been relatively protected from the ravages wrought by reform have turned to the Communist Party. Workers' support for authoritarian leaders at all political levels is considered here in the context of changes within the workplace, in particular the struggles over the redefinition of the nature of enterprise collectivism that have been unleashed by transition.

The labor collective of the past is under pressure. The state is no longer prepared to fund social provisioning, once the most tangible expression of collectivism within the enterprise, and the form of collectivity that exists within the microworlds of individual work groups is also contested as management attempts to reimpose its eroded authority. Workers are not indifferent to the loss of security provided by the social guarantees of the past or to the destruction of the collective institutions of social and welfare provision. But rather than seeking to build a new relationship between individual and collective in which the workers would take control of their collective institutions, they remain locked into the alienated forms of symbolic collectivism inherited from the past. They treat the collective as a resource imposed from above and seek their salvation in a paternalistic leader who can promise to restore the security of the past—a salvation that the Kuzbass mineworkers seek through their support for the Communists, and other brands of authoritarian leaders, at the local and national level. Yeltsin belatedly appealed to such sentiments in his election campaign in 1996. Meanwhile, as a complement to their search for collective salvation from above, workers are also very active in pursuing individual survival strategies.[1] Such strategies are not pursued through the social relations of the work collective, however, but through networks of family and friends that are in most cases independent of the social relations of the immediate work collective. Enterprise collectivism is thus also coming under pressure from below as workers increasingly look outside the enterprise for their survival—and this in turn reduces the possibility of their mounting a collective response to the transition and reinforces their dependence on authoritarian leaders. The complementary perspectives of individualism and "alienated collectivism" adopted by workers are a key force in shaping the labor collective—and the Russia—of the future.

The arguments developed here are based on a case study of one mine, referred to as "Taldym," situated in the South Kuzbass. The mine employs just over 3,000 workers, 700 of them women, and is the main employer in the mining settlement of Vishnovka, which has a population of 11,500. The research was conducted on four field trips, two in 1994, one in 1995, and one in the summer of 1996. All of the brigades selected for detailed research were from auxiliary shops, although a selection of individual miners from both production and development shops were interviewed outside work. This focus was partly determined by an interest in women's collectives in the mine, and partly by ease of access: it was possible to sit for long periods observing the work of surface workers (as well as maintenance workers who worked both on the surface and underground), an approach that was precluded in the case of miners.

The women's collectives selected for detailed research were: the *lampovaya*, where the miners arrival at and return from work is recorded and their lamps are recharged and serviced; the *zaryadnoe depo* (known locally only as the *zaryadnoe*), where the batteries used for in-mine transport are recharged; the central *kotel'naya* (boiler house), which provides heat and hot water for Vishnovka; and one of the mine's two technical complexes, where the coal is improved by the manual removal of lumps of rock as the coal passes on a conveyor. The men's collectives studied were a brigade of fitters from one of the in-mine transport shops, responsible for maintaining the conveyors in the mine; a brigade of fitters responsible for repairs in the *kotel'naya;* and one of the brigades responsible for the "modernization" and adaptation of newly acquired mine machinery and the upkeep of the old.

All names connected with the main case study have been changed to protect informants; the names of other mines and places have not been changed.

Taldym

Taldym is a particularly appropriate place from which to analyze mineworkers' desertion of the reformers in favor of the communists. The mine was formerly in the forefront of the democratic miners' movement: it was one of the first mines to strike in 1989, before the general miners' strike that began in neighboring Mezhdurechensk in July. Taldym was the first mine to follow the lead of Mezhdurechensk in summer 1989, and its workers refused to settle after the miners in Mezhdurechensk had gone back to work. The president of the mine strike committee became one of the most respected leaders of the regional strike committee and in 1993 was elected to the upper house of the Russian parliament on the democratic ticket. In autumn 1995, however, the workers at Taldym elected well-known local communists as mine director and as president of the company and voted heavily for the Communist Party in the 1995 parliamentary election.

The reversion to the communists at Taldym cannot be understood simply as a reaction to acute hardship. The coal mining industry has been heavily subsidized throughout the period of reform, so both employment levels and relative wages have largely been maintained. Although Vishnovka has not escaped the impact of reform, the mine has been relatively protected during the transition period and is one of the most prosperous in south Kuzbass. The mine privatized to the labor collective in 1992, but this has not resulted in significant internal restructuring. This fact is strikingly illustrated by the fact that despite falling production in 1995, there was no staff reduction; indeed, although the mine had supposedly frozen recruitment, its workforce *increased* by 230 in 1995 at a time when all of the other mines in the south Kuzbass concern were laying off workers (*Gornyatskaya solidarnost'* [Novokuznetsk], 14 December 1995: 2). Wages at Taldym remain relatively high compared with those in other mines and in other branches of production, and although miners are convinced that their living standards have deteriorated significantly since 1991, statistically, wages are significantly higher than they were in the

Soviet period. Although the mining industry has suffered from acute delays in the payment of wages, Taldym has again been relatively privileged; until mid-1996 delays in payment rarely exceeded one month.

Soviet Enterprise Collectivism

It is well-known that the Soviet enterprise was one of the central institutions of Soviet society. Within the ideology of state socialism work was central to the self-identification of the individual and the group, while within Soviet society the work collective was a key site of social integration. The labor collective accordingly had a dual significance: it was simultaneously a locus of social control and a locus of self-realization, the point of intersection between the totalitarian aspirations of the party-state and the individual and collective aspirations of the workers in whose name the state ruled.

Soviet enterprise collectivism is a complex phenomenon. First, the term *collective* (*kollektiv*) is used to refer to both the entire workforce of an enterprise and its individual subdivisions. Managers and workers use the term to refer to the different work groups within the mine—the workers in the *lampovaya* would describe themselves as a collective, for example. All of the employees of a particular enterprise are also referred to collectively as the *labor collective* (*trudovoi kollektiv*). In practice, the distinction between the two forms of collective in everyday speech is rather blurred, but to understand the character of collectivism it is important to distinguish between them. To avoid confusion, I use the term *labor collective* in this chapter to refer to all of the mine employees, whereas individual work groups are referred to as *immediate work collectives*. In addition, the collective is at the same time an ideological construct and a material reality, and the term is used here in both its ideological and concrete senses. This reflects workers' usage of the term, which constantly shifts between the ideal and the real.[2]

The labor collective is a reality, but it is also a rhetorical device, appealing to the unity of interests of workers and management in the face of external forces. The collectivism of the labor collective is expressed in various symbols and rituals, slogans and icons, which since 1992 has been supplemented by the nominal ownership of the mine by its employees. The nearest thing to a tangible expression of the collectivity of the labor collective, however, is the biannual delegate meeting of the collective, which gathers to hear the director and trade union president report on the fulfillment and revision of the collective agreement; also, there is now an annual shareholders' meeting. Since 1989 these meetings have not been purely ritual; since privatization, no chief of the labor collective has succeeded in being reelected. (The mine director and president of the joint-stock company are required to stand for reelection every two years.) Nevertheless, despite such episodic eruptions when the collective dismisses its leaders with abandon, the leader remains, for good or ill, the embodiment of the collective. It is the chief who is responsible for the good or bad fortune of the collective, and the immediate solution to bad fortune is not to give more reality to the collectivism of the labor collective, but always to elect a new chief.

Although the collectivity of the labor collective is largely symbolic, it finds very real expression in the authoritarian paternalist system of social and welfare provision, which is the tie that binds individual workers and work groups to the labor collective. The collective is the site of social provision and in this sense is a focus for workers' aspirations, but the distribution of various benefits is also a powerful lever of management control over individual workers and work groups. The labor collective is neither perceived nor realized as the product of the collective organization of individual workers or the association of their immediate work collectives; it is seen as an entity external to individual workers and work collectives, an entity from which they receive and to which they appeal, an entity personified in the chief who represents them and who bestows or withholds favor from them. In this sense the labor collective is an alienated collectivity in which workers relate to their own collective existence as something standing outside and opposed to them. Although this alienation has been weakened by the collapse of the Party-state, which has largely removed the repressive force with which collectivism was imposed on workers, it nevertheless persists. Indeed, management makes every effort to see that it does persist by seeking to ensure that forms of active collectivism do not develop, from carefully organizing and controlling meetings of the collective as delegate meetings to holding trade union meetings on a shift rather than a shop basis, thereby cross-cutting the solidarities of immediate work collectives.

Nevertheless, despite its alienated form, workers identify with and are attached to the labor collective, which they see as their immediate guarantee of security. As long as the collective retains an alienated form, however, workers are ultimately dependent on the will and whim of the director and on the director's ability and willingness to protect them against the whirlwind of reform. Therefore, to assess workers' ability to give the collectivism of the labor collective a more substantial reality, we must turn from considering the collective as a whole to the immediate work collective.

The collectivism of the immediate work groups also has a symbolic dimension, but it has a more tangible reality in the particular social relations formed at the level of the work group. If a new form of collectivism is to emerge, it can do so only on the basis of the collectivism of the immediate work group.[3] The next section of this chapter focuses on the immediate work collectives and the nature of workers' relationships to their work groups. Then, on the basis of a case study of one such collective, I chart the development of social relations in these collectives from the late perestroika period onward. I argue that although the collapse of the Communist Party and the erosion of discipline at the mine gave the work collectives more autonomy, workers proved unable to develop the collectivist potential immanent within immediate work collectives. At the same time, networks outside work and the household as a productive unit assumed greater importance as means that enabled workers to weather the transition. This process, as I will argue in the section entitled "The Collective Between Past and Future," is replicated at the level of the labor collective. Workers' collectivist aspirations take the alienated form of dependence on the authoritarian personification of the collective—the mine director. But their needs cannot be met within the alienated collectivity of the mine; thus, they are increasingly thrown back on their own resources.

"My Collective—My Second Family"

The immediate work collective was the point at which the individual's integration into the system was monitored and regulated,[4] but it was also a focus of sociability in which workers spent half their lives together. The effectiveness of the work collective as a locus of social integration and control depended on the fact that individuals were attached to their collectives. This section describes the relationships of workers to their collectives and highlights the centrality of the collective in their lives.

Soviet communism imposed a particular form of relation to the work collective that had both a material and an ideological basis. First, the impoverishment of the material conditions of private existence was the corollary of the provision of social and cultural facilities through the workplace. Cramped housing conditions and the lack of leisure facilities in the Russian urban context mean that work is both an escape from the drudgery of home and a welcome opportunity for communal sociability. As Alasheev has argued, workers "live in such conditions that work . . . is the single socially approved possibility of self realization" (1995: 71). This material basis of workplace collectivism has outlasted the system that gave rise to it.

Second, communist authorities continually stressed the value of "the collective," and although workers did not relate uncritically to communist categories, those categories did have a lasting influence on their perception. Thus, although the precise significance workers accorded to the collective differed from that prescribed in official discourse, the idea that the work collective was a crucial reference point was common to both and was true for both male and female workers. Men and women do not relate to their collectives—which in the mine are almost exclusively either all male or all female—in precisely the same way, but both sexes attach similar levels of importance to their lives within the collective.[5] The same point can be made about different categories of workers, such as male surface workers and miners.

The following discussion of realtionships to the collective draws on interviews with male and female workers at Taldym conducted during the years 1994–1996. The quotations in this section illustrate a particular kind of attachment to the collective that still exists, but it is important to point out that workers increasingly note that their collectives are becoming less "close," that life at the mine is "less interesting," and that work is less important because "they don't pay us." These sentiments were especially marked in August 1996, when the mineworkers had not been paid for three months. The rest of this section thus isolates a set of attitudes that appear to be changing in the present stage of transition, although they still inform workers' normative expectations. Work and the collective may be becoming less important, but that development is far from welcome. Indeed, the pervasive sense of loss induced by the waning of this communal sociability fuels the longing for security and protection that characterizes contemporary Russian political life. This development is the subject of the section entitled, "The Collective Between Past and Future."

Both male and female workers describe the collective as a welcome retreat from the pressures of home, although since men and women face different domestic pressures, they tend to look for a different kind of relief at work. For women, two main themes emerge. First, female workers often claim that their work within the collective is less arduous than their work at home. At home they feel isolated and under constant pressure, whereas at work their load is lightened by companionship. Work at home involves not only traditional "women's work," such as doing laundry and cooking, but also includes fruit and vegetable production and often, in mining settlements, animal husbandry as well. Work at home is thus often at least as physically exacting as work at the mine, if not more so. This was the view of a brigadier from the *zaryadnoe*, who kept cows, pigs, and chickens:

There are breaks at work when you can rest. You can't rest at home. There is always something to be done. I have the cows to look after. My mother helps me a lot, but there is still a great deal to be done. The home has to be in order. . . . Work is hard, but not always. Perhaps it's because you are in a collective that the time goes quicker. It seems that soon after you arrive it's time to leave. You can chat, and you don't notice the time going by. At home you work on your own.

Thus for women, rather than home being viewed as a refuge from work, the collective in some respects acts as a haven from the pressures of running a household.

Second, women describe the collective as a vital source of emotional support—a "second family" that acts as a buttress to the actual family, which is usually portrayed as the cause of distress. This formulation of a worker from the *lampovaya* is typical: "We are like a family. We can discuss personal problems together, for example, if someone has a problem with her husband. We give advice. Everyone has someone in the collective whom they trust." Or, as the brigadier from the *zaryadnoe* put it: "We all know each other's problems here. The collective is your second family. You come to work and you can express your feelings, talk about your problems, and then you'll feel better. That is how it should be."

The idea of the collective as a second family constantly recurred in interviews with female workers; not only was the collective seen as an emotional haven, it was also a vital alternative social focus.[6] The latter point is well captured by a retired worker from the *lampovaya* explaining why she wanted to return to work: "The collective is your second family. I, for example, do not need to work for the money—my husband and son are miners. But I will look for work in the winter because I need to be in a collective. I need to be with people. Housework gets very boring. And your family, well you can get bored of them too if you don't see anyone else. Human beings need to socialize."

Male workers do not express their attachment to the collective in these terms and only occasionally refer to the collective as a family. This is in part because prevailing norms of masculine behavior mean that it is less appropriate for men to describe their relationships using "feminine" family imagery, but the men's attitudes also reflects the different nature of the respite provided by male collectives; whereas female collectives tend to have a confessional, confiding culture, for men the collective offers light relief. The difference is well captured by the comments of a group of fitters in an in-mine transport shop:

Fitter 1: How could we survive now without the collective?

Fitter 2: You come to work and the collective raises your spirits . . . we're a cheerful collective.

Fitter 3: Yes, we've got our own "circus" here, we don't need to go and pay for it. He's on leave at the moment, although our clown's still here.

Such collectives commonly go drinking together after work a few times a month,[7] and many workers go fishing with coworkers in the summer. Much of the pleasure of these encounters is derived from the all-male company, which provides a haven from what male workers tend to portray as the female-dominated domestic world. The value placed on the all-male company of the work collective is well captured in the bemused response of the fitters quoted earlier when asked why they didn't drink with women:

Fitter 1: How could we? It's not possible. It's after work and we're together, and she's got things to do at home.

Fitter 2: We're an exclusively male collective. The only time we drink with women is on holidays and birthdays. They drive us out [of the home].

The collectives offer both male and female workers companionship and an important forum for self-expression, although, as indicated earlier, the nature of the interaction within the collectives differs. In part as a consequence of the different functions of the collective in the lives of men and women, a notable distinction between the two groups is that male collectives tend to socialize together outside work time, whereas women tend to have separate networks of friends outside work.[8]

Another distinction in the attitudes of the two groups is that men, unlike women, do not see work at the mine as less onerous than the work they perform at home, which includes tasks such as tending the family plots, chopping wood, and, for those with livestock, hay making in the summer. In part, this difference can be explained by the nature of the sexual division of labor in the home. Women not only have more work, but they also feel their work at the mine is more meaningful and socially valuable than cooking and housework—an attitude well captured in the comment "You cook a meal, it gets eaten, and then what have you got to show for it?" Meanwhile, the productive and creative nature of work on family plots, which constitutes the bulk of the male contribution to the household, means both men and women tend to view it not only as a necessity but also as a hobby.

Both men and women workers have a strong sense of identification with the collective, which gives them support and a sense of meaning. The importance attached to the cooperative culture at work and the value of the relationships built up over time are well captured by the warmth and feeling with which the miner quoted here spoke of the (model and highly productive) brigade to which he had belonged for nearly his entire working life. The brigade had been transferred en masse from a mine near Taldym where it had worked for several years before being disbanded. Recently, its members had been reunited when the locally famous brigadier agreed to return to work after a long illness—a history that says a good deal about the strength of relationships within the collective. The miner portrayed a solidaristic culture of mutual support and understanding:

Once they divided us up. I don't know why. It was simply stupid. . . . It seems to me that when a collective's friendly, as they say tight-knit [*skolo-chennyi*], where everyone knows each other, you work better because you understand each other in half a word, half a look, even. . . . We're very close [*splochennyi*], not quite as much as before . . . but before we were very friendly. The collective alone decided everything. For example, if someone worked with us in a low skill category, and the collective decided it wanted to, we'd go to the brigadier and say, "this person works with us and like us, and he should be paid the same as us, regardless of his category."

The attachment to both the social reality and the *idea* of the collective that comes across in this quotation and in those of the women workers cited earlier is a distinctive feature of Russian working life. But as already mentioned, many workers are distressed by the fact that the cohesion of their collectives is threatened as a result of social and economic transition. Can work collectives—once apparently so united—act as a focus of resistance to change? This question is analyzed in the next section on the basis of a case study of one women's collective, the *lampovaya*.

The *Lampovaya:* "The Collective Can Do Nothing"

The immediate work collective, as the previous section indicates, has always been an important arena for self-expression, although in the communist period this was balanced by its function as a locus of control. But the change in the political landscape in the late perestroika era created a space in which the emancipatory aspects of the communal life of the collective could potentially develop. After 1989, much of the disciplinary apparatus was dismantled: the draconian disciplinary code that applied to the mines was suspended in 1989, the party and state security bodies have since been removed from enterprises, managerial authority has been substantially undermined, and workers can now democratically remove their managers. The combined effect of these developments has been a shift in the balance of power in favor of workers, allowing them to increase their collective control over the production process and to order their collectives in a way that suits them. But this flowering of collectivism also had limitations, the nature of which became more apparent as the optimism generated by Gorbachevian reform dissipated in the cold light of the Yeltsinite new dawn. The stunted growth of collectivism can be clearly illustrated by an account of the development of work relations in the *lampovaya* during this period.

The years 1988–1992 represent the high point of collectivist development within the *lampovaya*. In 1988 the *lampovaya* became the first collective in the mine to remove its line manager through democratic vote; as the eventual successor to the deposed forewoman proudly put it, "Democracy came first to the *lampovaya*."⁹ The forewoman of the collective, Daria Nikolaevna, was voted out of office after she attempted to disrupt the stability of work relations by introducing a regime of three monthly changes in shift teams. As a brigadier from the collective reported: "She first of all broke up all the shift teams, then terrorized everyone . . . she did everything awful she could to the collective and annoyed everyone so much that we simply got rid of her."

After a brief time with another forewoman who was deemed unsatisfactory, the collective elected a former teacher, Anna Petrovna, whose four years in office are remembered as a golden age. In 1992 Anna Petrovna resigned as forewoman because of ill health. The mine director reappointed Daria Nikolaevna to the post; the collective did not resist, believing she had "learned her lesson" and was no longer a threat. At first that proved to be the case, and the working practices developed during the Anna Petrovna era persisted for some time.

After 1988, the *lampovaya* workers were able to create a highly favorable working environment. One of the most important aspects of the improvement was not restricted to their collective. The shift in the balance of power in favor of workers after 1989 meant the women's collectives at the mine were able to secure a change in their shift system (*grafik*) from an eight-hour to a twelve-hour regime. Thus, instead of a grueling regime of three days on a first shift followed by three days on the second shift and then three on the night shift, with each three days on shift separated by only one day off, the women now worked one twelve-hour day followed by a twelve-hour night shift with two days off between each stint. The campaign for the change in the *grafik* represents the most significant achievement of collective action among women workers at the mine.¹⁰ It is cited by all of the women on this *grafik* as a positive aspect of their work—not only does it allow women to combine their home and work lives more conveniently, it also weakens managerial control because line managers usually work on different shift systems. The changes in forewoman and the *grafik* gave the *lampovshchitsy* (the collective name for the *lampovaya* workers) much more autonomy over the organization of their work.

The collective is divided into four brigades of seven workers each, and each brigade constitutes a shift team. The brigades are led by brigadiers who are responsible for ensuring that the shift performs the required amount of work, but the relationship between the brigadier and the brigade members is egalitarian. Rather than being seen as an enviable position of power, the post of brigadier is seen as a burden because the brigadier is responsible for any mistakes made by her workers. For this reason the forewoman, who appoints the brigadiers, tends to rotate the position among the most senior members of the collective. As one brigadier commented: "Even if everyone who should be on shift is at work, I still have to answer for any mistakes that are made. If I don't notice and correct a mistake in time, it is counted as my mistake. . . . No one wants to be brigadier, so we only do the job for a year and then change over. No one wants the responsibility."

Since the forewoman works only a five-day week, from eight A.M. to four P.M., and the brigades work on the continuous twelve-hour shift system, for the majority of the week the brigadiers are in charge of their shift teams' work. And since a brigadier is "one of the girls," for the majority of the time the collective is effectively self-managed. Workers were thus able to establish their own informal norms within their brigades and arranged their work in a way that suited them. As one women said of her former shift team: "Lena was the senior *lampovshchitsa* on our shift, and she was understanding. For example, if I had to get home early for some reason, I could ask her and she'd let me go—without, of course, Daria Nikolaevna knowing anything about it. And on the night shift we used to take it in turns to sleep. Of course, we'd have been punished if anyone had seen us—but we used to get all the work done."

Thus, not only was the *lampovaya* a close collective, but it also seemed that in the period after 1988 the collective developed a capacity for self-organization that might have provided a basis for furthering the workers' own interests. Later developments, however, starkly revealed the limits of the form of collectivism developed within the *lampovaya* in the Anna Petrovna era.

In January 1995 the forewoman of the collective suddenly announced that she was breaking up the established shift teams, the offense for which she had been removed in 1988. Women who had been working together in brigades for years were suddenly divided up and arranged into new teams without even being consulted as to whom they wanted to work with. One worker reported: "When Daria Nikolaevna said she was going to break up the brigades, everyone pleaded with her not to do it. She just said 'we'll see' and then went ahead and did it anyway. I think she didn't like the fact that we all got on so well and enjoyed work—I think she thought that it meant we weren't working properly. I don't agree with her. I think if you're happy you work better."

This action had a dramatic impact on the collective: an atmosphere of gloom was palpable on my return to the mine in June 1995. The workers reported that everything had changed: "We've fallen out with each other" (*my razdruzhilis'*), one of them explained. The cozy companionship of the old brigades had been destroyed and, with it, the autonomy the shift teams had previously enjoyed. For example, in the past the women had cooked and eaten lunch and supper together in a cubbyhole behind the lamp racks or in the "laboratory" where the functioning of lamps was checked, away from the eyes and ears of the forewoman.

Under the new regime Daria Nikolaevna led a melancholy luncheon party to the mine canteen every day. Moreover, because the brigades were not composed of workers who trusted each other, they were unable to organize their work informally as they had done in the past. One brigade in particular was deeply unhappy: it had ended up with the "good communist"[11] of the collective, who could be relied on to report any irregularities to the forewoman. One brigadier remarked of this worker and another close family friend of the forewoman: "There are tell-tales in the collective who tell Dasha [Daria Nikolaevna] everything. I suppose every collective has such people. No one wants them on their shift because a shift will always have something it wants to hide from the forewoman." Whereas in the past these workers had been kept under control by strong brigadiers and workers who knew them intimately, they created enormous tension in their new teams. One worker even claimed she had taken sick leave to avoid the "good communist."

Thus, the forewoman had dramatically increased her power over the collective. As one brigadier memorably declared: "I think Dasha's a vampire. She draws energy from us when we're all quarreling. It suits her far better when we're not getting on with each other." The forewoman again reorganized the shift teams at the end of June 1995, again without consultation, and announced that they would be reorganized every three months thereafter. Her plan ensured that most members of the collective would eventually have to serve alongside the "good communist" and that it would be extremely difficult for workers to reestablish informal working arrangements: the collective had been broken.

No collective response followed the forewoman's action. A few brave individuals remonstrated with her, but that was the extent of the protest. The collective was awash with talk of replacing the forewoman, but no one was prepared to step forward as an alternative candidate. Even when insult was added to injury with the announcement that the shift teams would be reorganized regularly, the workers did not foresee themselves resisting. Asked what would happen if the forewoman went ahead with her plans, one of the older and more outspoken members of the collective replied, "Nothing will happen. Everyone moans between themselves, but there are very few people who will say it to her face."

Why were the seemingly well-organized women of the *lampovaya* unable to resist this assault on their collective? The answer reveals the limitations of the development of collectivism after 1988 and the vulnerability of work collectives in the face of managerial encroachments connected with restructuring.[12] First, although in the heady days of the late Gorbachev era workers made many gains, those gains were facilitated by the vulnerability of managers as they accustomed themselves to life without the Communist Party. The *grafik* campaign is a good example. The campaign *was* a gain for female workers at the mine, but it was achieved without a high degree of managerial resistance. Moreover, it led to no lasting organization among the women. Similarly, once the *lampovsh-chitsy* had secured what they saw as a desirable amount of autonomy, they were not concerned about building on the incipient organization they had developed when they first took the decision to remove Daria Nikolaevna. Thus, as management has begun to reassert control over the enterprise (a process that is continuing but not yet complete), workers have become increasingly vulnerable. The changing possibilities for self-determination within collectives in the 1980s and 1990s are well captured by brigadier Lena's account of the period: "When perestroika and glasnost began, it was easier to change [the forewoman]. Now there isn't any glasnost, there's nothing. Now the managers decide everything again. But before perestroika it was absolutely impossible. Gorbachev gave us some rights. . . . He allowed the collective to decide everything. Now there's very little that's decided by the collective."[13] What is notable about this account is the passive role it accurately accords to workers in the process: rights are "given" and taken away rather than fought for or defended.

A major reason for the failure to develop the organizational potential immanent within work collectives lies in the structure of the traditional Soviet enterprise in which the line manager not only acts as a representative of management but also represents the interests of her collective to the enterprise administration. The role of the lowest level of mine managers is to *safeguard* the rights of immediate work collectives, to get the best deal for "their" workers, in the same way the role of the mine director is to get the best deal for "his" mine. Rather than defend themselves *against* the lowest level of mine management, therefore, workers would normally expect to be *defended by* this "representative" of the collective. In the Anna Petrovna era, that is exactly what occurred. Anna Petrovna saw it as her role to stand up for the *lampovaya*:

> When I was forewoman—I am the kind of person who can't bear injustice, and I always fought for justice, always spoke the truth. I got on well with the shop chiefs but [not] with the *kontory* [office workers] and the director. I complained if we didn't have normal conditions to work in—so that we had some ventilation and so on. Dasha never does that—she won't even ask for a lick of paint to make the place look a bit better. I was always going to the director, to the chief engineer; I was always speaking up for the workers because they worked well, but they would swear at them for any tiny mistake. I don't know why, but none of the directors before . . . have been fond of the *lampovaya*.

Workers confirmed that, in contrast to Daria Nikolaevna, Anna Petrovna had stood up for their rights:

When Anna Petrovna was forewoman, she defended our interests. If we needed something we could simply gather and talk with her either in the shop trade union committee or just between shifts. She would go to the trade union, the economists, the director with questions, with demands, saying that they needed to do something for us, that the collective was demanding or asking for something that needed to be done.

Daria Nikolaevna does not go—she doesn't want to draw attention to herself in the eyes of the president [the mine director] or the eyes of someone else. She doesn't want anyone to notice and say that she's going there and asking for something or other. She doesn't want it. She wants everything to be quiet and peaceful so that no one notices her and she can get on with her work.

This reveals why, having elected Anna Petrovna, the *lampovshchitsy* believed there was no cause for further organization: she would look after their interests. The problems with this perception were revealed only when Daria Nikolaevna redefined her role within the collective from representative to manager.

Nevertheless, workers' instinctive reaction to the unpleasant turn in the fortunes of their collective under Daria Nikolaevna was still to consider a change in forewoman. The alternative was to appeal to the mine director for protection, but at this stage he was not prepared to provide it.[14] The women felt unable to resist the change while Daria Nikolaevna remained forewoman; an alternative figurehead was felt to be a prerequisite for any kind of reaction. Just as the election of a benevolent paternalist was seen as the solution to the mine's problems, so the election of a better "mother" was seen as the solution to the *lampovaya's* problems. And since the self-organization of workers does not extend to collective defense, this estimation is perfectly accurate in the immediate term.

Contested Collectivism

Although the *lampovshchitsy* may be incapable of defending themselves against their forewoman, they had, as described earlier, carved out a comfortable communal life after 1988. Collectivism within the *lampovaya* is limited, but it does exist. The workers do feel attached to the co-workers with whom they have built up cooperative working relations, habitually shared mealtimes, concealed minor infractions of work discipline from the forewoman, and so on. It was this form of collectivity that the forewoman broke up when, as the disgruntled *lampovshchitsy* put it, she "scattered" (*raskidyvala*) the established shift teams.

Daria Nikolaevna claimed she had broken up the shift teams to increase the cohesiveness of the collective, saying:

I did it so that the shifts would all be friendly. So that the girls would all know each other. I did it for the sake of unity [*splochennost'*]. If you work on one shift with the same people forever, you get sick of it. You could work for years on the same shift and not get to know the other members of the collective. You could pass them on the street and not even say hello. To work as a collective, everyone has to know each other. Anyway, this is my personal opinion.

The forewoman asserted an abstract view of the collective and a formal view of unity: not a cohesiveness born out of informal, cooperative relations but a putative unity forced on the collective from above. Her attack on the collectivity of the brigades is reminiscent of the Soviet antipathy to what in Soviet-speak were referred to as "false collectives"—that is, from the official communist point of view, "sub-groups that might potentially challenge the supremacy of the *kollektiv* from within, or the devolution of the *kollektiv* into an in-group that does not aspire to support broader social values and pursues only narrow group interests" (Kharkhordin 1996: 30). The trouble with false collectives from the point of view of the communist authorities is that they command more loyalty than the so-called true collectives, which are subordinate to official control. The forewoman thus scattered the "false" collectivity of the shift teams, turning the collective into a mere aggregate of unhappy workers who were "unified" only in their common subjection to her will. This fact was clear to the workers, who had accurately predicted what the forewoman would say if asked why she had broken up the old shift teams. Their view of her concept of *splochennost'* was "*eto konechno chepukha*" (it's rubbish, of course).

The ease with which the forewoman accomplished her aims, however, reveals the vulnerability of the limited form of collectivism that existed within the brigades of the *lampovaya*. Within the old shift teams, workers had built up trust with each other over a long period and could ensure that work was organized in a way that suited them. But the relations that developed were based on cooperation over work: the brigades were work groups, not defensive alliances. This reality is highlighted by the fact that although the brigadiers could use their discretion in ways that benefited their brigades, when the forewoman decided to break up the shift teams the teams proved unable to resist. Covering up for each other is very different from acting as a group to defend a collective interest. So although collective cooperation does exist at the level of the brigade, it barely extends beyond the day-to-day detail of organizing work.

Meanwhile, workers express a loyalty to the collective—the *lampovaya*—but this form of collectivity is realized only through the medium of the line manager. The collective cannot represent itself, and workers therefore look for an alternative figurehead to act as their representative when they experience problems. In this sense, "the collective" amounts to little more than an aggregate of individual supplicants. Thus, although at one level Daria Nikolaevna's action can be seen as merely her whim, it strikingly reveals workers' vulnerability to authoritarian assaults from the same matriarchs and patriarchs to whom they look for their salvation. Workers lack the organizational resources required for systematic resistance.

This is just one example of mineworkers' inability to realize the promise of 1989 by developing new kinds of self-organization, a failure that can be seen on a wider scale in the inability to develop an effective independent trade union out of the workers' committees and in the similar failure to realize the potential implicit in the form of privatization in which ownership was transferred to the labor collective. It is not enough, however, to put these failures down merely to the system of line management and the lack of consciousness among the workers. For "the collective" (in all its forms) is also being redefined from below by the daily practice of workers as they increasingly look outside the mine to secure their survival.

The Erosion of the Collective in the Reform Era

Although workers look to a paternalist for their salvation at work, they do not confine their survival strategies to work-based activities but engage in various kinds of economic activity and build on networks of family and friends beyond the workplace. Some of these opportunities existed in the Soviet period, but many have opened up or become legal only with the development of market relations, sometimes replacing facilities formerly provided by the enterprise.

To understand workers' survival strategies, it is necessary first to sketch the nature of the pressures they face. Mineworkers in Vishnovka have never been rich, but previously their position was characterized by a strong sense of security. The high level of savings necessitated by the shortages of the Brezhnev era meant workers felt protected in case of hard times. More important, once an individual had secured a position at the mine she would not be dismissed, even if she was no longer needed; in that case she would simply be transferred to another section. Moreover, although the social safety net provided by the mine was far from adequate—in particular with regard to housing provision—a variety of discretionary payments and loans were available to those in need. For example, the mine would guarantee the loans of its workers who needed to buy furniture from local suppliers and would also give soft loans and grants to those who wanted to build their own houses in what is known as the "private sector." The latter was a very important form of payment in kind since flats were always in short supply; just over a third of Vishnovka's inhabitants live in the wooden houses of the private sector. Such grants and loans allowed young couples to set up homes without being weighed down by financial worries. In short, the mine was the universal guarantor; it was an extremely generous mortgage company, a guarantor of its workers' loans, and even an insurance company—workers whose wooden houses burned down were entitled, on the basis of a clause in the collective agreement, to compensation adequate to cover the cost of reconstruction.

Today, although wages are not significantly lower than they were in the past, the mine can no longer provide the same kind of social safety net, and savings have been destroyed by inflation. A general sense of crisis has been created by the fact that workers are habitually paid late. At Taldym, on average, they are paid only one month late, which is significantly less tardy than payments at other, less successful mines, but at times the arrears have been greater. In August 1996 wages had not been paid for three months, and although management was planning to pay May's wages in two installments in September, the director did not anticipate being able to eliminate the backlog in the immediate future. Although workers are able to survive physically when wages are paid late, doing so requires planning and hard work. Meanwhile, holiday and sick pay are no longer paid automatically. In summer 1996, for example, workers who wanted to take leave were asked to sign a document saying they had agreed to do so in the knowledge that they would not receive their holiday pay in advance. In such situations, the mine trade union and the administration are unable to give concrete information; their answer to disgruntled workers' inquiries is that they will be paid "when Moscow sends the money." The fact that the payment of wages appears to be so starkly contingent on the whims of "Moscow" obviously detracts from workers' sense of social protection. Insecurity is also exacerbated by fears of staff reductions: managers' assurances that they are going to try to avoid redundancies only alert workers to the fact that they are being considered as an option. Meanwhile, soft loans and grants are no longer easily attainable from the mine, employment there no longer guarantees credit elsewhere, and the "insurance" offered by the collective agreement has been rendered meaningless by inflation.

In addition, local services that are part of the *sotskul'tbyt* complexes of the local enterprises—the kindergartens, house of culture, *profilaktorii* (prophylactic care facility), and holiday camps—face an uncertain future. According to the 1994 Privatization Law, *sotskul'tbyt* is to be handed over to local authorities, and many mines have abandoned their social facilities. Taldym had not done so in August 1996, but the trade union and the mine administration expected that two of the three mine kindergartens would be given over to the local authority before the end of that year. It was unclear whether either facility would remain open after being transferred. Meanwhile, the mine's "pioneer camp"—a vital resource that liberated parents from their children for part of the growing season—had been closed because the other mines that shared the expense of running it are no longer able to bear the costs.

The housing program was halted in summer 1994 when the government stopped paying the building subsidy, which means the mine can no longer offer new state housing for workers to rent. All accommodations built in the mining settlement since 1995 are being offered for sale rather than for rent, and the cheapest one-room flat for sale in June 1995 cost 28 million rubles—at a time when the highest annual salary of a face worker at the mine was 2 million rubles and the average female manual workers' wage at the mine was 400,000 rubles a month. Moreover, as a result of financial problems the mine is unable to give loans and grants to young families who want to build their own homes in the private sector.

Workers' reaction to this situation neatly illustrates the combination of individualism and alienated collectivism that characterizes their general response to change. Although, as argued earlier, workers' collectives are important to them, their immediate survival strategies have been largely family centered rather than based on networks at work. Whereas in large urban enterprises workers are more likely to engage in paid secondary employment, often using skills acquired in their primary employment,[15] in mining settlements secondary employment largely takes the form of small-scale food production within the household. Mineworkers have always had allotments or kitchen gardens attached to the self-built wooden houses of the private sector and have grown potatoes on the large tracts of land the mine rented from local collective farms for its workers, and many kept cows, pigs, and chickens in the past. Workers generally felt, however, that such activity had assumed greater importance during the transition period; as one fitter put it, "what is 100 percent true now is that we'd die without our allotments." This sentiment was expressed in different forms in nearly every interview with workers in August 1996.

Small-scale food production had also become a source of monetary income for many workers, who reported that whereas in the past they had given their surplus to friends, now they would usually sell it. Meanwhile, keeping cows is increasingly popular, and the money that can be made from selling milk is more significant. One worker, for example, reported that she had kept cows for all of her working life, but in the past her wages had been worth far more than her milk money. At the time of the interview she made a million rubles a month (just under $200 at that time) from selling milk, whereas her monthly wage, when she received it, fluctuated between 600,000 and 800,000 rubles.

Although other forms of secondary employment are less common in Vishnovka,[16] the mine's financial difficulties increase the relative importance of the household and family units in relation to work and the collective. Ironically, whereas the changes in the shift system at Taldym can in one sense be seen as a "collectivist" achievement, they also mean that both male and female workers spend fewer days at work and thus have more time for individual and family-based activities. Wage delays in particular cause workers to disengage gradually from the mine; in the absence of wages, work obviously seems less important than production within the household.

Moreover, workers generally feel work is no longer the social focus and source of meaning it once was. This shift is not only a result of the greater importance workers attach to outside interests; the attitude of management has also changed with the collapse of the Communist Party. Managers are no longer required to foster the integration of communist citizens by promoting the collective; they now have a narrower concern with maintaining discipline and production levels. The change in atmosphere is well captured in the comments of a woman worker from the technical complex:

> Before, they [managers] kept us informed about what was going on. For example, they kept us up to date with all the *prikazy* [orders] at the mine, read them out to us at the *naryad* [the preshift task assignment meeting]. Now they don't. . . . According to the health and safety rules, we have to have a *naryad*. We have to go along there and sign to say that we've had it. But before it was more interesting; we found out more there. And we could tell management what was wrong and what we needed. We talked there. . . . Before I used to get up and I was happy that I was going off to work. Now I wake up and I don't want to go to work; we don't even get paid. And the collective was better before. Before I'd even say that it was very good. But now people have turned nasty because of all the difficulties, and that influences relations.

These sentiments were echoed by a brigadier from the *zaryadnoe*:

> I liked it better in the communist period. Then we had the plan. We had to run round and meet it, and if we did then we got rewarded—people had an interest in the work. . . .
>
> The collective has changed. It was much more united before. Now it's fragmented [*razroznennyi*]. And people have become aggressive. . . . Before, there was something to aspire to—there were the medal givings, the bonuses, it all meant something. I used to run around. I was in the shop party

committee, the shop trade union committee, the civil defense, I was bursting with energy and used to manage to get everything done. . . . Now if I'm honest I've lost interest in work a bit. For example, a wagon might come up dirty from the mine. Whereas before I would have hosed it down, now I can't be bothered—let it stay dirty.

Institutions such as the plan, the party, and medals had their downside; workers often complain about the divisiveness of the old system. But at the same time they miss the sense of common endeavor and belonging that was fostered in the past.

The Collective Between Past and Future

Workers not only regret the decline of the mine as a focus of communal sociability; they also have concrete concerns about the decline of social provision and the threat to employment. For although the relative importance of the household as a productive unit has increased, workers cannot survive without the mine; as one worker put it, "we don't bake our own bread." Indeed, the fact that many public services, such as hospitals and higher education institutes, have begun to charge fees means that in many ways workers are even more dependent on the mine as a source of monetary income than they were in the past. For example, the worker mentioned earlier who made a million rubles a month selling milk was still forced to apply to the mine for an urgent loan of 5 million rubles to pay for hospital care when her son was involved in a serious accident. Meanwhile, the mine still provides workers with a variety of other services such as free coal, loans of machinery for activities such as hay making, discretionary emergency financial support, and holiday vouchers. Thus, even if workers expect less from the enterprise than they did in the past, their jobs are still very important to them, and they continue to look to the mine for protection in times of acute need.

For this reason, it is inaccurate to portray the labor collective as simply being eroded by the individualizing pressures of the market economy. Individual survival strategies are complemented by the search for collective salvation within the context of the labor collective. This reality expresses itself mainly in workers' dissatisfaction with management and their restless search for a director who will insulate the mine from the chilly neoliberal winds. Since the mine was privatized in 1992 it has had four "presidents," none of whom has survived for more than a single two-year term in office. Thus, the situation described in the *lampovaya* is replicated at the mine level: although the workers do not generally attempt to defend their position through organized activity, they do attempt to address their problems by hunting for that elusive strong leader who will be capable of guiding the mine through the troubled waters of transition.

Workers' search for an adequate protector for the labor collective was clearly visible in the contest for the post of mine director at the end of 1995—as were the contradictory implications of their attempts to realize their collectivist aspirations through the election of a new leader. The previous director was a democratic populist whose main virtue was considered to be the fact that he did not erect barriers between himself and the workers. These compliments—the first from a miner and the second from a *lampovshchitsa*—are typical: "I like him. For example, he knows I live near him, and if he sees me he'll offer me a lift home. He'll give a few of us a lift at the same time. . . . He's attentive to people; he tries to help." "He doesn't raise himself above others. You can go to him with any question. If he's got the time he will definitely see you. You can ask him anything and he'll give you an answer."

The director had been elected because he was a popular section chief who was seen as being "close to the people," a qualification, it was felt, that would ensure he would look after the workers. As the previous quotations illustrate, he often did personal favors for individual workers, and he did not attempt to tighten discipline at the mine. But the labor collective as a whole suffered under his populist regime; production and hence wages fell relative to past levels, and the mine fell into debt. Moreover, because of his lowly (popular) status as a former shop chief, the director lacked the connections required to extract resources from the concern and from Moscow, and wage arrears began to grow as soon as he was elected. The director attempted to compensate by making concessions to particular groups of workers, the result of which was a growing belief that he had allowed discipline to collapse and had failed to protect the majority of workers.

The new director, a deeply reassuring paternalist and former communist mayor of a nearby town, directly appealed to workers' desire for security.[17] The most important plank in his program was the fact that he had good connections that he would exploit fully to gain resources for the mine. As he put it in an interview:

> At the moment I can help the mine through my personal contacts. They are crucial. If you don't have them, you could spend two days outside an office door waiting to be seen. Whereas I can just pick up the phone. For example, we've got a new complex. We haven't paid for it yet. We are going to pay for it in coal over several months. I was able to arrange that because they know and trust me. They know that I'll keep my word. While these possibilities exist, I will use them. I will get all I can from my contacts. . . . I am trying to resist the policies of Moscow. They told me to shut down Vishnov-

skii raion [part of the mine], I invested money in it; they told me to close one of the faces, I put money into it.

He also promised, as this quotation indicates, to revive the Vishnovskii raion and to find the money to finish building the blocks of flats on which construction had been frozen under the former director. The points workers recalled most often from his program were his strong contacts with the local coal concern and his promise to finish the flats (which he did, although workers were dismayed when they were offered for sale rather than free of charge). Having had a taste of leadership by an "outsider," workers were keen to return to experienced communist hands.

Workers' reasons for supporting the communist director underline the fact that the mine labor collective still constitutes a suppicatory unity in the face of the outside world of the concern, Rosugol', and the government. The entire labor collective shares an interest in securing survival in an increasingly hostile world, and workers look to the director to do battle on their behalf. It is difficult for workers to break out of this form of politics; even when they attempt to do so, as they did during the 1989 strike, their struggle for a decent standard of living ends up being fused with the managers' struggle to secure the best deal for the coal industry.[18] Their action thus reproduces precisely those structures underlying the problem that promoted the action in the first place. At the mine level, this phenomenon expresses itself in the fact that any incipient mobilization of workers reaches its climax with the election of a new director or line manager.

Alienated collectivism has its limits and contradictions, however. First, it is becoming increasingly difficult for managers to protect their enterprises, no matter how good their contacts. The new director of Taldym may be much better connected than his predecessor, but that has not insulated the mine from the problem of wage arrears, which was endemic in the south Kuzbass in summer 1996. And he is aware that contacts do not offer a long-term solution to the mine's problems: "If government policy doesn't change, then the mine will slowly die. That is definite. But I am going to do all I can—use every contact—to make sure it's the very last to close. . . . But there may come a time in the future when all the leaks in the system are shut off. I might phone up my friend and he might say, 'I trust you, you're a good friend, but there's nothing I can do to help you.' Life is life and economics is economics."

Second, the community of interests between workers and managers is not without contradictions. The director went on to say that since he did not anticipate increased government support for the coal industry, he was working on a plan to reduce the price of the mine's coal through staff reductions, although initially his proposal only went as far as laying off workers over age sixty. Although he was able to present this step in a populist light—claiming he was creating space for young people at the mine and allowing the renewal of the labor collective—if he begins to make more significant cuts it will be harder to avoid division. Even if the director avoids division, he is unlikely to deliver the sort of protection workers are looking for because their aspirations are very different from those of management. Both groups want to preserve particular elements of the "Soviet way of life," but they are nostalgic for different aspects of the authoritarian paternalism of the traditional Soviet enterprise. Whereas mine management focuses on authoritarianism and looks back to the days of order and discipline when the boss's word was law, the workers focus on the paternalistic features of the traditional enterprise and look back to the security that was guaranteed by the collective. Workers' desire for protection does express itself in the search for a strong leader, but they are nonetheless deeply ambivalent about such strength when its effect is to reduce their autonomy and increase the intensity of their work.

The return of communism at Taldym is therefore by no means an unambiguous yearning for the restoration of the past but rather expresses two very different perspectives on the future development of a new Russia. Neither management nor workers want to renounce the opportunities and independence they believe they have achieved with the destruction of the Soviet system and the development of a market economy. But for management, order and discipline will provide the framework within which the enterprise can adjust to the demands of the changing economy, whereas for the workers paternalism will provide the means by which they can be partially protected from the ravages of the market.

Workers' desire to be defended by strong leaders during the transition period does not manifest itself only at the mine level; it is also apparent in their attitude toward national politics, in particular in the Kuzbass where support for the communists is strong. Although workers aspire to the security of collectivism, they can only envisage its realization through the benevolence of a line manager, a paternalist director, or the president of Russia—each of whom personifies the collective at a specific level. This alienated collectivism is exerting a major influence on the development of Russian politics. On the one hand, workers scurry around, too absorbed in their daily struggle for survival to organize, while on the other their combined aspirations further the development of authoritarian-paternalist strands of politics in the enterprise, the region, and the country as a whole. Thus, ironically, workers' conscious attempts to improve their position do little to transform the structures that define their subordination: their dependence on increasingly authoritarian leaders only makes them more vulnerable. Meanwhile, however, their improvised individual survival strategies are transforming economic relations and, regardless of their intentions, helping to foster market relations in Russia.

Notes

Acknowledgments: My thanks to Simon Clarke and Michael Burawoy for their extensive help with this chapter.

1. The strategies are individual in the sense that they are independent of the collective; although they are often family based, they are nonetheless private.

2. For a fuller analysis of workers' relationship to enterprise collectivism, see Ashwin 1996.

3. Trade unions will not be considered in this context. At the mine level the former official union, Rosugleprof, does not act as an independent force but represents the common interests of workers and managers. Since workers have little influence on union policy, a consideration of unions provides little insight into *workers'* response to transition. For more details on Rosugleprof, see Ashwin 1995; Ilyin 1996; and Borisov and Clark 1996. The Independent Miners' Union that grew out of the miners' strike movement has very little influence in Kuzbass. For more details, see Clarke, Fairbrother, and Borisov 1995.

4. For example, in the case of an individual who has an opportunity to travel abroad, a reference would be required from the immediate work collective. The opinion of the collective would also be taken into account in court if a worker was charged with a minor offense, and a judge could place a defendant who had been found guilty under the supervision of his or her work collective.

5. For more details on women's attitudes toward work, see Ashwin and Bowers 1997.

6. Such ideas are not exclusive to women who work in mining. A recent study of a Samara chocolate factory revealed exactly the same attitudes; the conference paper in which they were analyzed was entitled "My Factory—My Home" (Romanov 1996).

7. Many male workers noted, however, that such impromptu gatherings were becoming less common. Explanations included the lack of funds for vodka as a result of late payment of wages and the fact that work on allotments was taking up so much of their time.

8. This distinction does not apply only within the mines; it has also been observed by Russian sociologist Marina Kiblitskaya in her ongoing research at a variety of Moscow enterprises.

9. After the 1989 strike, voting unpopular managers out of office became common practice throughout the mine. As one shop chief lamented in an interview, "After the strikes it even got to the point where it was obligatory to change managers—businesslike or not—hands up, let's have a different one."

10. The twelve-hour shift system was introduced at the initiative of the women workers of the *kotel'naya* who, in a period between shop chiefs, simply took a unilateral decision to reorganize their work hours. Their example was taken up by the other women's collectives, which persuaded the trade union to pursue their

case. The eight-hour shift for underground miners at Taldym, which means they work fewer days per month than they do under the six-hour shift, was a similar post-1989 victory for the miners.

11. In the past she had been an active member of the Communist Party and had a reputation within the mine for reporting things to the party.

12. Even though the actions of the forewoman of the *lampovaya* were not specifically connected to restructuring, her action did have the effect of "softening up" the collective. Any future changes desired by mine management will be much easier to push through.

13. This account was largely confirmed by interviews with workers from other collectives, although elite workers such as miners in the famous brigade mentioned earlier felt that even during the communist era they had the possibility of influencing the director or the mine party secretary. They would, however, have been able to resolve a dispute with their line manager only through recourse to a higher authority—an open, democratic rejection of a shop chief was impossible.

14. Just before he was voted out of office at the end of 1995, the director did intervene on behalf of the *lampovshchitsy*: at the weekly meeting of shop chiefs he publicly criticized the forewoman for upsetting her workers. After this, an uneasy truce emerged in the *lampovaya*. Again, however, the workers had not been able to protect themselves; they had to rely on a managerial benefactor.

15. For more details, see Donova and Varshavskaya 1996.

16. Although some workers with marketable skills, such as fitters and welders, are able to find paid work outside the mine, this possibility is not nearly as widespread as it is in urban areas. Since workers' food production enables them to survive, they will usually seek additional paid employment only if faced with a specific financial need; a good example is the mine kindergarten teacher, who had set up a business buying meat in the Altai to sell in Osinniki because she needed to pay for her son's higher education.

17. This alternation between populist and authoritarian directors has been a common feature of the postperestroika era, particularly in the coal mining industry.

18. For an account of how miner's demands were fused with those of their managers during the 1989 strike, see Clarke, Fairbrother, Burawoy, and Krotov 1993: 132–138.

References

Alasheev, S. 1995. On a Particular Kind of Love and the Specificity of Soviet Production. In *Management and Industry in Russia: Formal and Informal Relations in the Period of Transition,* ed., S. Clarke. Aldershot: Edward Elgar, 69–98.

Ashwin, S. 1995. Russia's Official Trade Unions: Renewal or Redundancy? *Industrial Relations Journal* 26 (3): 192–203.

———. 1996. Forms of Collectivity in a Non-Monetary Society. *Sociology* 30 (1): 21–39.

Ashwin, S., and E. Bowers. 1997. Do Russian Women Want to Work? In *Post-*

Soviet Women, ed., M. Buckley. Cambridge: Cambridge University Press, 21–37.

Borisov, V., and S. Clarke. 1996. The Russian Miners' Strike of February 1996. *Capital and Class* 59: 23–30.

Clarke, S., P. Fairbrother, and V. Borisov. 1995. *The Workers' Movement in Russia.* Aldershot: Edward Elgar.

Clarke, S., P. Fairbrother, M. Burawoy, and P. Krotov. 1993. *What About the Workers? Workers and the Transition to Capitalism in Russia.* London: Verso.

Donova, I., and L. Varshavskaya. 1996. Vtorichnaya zanyatost' rabotnikov promyshlennykh predpriyatiya. In *Restructirovanie zanyatosti i rasvitie rynkov truda v Rossii.* Moscow: Institute for Comparative Labor Relations Research (ISITO), 72–84.

Ilyin, V. 1996. Russian Trade Unions and the Management Apparatus in the Transition Period. In *Conflict and Change in the Russian Industrial Enterprise,* ed., S. Clarke. Aldershot: Edward Elgar, 65–106.

Kharkhordin, O. 1996. "A System of Responsible Dependency": The Collective as an Object of Knowledge and Action. Unpublished ms.

Romanov, P. 1996. Moi zavod-moi dom. Paper presented to the conference "Gender Relations in Transition," Soros Foundation East–East Programme, Samara, Russia, 24–27 May.

World Bank. 1994. *Russian Federation. Restructuring the Coal Industry: Putting People First.* Washington, D.C.: World Bank.

9

Portable Worlds: On the Limits of Replication in the Czech and Slovak Republics

Andrew Lass

Now that free elections, multiparty governments and an insistence on market economies seem firmly established in the countries of Eastern Europe, the concern with transition, of making a firm break with the previous era, is beginning to fade and take on the trappings of historical memory. An entire generation of Czech children—those who were around age twelve when the Berlin Wall came down and their parents rattled their keys in Prague's Wenceslaus Square—have become adults looking for jobs and starting their own families. To them, Slovaks are "real foreigners," communists are a matter of political opinion, and the call for a return to Europe sounds like a contradiction in terms. And there is definitely nothing special about McDonalds restaurants, skateboards, or green hair. These young adults take for granted what the older generations watched and helped to bring about. And in this "life as usual," everyone accepts that companies should be concerned with profits, bureaucracies with following the rules, and almost everybody, in their daily lives, with trying to work their way around both: "Not *that* much has changed, you know; this place is still Kafkaesque. People are mean to each other, and just about everybody wants to rip you off" *(Vono se zas toho tolik nezměnilo vís, furt je to kafkárna. Lidi sou na sebe hnusný a kdekdo tě chce vzít na hůl).* Apparently, the past that was rejected and the principles of capitalism that have been embraced both turned out to have longer and subtler fingers than had been imagined at first.

The fact is that Eastern Europe has not only become a part of a growing European economy but, for better or worse, has also been incorporated into a global one. As elsewhere, such globalization involves, inter

273

alia, what is commonly referred to as "technology transfer," which includes more than just money, equipment, or know-how. It may also embody different values and expectations, reorganization of work, and, perhaps most significantly, new operational standards. These standards, such as those of measurement and classification, are considered necessary for the rest of the transfer to take place and bring the enterprise up to par, yet in the name of success the introduction of international standards calls into question previously established norms more generally of the world as we knew it. As a consequence, the transfer seems to encounter resistance at every turn, and even recipients' best intentions appear to backfire.

But all of this has little to do with whether the old *nomenklatura* and its right hand, the secret police, are actually lurking in the background getting ready to take over. Instead, it is institutional inertia, values and expectations, and the habits of social action they inform that continue to play a decisive role as conduits in the implementation of new technologies and in the corresponding organizational change. Constituted in the past, these "legacies" are arguably constituting in the present and therefore—to voice the concern of many—being reproduced all over again. What exactly do these legacies interfere with and how? Are they best described as "socialist," or does their reproduction have other historical sources? Most important, is the conflict between the old world and the new world inevitable, or are some situations more susceptible to it than others? This chapter addresses these questions. By drawing on specific examples from a large-scale project that involved the introduction of computer automation and networking in several large research and university libraries, I offer a partial view, at times graphic, of organizational behavior undergoing radical transformation in a society that claims to be in the midst of a transition and to point to some of the theoretical implications the examples seem to suggest.[1]

The Library Project

The Czech and Slovak Library Information Network (CASLIN) was conceived shortly after my visit to Prague (then still Czechoslovakia) in March 1990, shortly after the "Velvet Revolution" that brought down the forty-five-year-old communist government. During my undergraduate years (1968–1973), as an American student at Charles University, I had frequented the main reading room of the Klementinum, the once Jesuit monastery and now the seat of the National Library, and so I was happy to accept the invitation of one of my closest friends and former classmates to revisit the place. The guided tour of a sacred site turned into a horror picture show of crates filled with books placed in the aisles between the overflowing stacks; of poorly ventilated attics with leaking roofs filled with more rows of crates covered with plastic sheets to protect the catalogued but never shelved volumes from dust, rain, and pigeon droppings; of rotting manuscripts and old books and of once-spacious hallways cut up into "temporary" (implying indefinite) offices made of poorly assembled plywood and laminated roofing material. And more pyramids of books, periodicals, and theses; old furniture, exposed cabling, pipes, and last year's Christmas tree. It was quite a contrast to the collection of old astronomical clocks and the Klementinum's original baroque library, with its corkscrew columns, incunabula, and collection of precious globes. Here, as if spared from the ravages of time and history, even the cool, musty air seemed to have dated back to 1777, the year the Klementinum had been turned into the state library by imperial decree. Undisturbed, the portrait of Austrian Emperor Joseph I hung high on the front wall.

On the other hand, it was interesting to see that computer automation was not new to the library. In addition to a restricted use of ISIS (a library software offered free of charge by the United Nations Educational, Scientific, and Cultural Organization) for technical services, the National Library had developed a Czechoslovak cataloguing exchange format and had been fairly successful in introducing it into other libraries.[2] But for all intents and purposes and in all public services, the paper card catalog was still the means of keeping track of, looking up, and borrowing books. Few people used it since of the little information that could be found in it, only a fraction could actually be brought down to the circulation desk. The condition of the physical plant reflected the low morale of the entire institution: this place was truly dysfunctional. One could only wonder, in the postrevolutionary enthusiasm of 1990 when nearly everything seemed up for grabs, how there could be so much talk of university reform and no mention of the library. It was as if one were to design a new car and forget about the wheels.

In the years that have passed, I have come to understand the full extent and implications of the low status and poor image of the National Library and, for that matter, of libraries in general. The previous regime had so thoroughly forgotten about libraries that five years later and three years into the project it was still not clear whether their importance to young democracies facing a world dominated by the new information lords had been fully recognized. As for the organizational inertia and micropolitical intricacies that appear to govern this and other libraries and that one encounters when trying to use them, I feel only marginally closer to understanding what is or may be involved—in part because I became part of a serious effort to try to change them.

Between the library philosophy that prevails on the European continent on the one hand, and that which informs library science and library automation in the United States on the other, lies a fundamental difference of emphasis. At the risk of oversimplification, the former is best understood as historically rooted in the medieval monastic library with its collection of precious manuscripts, lists of prohibited books (*libri prohibiti*), and hierarchy of rules of access. The driving principle has been preservation. The latter, in contrast, derives its vision from Thomas Jefferson, whose cataloging system and personal library lie at the foundation of the Library of Congress. With its ideal of open stacks, the typical U.S. university or research library is user driven. But whereas the cause for the sad state of the National Library in Prague—of its physical plant, collection, and employee morale—can be traced directly to the policies of systematic neglect under the communist regime, the basic problems faced by the new leadership of the National Library—the lack of shelf space and rising cost of publications—are shared by most libraries around the world today and certainly by university and research libraries in the United States.

Enter computer technology, which is seen as the logical step in the right direction. Converting the traditional card catalog to an automated one brings improvement to both sides—to the library's ability to process (catalog) new documents and make them available to the user and to the user, who has access to a more "intelligent" and faster search tool. A more dramatic change comes with the introduction of the on-line catalog and eventually, as its logical outcome, the on-line electronic document delivery service. In essence, interlibrary loan, long the library's crutch, becomes the main gate to a new kind of library (sometimes referred to as the "virtual library" or the "library without walls"). Most of us no longer have to enter the library in person to look into its catalog or, for that matter, the catalog of any library, regardless of its physical distance from the user, provided it is on-line. We can search periodicals and look at journal abstracts from our homes and even have an article delivered in electronic form to our computer through the modem-to-phone hookup. Library services now include a variety of other types of information databases, and libraries are becoming a kind of publisher of their own resources (e.g., publishing medieval illuminated manuscript facsimiles on CD-ROM). Finally, on-line networks have reinforced cooperation among libraries and breathed new life into library consortia—groups of libraries that make joint decisions on the purchase and upgrade of computer equipment and, most important, on book orders and journal subscriptions. In other words, the argument goes, library automation and on-line service are not only natural steps for the user-driven library and a new, practical fulfillment of the democratic ideal of equal access to information for all; they also offer the possibility of containing libraries most pressing and chronic financial woes: the rising costs of publications, particularly of scholarly journals, and, because of the growth of digital media and electronic publishing, of shelf space.[3]

The idea of building an integrated on-line library network in Czechoslovakia is directly related to these visions. These visions informed the decision of the Andrew W. Mellon Foundation to take its long-standing support of higher education and, in particular, university and research libraries and help fund such projects in the emerging democracies of Eastern Europe.[4] Behind the possibility of funding lay an innovative solution to some of the National Library's problems. The desperate need for storage space and the badly needed reconstruction of the Klementinum would inspire different solutions if the librarians at the National Library were willing to entertain an alternative vision of the end result—a more public service–driven library that would derive much of its strength from its membership in an on-line library information network. And since the conditions at the National Library typified those at others, it seemed logical to assume that a cooperative effort would be equally advantageous to all consortium members.

But the idea of a consortium-based project evolved only gradually. Between 1990 and fall 1992, when the CASLIN project proposal was submitted for funding, the focus of attention was the National Library. In January 1991 a group of library specialists from the United States visited Prague. They included, among others, the director of the Council of Library Resources (a Washington, D.C.–based coordinating body), an architect who had designed many libraries in the United States and abroad, and a specialist on book and document preservation technologies. The purpose of their visit was to evaluate the National Library's situation and to give the Czechs the opportunity to voice their concerns and learn from the experts. This experience was the first that underscored for those from abroad that two worlds had met: beyond different library philosophies lay different energies and mannerisms and different ways of perceiving and presenting problems. One side followed the "turn crisis into opportunities" approach and found it all "terribly interesting"; the other, deadly serious, sought to explain the present in terms of a chronology of historical burdens. There seemed to be no language for the future as an actual possibility. Its place was taken by what sounded like a ritualized (elaborated) code in which the existence of problems—we had just spent two days touring—had to be defended, as if we had sat down at a negotiating table and it was essential to save face. Who's to say how much of this was the habit of communist officialdom, how much the protective behavior of those who perceive themselves as always "in tandem" (*v závěsu*), and how much the customary response to foreigners?

Our response was not atypical: we arranged a visit to the United States for the new leaders of the National Library to have them tour a variety of libraries in the Northeast. The hope was that they would replace fantasies about *Amerika* with their own direct experience, that they would return empowered because their knowledge and professional contacts would be not mediated but their own, and, most important, that they would see the other library philosophy in practice. Ideally, any funding of a "technology transfer" would have been positively affected by a prior "vision transfer." The trip was apparently a success since the group mutually agreed that "from here on, user services will be the library's driving force."

The visit took place in September 1991. On the last day of the visit the director of the National Library was joined by directors of three other Czech and Slovak libraries in a meeting at the Mellon Foundation in New York, where the idea for a consortium-type project was first proposed. In addition to the National Library in Prague, the Moravian Regional Library in Brno (on the Czech side), the Slovak National Library in Martin, and the University Library in Bratislava (on the Slovak side) are large national research libraries. Since the four libraries had signed an accord several years earlier, they were the logical group to establish an interlibrary, on-line network that would span the entire country.[5]

By the end of 1992, when the CASLIN proposal was approved by the Mellon Foundation, the country had split in two, and, by default, ours became one of the few international library projects of its kind. The funds would cover the cost of computer hardware, the library software license, and two modern microfilm preservation labs—one for each National Library—to help improve the quality and speed of preserving documents, especially newspapers that had been printed on acid paper. Additional funds came from the Pew Charitable Trusts, which expressed interest in supporting the project's educational components—the technical training of librarians, public relations efforts, and three library management seminars. Together, these sums were calculated to cover the cost of establishing a working (now international) on-line library network strong enough to serve the four members and to become the core for other libraries to join in the future.[6]

The funding made the possibility of modernizing Czech and Slovak libraries a reality (and helped to bring them up to international standards), but, equally important, it tabled the often-heard argument that "if only there was money it would all be different" (*no jo, kdyby byly peníze tak by to bylo všechno jinak*). The question most on my mind was, if neither the Iron Curtain nor the lack of funds stood as obstacles to the localization of a desirable "other," then what else could stand in the way? The answer came once implementation began and the long string of frustrations and seemingly insurmountable problems was explained by the other standard phrase that applies to everything that has gone wrong or that "still doesn't work the way it does in the West/in capitalist/civilized countries" (*stále to ještě není jako na Západě/v kapitalistickejch/civilizovanejch zemích*): "It's in the people, what do you want? It's going to take at least a generation before they get used to it and learn to behave differently" (*Je to v lidech, co chceš? To bude trvat celou generaci než si lidi na to zvyknou a budou se chovat jinak*). In fact, three years later what the proposal set out to do had essentially been accomplished. The new library software was up and running, the various public services—including the card catalogs—were being transferred to on-line computers, and microfilm preservation departments were saving old news from turning into acid dust.[7]

From the technical point of view, there was nothing unusual about the project's implementation, and it is reasonable to expect that, like anywhere else in the world of technology, the bugs will eventually be worked out. But beyond technology, or, better still, behind it, lies a reality bemoaned in the previous quote: In the end, and again like anywhere else, the problems always turn out to be human. After all, the project is a social act in a cultural setting. From the outset, all of the CASLIN-related work was infused with past political history as well as that in the making, with histories of interpersonal relations, of institutional inertia informed by micropolitical agendas. This became particularly clear in the one part of the puzzle on which all other parts depend: the idea of a consortium, a quartet of institutions each benefiting from working together on a common goal. Sharing resources and agreeing on uniform standards that depend on and further reinforce interinstitutional dependency, at a time when institutions are competing for limited state funds, while simultaneously advocating administrative and regional independence would not be easy. What was intended as an innovative solution to the kinds of problems that plagued the National Library in Prague contained, from the point of view of the libraries themselves, a condition that would pose the greatest challenge to the project's implementation and that will likely continue to constrain the ability of the project to deliver on its promise for some time.

How exactly are the technical and social bugs intertwined? I wish to address this question here and, in the process, offer some insight into a dilemma that looms high over the landscapes of our time: Why is it so much easier, or so it seems, to clone McDonalds restaurants (for which no local precedent exists) in so many different locations in the Czech and Slovak republics and satisfy customers with the same predictable Big Mac than it is to introduce computer technology (for which there is abundant local expertise) and with it the "enlightened" (*osvícená*) library philosophy the new board of directors claims it wants? Are some things more portable than others? And if so, why?

Portable Worlds

The case of McDonalds restaurants and what is perceived—from a commercial point of view—as a worldwide success illustrates what has become increasingly characteristic of a wider range of phenomena termed, appropriately, McDonaldization (Ritzer 1993). The ideals of efficiency, quantifiability, predictability, and control are those qualities Max Weber identified as typical of the modern bureaucracy ("the iron cage of rationality") and that found their fulfillment in F. W. Taylor's theory of scientific management and Henry Ford's assembly line. In both cases the efficiency of production and the predictability of results are predicated on control of the workforce, initially through rules and regulations, then by breaking down workers' movements into more efficient motions, and finally by minimizing the human factor as much as possible by replacing it with machines. This (now standard) analysis goes a long way in explaining what it is, in principle, that governs the McDonalds-type enterprise and why the results are always the same independent of the geographic location of the franchise. A self-contained, relatively dehumanized production process is highly portable.

But there is much the McDonaldization model does not address. For one, certain conditions must *already* be in place—from economic, legal, and infrastructural factors to the habits, values, and expectations of the relevant population—for the transfer to take place. And it is easy to forget, especially in what appear to be clear-cut cases (such as a fast-food franchise), that such conditions have their own microhistories that continue to exert influence. It is the *process of transition*, in which established cultural values and social habits are contested and eventually the rules of engagement are reset, that demands closer scrutiny.

Such inquiry is suggested by recent work in the social studies of experimental science. Analyses of laboratory life (Latour and Woolgar 1986), of the social history of the air pump (Shapin and Schaffer 1989), and of the "pasteurization" of France (Latour 1988) all make the point that replication—that is, the ability to produce the same results (facts) more than once, the key condition of success in experimental science—takes on a new level of difficulty when it involves other scientists in other places. It becomes clear that the production of consensus is a micropolitical process, that the facts of experimental science do not exist outside the complex "laboratory" conditions of their production, and that the portability of results is conditional on the portability of their rules of engagement.

In other words, the success and proliferation of science result from the network of identical (experimental) worlds in different locations, of bundles of networks of the political economies of the practice of science, of social actors, of rules of behavior, and of carefully calibrated equipment. But such a process is tedious and costly, and in the end this special environment is still one in which the "facts" produced are the results of a social process: of the contingent as much as of the necessary. The fact remains that although it is possible to build another laboratory in another location, following the same rules and using the same equipment does not in itself guarantee the same results. This reality stands in contrast to the industrial production line and suggests that in the move from basic experimental science through applied science to well-tested technologies of production, a concerted effort is made gradually to reduce and transform complex laboratory conditions into fixed rules of specialized machines.

But even with the production process as the epitome of rationalization, other, less visible sides of the enterprise do not come across as at all rational. Where in this spectrum lies the example of a computerized library? On one hand, the automation process is simple enough and is designed around the same criteria of rationalized production discussed earlier: efficiency, quantifiability, predictability, and control. On the other, that process is only part of a larger organizational structure in which the contingent (such as an unpredictable request by a library user) is a necessary component of its mission and with which the computerized process must articulate well for both to work. Is this more like a laboratory environment? Either way, it could be argued, the success of the CASLIN project—a project that reproduces mechanisms that have already been tested and are running in one location (e.g., U.S. libraries)—is dependent on the existence of near-identical conditions in a new location. This is not to insist that those mechanisms must already be in place but rather to ask whether, how, and under what conditions they come to be so.

Rather than thinking of the library as an institution with a definable organizational structure, a mission, and a set of rules that help to fulfill it—in other words, as a local tradition into which a new and different tradition is being introduced—it seems more productive to view the library, along with its history, as a confluence of complex interlocking networks of books, religious wars, worldviews, political agendas, and influential individuals and as essentially porous and unbounded. The conditions that are in place and that appear to offer resistance to the introduction of new rules and technologies are themselves the result of earlier influences that managed to set other standards in place. Perhaps the ideology of the Counterreformation, and the Jesuit order designed to implement it, was successful precisely because it established itself as a complete social order that included the monastery with its seminary and splendid library in the center of Prague. The Enlightenment, on the other hand, arrived mediated through the rules and legislation of the Vienna court. In fact, the introduction of the modern state in the postrevolutionary eras of Western and Central Europe (in 1789 and 1848, respectively) left in place a legacy of bureaucratic traditions (e.g., the Napoleonic code in France or the reforms of Austrian rule) and a habitus of adaptations to that legacy, a world (or space) within which these countries have been operating ever since.

From this perspective, the forty-five-year period of communist rhetoric, rules, and regulations imported from "the East" (*z východu*) and mediated through the local *nomenklatura* failed to produce the "socialist person" it promised (although, as the saying goes, they got exactly what they asked for). The world that period left behind can be said to be devastated and corrupt (Havel 1990), although not without a logic probably best understood as a further deformation of the world reinforced over generations and inherited from the Austrian Empire. So where does one turn for insight into the world encountered in the library project? That world seemed to me to be filled with contradictions, tensions, and even resistance. If these problems are characteristic of all organizational change, what typifies them as Central European or transitional? There is much to be said for the argument that faulting the communist era for most of what is wrong about the present (as almost everybody I know does) is itself symptomatic of that era. Conversely, much of the Western attention lavished on the post-1989 countries of Central and Eastern Europe would be well-advised to pay as much attention to the continuities with the *pre*communist histories as it does to those that inform the so-called transition.

Nevertheless, for anyone intimately familiar with the "era of normalization" (*období normalizace*)[8] there remains a strong sense of its *habitus*, that pattern of dispositions, meanings, and behaviors that created a horizon of sense then and that continue unabated to inform and be reinforced in the present. And as before, this habitus is as much lived and acted out as they are thematized and discussed. As integral parts of social interaction, they often strike me as the very energy that maintains the bundles of networks that create this particular world: a rhetoric of suspicion ("You can't trust anyone" [*Člověk nemůže nikomu věřit*] that lends its support to "in-depth" interpretations and brings new levels of confusion to the familiar distinction between saying what you mean and meaning what you say. This failure of trust in surface behavior not only reinforces the establishment of trustworthy, informal networks that carry real decisionmaking power but also demands increased diligence when it comes to official office work. Responsibilities are best shared ("People just don't take any responsibility" [*Lidi prostě nejsou schopný brát za sebe zodpovědnost*]. Yet another signature, yet another rubber stamp. As a result, my friends concur, one ends up with that agonizing double standard. The only way to get anything done is to "look out for yourself" (*starej se sám vo sebe*), which explains the proliferation of small entrepreneurs. But in a group setting the old habit takes over. Since some untrustworthy institution was always present and above you taking care of things, why participate or even listen; in the end "it will get done somehow" (*Vono se to nějak zařídí*). Hence the difficulty of setting up a self-governing consortium or of even running a meeting to discuss doing so.

The fall of communism and the embracing of capitalist market economies and Western democratic ideals and procedures, therefore, show up on the map of the library tradition as just another, albeit the most recent, discursive practice enacted in and through that tradition. This discursive practice intersects equally with the institution's organizational structure *and* the actual existing web of ego-centered networks that interfere with and manage the organization's daily activities through the powerful means of accumulated debts, gossip routes, jealousies and alliances, paranoid memories, and unofficial histories. The same is true of the legislative changes that affect the institution's governance and the real, as well as the official, relationships with the government itself (the Ministries of Culture and Finance and the Customs Office). Finally, the introduction of new technologies and with them—I have hoped—of a new library philosophy contests the habitual practices, ideas, and expectations already in place. If we agree that the library is not a circumscribed set of rules or historically mediated traditions (regardless of the image it presents), then CASLIN is also nothing more than a new articulation on a repeatedly reconstituted web. Although the project exists on more than just paper—it is not an indefinitely postponed promise—its implementation is caught up in a world other than its own.

Micropolitics

In signing an accord (Statement of Intent), the directors of the four CASLIN libraries agreed on several points of critical importance to the project's implementation, features that would define its purpose. Perhaps the most important point is the vision of a CASLIN union catalog—a jointly maintained database of all existing and future bibliographic records of domestic and foreign publications owned by the libraries. Such a "virtual" catalog offers hitherto unthinkable possibilities, including use of a public-access catalog that allows anyone anywhere to do a library search on a larger database (including call numbers, location, and current availability status) than that in the collection of any of the libraries. The database offers libraries the possibility of much more efficient coordination of their acquisition policies, cataloging, interlibrary loan services, and so forth. Participation in a union catalog depends on two things: sufficiently powerful technology (in place and running) and agreed-upon standards with which all records are entered, maintained, and made available to other libraries and to the public. The latter in particular requires coordinated work since the decision was reached to introduce and then adhere to international standards for the structure of electronic records, as well as to the widely accepted Anglo-American cataloging rules.[9] The seriousness of the commitment to these principles and goals is underscored by the closing statement of the accord: "Detailed steps to reach the above goals, all unforeseen troubles, and further development after accomplishing this Intent will always be negotiated and agreed upon jointly. The Consortium of Czech and Slovak Libraries should be founded as a standing base for the negotiation and agreement in the future utilization and development of the network."[10]

Sadly, the Consortium of Czech and Slovak Libraries was never established as promised. Unclear developments in legislation pertaining to associations of state organizations and now involving two countries created a major stumbling block, and there seemed to be no collective will to find a common solution to the problem and follow through on the initial intent. As a result, CASLIN remained an informal organization held together as much by momentum and the fact that some of the project's management was located in the United States (as were the funds that made it all possible) as by a common vision or its own simple organizational rules. Practically speaking, implementation entailed the complex and often convoluted interplay of social networks steeped in the micropolitics of work and knowledge, of conflicting interests as well as truths. When things became difficult the Statement of Intent would be quoted and, occasionally, the stern hand of the Mellon Foundation raised. Not surprisingly, "it all somehow got done in the end" (*vono se to dycky nějak sesmolí*).

As the project drew to a close (spring 1996), the money had been spent basically according to schedule, and both of the conditions mentioned earlier had been met: the technology was in place and running, and the various library standards had been agreed on and implemented. But the vision of a CASLIN union catalog remained unfulfilled, and the future of the as-yet nonexistent library consortium remained a question mark. The four original CASLIN members had to be reminded that the CASLIN project and Mellon are not coterminous, that the whole point (from the foundation's perspective) was to help to establish an association that had its own reasons for existence. The situation was complicated further by other Mellon-funded library projects that were in the works (referred to as CASLIN Plus projects). Those projects' representatives were invited to participate in all CASLIN board meetings, seminars, and work groups; yet, they were neither signatories to the Letter of Intent nor bound to each other or to the original group by any specific agreement. Once again, personal relations, prior cooperation between some of the institutions or animosity among others, and the fact that they had been selected by the Mellon Foundation drew more of their attention than the fulfillment of a common vision, a CASLIN consortium.

Among the general public there was (and still is) minimal awareness of the CASLIN initiative; among Czech and Slovak libraries the acronym has become a household word. Interest in joining has been high, although for a long time there was nothing to join in spite of the commitment of openness stated in the Statement of Intent: "The system will be open to any other institution and through them its services will be available to anybody." And so, starting in October 1995 the first joint meetings were held to try to resolve the problems and move from the Statement of Intent to a library consortium, from a group of four to an all-inclusive membership covering two countries. The first meeting was a disaster, I am told, and the many that followed are also remembered more for what they did not accomplish and why than for any steps in the right direction that may have been initiated. Finally, a proposal emerged to have two national consortia joined together by an "international agreement" between the two national libraries, whose primary responsibility would be to maintain the CASLIN union catalog. This proposal was countered by one of the CASLIN Plus libraries that was eager to participate in CASLIN as it existed up until that point, a singular organization covering two countries. The difference was not lost on anybody. The founding members were fumbling for a way to regroup as if, now that the financial incentive was gone, it was not entirely clear why they should do so.

Meanwhile, CASLIN had gained in prestige among libraries in both countries, and many were eager to join. Why, then, not establish CASLIN anew; why should those who had already been involved as CASLIN Plus members not have the right to do so? After all, CASLIN was meant as an organization of equals. I was concerned that a hierarchy of members would be legislated, reproducing the unofficial yet very tangible one already in existence—a hierarchy of those who came first, second, or third or ranked according to degrees of importance as defined by their institutional mandates. I raised this issue with the director of one of the CASLIN plus libraries. He believed an agreement between the two national libraries, in which each would become the center of a national organization of member libraries, seemed fair but was of little concern to him since he had a previous agreement with the National Library: "I just look to the National Library with respect, as they say, toward my superior institution." He commented on another regional library's wish to join an organization that would not privilege national centers: "They'd like to connect directly, wheras I already have it taken care of."

The director's comments are not only perceptive regarding others' intentions but are also characteristic. They exemplify what they criticize: the game of self-centered politicking, of how alliances are built and continually evaluated in a negative discourse in which virtually anything anyone else says or does is suspect. It is as if the whole point of a decentered, Internet-based network, in which the success of the total enterprise would add directly to the quality of services and prestige of each institutional member, was lost on those members.

Throughout the years most problems had a single underlying theme: "Why aren't the others doing their part for the whole instead of just looking out for themselves?" The institutional self-centered behavior was marked by an often confronted inability to see the collective as desirable and not as subtracting from the benefit, fame, and power of the individual institutions. The most obvious reason for this attitude is the historically long-established pattern of competition for money and legislative advantages among institutions coming under a single authority. Relations seem particularly stressed in situations marked by differences in status (usually vis-à-vis the national libraries) or generally felt core-periphery relations, such as the anti-Prague sentiment felt in the region of Moravia, which would translate into strained relations between the National Library in Prague and the Moravian Region Library in Brno. Similar tensions exist in Slovakia.

On the other hand, as the previous quote illustrates, "natural" alliances seem to form among "unequal" institutions in which other ties, even personal or regional, may override the deference that in any case may be taken as necessary or even comforting. One only needs to take part in any of the many meetings in which all of this constitutes the official agenda's subtext to observe the micropolitics of the decisionmaking process. Each participant's action is positioned with respect to (1) how he or she perceives himself or herself in relation to others present, (2) who represents authority (in his or her view), and (3) to whom he or she turns for legitimation of truths.[11] An excerpt from my field notes gives a more candid feel for the dynamics involved in one such meeting:

When I returned to the library director's office in the town of O. [In the Czech Republic], I found the director sitting with his counterparts from the Slovak regional library in X. The topic of CASLIN privileges came up shortly after I sat down. Speaking in allusions B. made reference to the existing tensions between libraries X and Y and to the former's concerted effort to uphold its statutory privileges, which it felt were being undermined by the advantages recently wheedled out of the Ministry of Culture by Y. (I had heard the reverse version of this complaint from the other side just a few days earlier.) Now X was concerned that in the new CASLIN agreement the special position of the original, founding members should be retained to guarantee that things agreed on wouldn't be overruled by other (i.e., new) members. It became clear that this was a little meeting in which, the hope was, things could be arranged. . . . The main meeting was held in a newly renovated lecture hall, arranged as a classroom, somewhat pointed toward the front. Dr. L. and I sat at the teacher's desk, blackboard behind us and the others, like pupils, facing us. Except for the fact that all present were adults ages thirty to sixty-five, the proxemics replicated the grade school experience. And so it was. We lectured them and they misbehaved. Throughout the afternoon I could observe the following patterns: since the different libraries were represented by twos or threes always sitting together, they all had a tendency to engage in conversation among themselves without paying attention to what was going on up front. The situation was eerie since it appeared as if these mutterings (which, by the way, made for a kind of uniform background noise) were all timed to correspond to the precise moment when what was being said was important (such as dates, amounts, procedures). T. and D. were the worst offenders. They engaged in a lengthy conversation to figure out some finances. Had they continued to listen instead they would have also heard answers to some of the concerns that were clearly informing their private discussion. All of this went on in front of my eyes since they sat in the first row. . . .

The second part of the meeting was devoted to the future of CASLIN. A new version of a possible agreement (which we had prepared) had been sent out a week earlier. The hope was that the final discussion of the document would take place here at this meeting so that an open meeting could be called for later in the spring when the founding document could be signed by all interested libraries. At this point in the meeting I chose to change seats and moved from the head table to the back row. Dr. L. introduced the topic by reviewing the situation, the legalities, and the points that the present version of the document was meant to cover. Tedious and monotonous, he went on too long. By the time we got to the discussion we had lost most of the time originally planned for the meeting (the Z librarians would soon have to dash out to catch trains for the "distant East"). The discussion was bogged down by individual institutions expressing their concern over one or another thing that would hinder, not be possible, or clearly not offer anything to their respective institutions. There was no sense of constructive criticism by members of a new collectivity with a joint purpose that brought us all together. Rather, it was the defensive behavior of individual subjects. Furthermore, all of the criticism was directed at L., who chaired the meeting and sat at the head table. The dynamics were odd to watch: as one person spoke *at* L., others were talking *to* each other or writing and sending notes across the room. I received two. Some were beginning to fall asleep, most notably N. Best of all, while someone was speaking to a point from the back row (and *at* L.), T. and D. were offering their view on the matter directly *to* L., who was sitting behind the desk facing them but only about a foot away. Finally, membership privileges came up again as S. (from rival library Y) expressed concern that the new CASLIN board include the original founding members as a guarantee that the future development doesn't stray off course.

I just couldn't take it any longer and asked to speak: of the necessity to make the association open to all and to start anew with a level playing field, a single voice per member institution. To do otherwise was to risk embodying in the text the very institutional differences already in place, their privileges, mandates, or dependencies. To make of the first corners the forever first is to make of the second comers the forever second. Wasn't it bad enough that CASLIN Plus librarians felt that the original CASLIN members had something "among themselves" (*mezi sebou*) that made them special? It would be fine to credit the founding members with an honorable mention in the opening lines of the text. But otherwise, history—of which they had plenty here—did not make for a well-functioning democracy. I gave the example of the married couple I had dinner with in Prague who ended up having a dreadful fallout over their differing views on what *actually* happened at the Battle of the White Mountain in 1620. At this point N. woke up and offered a rebuttal, something to the effect that "America had fine democratic institutions, but for us it is important to maintain historical traditions" (*zachovat historické tradice*). A strong sense of embarrassment filled the room, and a few more people left. Finally, the deputy director of the National Library in Prague suggested that they retain the first few paragraphs of the text, which seemed to be acceptable to all and best defined the purpose of the association. All agreed, and a series of dates was established for the next meeting to work on this text. It was 6:30 P.M. The meeting was scheduled to end at 4:00 P.M.

It is within this world, not outside or against it, that the presumably straightforward world of technology works (or doesn't) and on which, in turn, the actual functioning of CASLIN on-line depends. Thus, the disjointed quality of the meeting and the fact that the formation of a functioning consortium was once again delayed surfaced a few months later in negotiations between a library and a software vendor.

The computer hardware and, most important, the library program are supplied by foreign companies, and their purchase requires complex and sometimes protracted negotiations over contracts that are meant to assure both sides that beyond the costs and schedule, they have also agreed on the outcome. Although the vendor is chosen on the basis of proposals, demonstrations, and bids (in the case of CASLIN, *Aleph* from ExLibris/Israel was the system of choice), not until implementation do possible difficulties become apparent. Even then, it is not always clear which side caused the problem. Did the vendor promise something it cannot deliver, or did the client expect something that does not exist? Is the software architecture able to accommodate the particularities of the local library science, or is the new technology introducing new standards and therefore new procedures? In that case, the vendor would argue, it is incumbent upon the libraries to shift gears and discover that the engine works. The lengthy process of localization, during which the software is tailored to work in the client's language environment and many of the troubles surface, is therefore preceded by a contractual agreement that stipulates, among other things, the criteria and methods for the client's final acceptance of the product.

In the case of CASLIN, the acceptance procedures—which commenced two years after the initial contract was signed—were difficult, if not nasty, leaving both sides exhausted and disappointed. Yet, *Aleph* is running (more or less) in all four libraries, and CASLIN has joined the world of *Aleph* users.

ExLibris later won the bid and entered into contract negotiations with one of the new CASLIN Plus projects. By choosing *Aleph*, the Eastern Slovak Library Consortium followed CASLIN's lead and also complied with an overall understanding that using the identical system would be the best and most cost-effective guarantee of success.[12] But at what was supposed to be one of the last meetings before the signing, a series of disagreements arose, and a complete breakdown of communication between the vendor and the client nearly brought the process to a halt. The acceptance procedures were at the core of the mutual mudslinging. The libraries expected that the implementation would be concluded according to a protocol, a list of individual functions for which the system would be tested on the day of acceptance. This list, drawn up ahead of time, would be binding and would become an appendix to the overall contract. This was the procedure in the first CASLIN installation and seemed to be the best guarantee against undelivered promises.

The vendor would not agree to those terms. Not only did its representatives wish to avoid what had been a costly and unpleasant experience, but they argued—persuasively enough for me but not for the client—that such a repeat performance made no sense in the purchase of a network software license that was an expansion of the system already in place. Instead of treating this situation as an entirely new localization, the product should be accepted as a CASLIN system in which the criteria of functionality were already established. In the words of the vendor's chief executive officer:

> There is only one version of the *Aleph* system. The versions are marked by number, and during the interim from one version to another, updates are

numbered by "patch number." For example: if CASLIN has version 3.2.5–12, it means that they have version 3.2.5 and they received all the updates and additions up to patch number 12. The ExLibris system is [such] that when a correction is made, it receives a consecutive number, and is sent to the party involved. The "patch" includes all the changes and corrections up to this point. We will supply the version with the latest patch, at the moment of supply, and this will, of course, include whatever CASLIN has. (E-mail, June 1996)

As for the acceptance procedure, the following was proposed:

First, we will install the then current version. Second, our installing person will check the system and will approve, in writing, that according to his checks the system is installed and fully functional. Third, the libraries, upon facing any faulty function, will refer to our support center and will be serviced like any other customer. Usually the "bugs" are not "bugs" but users' wish that things will work in another way. This will be answered. However, there are always "bugs." If our support confirms to them that this is a "bug" or a malfunctioning of any kind, the test will be CASLIN. Libraries will call CASLIN and find out if they have the same problem. If positive, then it is taken care of by us (already reported and acted upon) as we do other CASLIN reports. If this is a problem in the new installation and works fine in CASLIN then we will fix it within 72 hours. It must be clear that computers have the funny habit of doing always the same thing. . . . The chances that they will have a malfunction that does not occur in CASLIN are practically Zero. Another very important note is that there are "bugs" and there are "bugs." *Nobody in the world of Aleph will find a bug in the main stream of work. This is used by so many people, around the world, that a "bug" of this kind would have already been found and corrected.* "Bugs" may be found in remote "corners" of the system, which may be used by very few and thus a combination of some sort, which never occurred earlier, produces a bug. This does happen often and would be corrected according to the importance of the "bug." (E-mail, June 1996; emphasis added)

In spite of these explanations and gentle nudging from the Foundation, the librarians felt more secure with the familiar acceptance procedure based on a predetermined list of functions the system would perform: "We have not understood how this [other] approach would be to our advantage and what would in such a case become of Appendix B. We would like it if Appendix B consisted of 'Yes' or 'No' answers to our list of functions" wrote one of the librarians (E-mail, June 1996). It seemed impossible to make any headway on this sticky point in spite of the assurances, so ExLibris agreed to an acceptance protocol and asked to see the list.

Several additional rounds followed, and, ultimately, it was ExLibris that got its way. In early September, 1996, the contract was finally signed, but only when the system is installed will we (maybe) have a better sense of who was right. Whatever the outcome, the issues that the process of negotiation raised were reminiscent of the problems with replication and verification encountered in the first air-pump experiments during the 1660s. Constructing a successful copy of a device and, following that, achieving the same results in a new place have never been based on written instructions alone. Such a feat demanded the transfer of people first, and not just of anybody; it required establishing a community of experts who were the bearers of authority and the direct witnesses of scientific experiments. Only with time did the standards of measurement themselves become authorized devices against which the reliability of other (new) devices could be measured, although these were nothing but agreed-upon events: "The establishment of a set of accepted matters of fact [about pneumatics] required the establishment and definition of a community of experimenters who worked with shared social conventions; that is to say, the effective solution to the problem of knowledge was predicated upon a solution to the problem of social order" (Shapin and Schaffer 1989: 282).

In the case described here, it was ExLibris whose behavior assumed the existence of a functioning consortium (CASLIN) with an established (i.e., localized) system (within the "world of *Aleph*") and therefore of a set of standards with which any newly introduced addition—whether as a new (local) installment or advancements to existing ones—must comply. Even its low price, the company argued during arbitration, was meant to reflect this fact. After all, once the localization of CASLIN *Aleph* has been accomplished, so has the world *within which* more *Aleph* is imminently portable. It is not necessary to start over again.

Two conclusions can be drawn. First, like any other technology, computer technology, specifically software, both embody and are embedded in social relations of their invention, reproduction, and use—only more so since it seems the manner in which software products are developed and enhanced is intricately tied to the way they travel and are tested, repaired, and used: through an electronic network that constitutes and depends on a social network. This situation poses a direct, even unprecedented challenge to the movement of people and the direct witnessing of events. Second, the software vendor had assumed a reality that was not functionally in place: an acceptance of piecemeal verification procedures that would use other *in situ* devices (in the world of identical devices) as the criteria of functionality and the existence of a working consortium in which the principle of cooperation exists not just on paper but by now is a well-established fact.

On the first point, and in all fairness, the lengthy implementation in those "other places" (notably CASLIN) has been marked by an endless string of technical problems. The system librarians argue that until recently they have spent their time fine-tuning the system and "catching bugs." Regarding the second point, it would also be unfair to maintain that cooperation among CASLIN libraries does not exist when it does (even if not as it was imagined); the question is how and why. In other words, the lived reality (even that of technology) is always more fuzzy, overdetermined, and just plain "human" than the ideal model admits. Slovak librarians' perspective on the issue of acceptance reflects such a reality in which the lack of experience, the overwhelming size of the project, the degree of individual responsibility it demanded, and an acute awareness that things are *not* perfect in other locations were reinforced by an a priori lack of trust. The unresolved CASLIN negotiations and the librarians' own positioning vis-à-vis their Slovak CASLIN partners necessarily reinforced what seemed only logical—that their *Aleph* installation should be an independent implementation that contained the same safeguards against a faulty product and a potentially unresponsive company as those of the original installation. After all, the arrival of a market economy and direct negotiations with vendors are not only new experiences but are imagined to be tough, dangerous, and individualistic. From this perspective "acceptance as a CASLIN system" lacks familiar (legal) assurances; it seems less tangible and more indeterminate—it is suspect.

Can the principle of the electronic library override these differences? Will it work in spite of them, or will the tradition override the potential for a radically different setup? Perhaps in the long run one can expect a new organizational structure to emerge as the necessary consequence of technology-driven change.[13] For the present, three networks have become intertwined. First is the one *desired* and located on the Internet; it involves computer technology. The second, *required* for the first one to work, is based on rules of cooperation between libraries and, as the previous example demonstrates, is also embodied in the technology. A third network stands already *in place*—the web of (ego-centered) social relations, the real lived world.

Conclusion

Why, then, is a McDonalds restaurant more portable than the idea of a Jeffersonian library? There are many reasons, but two are key to the present argument. First, as was suggested earlier, McDonalds is not only simpler, it is also the more self-contained system. The high replicability of the result in different locations is linked to the portability to the total environment of production. Designed around the idea of the assembly line, it is most like a construction set, ready to be shipped and reassembled basically anywhere where certain economic (legal) and infrastructural (water, electricity, and other) conditions are met. Plug in and play! Or so it seems. The principles of "scientific management" (Taylorism) are literally embodied in the actual technology (machinery) of food production; a simple and direct connection exists between the highly mechanized and rationalized work environment and the organization of work. In other words, the micropolitical process and the production process are kept apart; the susceptibility of Big Mac to the human factor has been reduced to the minimum. If, as is beginning to be the case in Prague, a high turnover of employees should occur, it will not affect the result: the carefully calibrated Big Mac and french fries.

A second reason, and more important to the present argument, has to do with the symbolic value of the enterprise. As was the case with Pepsi-Cola and, later, Coca-Cola (both of which had established themselves as desirable goods years earlier), the association with the West, in particular *Amerika,* is a determining factor. One could even speak of a "fame factor," the often noted phenomenon of the name preceding the named. And because there is no precedent, the quintessential fast-food restaurant had only the "other" to compete with. The dirty, dreary, beer-smelling stand-up buffets of the socialist period compete poorly with the clean, bright, and efficient locale with pleasant service, working bathrooms, and a phone. Combined with aggressive advertising, the "difference" associated with and observed in the West was now here, and that made all the difference. A real, stand-alone piece of *Amerika!* In contrast, the library automation project was an idea that involved implementation *within* already existing institutions that offer library services and that consisted of well-entrenched habits, library procedures, and the micropolitics that characterize formal and informal networks.[14]

It seems self-evident that a library is not meant to be McDonalds. The comparison may even appear far-fetched, if not odd. Clearly, the Mellon-funded library project is an attempt to put in place an idea that is in many ways utopian, if not entirely foreign, and that has no commercial value. Jeffersonian ideals are just that; they are good for thought and maybe even a little political clout. In fact, talk of citizenship, participatory democracy, education, and freedom of information was an effective marketing strategy in the project's first two or three years when the country was still breathing the values of the 1989 Velvet Revolution, and the willingness of a U.S. foundation to fund a national symbol caught the media's attention. But unlike the Big Mac, these symbols lack simple visual concretization. More important, the economic value of the project, outlined at the beginning of the chapter, is yet to be tested, and it will not be until a modern telecommunications infrastructure is in place and readily available throughout both countries.

Finally, as we saw, a library system was already in place, but no one had experience with an interlibrary on-line network. If anything, the long-standing tendency is for institutions to act on their own since cooperation is difficult at best and legislation in the two countries is developing in different ways. This reality, coupled with the complex micropolitics within each participating library and between libraries and the respective institutions of adminstrative oversight, accounts for the exasperation that seems to frequently accompany the project's implementation. We have also seen how these feelings of futility, frustration, and anger—like the discourse of cynicism and suspicion they reinforce—play themselves out and at what cost.

One feature, however, is shared by the fast-food chain and the on-line library: the automated processing line. Although no library comes in a kit that can be reassembled in a new place to guarantee the same results, the principle of library services depends on the system of technical services, of assembly lines that "process" documents and make them available to users. These production lines consist of a series of distinct steps that fit into an overall notion of the "properly processed" document and therefore into one or more services the institution has in its mandate.[15] Clearly, the public and technical services are highly rule-defined procedures anchored in long-standing (local) traditions, which means the move toward on-line catalog services, electronic documents delivery, and, most of all, the interlibrary consortia discussed earlier also means embracing standardization *across* libraries and library traditions. Since technical services (like computer technology) are by nature based on the repetitive application of identical rules, the argument goes, it should follow that the introduction of automation is a logical step for everyone to take. Between the technology and the rules, little space should be left for anything but repeatable identical results.

A recent review of the now fully operational document processing lines (*linka zpracování*) at all of the CASLIN libraries made it clear that essential changes in the nature of work could be introduced as part of the conversion to the *Aleph* system. For example, the computer cataloging screen can be programmed to make it impossible to enter certain fields at certain stages in the work line, which speeds up the process since it keeps individual catalogers from getting lost in the complicated system and making mistakes. It is possible to isolate and routinize some aspects of the process so it can be completed by less qualified students (at lower pay) and to use laptops that permit employees to take work home during sick or maternity leave.[16]

Finally, the physical document is accompanied on-line by an increasingly more complete electronic record. It is even possible to trace the document and know who worked on it at what stage; the record can be "stamped" with the time, date, and name of each cataloger in sequence as it moves from the acquisition department through author and subject cataloging to book binders and, finally, to the shelving and loan records. It seems clear that scientific management has sneaked into the library and threatens to further transform librarians' work into office work governed by essentially the same rules that operate at McDonalds (and nearly everywhere else), thus changing the social relations of the workplace and possibly further demoting the value of this profession (cf. Braverman 1974).

But the hopes as much as the concerns may have been premature. Whereas the initial introduction of the new system was difficult in all libraries, in two of them, after an initial and rather dramatic improvement in the average time it took to process a book, things slipped back to the previous level of underproduction, albeit on the new system.[17] Once again there were bottlenecks, and once again the bugs turned out to be human. The results are mixed: everyone will agree that automation has resulted in a more uniform catalog record and in opening up the library to the world. In that sense the project has succeeded in literally transforming the libraries' raison d'être. What the project has not yet done (automatically or uniformly) is to speed up the cataloging process; further, it is not impervious to the micropolitics of the workplace. If anything, it may have fueled an already divisive situation.

If portability of a system and the replication of results are at the core of both of my examples, the CASLIN case unveils more clearly the *process* of replication and, even more important, its possible limits. The ease of introduction of a new technology is clearly affected by the extent to which it confronts an established situation that is amenable to the new procedure, both by virtue of its purpose and by the organization of work already in place. It is even better if the technology and the values and power it is thought to embody are themselves desirable (e.g., computers, capitalism, *Amerika*), although in the case of the CASLIN libraries these Western values are not desired equally by all. They are contested by many who find the changes an unwelcome imposition. One could also argue that those values, ideas, and social relations most clearly embodied in a technology are also those that are most portable, if only because the implementation of the technology will induce the kind of transformations of local conditions that are required to obtain the same results. Although this may be the case in some situations (such as McDonalds), in others it may take a long time for the "new" habits to settle in (presumably true for the libraries); therefore, their direct tie to an "original" cause (such as the introduction of a new technology) may be weakened. Either way, the progression is never linear; if "things seem to take forever" (*všechno se věčně táhne*) it is because the delays in implementation are primarily micropolitical in nature and although they are frustrating and may even spell disaster, they are also the very moment in which realities are being contested, social relations confirmed, and new meanings taken on "as one's own."[18]

At last, there is nothing earthshaking about the insight that the rationalization of production (and the values of prosperity and progress so typically associated with it) is first and foremost technology driven; nor does it help to distinguish capitalist from socialist notions of industrialization. (Lenin was the first to advocate the importance of introducing ideas of scientific management to Soviet industrialization.) What needs further exploration, particularly in any European society undergoing a lengthy period of transition, is the complex interplay among the recent and distant legacies in the rationalization of office work, the actual lived micropolitics that informs the bureaucratic experience but extends beyond organizations into the experience of everyday life, and, finally, the advent of new information technologies with their own demands on networking and organizational behavior.[19] Bureaucratic systems established much earlier (in the late eighteenth century) have reproduced themselves up until the present and, with them (as discussed earlier), the particular official and unofficial ways of getting things done (the most recent, socialist "layer" is the most clear). It is into this established world that the other world, equally established, is being introduced. In this sense the library project offers a unique opportunity to observe this transition, its limits, and resistance to it in close detail. If we take the view that some of the most successful production technologies of late capitalism are those that emulate the ideal principles established by experimental science—for in both cases mastering replication is the key to establishing portability, a system of practices well equipped to penetrate, consume, and replace other worlds—we can then turn to describing in greater detail what is involved in these transitions and, just as important, what happens to those things, ideals, and individuals (i.e., networks) that are less directly or as yet unaffected by or embodied in these practices and why.

Notes

Acknowledgments: An earlier version of this chapter was presented at the conference Ethnographies of Transition, held at the Center for Slavic and East European Studies, University of California, Berkeley, 22–24 March 1996. This considerably revised version is in part a response to the many important issues raised at the conference and to the many subsequent comments, particularly those of Katherine Verdery, for which I remain grateful. I wish to thank the Andrew W. Mellon Foundation, which has been very generous over the years (1991–1998), and the librarians in the Czech and Slovak Republics who have been so patient in putting up with the anthropological gaze. Special thanks are reserved for Gregoire C. de Changy for sharing his insights on McDonalds.

1. In view of the recent discussions of the experience and practice of participant-observation, a crucial point should be made about the present study. It is the result of fieldwork with a particular twist: I am trying to make anthropological sense of a reality in which not only am I an active player but that is—initially at least and largely—the result of my initiative. Since I have yet to find my own voice, I have chosen not to make this theme a significant part of the present analysis. The pronouns "we" and "our" refer to the U.S. side of the project discussed in this chapter.

2. In library terminology, technical services designate those functions that must be in place for the library to fulfill its duties to the public—that is, public services. The circulation and reference desks are examples of public services. Typically, technical services take place "in the background" and include, among others, book ordering and cataloging. The Modular Automatic Library System (MAKS) was among the last state-sponsored projects in Czechoslovakia prior to 1989. The plan was to develop a modular library software (including all functions such as acquisitions, cataloging, lending, and the like) in a uniform, machine-readable format. Although only the cataloging module was developed and the format does not exactly match the international standard (UNIMARC), the software played a decisive role in introducing libraries to computer automation. It is still used in some libraries, and the conversion of data stored in this format into the UNIMARC format has been resolved. The history of automation at the National Library is reviewed by Svoboda (1992).

3. For a detailed analysis of the economic benefits of interlibrary cooperation and electronic text delivery, see Ekman and Quandt (1994).

4. Since 1990, in addition to the Czech and Slovak projects discussed in this chapter, the Andrew W. Mellon Foundation has funded several consortia-based library automation projects in Poland and Hungary and, most recently, in the Balkan countries. Funding for these projects has also come from the Open Society Fund (the Soros Foundation) and the Pew Charitable Trusts.

5. In January 1992 a third visit took place; the original U.S. team returned to participate in a one-day seminar organized by the Ministry of Culture to discuss the library building. The hidden agenda was to get the ministry that holds administrative and budgetary authority over the library involved and on our side from the beginning, especially since the relationship between the two institutions was (and remains) tense. On the basis of the recommendation of the minister of culture, the Czech government assigned a building to the National Library for reconstruction as the new book and document depository. What was furthest from anyone's mind—an improvement to the physical plant of the National Library and especially to the book storage crisis—has become a reality. The Hostivar depository was officially opened on 25 January 1996. While the initial architectural plans were designed by the American architects (The Hilliar Group), the construction firm was Czech. Funding came from the Czech Ministry of Culture.

6. The opening paragraph of the agreement (Statement of Intent) signed by the four libraries in November 1991 reads: "To lay a solid foundation of a nation-wide library network providing both home and foreign users with easy, fast and unrestrictive access to the information stored in or mediated by the libraries

and information centers" (CASLIN Group 1992). Of the total amount of $1.3 million earmarked for the CASLIN project, $200,000 was provided by the Pew Charitable Trusts. In the following year several other projects were funded by the Mellon Foundation, all conceived as extensions or add-ons to the original one and known as the CASLIN Plus projects. They included LINCA, a library automation proposal for the Czech Academy of Sciences ($350,000); RETROCON, a retrospective conversion project to help transfer the paper card catalog into electronic (machine-readable) form ($150,000); KOLIN, a library automation project that would join two university libraries and one state scientific library in eastern Slovakia ($750,000); and MOLIN, a consortium of four university and scientific libraries in the Moravian region of the Czech Republic ($350,000).

   7. A detailed official assessment of what was accomplished in the three years (1993–1995) for which the project was planned is presented in Svoboda (1996). For more on the situation at the National Library, see its 1995 Annual Report (Národní knihovna 1996).

   8. *Normalizace* was the official term used by the Husák government in the immediate years after the August 1968 invasion of Czechoslovakia by the Soviet-led Warsaw Pact armies. It became the generally accepted term for the atmosphere so poignantly discussed in Havel's work from that period.

   9. The head librarians and technical experts agreed to adopt international standards that guarantee that the card catalogs will not only be *readable* from within any other on-line library system around the world (regardless of the national language or even the character set) but, most important, be *exchangeable* among libraries. The universal machine-readable catalog format (UNIMARC) and the Anglo-American cataloging rules (AACR2) allow librarians to catalog a foreign book by downloading its already established UNIMARC record from an on-line catalog. In other words, the same document has an identical record in different countries, just as all documents are cataloged according to the same rules in different countries.

   10. CASLIN Group, 1992: Appendix I-A.

   11. An interesting analysis of the micropolitics of meetings and of truth claims made in organizational meetings (and coming out of the sociology of knowledge) is offered by Lazega (1992), although he does not consider the role memory plays in this context. The decisiveness of memory in the production of truth is familiar to anyone who has worked in Eastern Europe. For example, in speaking of other library directors attending a meeting, my informant supports her insights on their behavior with a reference to their past Communist Party membership. In telling me that "those two are bolsheviks, I remember them quite well," she is both disqualifying their claims (for, obviously, who in their right mind would trust one of those) and distancing herself from them. Most important, in cutting them down to size she is also drawing me (an authority with decisionmaking powers) into her confidence.

   12. Second-generation CASLIN projects would benefit directly from the experience and training of their predecessors, which in an ideal world of economics and engineering would lower costs, simplify and shorten the implementation schedule, increase performance, and reinforce the consortium's growing social

capital. But the idea of a library automation network using a single system ultimately faltered because of gossip—generated through the existing informal networks of (mostly) librarians—that reinforced negative evaluations of the system
by adding unfounded rumors about payoffs.

13. The impact of technology on the changing nature of work and therefore
on the workplace and organizational structure is the classic argument represented
best by the work of Braverman (1974). A rather harsh example of this view, encountered in Eastern Europe as "common-sense" practice, was expressed by a
middle manager at one of the libraries. In response to a concern about what appeared to be a confused cataloger who could not explain what she was doing on
the computer, he observed, "The technology will force them to get it straight"
(*vona je ta technologie k tomu donutí*). Thomas (1994) argues persuasively that
there is much machines cannot do.

14. This argument assumes a distinction between the identity of an object
(e.g., a hamburger sandwich), understood here as an aspect of repetitiveness, and
its meaning. The relationship between the two (reproducibility and meaning) is
only hinted at; a fuller exploration is reserved for a separate study. The meaning
of McDonalds (and its Big Mac) is clearly different in different locations, and it
shifts over time and social strata. For example, in Prague the newness factor has
worn off, and after the initial, cautious rejection of the McDonalds experience by
my more urbanite, sophisticated friends, McDonalds seems to have settled into
general acceptance as a clean, reliable, and convenient place. Apparently, over-
seas McDonalds do accommodate the local situation. Although the menus have
the traditional standards (such as the Big Mac), they offer a variety of other meals
as well. Napkins are given with each order instead of having dispensers accessible
to all ("people just come here and steal them" [*lidi si sem choděj a kradou je*]).
On the other hand, the same dripped, stewed, and diluted coffee familiar in most
U.S. restaurants is also served here, in a country that has an established tradition
of serving excellent Turkish and Italian coffees. Rumor has it that people have
been seen drinking it!

15. For example, within the hierarchy of libraries an institution such as the
National Library or the U.S. Library of Congress may (in addition to offering
readers access to books, periodicals, and other materials) also register the International Standard Book Number (ISBN) all books are supposed to have or be the
recipients of the "legal deposit," the copy all publishers are requested to place
with the library to guarantee that a complete deposit of the national book and
journal production is maintained. Other services may include providing specialized catalogs and offering legal copyright registration.

16. The head cataloger took great pride in the possibility of using laptops to
make work portable since, as she complained to me, "most of the librarians are
women and so we face an incredibly high amount of absenteeism."

17. Although the time it takes to get a new book on the shelf is an important
indicator, whether a library has a backlog of uncataloged books and, if so, how
many is a better overall measure of a library's health.

18. For a systems theory approach to delay as a key component in organizational behavior, see Senge (1994).

19. See Rabinbach's (1992) excellent study of the competing trends in the science of work and the arrival of scientific management in Europe.

References

Braverman, Harry. 1974. *Labour and Monopoly Capital.* New York: Monthly Review Press.

CASLIN Group. 1992. *CASLIN: Automation and Preservation Project: A Proposal Presented to the Andrew W. Mellon Foundation and Pew Charitable Trusts.* Mount Holyoke College, South Hadley, September.

Ekman, Richard, and Richard E. Quandt. 1994. *Scholarly Communication, Academic Libraries, and Technology.* New York: Andrew W. Mellon Foundation.

Havel, Vaclav. 1990. The Power of the Powerless. In *Living in Truth: Twenty-Two Essays Published on the Occasion of the Award of the Erasmus Prize to Vaclav Havel,* ed., Jan Vladislav. London: Faber and Faber.

Latour, Bruno. 1988. *The Pasteurization of France.* Cambridge: Harvard University Press.

Latour, Bruno, and Steve Woolgar. 1986. *Laboratory Life: The Construction of Scientific Facts.* Princeton: Princeton University Press.

Lazega, Emmanuel. 1992. *The Micropolitics of Knowledge: Communication and Indirect Control in Workgroups.* New York: Aldine de Gruyter.

Národní knihovna České republiky. 1996. *Výroč ní zpráva 1995.* Praha: Národní knihovna.

Rabinbach, Anson. 1992. *The Human Motor: Energy, Fatigue, and the Origins of Modernity.* Berkeley: University of California Press.

Ritzer, George. 1993. *The McDonaldization of Society: An Investigation into the Changing Character of Contemporary Social Life.* Thousand Oaks: Pine Forge.

Senge, Peter. 1994. *The Fifth Discipline: The Art and Practice of the Learning Organization.* New York: Currency Doubleday.

Shapin, Steven, and Simon Schaffer. 1989. *Leviathan and the Air-Pump: Hobbes, Boyle, and the Experimental Life.* Princeton: Princeton University Press.

Svoboda, Martin. 1992. Automation in Libraries—How to Proceed? Paper presented at the *LIBER* conference, Budapest, July.

———. 1996. CASLIN: From Project to Consortium. Paper presented at the International Conference on Library Automation in Central and Eastern Europe, Open Society Fund, Budapest, March.

Thomas, Robert J. 1994. *What Machines Can't Do: Politics and Technology in the Industrial Enterprise.* Berkeley: University of California Press.

10

Afterword

Michael Burawoy

As ethnographers, we focus our research on the rituals and routines of daily life. We immerse ourselves in the spatial and temporal rhythms of the people we study. We train our ethnographic microscopes on the experience and self-understanding of our subjects. But we always bring our own theoretical lenses, which we continually shape and polish in the light of what we observe and whom we eventually want to persuade. These portable lenses not only give us access to the world of our subjects and not only demarcate the visible from the invisible; they also enable us to locate the field in its wider historical and geographical context. Living in villages or towns, working in factories or fields, hobnobbing with teachers or priests, passing the time of day in bars or kitchens, we deploy our theories to reach upward and outward to the movement of society as a whole, to the convulsions and continuity of national political regimes and economic systems, and, beyond these, to global transformations. Only through theoretical work can we connect microworlds to their macrodeterminations. I close our book with some ruminations on the theories we import to make this last leap outward.

All of us have spent many years in the countries we study. We do not migrate with international consultants and advisers from one country to the next as fashion and demand dictate. We are regional specialists who have made the study of the Soviet and post-Soviet world a lifetime engagement. Nevertheless, we are also deeply rooted in the Anglo-American academy. Since our guiding interpretations draw on Western social theories, it is reasonable to ask how well such theories travel eastward first to Eastern Europe and then to Russia.

I should acknowledge immediately that the flow of theory is never one-way. Both the practice and the ideology of "communism" profoundly shaped the real and imaginary worlds of Western social science. The Sturm und Drang of the 1930s Depression era, whether for or against socialism, was played out against the background of the Bolshevik Revolution. Whether it was Schumpeter's thesis of the self-transformation of capitalism, Hayek's road to serfdom, Burnham's managerial revolution, Lange's market socialism, or Popper's enemies of the open society, the Soviet Union was deeply embedded in their collective consciousness. In the Cold War era, much Anglo-American social theory was driven by the "totalitarian" Soviet Union as liberal democracy's repudiated Other.

Although the Soviet Union cast a shadow on Western scholarship, the communist world was only rarely the object of theoretically innovative empirical studies, especially in sociology and anthropology. Typical in this regard is Barrington Moore, one of the great Soviet specialists of the period, who is remembered not for his disquisitions on Russia but for his analysis of the historical origins of democracy and dictatorship. Although profoundly shaped by his engagement with Soviet history, he omitted Russia from his six-country analysis. The specter of communism haunted Western social science but without delivering classics that live on in our imagination.

The specter has evaporated, and we must now ask whether the collapse of communism will remain as a broad shadow, informing what we do and how we think rather than invigorating social theory with new innovative studies. Certainly, the collapse of the Soviet order created an ideological vacuum that sucked in Western visions celebrating markets and democracy. But once the first rush died down, more critical social theory gained ground. As the initial euphoria evaporates, the transition falters, and postsocialism enters a dull normality or erupts in violent conflagration, a second generation of theorizing probes more deeply into the fabric of society. Ten years after the collapse of the Berlin Wall we can begin to contemplate how successive waves of Western theory have fared in these new surroundings and whether they are sketching out new cognitive maps.

The first theories to fly across the Atlantic, in jets hired by the IMF and the World Bank, were the economic theories of neoliberalism. Shock therapy aimed to jolt Eastern economies out of their socialist rigidity and degeneration; it would miraculously rectify the inherited pathologies of planning. Shock therapy was to be the "big bang" that would eclipse the old order and set in motion an irreversible expansion of a market economy. As virtually all of the chapters in this book confirm, although markets can be created overnight, their character and consequences cannot be controlled. Markets can generate a retreat to barter relations or criminalized trade, as well as to monetized exchange; markets can lead to involution rather than revolution or evolution; markets can be the engine of primitive disaccumulation rather than advanced accumulation. To a lesser or greater extent, we can observe such alternative scenarios all across Eastern Europe, not just in Russia and the other former Soviet republics.

Those economists who recognize the failure of neoliberal practice have turned to institutional theories of the economy that advocate evolutionary transformation: instead of destroying the old in the pious hope that the new will spring forth like a *deus ex machina,* they propose constructing the new within the framework of the old. The IMF and, especially, the World Bank find themselves rallying against their own neoliberalism, against unrestrained privatization, against privatized pensions, against extravagant promises of what the market miracle will deliver. The more successful economies of Eastern Europe—Poland, the Czech Republic, and Hungary—have been wary of shock therapy and have pursued a more cautious road that recognizes the signal role of the state in creating and nurturing modern capitalism.

Of course, there is nothing new here from the standpoint of classical social theory. Sad to say, we have still to relearn the lessons of Weber, Durkheim, and Marx. In moving social theory forward, therefore, we would do well to begin by interrogating their insights into earlier transitions to capitalism. Max Weber is an obvious point of departure. Throughout his life he wrestled with the Janus-faced character of modernity, what Horkheimer and Adorno later called the dialectic of enlightenment. Weber's pessimism is well suited to the uncertain transitions studied in this book, which also provide fertile soil for reexamining his account of the sources of modern bourgeois capitalism—the fecund mixture of rule of law, the organization of formally free labor, elaborate systems of budgeting and accounting, and that uniquely occidental ingredient, the "spirit of capitalism."

Today's postsocialism, however, looks very different from seventeenth- and eighteenth-century Europe. One searches in vain for that originating class of capitalist entrepreneurs. Rerunning Max Weber's *Protestant Ethic and the Spirit of Capitalism,* Gil Eyal (1998), for example, uncovers the sources of elective affinity not between Calvinists and bourgeoisie but between dissidents and technocrats in the making of a Czech managerial capitalism. Eyal, Iván Szelényi, and Eleanor Townsley (1998) extend the argument across Central Europe. Adding Bourdieu to Weber, they describe a dynamic social space of strategic actors possessing different forms of potentially convertible capital—economic, social, and cultural. Postcommunist capitalism, they claim, is being made not by an economic bourgeoisie or by the old political elite but by a cultural bourgeoisie, an intelligentsia formed under communism.

This making of "capitalism without capitalists" is a forward-looking scenario. It suggests an entirely novel form of corporate capitalism manufactured from the ruins of socialism. By contrast, a backward-looking scenario, also from Weber, maps the gestation of a capitalism that *predated* Western bourgeois capitalism—merchant, adventure, speculative, or even booty capitalism in which profit is sought in the realm of trade and exchange rather than production. Certainly, as Caroline Humphrey shows (chapter 1), Russia exhibits features of a latter-day merchant capitalism, a capitalism based on the export of raw materials, the import of cheap foreign consumer goods, and regulation by high finance. Instead of Weber's ascetic, sober, autonomous bourgeoisie we discover the formation of a class of oligarchs embedded in global capitalism who have expropriated the state for their own ends, who in the style of new classes are impressed by their own conspicuous consumption, and who surround themselves with an elaborate security apparatus that separates them from outsiders clamoring to join them. One is reminded less of Max Weber's occidental bourgeoisie than of Frantz Fanon's African national bourgeoisie—an appendix of multinational capital, a parasite on its own popular classes, mimicking the West rather than seeking its own innovative road.

To turn from Weber's specification of Western bourgeois capitalism to its cultural and political *preconditions,* not surprisingly, generates a catalog of deficits—from entrepreneurial culture and the rule of law to the modern nation-state with its monopoly of legitimate violence. Countless commentaries, such as that of Stephen Holmes (1997), show the Russian state as having failed in every area of endeavor—human, economic, political, and social rights. Once again the Russian state has failed to meet Western norms, and if the blame was earlier laid at the feet of totalitarianism, now the problem is the opposite: state weakness and incapacity. Deficit models that cast Russia in darkness not only stigmatize but also fail to deliver any insight into the character and dynamics of contemporary Russian society.

To compare, differentiate, homogenize, and hierarchize countries according to their deviation from a single Western norm raises the question of exclusion, of whether some countries fall outside the standard, lie beyond the pale. Can Russia be put under the same microscope as its erstwhile satellites? Do the heavy weight of Russia's past—its imperial role, its repeated failure to catch up with the West, and the longevity of its communist period—and its enormous size put it in a category of its own when we consider transitions beyond socialism?

In her comparative study of the fortunes of liberal democracy in Eastern Europe, Ellen Comisso (1997) significantly omits Russia. Yet even within Eastern Europe, Western theories of liberal democracy travel better to some countries than to others. Comisso utilizes the Weberian distinction between formal democracy and substantive democracy. In terms of formal democracy broad and remarkable success has occurred, but in terms of substantive democracy—that is, what democracy is supposed to deliver—the picture is bleaker. Comisso considers three substantive dimensions: egalitarian, national, and liberal. In each instance postsocialism is found wanting: equality has suffered, national rights have been weakened, and the protection of property rights has been inadequate. Her model does not end up as a catalog of deficits, however, but attempts to make sense of government policies as reflecting particular constellations of national, egalitarian, and liberal interests.

Still, what shall we do with Russia? Is the Russian political order sui generis, a product of its own *Geist,* unreceptive to Western institutions (McDaniel 1996)? Is the Russian state conjuring up ghosts from the past? Would we more appropriately see in it the antecedent and antithesis of Weber's bureaucratic order? Does it make sense to talk of the Russian state as an "industrial patrimonialism" (Garcelon 1997) or a feudal state in its parcelized sovereignty (Humphrey 1991; Verdery 1996)? Are historical analogies relevant to its double existence—formal public institutions with a legislature, judiciary, and executive coexisting with a shadow "private" state that also exercises violence, collects taxes, and enforces economic transaction? Inseparable and interpenetrated, do these two sides generate something altogether new? Is the Russian state, rather, a member of the family of predatory states that include Mexico, Zaire (now Congo), and Indonesia? Again, if the communist legacy is so important, perhaps we should compare Russia to an equally complex and enormous society such as China, even though its history, its stage of industrialization, and even its experience with communism are so different.

These questions have no definite answer. By themselves, comparisons are neither appropriate nor inappropriate; they depend on the questions behind them. If one is interested in the conditions under which market reforms can stimulate economic growth, then indeed it might make sense to compare Russia's descent with China's soaring economy. Comparisons that seem senseless at first sight can be made inviting when correctly framed. Who, for example, would think a comparison of Yugoslavia and the Soviet Union could bear fruit? Veljko Vujacic (1996), however, trains his Weberian lens on Serbian and Russian nationalisms. Given that constitutionally and structurally Serbia's relationship to the other nations of the former Yugoslavia was parallel to Russia's relationship to the former republics of the Soviet Union, why should the former break up violently and the latter relatively peacefully? Our theories would suggest, if anything, the opposite outcome. The methodological point is simple: comparisons are constituted by theories and the empirical puzzles they stimulate rather than by some "intrinsic" difference or similarity.

Through the Weberian lens we see a thick smog settling over Russia, spreading unevenly across its former satellites. But then, Weber's account of Western rationalism, emanating from the tortured Prussian road to modernity, cast a suffocating pallor everywhere. For a more optimistic picture, one reflecting France's cleaner break with its feudal past, we might turn to Emile Durkheim. How do the uncertain transitions appear through his lens? Is there a parallel to the transition from mechanical to organic solidarity? Hannah Arendt's conception of totalitarianism as a terrorized and atomized mass, fused together by an iron band, can be likened to a society of mechanical solidarity. The transition to democracy and markets simulates the rise of organic solidarity, but as in Durkheim it is an unsure transition, likely to produce abnormal forms. Durkheim would find plenty of those in the former communist world and would argue that making them "normal" rests on a moral regeneration. As Hans Joas (1996) argues, Durkheim is the theorist par excellence of "new values" and institutional creativity. Aside, however, from such visionary leaders-cum-intellectuals as Václav Havel and Adam Michnik, few regenerative visions are found in the field of post-Soviet studies. Among Western scholars Ken Jowitt (1992) comes close when he talks of the Leninist extinction and the genesis of a new order emerging from the ashes of the old. But this new order proves more dangerous and fractious than benign and solidary, and its Leninist legacies repeatedly thwart a regenerative beginning.

Katherine Verdery (1999) maps out new beginnings more suggestively. She transports us from the Weberian politics of disenchantment to a politics of enchantment. Like Ellen Comisso she delves beneath the formal democracy of voting, parties, legislatures, the monopoly of violence, and so forth to a transfigured moral order mapped by traveling dead bodies, by the organization of national rituals around death and rebirth. In memorializing the dead, nations resignify space and time, create and consolidate new identities, and sacralize new authorities. Verdery reminds us less of Durkheim, however, than of Gramsci. Recomposition of the moral order takes place not through a spontaneous collective effervescence but through continual social conflict. The practices of taking Lenin from Red Square or using reburials to mark the boundaries of Serbia, Bosnia, and Croatia are vigorously and often violently contested. Like Weber, Gramsci travels East more easily than Durkheim—intellectuals reconfiguring past traditions, building a political order from below as well as imposing it from above, forge a new political hegemony.

Politics, then, is not confined to the official or the formal; power is not the monopoly of the state but extends throughout society. This is the Foucauldian move in social theory, matching dissident perspectives on antipolitics in which withdrawal behind the barricades of the private sphere was as political as engagement in the official realm. Not all Western theory that emphasizes the microphysics of power, however, has met with a warm reception in the East. Neither has feminism, with its mantra of the personal as the political, which also conveys the Foucauldian expansion of politics. There are at least two reasons for this cool response. At the level of *discourse* socialism had already contaminated the universalism espoused by Western feminists. At the level of *practice* the family, the veritable fountain of patriarchy, was the last defense against the rapacious socialist state. The result was what Joanna Goven (1993), referring to Hungary, calls the antipolitics of antifeminism. As Lynne Haney argues in chapter 5, by defending the family against the state women played into the hands of the new postsocialist conservatism that would confine them to the domestic sphere.

In trying to comprehend the reception of theories, one has to understand the conditions of their birth as well as the places to which they travel. If Western feminism was born with the illusion of the state liberating women from private patriarchy, in the East the opposite illusion was more popular—that of the family as a bulwark *against* the state. Western feminism may have received a cool reception as it traveled East, but that was nothing compared to the frosty reception of Western Marxism, at least in the twilight years of socialism. The reasons are perhaps obvious: whereas in the one regime Marxism poses as a critique of the market economy, in the other it acts as legitimating ideology of an oppressive order. Yet, some of the most imaginative critiques from within state socialism have been Marxist, from Trotsky's *Revolution Betrayed,* Djilas's *The New Class,* Kolakowski's *Towards a Marxist Humanism,* and Bahro's *The Alternative in Eastern Europe* to Fehér, Heller, and Márkus's *Dictatorship over Needs.* Marxism is itself a complex and contradictory terrain of struggle.

At the same time, one is hard-pressed to discover such powerful Marxist treatments of postsocialism. This phenomenon is especially paradoxical since the concrete effects of neoliberal economic policy confirm the most dire Marxist anticipations—concentration of capital, polarization between rich and poor, the ebb and flow of economic crisis, and the commodification of needs. Russia and Eastern Europe offer resounding corroborations of Marxist theories of global capitalism, whether they draw inspiration from Manuel Castells's ideas about the information society, David Harvey's on flexible accumulation, or even Hilferding's classic analysis of finance capital.

There is a Marxist answer to the paradox of Marxism's demise, an answer that interweaves the content of theory with the class position and class interests of intellectuals. George Konrád and Iván Szelényi (1979) argued that intellectuals were on the road to power in Eastern Europe, a trajectory that bifurcated them into two groups: an elite of "rational redistributors" who embraced Marxism as ideology and a marginalized group of dissidents who initially tried to use critical Marxism against the

elite but after 1968 abandoned Marxism as irredeemably tainted by oppression. The collapse of state socialism brought with it the collapse of
Marxism among both the included and the excluded. In the West, however, the trajectory of Marxism was always different because intellectuals
were never on the road to class power but instead occupied their own
contradictory class location. Daniel Bell and Alvin Gouldner were only
half right—intellectuals formed an incipient new class not in the West but
in the East. It is ironic that only with the fall of communism have intellectuals flooded ministries and parliaments—not at the apogee of socialism
but at its moment of disintegration. Ill suited for the rough and tumble
of real politics, oppositional intellectuals have slowly retreated or been
transmogrified. One wonders how long it will be before disillusionment
will lead back to Marxism's critique of markets and liberal democracy.

So far I have traced separate strands of classical theory forward, but
they can also be woven together into new fabrics. Szelényi's theory of intellectuals is a case in point, embedded as it is in an analysis of political
economy that draws together Marx, Weber, and Durkheim. From Marx
he took the centrality of *class* defined by property relations that divide
socialism from capitalism, from Weber different modes of *legitimation*
called for by redistributive as opposed to private appropriation, and from
Durkheim the *functionalist interdependence* of state and economy.
Armed with this theoretical apparatus, he extended Karl Polanyi's argument that state intervention corrects for market failures whereas the state
redistributive economy calls forth the market as a subordinate, balancing
mechanism (Szelényi 1991). David Stark has called such inverted combi-
nations of types "mirrored comparisons." He showed how Hungarian
enterprises spawned marketlike institutions—systems of inside contracting—as adaptations to the state-induced shortage economy, whereas in
the United States enterprises bureaucratize labor allocation to alleviate
the pressures of market competition (Stark 1986). Markets compensate
for hierarchies in state socialism, whereas hierarchies compensate for
markets in advanced capitalism. Like the chapters in this book, Stark and
László Bruszt (1998) pursue this understanding of the diversity and complexity of socialism toward "postsocialist pathways" that reorder, reconstitute, reconfigure, and recombine institutions—such as property relations—inherited from the past.

Although they come to similar conclusions, Stark's *recomposition*
within a Bourdieu-type *field* is very different from János Kornai's (1992)
analysis of *transition,* which theorizes *systems* and the difficulty of moving from one to another. Capitalism is an economic system based on private property and constrained by demand, whereas the socialist system is
based on public ownership and constrained by supply. In contrast to the
indeterminacy-within-continuity implied by the *field* metaphor, *system*

conveys a distinct dynamics and rationality. It demands that we interpret any empirical phenomenon, from practices on the shop floor to those in the home, against the specific rationality of the wider system within which it is embedded. Or to use Habermas's framework, life world and system come in pairs, and we should not cross-match them, thus criticizing the socialist factory from the standpoint of the functional imperatives of the capitalist system—or, for that matter, projecting an emancipatory workplace for the United States that ignores the imperatives of capitalism. The insistence that socialism is a system with its own logic means that miracles cannot be expected from shock therapy and that change must be gradual and negotiated. Perhaps because he is resistant to the idea of "mixed types," Kornai is deeply cautious about expecting ready transitions from one system to the other.

The methodological and theoretical moral of this discussion is simple. Whether we operate with the concept of field or of system, two ideal types are better than one. They can purchase fruitful comparisons between widely differing countries. On the one hand, they avoid the deficit models of single ideal types; on the other, they can capture rich specificities through their combination. Such strategies of comparison, which theorize divergence as well as convergence and particularity within a common and general framework, do away with those teleologies and counterteleologies that underpin the use of singular Western models as a yardstick of postsocialist development. In keeping with poststructuralist opposition to the grand narratives of progress or decline, this methodological-cum-theoretical move leaves trajectories of transition more open and indeterminate.

Postsocialist theorizing still relies on socialism as a negation or a comparison—as a celebration of capitalist supremacy or, more rarely, a source of capitalist critique. As socialism retreats into the past, the danger is that we will become ever more enthralled with a single model—an ideal typification of liberal capitalism—against which to compare reality, inevitably making of the post-Soviet world a black hole. We will lose sight of alternatives, whether alternative capitalisms, alternative socialisms, or other utopias that offer novel lenses through which to interpret the present and the past, as well as the future. We must maintain a hold on a critical consciousness, what Edward Said (1983: 247) has called the "unstoppable predilection for alternatives."

From where might such alternative visions emerge? One might imagine that the intellectuals of the former Soviet Union and Eastern Europe, reacting to their national marginalization, will once more divide into two camps—Westernizers and nativists. Disillusioned with the promise of Western liberal theory, a new generation of dissidents would abandon the optimism and teleology of so-called transitology and turn to something more akin to postcolonial theory. After all, anticolonial struggles, like those against communism, embraced Western ideas of economic development and national independence only to discover that they promoted backwardness and oppression in a new guise. So in postsocialism, when humanitarian aid expires and underdevelopment deepens, markets and democracy will evoke skepticism. What indigenous theorizing will arise to supplant or reconfigure Western imports, settling accounts with twentieth-century trajectories through socialism? What will be the contours of postsocialist theory in the twenty-first century, and how will that theory flow back to the West?

Note

Acknowledgment: Thanks to Katherine Verdery for her comments on this chapter and to participants in the Berkeley seminar Traveling Theories, sponsored by the Ford Foundation, from which this chapter emerged.

References

Comisso, Ellen. 1997. Is the Glass Half Full or Half Empty? Reflections on Five Years of Competitive Politics in Eastern Europe. *Communist and Post-Communist Studies* 30(1): 1–21.

Eyal, Gil. 1998. Anti-Politics and the Spirit of Capitalism. Unpublished manuscript, Department of Sociology, University of California, Berkeley.

Eyal, Gil, Iván Szelényi, and Eleanor Townsley. 1998. *Making Capitalism Without Capitalists: Class Formation and Elite Struggles in Post-Communist Central Europe.* London: Verso.

Garcelon, Marc. 1997. The Estate of Change: The Specialist Rebellion and the Democratic Movement in Moscow, 1989–1991. *Theory and Society* 26: 39–85.

Goven, Joanna. 1993. *The Gendered Foundations of Hungarian Socialism: State, Society, and the Anti-Politics of Anti-Feminism, 1948–1990.* Ph.D. dissertation, University of California, Berkeley.

Holmes, Stephen. 1997. What Russia Teaches Us Now: How Weak States Threaten Freedom. *American Prospect* 33 (July–August): 30–39.

Humphrey, Caroline. 1991. "Icebergs," Barter, and the Mafia in Provincial Russia. *Anthropology Today* 7: 8–13.

Joas, Hans. 1996. *The Creativity of Action.* Chicago: University of Chicago Press.

Jowitt, Ken. 1992. *New World Disorder: The Leninist Extinction.* Berkeley: University of California Press.

Konrád, George, and Iván Szelényi. 1979. *The Intellectuals on the Road to Class Power.* New York: Harcourt Brace Jovanovich.

Kornai, János. 1992. *The Socialist System.* Princeton: Princeton University Press.

McDaniel, Tim. 1996. *The Agony of the Russian Idea*. Princeton: Princeton University Press.

Said, Edward. 1983. Traveling Theory. In *The World, the Text, and the Critic*. Cambridge: Harvard University Press, 226–247.

Stark, David. 1986. Rethinking Internal Labor Markets: New Insights from a Comparative Perspective. *American Sociological Review* 51: 492–504.

Stark, David, and László Bruszt. 1998. *Postsocialist Pathways: Transforming Politics and Property in East Central Europe*. Cambridge: Cambridge University Press.

Szelényi, Iván. 1991. Karl Polanyi and the Theory of a Socialist Mixed Economy. In *Markets, State, and Society at the End of the 20th Century*, eds. Marguerite Mendell and David Salee. New York: St. Martin's, 231–248.

Verdery, Katherine. 1996. *What Was Socialism, and What Comes Next?* Princeton: Princeton University Press.

———. 1999. *The Political Lives of Dead Bodies: Reburials and Postsocialist Change*. New York: Columbia University Press.

Vujacic, Veljko. 1996. Historical Legacies, Nationalist Mobilization, and Political Outcomes in Russia and Serbia: A Weberian View. *Theory and Society* 25(6): 763–801.

Index

About the Contributors

Sarah Ashwin is a lecturer in industrial relations at the London School of Economics. Her doctoral research was on workers' organization in Russia during the transition from socialism; other research interests include gender and employment in Russia and the response of Russian trade unions to economic and political change.

Michael Burawoy teaches sociology at the University of California, Berkeley. He has carried out industrial ethnography in Hungary and Russia. Among his books are *The Politics of Production* and *The Radiant Past* (with János Lukács).

Gerald W. Creed is associate professor of anthropology at Hunter College and the Graduate School of the City University of New York. He is the author of *Domesticating Revolution*, a monograph examining agrarian reform in Bulgaria from the beginnings of collectivization to the postsocialist land restitutions.

Elizabeth Dunn completed her Ph.D. in anthropology at Johns Hopkins University, specializing in postsocialist privatization. She conducted research in Poland, investigating ways the introduction of Western management practices into a Polish factory transforms notions of the person. She is coeditor (with Chris Hann) of *Civil Society: Challenging Western Models*.

Lynne Haney is assistant professor of sociology at New York University. Her research, based in Hungary, examines changes in the Hungarian welfare state throughout the communist period and into the present, with particular emphasis on issues of gender.

Caroline Humphrey, reader in Asian anthropology at Cambridge University and author of the prize-winning monograph *Karl Marx Collective,* has done fieldwork in Russia, Mongolia, and Siberia—both before and after the collapse of Communist Party rule—as well as in China, Nepal, and India. Her present interests center on trade and consumption in the postsocialist transformation.

Andrew Lass, associate professor of anthropology at Mt. Holyoke College, has conducted extensive multidisciplinary research in the Czech and Slovak Republics. Continuing his past work on Czech nationalism, he is researching and participating in social and cultural change in the Czech Republic since 1989.

Katherine Verdery is professor of anthropology and associate in East European Studies at the University of Michigan. She has published *Transylvanian Villagers, National Ideology Under Socialism,* and *What Was Socialism, and What Comes Next?,* all resulting from fieldwork in Romania. Her current research concerns property restitution in Transylvania.

David Woodruff is assistant professor of political science at MIT, specializing in the political economy of transformation in Russia. Based on lengthy field experience, his work focuses on problems of monetization and interenterprise debt and barter in Russia since 1990.

Slawomira Zbierski-Salameh is assistant professor of sociology at Haverford College. Her research focuses on the political economy of postsocialist agrarian transformations in Poland.